Police L Administration

William Walsh and Gennaro Vito have adapted the strategic management process to the police organizational world in this innovative new text, *Police Leadership and Administration: A 21st-Century Approach*. Focusing principally on the police executive, this book covers pioneering management techniques for leaders facing the challenges of today's complex environment, providing the police practitioner instruction in planning, setting direction, developing strategy, assessing internal and external environments, creating learning organizations, and managing and evaluating the change process. It also tackles how to handle the political, economic, social, and technical considerations that differ from one community to the next.

Police Leadership and Administration trains individuals to search for solutions, rather than relying on old formulas and scientific management principles. It shows how to tailor responses to the unique problems and issues that professionals are likely to face in the field of law enforcement, providing a foundation with which to adapt to an ever-changing criminal justice climate. This book is essential for forward-thinking police leadership courses in colleges and professional training programs.

William F. Walsh is the former Director of the Southern Police Institute and Professor Emeritus in the Department of Criminal Justice. He holds a BA in Behavioral Science, an MA in Criminal Justice from John Jay College of Criminal Justice, and a PhD in Sociology from Fordham University. A former Lieutenant with the New York City Police Department with 21 years of service, he has conducted research on police and security issues, and authored several articles in scholarly journals, monographs, book chapters and books on police administration, supervision, and management. Before joining the University of Louisville, he served on the Administration of Justice Faculty at Pennsylvania State University, where he received the National Continuing Education Association Faculty Service Award in 1988. He has been a consultant to numerous United States law enforcement agencies and the national police forces of Hungary and Romania. The Academy of Criminal Justices Sciences awarded him the O. W. Wilson Award for his outstanding contributions to police education, research, and practice in 1999. In 2003, he received the Governor's Award for his contributions to Kentucky law enforcement. He was awarded the Melvin Shein Award by the Kentucky Law Enforcement Council in 2004 for Distinguished Service to the Kentucky Police Community. In 2006, he was named the first recipient of the James J. Fyfe Award for a lifetime of service and scholarship to the law enforcement profession by the Police Partnership of New York City. In 2008, Mayor Jerry E. Abramson of the city of Louisville, Kentucky, presented him with the Community Partnership Award for his services to the Louisville Metro Police Department.

Gennaro F. Vito is a Professor in the Department of Criminal Justice at the University of Louisville. He also serves as a faculty member in the Administrative Officer's Course at the Southern Police Institute. He holds a PhD in Public Administration from Ohio State University. Active in professional organizations, he is a past President and Fellow of the Academy of Criminal Justice Sciences and recipient of its Bruce Smith Award in recognition of outstanding contributions to criminal justice as an academic or professional. He is also the recipient of the following awards: Educator of the Year Award from the Southern Criminal Justice Association (1991), the Dean's Outstanding Performance Award for Research and Scholarly Activities from the former College of Urban and Public Affairs at the University of Louisville (1990), the Dean's Award for Outstanding Research from the College of Arts and Sciences, the President's Distinguished Faculty Award for Excellence in Research (2002), and as a Distinguished University Scholar (2008). He is the author of more than 100 professional, refereed journal articles (in such journals as *Criminology*, *The Journal of Criminal Law and Criminology*, *Justice Quarterly*, *Police Quarterly*, and *The Prison Journal*) and more than 50 technical research reports. He has published on topics including capital sentencing, police consolidation, police traffic stops, policing strategies for drug problems in public housing, attitudes toward capital punishment, and the effectiveness of criminal justice programs, such as drug elimination programs, drug courts, and drug testing of probationers and parolees. He has made more than 100 presentations at professional meetings, including the American Correctional Association, the International Community Corrections Association, and the Kentucky Bar Association. He is the co-author of nine textbooks in criminal justice and criminology.

Police Leadership and Administration

A 21st-Century Strategic Approach

William F. Walsh and Gennaro F. Vito

Routledge
Taylor & Francis Group

NEW YORK AND LONDON

First published 2019
by Routledge
711 Third Avenue, New York, NY 10017

and by Routledge
2 Park Square, Milton Park, Abingdon, Oxon, OX14 4RN

Routledge is an imprint of the Taylor & Francis Group, an informa business

Library of Congress Cataloging-in-Publication Data
Names: Walsh, William F., author. | Vito, Gennaro F., author.
Title: Police leadership and administration : a 21st-century strategic approach / William F. Walsh and Gennaro F. Vito.
Description: New York, NY : Routledge, 2018. | Includes bibliographical references and index.
Identifiers: LCCN 2018006036 (print) | LCCN 2018006545 (ebook) | ISBN 9781351244435 (master) | ISBN 9780815373001 (hardback) | ISBN 9780815373018 (pbk.)
Subjects: LCSH: Police administration—United States. | Police—United States. | Leadership.
Classification: LCC HV8141 (ebook) | LCC HV8141 .W348 2018 (print) | DDC 363.2068—dc23
LC record available at https://lccn.loc.gov/2018006036

ISBN: 978-0-8153-7300-1 (hbk)
ISBN: 978-0-8153-7301-8 (pbk)
ISBN: 978-1-351-24443-5 (ebk)

Typeset in Minion Pro
by Apex CoVantage, LLC

Visit the eResources: www.routledge.com/9780815373018

Dedication

We dedicate this work to all our police students who during the last two decades and a half at the Southern Police Institute have freely shared their knowledge and experiences with us in the dynamics of the classroom and as a result enriched their professors and profession.

Dr. Vito dedicates this text to the memory of Officer Ronald D. Vito of the Niagara Falls (NY) Police Department.

Contents

Preface

This book provides a primer on strategic management in policing. Policing is presently going through a period of tumultuous change and challenge. Rapid transformations in technology, community demographics, individual rights, cultural values, economics, social unrest, violent crime, transnational terrorism, and challenges to their legitimacy and government regulations have created a challenging world that is experiencing a variety of legal and social problems. For the last three decades, police executives and criminal justice scholars have been rethinking what constitutes effective policing. It takes a special type of organizational leadership to position a police department to deal with these forces. This challenge has led to the selection of strategic management as the defining concept of this book.

The purpose of this book is to addresses current trends and strategies in police leadership and administration. Specifically, it focuses on the evolution of professional policing, the leadership role of the police executive, and the strategic management of the police organization. In addition, it examines the latest in management techniques that are directly related to the emerging role of the police executive as they face the challenges of today's complex environment.

Written from the perspective of the chief executive, it begins with an examination of the history and development of professional police administration and leadership. It defines, discusses, and identifies the concepts, techniques, and issues relating to managerial authority, leadership, administration, and command. It explores police leadership and administration by an examination of the issues and challenges of setting organizational direction, managing change, and strategic analysis. It examines the process of strategic management through the development of organizational strategy, strategic planning, operations, and human resource management. It discusses performance measurement, organizational integrity, and professional standards. This book also functions as a guide for the development of police organizations as learning organizations. Lastly, it covers the issues related to creating safe communities, police legitimacy, and preparing for the future.

1 The Evolution of Police Leadership and Administration

Police administration is not applied mechanics, but a living-breathing organism shaped by the political, social, and economic trends of time and place.
Thomas Repetto, *The Blue Parade* (Repetto, 1978, p. 4)

Learning Objectives

1. To describe the evolution of policing.
2. To identify the police functions.
3. To describe the types of police departments in the United States.
4. To define the administrative challenge of today's policing environment.
5. To identify the relationship between the learning organization and strategic policing.
6. To understand the impact of Peel's London police model on professional policing.
7. To describe the relevance of Peel's *Principles of Law Enforcement*.
8. To define the different paradigmatic shifts in 20th-century American policing.
9. To identify the characteristics of the Community Problem-solving Paradigm.
10. To be able to list the characteristics of the top suburban police departments.
11. To describe the difference between an open and closed management system.
12. To identify the characteristics of strategic policing.
13. To define the Compstat management system.
14. To describe Intelligence-Led Policing.

Introduction

The *"Police"* are an organized body of individuals that represent the civil authority of a government. The origin of the word "police" can be traced to the Greek word *politea*, which refers to the internal administration and government of the city (Fyfe, Greene, Walsh, Wilson, & McLaren, 1997, p. 4). Since the emergence of professional policing in the 1830s, the word has come to define the personnel and organizations whose principal concern is the maintenance of order and the enforcement of law. Members of the police profession may be referred to as police officers, troopers, sheriffs, constables, agents, rangers, and peace officers. Police departments are products by their political, historical, and community environments. In the United States policing has evolved into a local governmental function responsible for public order and safety within a defined political jurisdictional area such as a city, town, county, and borough or state. The police in the many municipalities are the only public service who will respond when called 24 hours per day, 7 days a week. As a result, police officers are the most visible representatives of local governmental authority. As such, their enforcement activities determine the limits of public safety, the level of governmental service, and individual freedom. Since American police departments are primarily local institutions, they are influenced by and responsive to pressure and politics of the community within which they serve.

Our nation has developed from an agrarian-based group of former English colonies into a complex technological society that is interconnected to the entire world. The strains and pressures created by this transformation have brought about economic and social changes that affect all aspects of our society including public safety. The effective use of police resources is essential to the maintenance of community safety and security. However, the events of 9/11 and the resulting national emphasis on homeland security have accelerated the need for police departments to understand and effectively respond to the shifting demands and uncertainty of these times. Changing economic systems, multiculturalism, demographics, community confidence, family structures, limited resources, technology, and transnational crime are increasingly placing greater demands on police services. As these demands have expanded, public expectations of what the police should be doing and how they should do it have also changed. Today's police organizations are expected to take responsibility for traditional order-maintenance functions as well as many new ones, requiring different skills and ways of working (Flanagan, 2008).

United States Policing System

The United States has one of the more decentralized and complex policing systems in the world. This system is an outgrowth of the nation's founders' fear of a strong centralized government. This fear led them to emphasize local autonomy over centralized authority while delegating policing powers to state and local governments. A Bureau of Justice Statistics survey conducted in 2008 found there are nearly 800,000 full-time sworn law enforcement officers, serving in 17,876 law enforcement agencies that provide protective services to 312 million people in the United States. These departments consist of:

- 12,766 General-purpose Local (municipal) Police Departments.
- 3,067 Sheriff's Offices.
- 49 State Police Departments.
- 731,903 sworn employees and a combined annual budget of about $3 billion.
- 1,481 Special police agencies for highways, port, transit, causeway, housing, school, and/or capitol police.

American police organizations may also be described beyond these raw numbers as:

- **Urban—multilevel departments**: These are large bureaucratic hierarchical organizations with a high degree of task specialization. They are usually staffed with over a thousand sworn and non-sworn employees. Their service areas are characterized by diverse socio-economic urban communities consisting of high-density zones of crime and human service demand.
- **Suburban departments**: These are medium-sized organizations of less than a thousand sworn employees. They usually have a strong resource base with limited task specialization. Suburban police departments are presently experiencing an increase in service demand. Most departments with 100 or more officers had full-time specialized units to address child abuse, juvenile crime, gangs, and domestic violence (Reaves, 2015).
- **County police/full service sheriff's office**: These organizations have a variety of organizational structures, service demand and development. Structural change is occurring in which smaller municipal police departments are being merged with the countywide agencies or contracting with them to provide police services.
- **Small community**: These departments have a small number of personnel, usually less than 25 officers, lack resources but have a close relationship with the communities they serve. Their operational officers are expected to perform all police tasks. About half (48%) of police departments in the United States employed fewer than 10 officers (Reaves, 2015).
- **State and highway—state-wide jurisdiction**: These are large bureaucratic organizations that either perform full service policing state-wide or are restricted to the enforcement of highway safety regulations and laws. They are noted for their traditional military-style culture and high levels of integrity. In states where they have full state-wide police powers they support local police in serious or complicated cases and help to coordinate multijurisdictional task force activity. There are 49 State Police Departments in the United States. The state of Hawaii is the one exception.
- **Special function**: These are organizations whose authority is limited to the enforcement of special laws, control areas, and specific functions. Campus and Fish, Game and Wildlife police organizations are typical examples of these types of agencies.

Our policing system is responsible for three distinct functions: crime control, order maintenance, and service provision (Glensor, Correia, & Peak, 2000). Noted police scholar Herman Goldstein (1977, p. 23) identified the complex multiple objectives of policing as follows:

1. To prevent and control conduct widely recognized as threatening to life and property (serious crime).
2. To aid individuals who are in danger of physical harm, such as the victim of a criminal attack.
3. To protect the constitutional guarantees, such as the right of free speech and assembly.
4. To facilitate the movement of people and vehicles.
5. To assist those who cannot care for themselves: the intoxicated, the addicted, the mentally ill, the physically disabled, the old, and the young.
6. To resolve conflict, whether it be between individuals, groups of individuals, or individuals and their government.

7. To identify problems that have the potential for becoming more serious problems for the individual citizen, for the police, or for the government.
8. To create and maintain a feeling of security in the community.

On a daily basis police departments seek to fulfill these objectives by responding to emergency calls for service, preventing crime, enforcing laws and ordinances, rendering first aid, resolving disputes, regulating traffic, investigating crimes, and arresting violators. However, the way police departments administer and deliver their principal programs and services have evolved over the last two centuries.

Administrative Challenge

As one might imagine, administering a police organization today is a challenging task. The modern police agency is expected to take responsibility for traditional order-maintenance functions as well as many new ones, which require different skills and ways of working. The complex nature of today's policing and the economic climate in which police organizations operate has fundamentally changed the leadership expectations of police executives (Flanagan, 2008). Every day police leaders face issues of complexity, uncertainty, and sensitivity that require a different level of thinking and decision making. Police executives are challenged to create effective organizations that are adaptable and proactively responsive to changing public safety needs and community relationships. Conventional ways of thinking, analyzing data, solving problems, making decisions, and responding to organizational demands are changing. Few situations are easily resolved with methods developed to address issues in the past. Today's challenges require thinking at different analytical and strategic levels.

William Geller (1997) assessed this challenging administrative environment by asking, "Can our police and sheriff departments find ways to work smarter, not just harder?" He answered by suggesting that police departments should become "*learning organizations*" just as many of our nation's most successful business organizations have. Geller believes that this development will allow police departments to innovate and create new strategies to provide public safety. In this manner he believes that they will serve their communities more effectively, efficiently, and legitimately. A *learning organization* is one that enhances its effectiveness by adapting to the needs of its environment (Senge, 1990). It actively engages, evaluates, and adapts by continually assessing its environmental demands and operational methods. It learns from its own and the similar experiences of other organizations in order to adjust and respond to the environmental demands it faces.

Managers in learning organizations actively seek to expand their capacity to understand the environmental pressures they are facing by consistently gathering and analyzing information. The knowledge gained from this process forms the basis for the creation of data-driven strategies and tactics that are designed to respond to changing operational demands. In learning organizations, information collection is a constant process, along with ongoing verification and analysis. In order for police organizations to become learning organizations they must develop the ability to restructure their operational tactics to meet both current and changing needs of their communities (Silverman, 1999). In these departments the development of operational tactics and strategies is an information data-driven analytical process. Operational success and sustainability are maintained through an ongoing process of information gathering, analysis and sharing, strategy and tactical development, implementation, and continuous assessment.

Managerial decisions in learning organizations are influenced by a diverse set of factors that are derived from without and within these organizations. Externally, these factors include but are not limited to changes in government, community demographics, cultural values, economic conditions, both local and transnational crime, global terrorism, and the degree of community confidence in the police organization and its officers. Internally, clarity of an organization's mission and goals, recruitment and retention of personnel, organizational values, internal politics, accountability, training, unions, and managerial ability affect police organizational performance. These forces place increased pressure on how police executives and administrators plan and decide their organization's response to community's needs.

This challenge has led to the selection of strategic management as the unifying theme of this book. **Strategic management** is the art and science of formulating and implementing strategies to accomplish organizational goals and objectives (David, 2009). The primary purpose of strategic management is to achieve an organization's mission by matching its strengths and capabilities with the demands placed upon it by its environment (Dessler, 2004). Strategic management is the process by which learning organizations are created. It is currently being practiced in police departments whose executives are developing management systems that are operating under a variety of mega-strategies such as Compstat, Intelligence-Led Policing, Predictive Policing, and Evidence-Based Policing. Strategic management and the variety of ways in which it has been adapted in policing is the primary focus of this book.

In policing, strategic management involves the development of innovative strategies whose characteristics involve information analysis and technology, strategy and tactics development, managerial accountability, creativity, and continuous assessment to control crime and provide public safety. Strategic management requires that a police department's chief executive and his or her administrative team create a "*strategic vision*" for the department that consists of clear measurable goals that are focused on integrating organizational elements such as information gathering, computer information systems, patrol, specialized units, and staff support systems to respond to the public safety needs of the community. On the unit level, strategic management refers to the managerial integration of information, strategy, tactics, personnel, and evaluation to achieve organizational goals and objectives. This is a proactive instead of a reactive approach to organizational leadership that is appropriate for responding to changing environmental demands. The first adaptation of this form of management in United States policing occurred in 1994 in New York City when then Police Commissioner William Bratton and his command staff reengineered the police department through the development of the Compstat process (Bratton, 1998).

This chapter will identify and explain the historical events that have led to the development of contemporary police administration and strategic management in policing. Many students tend to think of history as just a dry recitation of "facts": dates, names, and places from the hoary past. Although a chronology of events is an important part of the process, the study of history offers much more. Examining the development of an important societal institution like the police explains the basis for its current practices as well as provides answers to pertinent questions such as the following: How has the police mission developed over time? How have police organizations evolved? Where are the police going as an institution? In today's world how can police departments provide public safety? Naturally, before we can consider these, we must understand where the police (as an organization) have been. History provides a starting point for the understanding of police organizational leadership and administration as well as enhances our understanding of the present.

Professional Policing: The Early Years

Policing has always existed in some form or another in every society. Tribal groups practiced self-policing through the enforcement of behavioral standards by their leaders, councils of elders, religious leaders, and adult members. As societal groups became more complex and industrialization occurred, governing groups and national states saw the need to develop a more structured and organized form of policing. France established a police department for the city of Paris as early as 1544 (Palmer, 1988, p. 69). Urban police forces founded on the French model were created in Russia's St. Petersburg (1718), Prussia's Berlin (1742), and in the capital of the Austro-Hungarian Empire, Vienna (1751). European police forces were armed military-style organizations whose purpose was to serve the national state and maintain public order. These departments acted as both a social and political control system which drew their power from and gave their service to the government that created them (Critchley, 1972, p. 52; Bayley, 1975). Reaction to the pervasive nature of the continental policing systems is the basis upon which rests the Anglo-American belief that excessive centralization of police power should be avoided. However, the origins of what is known today as "Professional Policing," a department of individuals specifically created, trained, and empowered to enforce the law and maintain public order, can be traced to the creation of the London Metropolitan Department in 1829.

In the late 18th and 19th centuries English society was transformed from an agrarian to an urban, industrialized one. This brought about mass migrations of people from rural areas to urban centers in search of employment. One outcome of this process was a breakdown of both civil and social control that necessitated a change in public order control methods. The traditional English fragmented policing system based on watch and wards, constables, and justices of the peace became overwhelmed and ineffective. London, the capital of the British Empire, was a violent, crime-ridden city policed by a fragmented antiquated public safety system.

London Metropolitan Police Model

After many years of debate on the subject of policing the city of London, the English Parliament in 1829 passed the Metropolitan Police Act. It authorized the creation for the city of London of a 3,000-member full-time, uniformed police department. The Metropolitan Police transformed London into one of the safest cities in the world at that time and as a result its police department became a model for the development of urban police departments world-wide (Lee, 1901, p. 228). Sir **Robert Peel,** the Home Secretary of England, is credited with the Act's passage as well as providing the organizational vision and direction for the new police force (Fyfe et al., 1997, p. 7). Peel, in his wisdom, knew that a police force created by the government would be rejected by many English citizens as a foreign form of coercion that would usurp their traditional rights. There was considerable public and parliamentary suspicion of Peel's efforts. The new department met with fierce opposition both before and immediately after its creation (Lee, 1901, p. 245).

From a developmental perspective, it is important to understand why this department succeeded and became the model for so many police organizations. The answer lies in its executive leadership, vision, clarity of mission, organizational strategy, accountability system, administrative practices, and the appropriateness of these for that society's demands at that time. Peel understood that gaining the support of the people was a necessary factor in achieving both acceptance and legitimacy for his "New Police." Current community unrest and protest against police departments in United States reflects that this factor is as important today as it was in Peel's time. The Metropolitan Police Department from its beginning was based upon the principle that "the people are the police and the police are the people." From its origin Peel designed the London Metropolitan Police Department as an organization that drew its authority from the legal system and the people it served. He envisioned that his police officers would do things that any citizen would do to make the society safe if they had time to do so (Moore & Braga, 2003, p. 13).

To implement his vision and achieve its acceptance by citizens, Peel and his associates selected men who were even-tempered and reserved; chose a uniform that was unassuming (navy blue rather than military red); insisted that officers be restrained and polite in their dealings with the public (Uchida, 2010). Peel's police constable constitutionally had original authority and personal responsibility for his actions. However, he was beholding to the law, not a national or local government.

A key factor in Peel's achieving his objectives was the department's executive leadership. He appointed jointly two Commissioners of Police to administer and lead the department. Richard Mayne (1796–1868), an Irish barrister, was selected because of his legal experience and Lieutenant Colonel Charles Rowan (1782–1852), a military officer, for his experience with military organization and discipline. These joint-commissioners combined Peel's strategic vision, executive power, administrative knowledge, and organizational strategy with the strong application of discipline to instill a department-wide cultural value system based on impersonal public service into the structure and practice of the department (Klockars, 1985, p. 42). The "Prevention of Crime and the Maintenance of Order" was established as the department's primary mission. Peel and his commissioners decided that the "true test of the department's effectiveness would be the absence of crime and disorder, and not the visible evidence of police action in dealing with them" (Lee, 1901, pp. 228–244).

The operational strategy used to achieve this mission was a visible uniformed patrol system based on interlocking foot patrol beats that covered the city's streets. These foot beats were designed so that each officer should be able to see every part of his beat at least once in 10 minutes or a quarter of an hour; and this he was expected to do. The objective of this tactic was to have a highly visible uniformed patrol force guarding the streets to prevent crime and ensure citizen safety. The patrols were expected to prevent street robberies, vandalism, and disorder as well as control juveniles, street prostitutes, and drunks. The officers were unarmed except for a small hardwood truncheon that they kept concealed.

The department was organized as a military-style bureaucracy with a hierarchical staffing structure based on a ranking system. For the guidance of all ranks a set of rules and regulations was established. Promotion was achieved through merit but improper behavior or poor performance would receive harsh discipline. "Between the years of 1830 and 1838, there were nearly five thousand dismissals, and more than six thousand resignations from the department" (Lee, 1901, p. 240). Sir Robert Peel's *Principles of Law Enforcement* guided the use of the department's policing powers, operations, and interaction with citizens. These principles were set out in the "General Instructions" that were issued to every new police officer beginning in 1829.

Sir Robert Peel's Principles of Law Enforcement

1. The basic mission for which the police exist is to prevent crime and disorder, as an alternative to their repression by military force and severity of legal punishment.
2. The ability of the police to perform their task is dependent on public approval of their existence, actions, behavior, and/or ability of the police to secure and maintain public respect.
3. The police must secure and maintain the respect and approval of the public, means also the securing of the willing co-operation of the public in the task of observance of laws.
4. To recognize always that the extent to which the cooperation of the public can be secured diminishes proportionately, the necessity for the use of physical force and compulsion for achieving police objectives.
5. To seek and to preserve public favor, not catering to public opinion, but by constantly demonstrating absolutely impartial service to law, in complete independence of policy, and without regard to the justice or injustice of the substance of the individual laws; by ready offering of individual service and friendship to all members of the public without regard to their wealth or social standing; by ready offering of sacrifice in protecting and preserving life.
6. To use physical force only when the exercise of persuasion, advice and warning is found to be insufficient to obtain public cooperation to an extent necessary to secure observance of law or to restore order; and to use only minimum degree of physical force which is necessary on any particular occasion for achieving a police objective.
7. To maintain at all times a relationship with the public that gives reality to the historic tradition that the police are the public and that the public are the police; the police only being members of the public who are paid to give full-time attention to duties which are incumbent on every citizen, in the interest of community welfare and existence.
8. To recognize always the need for strict adherence to police executive functions, and to refrain from even seeming to usurp the powers of the judiciary or avenging individuals or the state, and of authoritatively judging guilt and punishing the guilty.
9. To recognize always that the test of police efficiency is the absence of crime and disorder, not the visible evidence of police action in dealing with them.

(Lee, 1901)

Peel's *Principles of Law Enforcement* defined the organization's core mission, its relationship with citizens, operational standards, including use of force standards and identified the absence of crime and disorder as the measure of police effectiveness (Lee, 1901, p. 243). Former New York City Police Commissioner William J. Bratton believes that many of today's police problems can be resolved by these principles (Goldstein & Goodman, 2014). The London police officers' authorization to control citizens was drawn from the social authority and power of the institution of which they were a part (Klockars, 1985, p. 49). The centrally administered, disciplined, semi-military organized police department eventually won the respect and support of not only the citizens they policed but also the world. During the mid- to late 19th century similar professional police departments based on this model were established throughout England and beyond (Repetto, 1978).

Development of Professional Policing in America

In the United States, policing evolved from the responsibility of the 17th- and 18th-century colonial sheriff, volunteer posse, slave patrols, constables, and civilian night watch to an organized, 24-hour governmental function. In the early 19th century, industrialization, immigration, socio-economic conditions, riots, and pervasive urban crime created social unrest, disorder, and fear among citizens. Urban riots, sensational murders, fear of immigrants, and unsafe conditions in American cities resulted in many municipalities creating police departments that were modeled after Peel's London force. The police departments created in New York City (1844), Chicago (1851), Cincinnati and New Orleans (1852), Philadelphia (1854), Boston (1855), Newark and Baltimore (1857), and Kansas City and St. Louis (1861) adopted the London department's organizational structure and patrolling system but not its guiding principles and organizational culture. As a result these departments did not develop an efficient, respected, or ethical police service or create safer cities (See Lane, 1967; Repetto, 1978).

In 19th-century America, local governmental authorities were evolving and as a result, organized policing began as a decentralized, partisan, politically controlled, and corrupt function in most major cities of the day (Repetto, 1978). Police chiefs and officers owed their loyalty to the local political bosses who were responsible for their appointment. They in turn used their police powers to serve the objectives of these individuals (Kelling & Moore, 1988). This development ensured that politics would be a major factor in the development of professional policing in the United States.

The Boston Police Department led by Stephen James O'Meara from 1906 to 1918 was the one department that was an exception to this practice. Raymond Fosdick in *American Police Systems* (1915, pp. 121–122) identified Boston as the best police department in the United States. O'Meara's appointment in 1906 was an outcome of the municipal reform movement that began at the end of the 19th century and extended into the 1920s. O'Meara's leadership abilities and the way in which he used the power of his office contributed to his success. Under O'Meara's leadership, the Boston Police came closest to implementing that administrative ideal of both Peel and America's municipal reformers. The following characteristics led to his successful administration.

1. O'Meara was appointed police commissioner for a 5 year term.
2. He had full authority over personnel matters that included, hiring, firing and promoting virtually at will.
3. The officers were selected from the working class of Boston.
   Like in London they were recruited from the people they policed.
4. The department maintained a relatively high ratio of police to population, which permitted full utilization of a beat patrol system similar to that used in London.
5. Management and supervision insured that a high standard of integrity and legality was maintained.

(Fyfe et al., 1997, p. 12)

O'Meara employed a strong authoritarian leadership style not unlike that used to administer the London Police. This example of a strong chief executive using coercive power to create and sustain a positive police organization has been repeated throughout the history of modern police administration beginning with Rowan and Mayne. Unfortunately, the impact of strong police chiefs usually lasts only during their tenure in office. O'Meara died in 1918. The following year the officers of the Boston Police Department conducted an unsuccessful strike to gain recognition for their trade union and improve their working conditions. The city of Boston dismissed the striking officers and hired a new force of 1,000 officers. Police officer attempts to unionize nationally were set back for 20 years and the achievements of O'Meara's administration were destroyed (Repetto, 1978, pp. 97–105).

Kelling and Moore (1988) analyzed the organizational development of American professional policing by dividing it into three eras: political, reform, and community policing. They identified each era with a specific policing strategy or paradigmatic view that structured the way police managers viewed their leadership role, administered their departments, and responded to the problems of the time. A *paradigm* is "a mental screen or cognitive filter through which information passes before it can be integrated into human thought processes and behaviors" (Kuhn, 1962; More, Vito, & Walsh, 2012, p. 139). Paradigms serve as a basis and guide for decision making. They also limit a decision maker's ability to recognize and develop new ways of doing things by restraining their thought processes to existing methods that have proven to be successful in the past (Covey, 2004, p. 26; More et al., 2012). According to Kelling and Moore's perspective, the organizational development of professional policing in the United States is a product of the issues, thinking, values, and beliefs of a specific historical era. It is also a tale of resistance to new ideas before accepting them in the face of crises (Wadman & Allison, 2004). The impact of the Boston police strike described earlier is an example of this process.

The period in which the development of American urban police departments began in the 1840s and lasted into the early part of the 20th century Kelling and Moore identified as the *Political Era*. City departments were controlled by local political powers. Police officers served their public and political bosses by maintaining public order through a watchman style of policing and were more deeply involved in the community through the provision of a variety of social services. The 19th-century police officer performed more as a street social worker than do police officers today (Whitehouse, 1973).

Toward the end of the 19th century and the beginning of the 20th century, municipal reformers and police administrators sought to end political control and corruption through the professionalization of the police. This *Reform Era* lasted in varying degrees until the beginning of the 1980s, when community problem-solving policing emerged. During the reform period, a number of influential police chiefs and police scholars redefined the police function and organization. The primary police mission changed from the 19th-century focus on maintaining the peace and the provision of social services to a narrow emphasis on crime fighting through law enforcement and managerial control by a bureaucratically administered police department. The reformers believed that the administration of police departments should be separated from the influence of politics and its values (Conser, Russell, Paynich, & Gingerich, 2005). They theorized that an administratedly controlled police department commanded by a strong independent police chief with powers similar to that of Stephen James O'Meara of Boston was the ideal administrative model. These beliefs dominated police administration until the 1960s when increases in crime, the civil rights movement, anti-war protests, riots, and Supreme Court decisions seriously challenged them and created an intense examination of the practice of policing in the United States (Fyfe et al., 1997, pp. 3–27).

During the 1980s, the ***Community Problem-Solving Policing Era*** emerged out of the desire to create a more effective, responsive, and just police service that would have a closer relationship with the citizens and community they served. The central precept of community problem-solving policing is the creation of public safety through the formation of partnerships between police and citizens to solve community safety problems.

The authors of this text believe a fourth era, the ***Strategic Policing Era,*** should be added to this schema. This era began with the adoption of strategic policing strategies by urban police departments in the last decade of the 20th century and continues today. As a result of these efforts, a shift in the basic methods of policing marked by the development and adaptation of the data-driven police operational strategies is now occurring (Kelling & Bratton, 1993).

Each of these eras has left its mark on today's police organizations. The legacy of these paradigmatic shifts currently drive the way police departments define their primary mission, articulate their operational philosophy, structure their organization, interact with the community, and provide service delivery. During the 20th century, the police profession changed the focus of its administrative and operational strategies three distinct times.

Paradigmatic Shifts of the 20th Century

Reform Paradigm

As policing emerged out of the 19th century, corrupt politicians and political machines controlled many local and city governments. Corruption and inefficiency were rampant. Municipal policing provided a source of patronage that regulated businesses, operated election machinery, and exercised power over the daily life of citizens (Repetto, 1978). Politics influenced personnel hiring, while standards for hiring and training were almost non-existent. Most officers were native-born citizens with limited education and skills who learned their craft on-the-job. Only the largest municipal police departments formally trained new officers in a police academy. Officers often responded to the problems they confronted on their patrol beats with brute force. The majority of police executives administering local police departments were appointed and removed for political reasons. Positional qualifications, leadership training, and development for police managers did not exist.

In response to these conditions, civic reformers began efforts to change the administration of police departments in the United States. The reformers included scholars like Leonhard F. Fuld, Raymond Fosdick, Bruce Smith, and Elmer D. Graper, and police executives such as August Vollmer, Orlando W. Wilson, J. Edgar Hoover, and Los Angeles Police Chief William Parker. The reformers ideal was a politically neutral police organization that was centrally administered and controlled by professionally trained managers and a tenured police chief. They sought to create a new legitimacy for policing based on law, scientific methods of investigation and crime control operations. Their efforts helped to create a nation-wide effort to transform politically dominated police departments into rational-legal, bureaucratically controlled organizations focused on crime control and criminal apprehension as their primary mission (More et al., 2012).

The reformers advocated:

1. Elimination of political interference.
2. Specialization of police duties.
3. Clearly defined duties.
4. Constant supervision of duties.
5. Strong executive leadership.
6. Constant auditing by inspectors.
7. Maintenance of internal discipline.
8. Comprehensive training of police officers.
9. Careful selection of personnel based on merit and qualifications.
10. Elimination of police duties not associated with crime control and law enforcement.

(Fuld, 1910; Fosdick, 1969; Graper, 1921)

In the years between 1930 and the 1980s, this reform movement's efforts resulted in the emergence of a bureaucratic command-and-control style of administration dominating policing. Police departments were administered through an integrated and coherent semi-military organizational control structure that sought authority in criminal law enforcement; emphasized bureaucratic organizational structure; relied on motorized preventive patrol, rapid response to calls for service, and reactive criminal investigation as crime control tactics. Departments measured their effectiveness in crime reports, arrest, and clearance data. Unfortunately, these, as foresaw by Sir Robert Peel, are measures of police response to crime but not how effective police were in preventing crime.

The first great visionary of this reform movement was *August Vollmer* who served as chief of police in Berkeley, California, from 1905 to 1932. He envisioned the creation of a professional police service through the adaptation in policing of theories and concepts drawn from the fields of management, sociology, psychology, social work. Vollmer was the first police executive to advocate business management principles, ethical standards, and a sense of professionalism for policing. He was also the first police chief to hire college-educated police officers, many of whom went on to command other police departments. The administrative architect of Vollmer's vision, *Orlando W. Wilson,* was one of Vollmer's college-educated officers and his protégé. Wilson became the originator of this movement's organizational strategy (Fyfe et al., 1997, p. 13). He had great influence on police managers across the United States through his authorship of the first published texts on police administration such as *Police Records* (1942), *Police Planning* (1957), and several editions of *Police Administration* beginning in 1951, all of which became mandatory reading for police managers. Through his writing, Wilson successfully laid the foundation for a professional police management and service delivery strategy that governed policing until the 1980s.

These reform efforts produced an administrative-oriented police leadership that transformed many departments into bureaucratically controlled organizations with an emphasis on crime control (Guyot, 1991). The major operational strategy of the reform era included: (1) a motorized patrol force dispatched by radio to create an impression of omnipresence and rapid response to incidents of crime, and (2) investigative units trained in methods of criminal investigation, such as automated fingerprint identification and the use of criminal histories (Moore & Trojanowicz, 1988, p. 5).

The basic principles of the Reform model of policing are that:

1. The primary function of policing is crime control.
2. Police Departments should be independent of politics.
3. A highly centralized command structure and standardized operating procedures can produce an effective and efficient police service.
4. The police organization should be hierarchical and subdivided according to a division of labor and task specialization.
5. Officers should be selected based on established recruitment standards.
6. Officers should be well trained and disciplined.
7. Preventive random motorized patrol deters crime.
8. Policing should use modern technology.
9. Police officers should enforce laws impartially.
10. Crimes are solved by scientific investigative methods.

(Goldstein, 1990, pp. 23–25)

Many of these principles still influence police organizational administration today.

In support of this administrative perspective, O. W. Wilson developed nine tenets of organizational administration to guide police organizational development during this era. He advised that:

1. Tasks similar in purpose, method, or clientele should be grouped together in one or more units under the control of a single person.
2. Duties should be defined precisely and made known to all members of the organization so that responsibility can be placed exactly.
3. Channels of communications should be established so that information can flow up and down the organization and authority can be delegated.
4. The principle of unity of command that states that an employee should only be answerable to one person must be applied.
5. Span of control which is the number of employees that a supervisor or manager can control should be limited.
6. Each task should be assigned to a member of the organization.
7. Line personnel must be supervised around the clock.
8. Each assignment of responsibility must carry with it a commensurate authority to accomplish the task.
9. Persons to whom authority is delegated are held accountable for its use.

(Wilson & McLaren, 1977, pp. 73–74)

These tenets helped to create administratively controlled bureaucratic police departments whose primary functions were random patrol, crime control, and criminal investigation. A shift had taken place away from the 19th-century politically controlled order-maintenance policing to a highly structured reactive crime fighting model (Bratton & Kelling, 2012). The order maintenance and social services of the political era were rejected as not true police work. Organizational principles, such as the division of labor and unity of command, became the vogue, and task specialization was implemented along with hierarchical control of employees (Fayol, 1992, pp. 37–43). Attempts were made to standardize and control officer discretion, decision making, and behavior through development of policy and procedures. The desire to control the discretionary activities of officers led to structural changes such as a shorter span of control for closer supervision of officers and the creation of additional hierarchal layers of management. Meticulous record keeping was emphasized, and following the chain of command was the desirable channel of communication (Fyfe et al., 1997; Harring, 1982, pp. 25–35). O. W. Wilson also developed the theory of preventive patrol. He advocated that if motorized police officers drove conspicuously marked cars randomly through city streets and gave special attention to certain "hazards" (bars and schools, for example), a feeling of police omnipresence would be created. In turn, this sense of omnipresence would both deter criminals and reassure good citizens. Moreover, it was hypothesized that vigilant patrol officers moving rapidly through city streets would happen upon criminals in action and be able to apprehend them (Kelling & Moore, 1988).

The reform era's approach to organizational administration paralleled the concepts suggested by the works of the classical organizational theorists that dominated managerial thinking into the 1930s and that remain influential today in policing. Classical theorists emphasized stable, clearly defined machine-like organizational structures and procedures to control employees and effectively attain goals and objectives. They envisioned organizations working like the carefully designed interrelated parts of a well-constructed machine. People are a part of this machine, but the organization and its mission took priority over people (Morgan, 1997).

The organizational model that exemplifies this theoretical perspective is the *bureaucracy*. German sociologist **Max Weber** (1864–1920) described the bureaucracy as a centralized managerial authority system based on a logical hierarchical ordering of positions from the top to the bottom of the organization (Weber, 1947, pp. 329–341). He believed that the characteristics of the bureaucracy made it capable of achieving a higher level of efficiency and effectiveness than other organizational forms.

The police department that emerged during this reform period used structure to centralize administrative control of the department. Laws, policy, rules, and procedures defined performance expectations. Individual initiative, enterprise, judgment, and creativity were controlled through the command staff's application of policies and procedures. The foremost example of this model of policing during this era was the Los Angeles Police Department during the administration of Chief William Parker (1950 to 1966). Parker took over a corrupt police department and transformed it into the nation's leading model of police bureaucratic professionalism (Walker & Katz, 2011, p. 44).

During the reform era, police operational tactics became grounded in random motorized preventive patrol, rapid response to calls for service, and reactive investigation of crime. O. W. Wilson's emphasis on the omnipresence and invulnerability of motorized patrol led to the assignment of the majority of a department's patrol officers to motor units (Fyfe et al., 1997, p. 540). This process required patrol units to randomly roam the streets at all times. Citizens were expected to call the police to activate officer response. The 911 emergency systems developed in the 1960s made it easier for the public to contact the police and obtain a quick response. As a result, the unintended consequence of this strategy is that answering calls for service became the most time-consuming patrol task. Patrol workloads increased to such an extent that operational units found it difficult to perform preventive patrol (Kessler, 1993). At the same time, the citizen's obligation for crime prevention was reduced and the police department's responsibility for community safety increased. Citizens turned into the passive recipients of crime control services. Patrol became a reactive function activated by crises instead of a crime preventive function.

The reform era police organization became a closed bureaucratic system that emphasized internal control and adherence to policy and procedures. Department policy and procedures covered every conceivable aspect of organizational life. Officers were discouraged from becoming too friendly with the people they served because policing was considered the responsibility of professionally trained officers only. This separation was further enhanced by the total motorization of patrol. In some departments uniform patrol officers were discouraged from making drug arrest in order to control corruption. The effort to prevent corruption and control officer behavior shaped virtually every aspect of the police organization, administration, and tactics (Kelling, 1995).

In the attempt to free policing from political influence, it became separate from and unresponsive to the communities it served. A technical form of professionalism developed based on skills and values associated with crime control, rather than focus on crime prevention and community respect. Instead of creating safer communities through the prevention of crime, the era's reactive patrol strategy emphasized responding to crime but did little to prevent crime (Kelling, Pate, Dieckman, & Brown, 1975). A powerful administrative orthodoxy emerged rooted in the traditions of military command and bureaucratic management that became the foundation for the theory and practice of police management (Moore & Stephens, 1991).

Table 1.1 summarizes the characteristics of the reform era. This era dramatically changed police administration through the creation of closed organizations isolated from both political and community influences. As a result, law enforcement agencies became the most autonomous and isolated public departments in urban government (Goldstein, 1990). In the final analysis, however, the reform movement failed in every conceivable way: it did not prevent crime; it did not solve crimes; and it lost the consent of the public, especially the minority community (Bratton & Kelling, 2012).

The concepts and principles of the reform era swept the country. The conclusion that crime fighting was the primary police task had a common sense appeal. In attempting to

TABLE 1.1 Reform Paradigm—1930–1980s

- **Mission**—crime control and rapid emergency response
- **Strategy**—random preventive patrol, response to calls for service, and after-the-occurrence crime investigation
- **Organizational system**—closed, command and control bureaucracy
- **Structure**—hierarchical organization defined by rank, policy, standards, rules and task specialization
- **Authority**—criminal law—technological expertise—command authority independent of politics and community control
- **Service tactics: 3 Rs**—random motorized preventive patrol—rapid response to calls for service—reactive investigations

avoid the pitfalls of the political era, this movement was successful in reducing political influ-ence and replacing it with managerial control. However, the era's dominant leadership style resulted in police managers becoming increasingly autocratic and remote from their oper-ational personnel. While professionalism was the ideal of this era, it did not extend to the lower level of the organization, the patrol officer. Management maintained the fiction that the total organization was designed to support patrol, but in reality this was not the case. Management continually tried to control and structure the behavior of patrol officers. This administrative style stifled officer initiative and communicated to them that management did not trust them to think on their own. Everything had to be done in accordance with the procedural manual. These efforts even extended to personal conduct of the officer when off duty. Specific rules and procedures supported by disciplinary punishments were developed to ensure strict compliance with departmental policy and values.

The emphasis on managerial control and decreased officer discretion produced a *deprofessionalization syndrome* that weakened the professional status of the patrol officers (see Sharp, 1982; Stokovic, Kalnich, & Klofas, 2012). As a result, in large urban police depart-ments any assignment except patrol was eagerly sought after, and over time, patrol was per-formed by the newest, most inexperienced officers and those who had been reassigned back to patrol as punishment for rule violations. In fact, patrol became the dumping ground of many departments (Sparrow, Moore, & Kennedy, 1990). Thus, the "best and brightest" offi-cers were often absent from the front line of police service delivery.

Another product of this command and control system with its deprofessionalization syndrome is the creation of two separate organizational cultures, the *street cop culture* and the management culture. In response to command and control management style, the work-ing officers (street cops) developed a self-protective culture consisting of a set of beliefs, val-ues, and norms that reinforced solidarity and support with fellow officers above professional standards of conduct and organizational integrity. Once officers were socialized into this culture, it shaped the way they performed their duties and viewed community members, their department, and its managers. Street cops believed that their managers' only concern is advancing their careers, and that these managers will not protect them from politicians, the media, civilians, and others who do not understand "real" police work, with its constant ambiguity and relentless pressure to "do something, now." Officers adapted the belief that they are on their own, forced to do society's dirty work but received little understanding and support from the public and their department's administrators (Reuss-Inanni, 1983; Kelling, 1995). The reform era's attempts at controlling officer discretion through its command and control administrative practices undermined the goals of police professionalization.

Crises and Paradigm Shift

During the 1960s and 1970s, the United States underwent a series of social changes that altered the relationship of government to its citizens. The civil rights movement and the due-process decisions of the United States Supreme Court had an impact on police prac-tices and this, followed by the anti–Vietnam War protests, challenged the methods police used to handle demonstrations, riots, marches, rallies, and citizens' constitutional rights. Television viewers saw minorities and demonstrators gassed, clubbed, and attacked by dogs. Police investigative tactics and interrogation methods were found to be unconstitutional by a number of Supreme Court decisions. This led to a comprehensive examination of police practices and the justice system that resulted in two national studies, The President's Commission on Law Enforcement and the Administration of Justice in 1967 and the National Advisory Commission on Criminal Justice Standards and Goals in 1973. The focus of these studies was the organization, personnel, education, training, and management of police departments. However, they also raised serious questions about police accountability and relationship to the communities they served (Goldstein, 1990, p. 10). A paradigm shift had begun to take place that challenged the basic conception of how policing should be conducted and organized in the United States.

The issues and questions raised at this time created an interest by scholars into police research. Funding for much of this research came from the Safe Streets Act created by Congress in 1968 and from private sources such as the Ford, Guggenheim, and Charles Stewart Mott Foundations. These efforts disclosed that police officers actually used a great amount of discretion in their work and that the majority of their calls for service were not crime-related. It became evident that policing was more complex than originally perceived by those within and outside of the profession. Lastly, a series of studies conducted during the 1970s found that the police operational strategies of random motorized preventive patrol, rapid response to calls for service, and reactive investigation were not the effective crime control tactics the police claimed they were. These conclusions added to a controversy associated with police strategies and tactics at this time (see Kelling et al., 1975; Spelman & Brown, 1981; Greenwood, Petersilia, & Chaiken, 1977).

Research conducted during the 1980s determined that citizens' view of their personal safety and fear of crime was more closely correlated with community disorder than with crime (Kelling & Moore, 1988). Unfortunately, order maintenance had been all but eliminated as a police tactic by the reform movement. Few departments collected data on disorder offenses or trained officers in how to handle such activities. Nor did they encourage and reward officers for successfully performing order-maintenance activities. The primary police focus was on serious crime, especially felonies, not on offenses that created disorderly neighborhoods (Wilson & Kelling, 1982, pp. 29–38). A shift in police strategy had taken place during the reform era that moved policing away from crime prevention and order maintenance to after-the-fact reaction to crime (Bratton & Kelling, 2012). Community problems became compartmentalized into unrelated single-incident response; crime prevention and Peelian policing ideals were forgotten.

The Community Problem-Solving Policing Paradigm

The 1980s marked the beginning of another paradigmatic shift in policing. The events of the previous two decades along with the impact of research findings and the unprecedented rising of crime rates beginning in 1965 created more questions than answers for police administrators about the effectiveness of their organizations. In addition, during this period, a new breed of officer who differed greatly from those in the past entered policing and began moving up the ranks to positions of authority. The "**new breed**" started entering policing in 1968 with the employment of the first of the "Baby Boomer" generation (born between 1943–1960) (Zemke, Raines, & Filipczak, 2000). This employment cohort was better educated than past recruits and included increased numbers of women and minorities as well as veterans of the Vietnam War. Minority and women officers earned equal treatment in hiring and promotion after numerous legal challenges to past discriminatory practices that eliminated them from police employment and advancement. These "New Breed" officers began to question the management practices, policies, and procedures they were subjected to on a daily basis. Also, during this period several police departments began to experiment with different operational tactics to create safer cities that included foot patrol, decentralization of patrol units, with an emphasis on community outreach and problem solving. These experiments were conducted by police departments in Boston, Massachusetts; Flint, Michigan; Houston, Texas; Newark, New Jersey; New York City; and Santa Ana, California. The neighborhood-oriented policing philosophy developed by the Houston Police Department defined its approach to public safety as:

> an interactive process between police officers assigned to specific beats and the citizens who either work or reside in these beats to mutually develop ways to identify problems and concerns and then to assess viable solutions by providing available resources from both the police department and the community to address the problems and/or concerns.
>
> (Oettmeier & Bieck, 1987, p. 5)

At this time, one of the foremost authorities on policing, Herman Goldstein (1979), articulated and later expanded on the concept of problem-oriented policing (POP). Goldstein suggested that the police should analyze a wide range of information that would identify the cause of the problems that affect communities and create crime. Then construct and implement responses uniquely suited to each particular problem. He urged police managers to consider implementing this approach to solving community crime rather than relying solely on rapid response to individual calls for service and arrest-oriented practices. Goldstein's suggestion challenged traditional police practice and the reform movement's claim to police crime control expertise by disclosing that systematic analysis was seldom applied to the underlying substantive community problems that generate the major proportion of a police department's service demand. A fundamental part of his argument is that community problems cannot be resolved in isolation one incident at a time. He claimed that successful problem control could only be accomplished if those members of the department and the community who have a stake in the problem are included in its analysis and solution.

Police departments experimented with problem-oriented policing in Baltimore County, Maryland; Madison, Wisconsin; San Diego, California; and Newport News, Virginia. A unique aspect of the problem-oriented approach is that it does not require a total organizational redirection by a department in its operational methods. Instead, it can be a process practiced by a specific unit or the whole department. In fact, many departments adapted this processes as part of their Community Policing programs (Reitzel, Piquero, & Piquero, 2005).

In less than two decades following the initial community-oriented experiments, Community Policing (COP) evolved as the new organizational orthodoxy of policing (Cordner & Bibel, 2005; Eck & Rosenbaum, 1994; Rosenbaum, 1998). In 2015, the Bureau of Justice Statistics found that nearly 70 percent of local police departments include Community Policing in their mission statement. That includes nine out of 10 departments serving populations of 25,000 or more (Reaves, 2015). Trojanowicz and Bucqueroux (1994, p. 2) define Community Policing as:

a philosophy and an organizational strategy that promoted a new partnership between people and their police. It is based on the premises that both the police and the community must work together to identify, prioritize, and solve contemporary problems such as crime, drugs, fear of crime, social and physical disorder, and overall neighborhood decay, with the goal of improving the overall quality of life in the area.

Theoretical support for this new community-oriented paradigm was published in a 1982 *Atlantic Monthly* seminal article entitled "Broken Windows: The Police and Neighborhood Safety" written by James Q. Wilson and George L. Kelling. They argued that police departments who focused solely on detection of serious crime are not truly helping communities survive. In addition, Wilson and Kelling claimed that it was community disorder in the form of broken windows, trash, street prostitution, and drug dealing that attracted criminals and bred fear among citizens. This fear created citizen apathy and insecurity, leading to community abandonment and even more crime in marginal communities. They concluded that fighting crime is important; however, fighting fear is essential in order for communities to survive.

A major impetus for the adoption of Community Policing occurred in 1994, when Congress passed the *Omnibus Crime Bill, 18 U.S.C.A. § 1033(e)* that provided funding for the hiring of 100,000 new police officers. The act specified that these new officers must engage in Community Policing. As a result, thousands of local governments directed their police to adapt Community Policing as an organizational strategy in order to gain additional police officers through federal funding.

At the heart of the community-oriented philosophy is a broad view of the police function that involves the creation of a partnership between the police and the residents of the communities they serve. This partnership is designed to improve the quality of community life through the creation of problem-solving strategies to enhance neighborhood safety. However, some early proponents of this form of policing have claimed that it returns policing to the original principles of Sir Robert Peel (Braiden, 1986). Operationally Community Policing is designed to move beyond incident-driven reactive policing by directing patrol officers' attention to the conditions that underlie and create disorder and criminal incidents. Officers are expected to work closely with neighborhood residents to identify and address issues of crime and disorder by using the resources and capabilities of both the department and local community. It is envisioned that with community cooperation, the police would obtain valuable information and support that will assist them in solving crimes, creating order, and in some instances, identify problems that were unknown to them (Trojanowicz & Bucqueroux, 1994). This perspective envisions policing with an expanded purpose that combines crime control with the responsibility to prevent crime and promote and maintain community order.

The operational strategy of Community Policing contains the following key elements:

- Decentralization of patrol units by geographical assignment. Officers are assigned to foot beats, substations, and community-policing zones to be closer to the community.
- Selection of a number of officers as community policing officers to liaison with the community as well as patrol and manage specific beats, zones, and/or substations.
- Selection of a line supervisor, usually a sergeant or lieutenant, to oversee the community patrol officers.

- Directed and structured patrol activities designed to develop a closer interpersonal relationship between citizens and community patrol officers.
- Citizen-police engage in joint efforts in problem identification, analysis, and resolution.
- Problem response strategies developed at the operational level.
- Enhancement of communication between the department, community, and other agencies within and outside of city government.

(Fyfe et al., 1997, p. 541)

Community Policing encourages departments to develop a close bond between the patrol officer and the community. Officers are urged to get to know the citizens on their beats and understand their needs, habits, and wishes (Farrell, 1988). The underlying belief is that the police must be able to relate and understand a community in order to identify its problems and develop creative responses to its public safety issues. Community Policing is the actualization of the concept that police in a democracy are not a closed organization that is insular, self-contained, or cut off from the communities from which their power truly derives (Skolnick, 1999). This is an actualization of the Peelian concept that "the police are the people and the people are the police." An initial evaluation of the community foot patrol program in Flint, Michigan, found that citizen fear of victimization was reduced, citizen satisfaction with the police was enhanced, and the attitudes of the police toward the public improved. In addition, many officers found foot patrol personally and professionally rewarding (Trojanowicz, 1982).

Advocates of Community Policing encouraged police departments to adopt proactive decentralized strategies designed to address issues of crime, fear, and disorder within neighborhoods. In return, community members were expected to take a proactive role in helping the police and other government entities set and implement community-oriented policy. It was envisioned that citizens would have input in setting organizational goals and objectives as well as establishing priorities for action. Ideally, each community or neighborhood would be policed in accordance with neighborhood needs and values (Kelling & Coles, 1996). In its ideal form, Community Policing foresees police assignments and strategies being set in accordance with local needs, norms, and values. This decentralized approach to operational strategy is assumed to provide citizens with protection that is tailored to meet the needs of diverse communities (see Table 1.2).

TABLE 1.2 Community Problem-Solving Policing 1980s–Today

- **Mission**—community safety, stablization, and problem solving
- **Strategy**—decentralized service delivery based upon community needs that are identified through community police problem solving partnerships
- **Organizational system**—open system
- **Structure**—hierarchical with decentralized, programmatic, and place-based officers and units
- **Authority**—philosophy—community partnership and engagement focused on problem identification and solving
- **Service Tactics**—line officer-based, foot patrol, bikes, teams, neighborhood police stations

In contrast to the reform era, Community Policing expands the function of policing beyond crime to the resolution of community problems (Peak & Glensor, 2012). In essence, Community Policing places more responsibility on the police department. Agencies committed to Community Policing must perform their traditional duties of law enforcement, order maintenance, and service as well as attempt to identify and solve local problems. The police function is expanded to include a proactive response to maintaining order, dealing with quality-of-life offenses, problem solving, and fixing community "broken windows."

Community Policing represents a major transformational change that redefines how the police organization understands its function, operations, and relationship to the community. It is not just a program but also an operational strategy and organizational philosophy designed to promote police-citizen, community-based problem solving. Analytical community problem solving beyond the resolution of specific incidents is a strategic redirection that is in contrast to previous efforts by reform era police management to limit officer discretion and standardize their administrative control. However, while this community problem-confronting approach contradicted many of the key features of the reform era, it did retain its bureaucratic organizational structure. Lastly, relying on citizen endorsement of order-maintenance activities (as a means of justifying police activities) acknowledges dependence on the political process and the broadening of the police function.

During the 1990s adoption of Community Policing methods increased markedly as many departments devoted a proportion of their patrol resources to Community Policing. In 1996, *Good Housekeeping*, a popular monthly magazine that is subscribed to by millions of American households, published a special report on a year-long survey that identified America's best suburban police forces. The survey focused on the suburbs because this is where a sizable portion of the country's population lived. The article claimed that, "Today's top departments do more than just arrest criminals—they help neighborhoods solve problems and stop crime before it starts." *Good Housekeeping* identified the following characteristics as those that each of the top police departments had in common:

- Excellent leadership epitomized by a police chief with vision and the skills to carry it out.
- An ability to identify trouble spots and act before there is a need to make arrests.
- Quick and thorough response to citizens calls for assistance, complaints and concerns.
- Innovative programs, often technology based, to fight crime more quickly and effectively.
- Officers who see policing as a career of choice and who are personally accountable for community stability.
- Intolerance of brutality and corruption within the ranks.
- Creative solutions to address traditional hard-to-handle crimes such as domestic violence and drug abuse in the schools.
- Citizens who are active auxiliaries of the crime-fighting team and who are encouraged to critique the department's performance.

(Domanick, 1996, pp. 82–92)

The significance of this article is that it reflects the extent to which the operational dimensions of Community Policing and problem solving had become the standard by which police organizational excellence is judged by mainstream America. The Office of Justice

Programs in 2000 reported that 65 percent of departments serving 50,000 or more residents indicate that they have a full-time Community Policing unit in their department (Reaves & Goldberg, 2000). It also reflects the emphasis on the use of technology-based innovation to address crime which has emerged as a defining characteristic of strategic policing.

Ideally, Community Policing is a bottom-up strategy that places emphasis on the police officer's use of information, judgment, wisdom, problem-solving abilities and expertise to solve community public safety issues. At the same time, it supports a strategic redirection in policing because it encourages police departments to actively engage their external environment and develop strategies to address public safety needs instead of just responding to single incidents. Thus, Community Policing represents a significant shift in organizational power and control from administration to operations.

This type of organizational shift requires police administrators to adopt a flexible leadership style that is different from the traditional "command and control" methods that departments had developed in the reform era (Moore & Stephens, 1991). Community Policing challenges police executives to be aware of their interdependence with the community and understand the factors that affect public safety. It provides a viable frame of reference and calls for integration between the department and its community. Unfortunately, research has determined that the process of organizational change needed to support this philosophy and make community-oriented strategies work is incomplete (Zhao, He, & Lovrich, 2003).

Despite financial support from the federal government, Community Policing has never fully become a complete organizational strategy. In many police departments, Community Policing is a programmatic function that is the responsibility of an organizational subunit. Police departments operating in this manner are divided into both a closed and open system organizational model. The majority of the department's officers are still subjected to traditional reform-style management and their primary operational strategy is random patrol and single-incident response policing. Today, almost every specialized program developed by a police department is labeled Community Policing. Stand-alone Community Policing units tend to evolve into operational ghettos whose officers are considered not to be engaging in real police work (Toch & Grant, 2005). Departments that claim to be Community Policing organizations are still bureaucratically structured and functioning with operational service delivery strategies similar to that developed in the reform era of policing (Greene & Mastrofski, 1988; Skogan, 1990). However, the central philosophy of Community Policing with its emphasis on listening to and working more closely with the community has become the dominant tenet of 21st-century police administration.

Strategic Policing: A Developing Paradigm

During the three decades before the 1990s the United States experienced its highest recorded crime rates. At the beginning of the 21st century, changing societal conditions and fear of crime increasingly created greater demands on police services and tested the limits of the traditional operational strategies that developed during the reform era. As the demands on policing expanded, public expectations of what the police should be doing also diversified and grew. The events of 9/11 created a national emphasis on homeland security. However, fiscal difficulties further enhanced by the financial crisis of 2008 affected the ability of local governments to provide services such as policing. A national survey of police departments conducted by the Police Executive Research Forum in 2010 found that 51 percent of the respondent's departments had experienced significant cutbacks in personnel and staffing levels. Thus, the police were expected to address increasingly demanding public safety needs and be more effective but had fewer personnel resources to accomplish these demands.

As they responded to these environmental demands some police administrators sought to change their operational methods and develop more effective responses to the challenges they were facing (Moore & Stephens, 1991; Kennedy, 1993; Bratton, 1998; Maple, 1999). Executives within this group began to experiment with new ways of policing. They sought to use their resources more effectively and resolve public safety problems while innovating their operational response strategies. New strategies such as Compstat, Hot Spots, Focused Deterrence, Intelligence-Led, and Evidence-Based Policing emerged as part of these new data-driven approaches to policing labeled by some as "Predictive policing" (Pearsall, 2010). The operationalization of these new strategies created another paradigm shift as they engaged an open-system organizational information perspective that was based upon the adaptation of data-driven strategic problem-solving tactics for their organizations. This form of management prevalent in the corporate world emphasized the linkage between the organization and the environment in which it existed and the outcomes it desired to achieve (Moore & Stephens, 1991).

An evolution of thought began to take place within the police profession. Police executives who learned from their own experiences were now generating new ideas about how to police the nation's communities. The strategies they developed paralleled organizational techniques drawn from the corporate world that used data analysis to anticipate trends in market conditions to drive sales strategy. Police departments began to use data analysis to anticipate and identify trends in community safety and crime and develop strategic responses to these conditions. These new strategies shared common elements that included developing information from various sources, analyzing these data, and using the intelligence that was produced to anticipate and respond to crime and problem conditions.

The idea of the strategic management of policing was initially discussed during the Executive Session on Policing 1985–1988 conducted at Harvard University's Kennedy School of Government. In a monograph developed during this session, Moore and Trojanowicz (1988) defined it as a strategy that increased police capacity to deal with crimes that are not well controlled by traditional methods. In 1991, Mark H. Moore and Darrel W. Stephens coauthored a text for the Police Executive Research Forum that made a strong case for policing to move beyond the administrative practice of command and control and adopt the practices of strategic management. David Kennedy (1993), however, warned that strategic policing, with its wider range of tactics, new responsibilities, and roles for officers and managers, would require hard choices for managers especially in regard to resource allocation to be successful.

For the purposes of this discussion, *strategic policing* is defined as the art and science of developing, implementing, and evaluating data-driven cross-functional strategies to accomplish organizational goals and objectives (David, 2009). It involves the integration of information analysis, strategy development, managerial accountability, operational tactics, and continuous evaluation. It represents a significant shift from the way managers traditionally conceive of their departments and how they conduct the process of policing. A central facet of this process is the alignment of a department's strengths and capabilities with the demands placed upon it by its external and internal environments. Operational managers are expected to formulate, implement, and evaluate cross-functional strategies and tactics that respond to the demands of their department's environment to achieve organizational goals and objectives. Departments engaging in strategic policing function as open learning systems that actively interact and understand and learn from the environment in which they exist and respond to its demands as proactively as possible.

All organizations interact with their environment; it is the degree in which they do and understand the demands the environment makes of them that varies. ***Closed systems*** such as the ones that emerged in policing during the reform era interacted minimally on an incident-by-incident basis. These organizations were perceived to be administratively self-regulating closed structures that were complete unto themselves, not affected by external forces. This is not an accurate view of the police organizational reality in today's world. Today police organizations are viewed as complex structures subjected to a variety of environmental influences and driving forces.

Strategic policing envisions police departments as ***open system* learning organizations** that acknowledges their dynamic interrelationship with their external environment. This concept of policing emphasizes the understanding and use of external environmental inputs (information about driving forces such as crime and community safety problems) and internal processes (organizational capability to respond to and manage demands) to create outcomes and services that are valued by the communities they serve (More et al., 2012, p. 10).

Open system police organizations engage with and understand their community and its problems. They engage in a continual process of transforming inputs (intelligence data, citizen complaints, governmental mandates, problems, safety issues, police observations) into a coordinated response by managing internal subsystems (calls for service processing, crime analysis, developing operational strategy, tactical deployment, investigation, arrests) that produce outcomes (e.g., public safety, crime control, traffic control, dispute resolution, fear reduction, community survival and justice). Effectiveness is based upon the adaptation of their operational practices and resources to community needs and expectations (Roberg, Kuykendall, & Novak, 2002, pp. 35–36).

Strategic policing involves the integration of information analysis, strategy, managerial accountability, operational tactics, and performance evaluation within the daily functioning of the police department. It is designed to create a more proactive police response to crime prevention and public safety through intelligence analysis, the identification and management of problems, and the deployment of department resources. In strategically managed departments intelligence becomes the basis for operational decisions about deployment of resources, tactics, impact assessments, performance outcomes, and community safety. Through strategic analysis departments are able to identify potential and current crime patterns and persistent offenders. This intelligence provides departments with the ability to anticipate crime trends and threats instead of just reacting to them incident by incident.

A central facet of strategic policing is the development and utilization of a contingency process to plan and develop tactics to respond to public safety demands. Contingency theory holds that the most effective organizations possess a degree of adaptably and flexibility that enables them to respond to the changing and contradicting demands they confront (Banner & Gagne, 1995). Strategic policing provides police operational managers with the discretionary flexibility to initiate and reshape operational tactics to meet changing demands. The department's response to crime and community safety becomes broader, more proactive, and more sophisticated. Strategic management organizes policing as an information-intensive learning endeavor (Pearsall, 2010). However, departments that engage in strategic policing still employ a centralized bureaucratic structure and an administrative style that controls intelligence and operational strategy.

Operational managers are responsible for using intelligence gained from community engagement and analysis to develop tactics and focus their attention on current and potential crime patterns as well as threats to community safety. The benefit of understanding, engaging, and building relationships with the community is one tactic learned by police managers during the community problem-solving policing era. As new intelligence data arises, commanders are expected to adjust their tactics to respond effectively. This process provides the department with the means to develop the capacity to initiate and reshape operational behavior to meet changing demands. As a result the police department is functioning as a learning organization.

Strategic policing represents the adaptation of the learning organization concept to policing by consistently expanding a department's capacity to restructure its operational tactics to meet both the current and changing needs of their communities (Silverman, 1999). Strategically managed departments continually evaluate and adapt to their environment instead of simply trying to maintain the status quo and operate in a reactive mode such as traditionally managed police organizations. Learning organizations analyze the forces that affect them, continually assess their ability to respond to these forces, and learn from their own and similar experiences of other organizations. They are working smarter, not harder (Geller, 1997).

Major examples of strategies currently in use during this developing era in policing that will be discussed in this text are Compstat, Hot Spots, Focused Deterrence, Intelligence-Led, and Evidence-Based Policing. As part of this chapter we will briefly discuss Compstat and Intelligence-Led Policing because of their significant impact on changing the course of police administration and leadership. Table 1.3 summarizes the organizational strategy of the strategic policing era.

Strategic policing is not one form of policing (i.e., traditional, community, or problem solving) but a blend of all these plus an organizational management process that is based upon ongoing analysis of the department's data drawn from the external environment and

TABLE 1.3 Strategic Policing 1994–Today

- **Mission**—prevent, control, and reduce crime; improve quality of life and community safety
- **Strategy**—combines information gathering, crime and problem data analysis with a geographic focus, and tactical development
- **Organizational System**—open system mission-driven outcome-focused adaptive learning system
- **Structure**—bureaucratic and geographical decentralized
- **Authority**—knowledge-based—system thinking—managerial accountability system
- **Service Tactics**—information gathering, timely and accurate analysis, incident mapping, community partnerships, intelligence-based development of operational strategies and tactics, and continual follow-up and assessment. Data analysis and pubic safety needs focuses and drives operational units' tactics.

the evaluation of its operational tactics. It builds on the past and present to engage the future of policing.

Compstat

The first adaptation of strategic management in policing occurred in 1994, when the New York City Police Department developed an organizational management and operational service delivery process entitled Compstat. (See Chapter 13 for an extensive discussion of this process.) Compstat employs a comprehensive, continuous analysis of current crime patterns, with the development of tactics based upon this data analysis, identification, and evaluation of results, and redirection of operational personnel to meet changing conditions (Silverman, 1999; Walsh, 2001). Once a police manager had monitored and analyzed the intelligence data, he or she could deploy their resources to reduce crime in the "hot spot areas" in a logical data-driven manner. It was not a one-shot incident-driven approach but a continuously updated daily accounting of data keyed to localities that held supervisors up and down the chain of command accountable for solving problems and preventing them from reoccurring. The NYPD executive team's organizational strategy set clear performance outcomes that concentrated on crime prevention and suppression and on managerial accountability based on real-time information analysis, integrated problem solving, and tactical development. Compstat also set a premium on monitoring, accountability, and maintaining managerial oversight of the entire organization (Henry, 2002; Silverman, 1999). Through this process NYPD used information technology, operational strategy, and managerial accountability to focus the department's resources on crime and quality-of-life problems that were affecting the entire city. It was the first development of the learning organization concept in policing. Compstat's emphasis on crime prevention and suppression, and on supervisorial accountability, would have a profound impact on increasing the effectiveness and efficiency of NYPD and other large city police departments that would adopt it (Domanick, 2015).

Operationally Compstat is radically different from the accepted concepts and practices that have guided police administration through most of its existence from the reform era. It utilizes methods and strategies similar to those used by corporate managers to achieve their mission (Henry, 2002). Compstat is based upon and emphasizes the vital link between timely intelligence information, operational decision making, and crime control objectives (McDonald, 2002). As a management tool, its utility rests in the fact that it is adaptable to constantly changing conditions and any organizational setting. The underlying principle of Compstat is the belief that police officers and police agencies can have a substantial positive impact on crime and quality-of-life problems (Bratton, 1998).

The New York City Police Department's Compstat process is credited with turning the city from a place that once represented the ultimate in urban lawlessness into a city safer than many other cities in the United States. Police statistics for New York City indicate that serious crime has decreased by double digits since NYPD developed Compstat in 1994. Since then, serious felony crime in New York City has dropped by 80.07 percent and murder by 86.4 percent (see NYPD website: www.nyc.gove/html/nypd). Compstat has been adopted by a majority of the larger police departments in the United States as well as police organizations in other countries.

Intelligence-Led Policing

Intelligence-Led Policing is a business model and managerial philosophy in which data analysis and crime intelligence are pivotal to an objective, decision-making framework that facilitates crime and problem reduction, disruption, and prevention through both strategic management and effective enforcement strategies that target prolific and serious offenders (Ratcliffe, 2016, p. 63). This process is based upon the fact that the police during the normal course of their work gather a great amount of data about crime and offenders. Community and problem-solving policing enhanced this informational gathering. At the same time, problem-oriented policing supports the belief that analysis of this data is useful in determining responses to crime and community problems.

Intelligence-Led Policing, like Compstat, employs a top-down hierarchical administrative control system like the one advocated during the reform era. Operationally it combines crime analysis and criminal intelligence to focus police resources on serious crimes and offenders (Tilley, 2003). In 1995, the Chief Constable of Kent, England, Sir David Phillips, pioneered the first use of Intelligence-Led Policing in a systematic manner. He positioned intelligence at the heart of his department operational decision making. The Kent Intelligence Unit directed aspects of daily police activities (Maguire & John, 2006). This policing strategy has been adopted by police departments in the United States, New Zealand, Australia, India, and Europe. The Bureau of Justice Assistance issued a report on Intelligence-Led Policing in 2005 noting that policing cannot function without collecting, processing, and using intelligence. The report emphasized that intelligence is vital for decision making, planning, strategic targeting, and crime prevention (Peterson, 2005). (See Chapter 13 for an extensive discussion of this process.)

 Analysis

Emerging out of the development of strategic policing is a new police leadership model similar to that found in corporate organizations. This model represents a change in how police administrators conceive of their department's organizational strategy as they analyze and convert information, prioritize resource allocation, develop tactics to prevent and respond to public safety demands. Police executives who practice this managerial approach are expected to proactively develop and implement an organizational direction based upon current intelligence that allows their departments to initiate and reshape their activities to meet the changing demands of their operational environment. Through a process of data collection and analysis, they are expected to align the capabilities of their internal organization with the demands and needs of their external environment. Properly implemented, strategic policing turns the police organization into an open, adaptive, learning organization.

The extent of the adaptation of strategic policing and its effect on community safety remains to be empirically tested. While knowledge about the effect of these developing strategies is still emerging, there is optimism about the future of policing (Braga & Weisburd, 2006). Strategic policing will require organizational changes that demand more than quick adaptations and limited structural changes. A properly designed organizational strategy must establish command accountability and integrity at all levels of the department or this process has the potential to degenerate into a numbers game without lasting impact (Eterno & Silverman, 2012). Ideally, it should focus the entire organization on its primary public safety mission. Strategic policing is a blend of the old and the new, retaining an organizational leadership style and structure similar to that employed by the Peelian Reform of 1829 and the Professional Reform of 1930–1980s (Willis, Mastrofski, & Weisburd, 2004). Time will tell the extensiveness of strategic policing's impact on police administration.

Conclusion

This chapter began with a quote from Thomas Repetto (1978) that described police administration as a living, breathing organism shaped by the political, social, and economic trends of time and place. Our descriptive history of the development of professional policing supports his position. In the 19th century, executive leadership and strong administrative practice were the critical elements in the success and acceptance of the London Metropolitan Police as a world-wide model of professional policing. The police paradigm shifts of the last century were also products of efforts by strong police leaders as they responded to the challenges they faced. August Vollmer in Berkeley, California; O. W. Wilson in Kansas City and Chicago; J. Edgar Hoover of the FBI; and William Parker of Los Angeles were the developers and disseminators of the professional police reform movement. Lee Brown of Houston, Texas; Hubert Williams of Newark, New Jersey; Neil Behan of Baltimore County, Maryland; and Darrel Stephens of Newport News, Virginia, are but a few of the police chief executives who were responsible for the community problem-solving paradigm shift (Sparrow et al., 1990). William J. Bratton, twice Commissioner of the NYPD and former Chief of the Los Angeles Police Department, along with the 1994 NYPD executive team, are the creators and implementers of the Compstat process.

William Bratton is an example of a strong strategic leader whose leadership style energized the bureaucratic structures of the police organizations under his command. These organizations were changed through the introduction of strategic management practices and the establishment of accountability measures that accurately determined levels of both production and performance. They became police learning organizations.

Today's police departmental structure, management, and service delivery strategies are the result of three organizational redirections that occurred during the 20th century. Disenchantment with political control of the police and widespread corruption at the beginning of the century led to the reform era. The ultimate goals of this reform were to free policing from political influence and professionalize the occupation. Services that could be described as social work were eliminated, and the primary mission of the police became crime control through enforcement of the law. Administrative control established through bureaucratically structured organizations became the dominant objective of the reformers, and every effort was made to reduce officer discretion. This movement established the bureaucracy as the dominant police organizational model. The vast majority of police organizations in the United States are still organized and managed in this manner.

In the 1960s, a series of societal changes and civil unrest in American cities challenged police legitimacy. In reaction to these external driving forces, unanswered questions were raised by critical research of the effectiveness police operational practice. The desire by many police executives for a change from the traditional police practices developed in the past led to the emergence of the community problem-solving policing models.

During the community problem-solving era, departments began to adopt a more open-system approach that involved customer engagement and service philosophy. Crime control remained as one of the primary functions of law enforcement, but attempts were made to broaden police objectives to include order maintenance, conflict resolution, and problem solving, and engaging in community partnerships. Input from members of the community was actively sought. Policing attempted to decentralize along programmatic lines, employing community-based substations and geographically based teams. Line officers were assigned to a specific beat for an extended period to conduct crime control meetings, engage in problem-solving activities, and work diligently to improve the relationship between the police and the public. However, the dominance of the reform era's bureaucratic organization with its control-oriented management culture resulted in a limited adaptation of Community Policing by many police departments.

Perhaps, the challenge of police reform is not to "banish bureaucracy" but to return it to functionality (Osborne & Gaebler, 1993; Osborne & Plastrik, 1997). In many police departments today, bureaucratic values still define their relationship with the public, shape organizational goals, and set performance standards. However, many managers are pragmatists who understand they must temper bureaucratic values with genuine empathy (for employees and clients) if they are to accomplish the department's mission, goals, and objectives effectively (More et al., 2012).

Strategic policing addressed the schism between bureaucracy and Community Policing. While many of the creators of strategic policing reject Community Policing as an effective organizational strategy, they retain its central philosophy—to work closely with the community to identify and address crime and disorder issues. Strategic policing is an attempt to reengineer police administration by blending the best of both the bureaucratic and community problem-solving organizational processes to develop proactive instead of reactive organizations.

Strategic policing provides police administrators with a way to retain the lessons of the past while constantly reassessing, learning, and redirecting the organization to meet future needs. It is not bureaucracy, or Community Policing, or problem-solving policing alone, but a combination of all of these that are being used by strategic administrators as they direct their organizations to meet the needs of public safety in United States. Lastly, it should be remembered that in a democracy policing should always respond to the needs of the people. It is a work in progress shaped by the political, social, human, organizational, and economic trends of time and place.

KEY TERMS

August Vollmer	Learning organization	Police
Bureaucracy	London Metropolitan Police	Political era policing
Closed system	Max Weber	Reform era policing
Community problem-solving	New Breed	Robert Peel
policing	Open system	Strategic management
Compstat	Orlando W. Wilson	Strategic policing
Deprofessionalization	Paradigm	Street cop culture
syndrome	Peel's *Principles of Law*	Types of police organizations
Intelligence-Led Policing	*Enforcement*	

References

Banner, D., & Gange, T. (1995). *Designing effective organizations: Traditional & transformational views.* Thousand Oaks, CA: Sage.

Bayley, D. (1975). Police and political development in Europe. In C. Tilly (Ed.), *The formation of national states in Western Europe* (pp. 328–379). Princeton, NJ: Princeton University Press.

Braga, A., & Weisburd, D. (2006). Police innovation and crime prevention: Lessons learned from police research over the past 20 years (2015, July 20). This review draws upon material available in Weisburd, David L. & Braga, Anthony A. (Eds.) *Police innovation: Contrasting perspectives.* New York: Cambridge University Press. Hebrew University of Jerusalem Legal Research Paper.

Braiden, C. (1986). Bank robbers and stolen bikes: Thoughts of a street cop. *Canadian Police College Journal, 10,* 1–30.

Bratton, W., & Kelling, G.L. (2012, December). Counts count, police matter: Of tactics and strategy. *The Police Chief, 79,* 54–59.

Bratton, W., & Knobler, P. (1998). *Turnaround.* New York: Random House.

Conser, J., Russell, G., Paynich, R., & Gingerich, T. (2005). *Law enforcement in the United States.* Sudbury, MA: Jones and Bartlett.

Cordner, G., & Bibel, E. (2005). Problem-oriented policing in practice. *Criminology & Public Policy, 4,* 155–180.

Covey, S.R. (2004). *The seven habits of highly effective people.* New York: The Free Press.

Critchley, T. (1972). *A history of police in England and Wales.* Montclair, NJ: Patterson Smith.

David, F.R. (2009). *Strategic management,* 12th ed. Upper Saddle River, NJ: Prentice Hall.

Dessler, G. (2004). *Management: Principles and practices for tomorrow's leaders.* Upper Saddle River, NJ: Prentice Hall.

Domanick, J.(1996, November). America's best suburban police forces. *Good Housekeeping,* 82–92.

Domanick, J. (1996, 2015). *Blue: The LAPD and the battle to redeem American policing.* New York: Simon & Schuster.

Eck, J., & Rosenbaum, D. (1994). The new police order: Effectiveness, equality and efficiency in community policing. In D. Rosenbaum (Ed.), *The challenge of community policing* (pp. 3–23). Thousand Oaks CA: Sage.

Eterno, J.A., & Silverman, E.B. (2012). *The crime numbers game: Management by manipulation.* Boca Raton, FL: CRC Press.

Farrell, M. (1988). The development of the community patrol officer program: Community policing in the New York City police department. In J. Greene, & S. Mastrofski (Eds.), *Community policing: Rhetoric or reality?* (pp. 73–88). New York: Prager.

Fayol, H. (1992). General principles of management. In J. Shafritz, & J. Ott (Eds.), *Classics of organizational theory* (pp. 37–49). Long Grove, IL: Waveland Press.

Flanagan, R. (2008).*The Independent review of policing final report*. Home Office: Gov. UK.

Fosdick, R. (1969, reprint of 1915 original). *American police systems*. Montclair, NJ: Patterson Smith.

Fuld, L.F. (1910). *Police adminstration*. New York: Putnam.

Fyfe, J.J., Greene, J.R., Walsh, W., Wilson, O., & McLaren, R. (1997). *Police administration*. New York: McGraw-Hill.

Geller, W. (1997). Suppose we were really serious about police departments becoming learning organizations? *National Institute of Justice Journal, 234*, 2–8.

Glensor, R., Correia, M., & Peak, K. (2000). *Policing communities: Understanding and solving problems*. Los Angeles: Roxbury.

Goldstein, H. (1977). *Policing a free society*. Cambridge, MA: Ballinger.

Goldstein, H. (1979). Improving policing: A problem-oriented approach. *Crime and Delinquency, 25*, 236–258.

Goldstein, H. (1990). *Problem-oriented policing*. New York: McGraw Hill.

Goldstein, J., & Goodman, J.D. (2014, April 16). A London guide for 1 Police Plaza. *New York Times*, A20.

Graper, E. (1921). *American police administration*. New York: Palgrave Macmillan.

Greene, J., & Mastrofski, S. (1988). *Community policing: Rhetoric or reality?* New York: Praeger.

Greenwood, P., Petersilia, J., & Chaiken, J. (1977). *The criminal investigation process*. Lexington, MA: Heath.

Guyot, D. (1991). *Policing as though people mattered*. Philadelphia: Temple University Press.

Harring, S. (1982). The taylorization of police work. *The Insurgent Sociologist, 4*, 25–32.

Henry, V. (2002). *The Compstat paradigm: Management accountability in policing*. New York: Looseleaf Press.

Kelling, G. (1995). How to run a police department. *City Journal, 5*(4), 1–13.

Kelling, G.L., & Bratton, W.J. (1993). Implementing community policing: The administrative problem. *Perspectives on Policing, 17*, 1–11.

Kelling, G., & Coles, C. (1996). *Fixing broken windows: Restoring order and reducing crime in our communities*. New York: The Free Press.

Kelling, G., & Moore, M. (1988). The evolving strategy of policing. *Perspectives on Policing, 4*, 1–4.

Kelling, G., Pate, T., Dieckman, D., & Brown, C. (1975). *The Kansas City preventive patrol experiment*. Washington, DC: Police Foundation.

Kennedy, D.M. (1993). The strategic management of police resources: *Perspectives on Policing, 14*, 1–9.

Kessler, D. (1993). Integrating calls for services with community and problem oriented policing: A case study. *Crime & Delinquency, 39*, 485–508.

Klockars, C.B. (1985). *The idea of police*. Beverly Hills, CA: Sage.

Kuhn, T.S. (1962). *The structure of scientific revolutions*. Chicago: University of Chicago Press.

Lane, R. (1967). *Policing the city—Boston, 1822–1825*. Cambridge, MA: Harvard University Press.

Lee, W. (1901). *A history of the police in England*. London: Methuen.

Maguire, M., & John, T. (2006). Intelligence led policing, Managerialism and community engagement: Competing priorities and the role of the National Intelligence Model in the UK. *Policing & Society, 16*(1), 67–85.

Maple, J. (1999). *The crime fighter*. New York: Doubleday.

McDonald, P.P. (2002). *Managing police operations: Implementing the New York crime control model—Compstat*. Stamford, CT: Thomson.

Moore, M., & Braga, A. (2003). *The bottom line of policing: What citizens should value and measure in police performance*. Washington, DC: Police Executive Research Forum.

Moore, M., & Stephens, D. (1991). *Beyond command and control: The strategic management of police departments*. Washington, DC: Police Executive Research Forum.

Moore, M., & Trojanowicz, R. (1988). Corporate strategy for policing. *Perspectives in Policing, 6*, 1–8.

More, H.W., Vito, G.F., & Walsh, W.F. (2012). *Organizational behavior and management in law enforcement*. Upper Saddle River, NJ: Prentice Hall.

Morgan, G. (1997). *Images of organization*. Thousand Oaks, CA: Sage.

Oettmeier, T., & Bieck, W. (1987). *Developing a policing style for neighborhood oriented policing*. Houston: Houston Police Department.

Osborne, D., & Gaebler, T. (1993). *Reinventing government*. New York: Plume.

Osborne, D., & Plastrik, P. (1997). *Banishing bureaucracy*. New York: Addison-Wesley.

Palmer, S. (1988). *Police and protest in England and Ireland, 1780–1850*. New York: Cambridge University Press.

Peak, K., & Glensor, R. (2012). *Community policing & problem solving: Strategies and practices*. Upper Saddle River, NJ: Prentice Hall.

Pearsall, B. (2010). Predictive policing: The future of law enforcement? *NIJ Journal No. 266*, May. Washington, DC: National Institute of Justice.

Peterson, M. (2005). *Intelligence-led policing: The new intelligence architecture*. Washington, DC: Bureau of Justice Assistance.

Police Executive Research Forum. (2010). *Critical issues in policing series: Is the economic downturn fundamentally changing how we police*. Washington, DC: PERF.

Ratcliffe, J. (2016). *Intelligence-led policing*, 2nd ed. New York, NY: Routledge.

Reaves, B. (2015). *Local police departments 2013, personnel, policies, and practices*. Washington, DC: Bureau of Justice Statistics.

Reaves, B., & Goldberg, A. (2000). *Law enforcement management and administrative statistics, 1997*. Washington, DC: Bureau of Justice Statistics.Reitzel, J., Piquero, N., & Piquero, A. (2005). Problem-oriented policing. In R. Dunham, & G. Alpert (Eds.), *Critical issues in policing* (pp. 419–431). Long Grove, IL: Waveland.

Repetto, T.A. (1978). *The blue parade*. New York: Free Press.

Reuss-Inanni, E. (1983). *Two cultures of policing: Street cops and management cops*. New Brunswick, NJ: Transaction Books.

Roberg, R., Kuykendall, J., & Novak, K. (2002). *Police management*. Los Angeles, CA: Roxbury.

Rosenbaum, D. (1998). The changing role of the police: Assessing the current transition to community policing. In J. Brodeur (Ed.), *How to recognize good policing: Problems and issues*. Thousand Oaks, CA: Sage Publications.

Senge, P. (1990). *The fifth discipline: The art & practice of the learning organization*. New York: Doubleday.

Sharp, E. (1982). Street-level discretion in policing: Attitudes and behaviors in the deprofessionalization syndrome. *Law and Policy Quarterly, 4*, 167–189.

Silverman, E. (1999). *NYPD battles crime: Innovative strategies in policing*. Boston: Northeastern University Press.

Skogan, W. (1990). *Disorder and decline: Crime and the spiral of decay in American neighborhoods*. New York: The Free Press.

Skolnick, J. (1999). On democratic policing. In *Ideas in American policing*. Washington, DC: Police Foundation.

Sparrow, M., Moore, M., & Kennedy, D. (1990). *Beyond 911: A new era for policing*. New York: Basic Books.

Spelman, W., & Brown, D. (1981). *Calling the police: Citizen reporting of serious crime*. Washington, DC: Police Executive Research Forum.

Stokovic, S., Kalnich, D., & Klofas, J. (2012). *Criminal justice organizations: Administration and management*. Belmont, CA: Wadsworth.

Tilley, N. (2003).Community policing, problem-oriented policing and intelligence-led policing. In T. Newburn (Ed.), *Handbook of policing* (pp. 311–339). Portland, OR: Willan.

Toch, H., & Grant, J. (1982). *Reforming human services*. Beverly Hills, CA: Sage.

Trojanowicz, R. (1982). *An evaluation of the neighborhood foot patrol program in Flint, Michigan*. East Lansing, MI: Michigan State University.

Trojanowicz, R., & Bucqueroux, B. (1994). *Community policing: How to get started*. Cincinnati: Anderson.

Uchida, C. (2010). The development of American police: An historical overview. In R. Dunham, & G. Alpert (Eds.), *Critical issues in policing* (pp. 17–36). Long Grove, IL: Waveland Press.

Wadman, R.C., & Allison, W.T. (2004). *To protect and to serve: A history of police in America*. Upper Saddle River, NJ: Prentice Hall.

Walker, S., & Katz, C.M. (2011). *The police in America*. New York: McGraw Hill.

Walsh, W. (2001). Compstat: An analysis of an emerging police managerial paradigm. *Policing, 24*(3), 347–362.

Weber, M. (1947). *The theory of social and economic organization*. New York: The Free Press.

Whitehouse, J. (1973). Historical perspectives on the police community service function. *Journal of Police Science and Administration, 1*(1), 87–92.

Willis, J., Mastrofski, S., & Weisburd, D. (2004). Compstat and bureaucracy: A case study of challenges and opportunities for change. *Justice Quarterly, 21*, 463–493.

Wilson, J., & Kelling, G. (1982, March). Broken windows: Police and neighborhood safety. *Atlantic Monthly*, 29–38.

Wilson, O.W. (1942). *Police records—Their installation and use*. Chicago: Public Administration Service.

Wilson, O.W. (1957). *Police planning.* Springfield, IL: C.C. Thomas.

Wilson, O.W., & McLaren, R. (1977). *Police administration.* New York: McGraw Hill.

Zemke, R., Raines, C., & Filipczak, B. (2000). *Generations at work.* New York: American Management Association.

Zhao, S., He, N., & Lovrich, N. (2003). Community policing: Did it change the basic functions of policing in the 1990s? A national follow-up. *Justice Quarterly, 20,* 697–724.

2   Administration, Authority, and Command

Effective executives do not make a great many decisions. They concentrate on what is important.

Peter F. Drucker, *On the Profession of Management* (1998, p. 19)

Learning Objectives

1. To be able to define the terms "Administration," "Authority," and "Command" in policing.

2. To know the attributes of Managerial Authority.

3. To identify the critical responsibilities of the three command levels.

4. To able to discuss the managerial functions.

5. To identify the elements of different styles of supervision.

6. To be able to explain the changing nature of police management.

Introduction

The **Administration** of a police department involves the logical coordination and arrangement of people, tasks, and resources in a manner designed to achieve its mission. Department managers accomplish this responsibility through the use of their authority to command and manage the organization's employees and assets. The goals of the administrative process are to ensure organizational effectiveness, enhance its potential, and organize it to achieve desired outcomes. It is important to note that all department successes and failures are products of human behavior. Historically, organizations have sought to ensure behavioral compliance and reduce uncertainty in employee performance through the establishment of an administrative system that involves a hierarchical authority structure; scalar levels of command; delineation of tasks, policy, rules, procedures, processes; and managerial accountability (Swanson et al., 2011). The organization's hierarchical structure delineates lines of authority tasks and sets responsibility. The majority of the police departments in the United States distribute command authority and responsibility through three distinct organizational levels, executive, middle management, and supervisory. The higher the administrative level, the greater the responsibility, authority, and power. The bureaucratic organization continues to dominate policing because it is designed to ensure control and accountability in the uncertain, complex, and often hostile environment faced by many police departments

Organizational administration and management involves the exercise of command authority to control, direct, and coordinate the department's personnel, resources, and activities (Fyfe et al., 1997). Command authority and responsibility is defined in the department's direction, policy and procedures, internal structures, mission, values, and practices. Managers at all levels of the organization are expected to achieve performance objectives, provide performance control, feedback and assessment of the areas of responsibility under their command authority. Managerial and organizational effectiveness, however, depends on the willingness and capabilities of the department's employees to support and follow managerial direction. Employees do not always achieve what their managers expect because of differences in their knowledge, skills, abilities, and their commitment to organizational objectives. As a result, the performance response to managerial direction is an uncertain variable phenomenon requiring oversight and direction. To understand the complexity of the relationship between organizational objectives, command levels, and employee performance requires critical analysis and comprehension of the concepts of managerial authority and command and human behavior. This chapter helps the reader develop understanding and knowledge of the police organization's administrative levels, authority at each level, and command responsibilities. So as Drucker (1998) advised at the beginning of this chapter, they know what is important and will focus on that instead of wasting their time on things that are not relevant to their organization's effectiveness.

Managerial Authority

Max Weber (1864–1920), the originator of the study of complex organizations, argued the bureaucracy constitutes the most efficient and rational way to organize, and that systematic processes and organized hierarchies were necessary to maintain order, maximize efficiency, and eliminate favoritism (Weber, 1947, pp. 329–341). Police departments are bureaucratic organizations not unlike that described by Weber. They are centralized managerial authority systems with task responsibilities based on a logical hierarchical ordering of positions. Organizational structure defines positional roles, departmental interdependences, and communication channels. It assigns authority, accountabilities, and responsibilities. It determines who is empowered to make decisions and the depth and extent of their authority. Management is accorded legitimate authority and power to direct and control a group of employees assigned to accomplish specific tasks. Each manager is responsible for the accomplishments of the employees under their command and consequently should have the authority to achieve this responsibility. The exercise of managerial authority involves the interaction of two organizational elements, the managerial (superior) and the employee (subordinate). Weber (1947, p. 324) defines authority within the bureaucratic system as "the probability that certain specific commands from a source will be obeyed by a given group of persons." In policing these concepts were structurally developed to achieve tighter managerial control, better performance, and more accountability to combat political influence, corruption, and lack of confidence that the political era of policing had created in American policing in the 19th and early 20th centuries (Goldstein, 1990).

Managerial Authority within a bureaucracy is both legal and rational when it is attached to the position an individual occupies and exercised through a system of rules and procedures. A common element for an authority relationship to exist and be effective is voluntariness on the part of a subordinate (employee). **Voluntariness** involves a choice made by the free will of the employee, as opposed to being made as the result of managerial coercion or duress. The department's effectiveness is thus inseparable from the accomplishments of its personnel (Covey, 1997). Using coercion or duress involving threat of punishment or sanctions may gain an employee's unwilling limited compliance but also their resistance. True authority and respect for command derives from employees who willingly follow managerial directives and accomplish tasks at the required performance level without direct supervision. It is important to remember that police patrol officers function the greater proportion of their tour of duty without the immediate direction of their managers. The internal motivation of the officer is directly affected by the manner in which they are managed and influenced by their manager. Good managers understand that their use of influence and respect instead of directing employees is an important managerial technique. Employees who are respected and feel good about themselves and how they are treated will produce good results (Blanchard & Johnson, 2003). Additionally, the ability to use coercive power in the current organizational world has been restricted by legal and social constraints. Laws and regulations such as the Fair Labor Standards Act, Title VII of the 1964 Civil Rights Act, Civil Rights Act 1991, and the Age Discrimination in Employment Act, Equal Employment Opportunity Act, and rulings by federal courts have resulted in restricting and limiting the power of managers (Dessler, 2012).

Command Levels

As noted in the previous chapter, police departments vary in size, complexity, and diversity of their mission from small organizations with fewer than 25 officers to large urban organizations employing a thousand or more people. However, almost all of these departments are internally divided by **levels of command** authority. As departments grow in size and complexity of tasks the number of individuals serving at these levels will increase. In a small police department, there will always be a chief of police but there may only be one lieutenant and/or one or two sergeants. In large urban police departments, there can be 10 or more individuals at the executive level alone. The majority of police organizations have three distinct but overlapping command levels: the executive level, the middle management level, and the supervisory.

Executive Level

Individuals at the **executive strategic level** have an assortment of titles, such as commissioner, director, chief, sheriff, colonel, and/or superintendent. The chief executive's position is a demanding, high-profile position that often is expected to maintain availability 24 hours a day, 7 days a week. The **administrative functions** of the executive strategic level involve Human Resource Development, Maintaining Organizational Integrity and Respect, as well as the Creation of a Positive Organizational Culture.

The qualifications required for the police chief's position differ depending on the size of the department and the region of the country. Small departments may have minimum requirements for the position while larger departments will have educational and experiential levels that will vary with the size of the department (Peak, 2012). For example, the International Association of Chiefs of Police in its nation-wide search for a chief of police for Leesburg (103 employees), Virginia, described the ideal candidate as being:

CHIEF OF POLICE
Leesburg Police Department

- A strong leader, both internally and externally.
- Able to demonstrate the effective use of modern organizational leadership practices.
- Engaged with community and have a visible presence.
- Committed to a community policing philosophy.
- Able to communicate well to build trust and transparency.
- Politically savvy and adept at working with and through political processes.
- Dedicated to building and maintaining collaborative partnerships, internally and externally.
- Focused on youth issues.
- Concerned with seeking solutions to mental health and domestic violence issues.
- Experienced in a growing and diverse community.
- Familiar with 21st century policing concepts, including procedural justice and the guardian vs. warrior perspective.
- Committed to building diversity within the department.

The police chief's principal responsibility is to administer the department and ensure that it effectively carries out its mission while at the same time gain the approval and support of the political structure and community for the department. They are expected to have the ability to conceptualize and define the role of their department to the communites they serve. Chiefs of police are praised for their department's achievements and held accountable for its failures. Recent events such as that in Ferguson, Missouri, in 2014 disclosed that a split-second decision by an unsupervised police officer to use deadly force can eventually lead to the dismissal or resignation of a police chief. The chief executive's most critical function is meeting their department's organizational needs and the community's current needs while simultaneously preparing it to meet future departmental demands (Reiss, 1985). Creating an effective department to meet future demands requires ensuring that the department's knowledge, skills, diversity, systems, and technology are ready for the task (Colvin, 2015). The responsibilities of the chief's position differ with the size and functions of their department. Chiefs of large departments are assisted by a command staff of other executives whose titles include assistant chief, deputy chief, assistant director, deputy commissioner, colonel, or lieutenant colonel.

Leading a police department is a complex, demanding task. Police executives provide their organizations with direction and performance oversight to achieve maximum use of their assets and capabilities (Moore & Trojanowicz, 1988). They must inspire and organize the activities of the department's employees. Police chiefs must also establish cooperative relationships externally with federal law enforcement agencies, surrounding jurisdictions, and related services such as Fire and Emergency Medical Transportation (Cunningham, Jones, & Behrens, 2011). They accomplish this through personnel management, budgeting, and operational management and community relations. The police chief executive with the assistance of his or her command team is required to establish a strategic direction for the department that unleashes the power and potential of the organization to impact the public safety demands facing the community it serves. They accomplish this by creating an organizational strategy that sets performance priorities for the department that meets the requirements of government and community.

The diversified and complex nature of today's public safety environment has fundamentally changed the leadership expectations of police executives. Every day law enforcement executives face issues of complexity, uncertainty, and sensitivity that require a different level of thinking and decision making. Before the August 2014 fatal shooting in Ferguson, Missouri, of Michael Brown, the effectiveness of most police chiefs was determined by crime rates and response to 911 calls (Williams, 2015). Now police executives must be astute in dealing with their community's safety demands and complex issues involving race, class, ethnicity, gender, and sexual orientation, not only in the context of the public served but also within their own police organizations. They must demonstrate an understanding of the importance of diversity from its broadest perspective such as education, training, career development, personal values, differing ages, race, color, creed, religious affiliation, nationalities, and sexes. Conventional ways of thinking, analyzing data, solving problems, making decisions, dealing with the public, and responding to organizational demands are obsolete. Few situations are easily resolved with old methods and today's challenges require critical thinking at different levels.

For example, when Ray Kelly was appointed New York City's Police Commissioner for the second time in 2002 the public safety challenges he was confronted with involved a consistent possibility of terrorist activity because of the events of 9/11 and the city's high value as a terrorist target. This factor demanded a fundamental rethinking of the role of the New York City Police Department. As a result he set into motion a complete reordering of the department's priorities to include a focus on counterterrorism and intelligence (Kelly, 2015, p. 143). The department developed a counterterrorism unit that is considered one of the more sophisticated in the world, complete with sea, land, and air capabilities.

Police chief executives are accountable for the following administrative activities:

1. Development of a departmental mission, vision, goals, and operational objectives.
2. Creation of strategic, operational, procedural, tactical, and budgetary plans.
3. Creation of an organizational structure and division of labor focused on ensuring fulfillment of mission and performance objectives.
4. Establishment of guiding principles, values, policy and procedures that supports an organizational culture that upholds its legitimacy in the eyes of the community as well as the department.
5. Employment of a leadership direction and style that, while focused on mission fulfillment, will also achieve willing compliance and support from employees of the department and members of the community.
6. Creating adequate resource levels, budget, personnel and technological capability.

7. Controlling and assessing departmental activities for integrity, efficiency and effectiveness through measurement, evaluation, and when necessary redirection.
8. Ensuring that all members of the department are competent and adhere to the highest standards of integrity and ethics.

(More, Vito, & Walsh, 2012, p. 38)

An assistant chief is usually the second in command of a department and normally functions as the alter ego of the police chief executive. Generally, deputy and assistant chiefs are responsible for supervising major functional subdivisions such as operations, investigations, or support services. For example, the city of Mesa, Arizona, Police Department has three assistant chiefs, one in charge of operations, another administration, and one the community engagement and employee services section. Assistant chiefs are central figures in the management team, with operational and administrative responsibilities. They may assist the chief executive in the development of the department's goals and objectives; assist in the administration of policies and procedures; manage, direct, and organize operational services; and conduct internal investigations as directed by the chief executive. The executive's management team is responsible for the creation of a quality, high-performance work environment through planning, directing, and coordinating of activities in the department. Their duties involve problem solving at the highest level and technical nature as well as formulating of departmental policies, planning, staffing, developing, and maintaining a positive organizational culture and sustaining accountability for operational efficiency and effectiveness.

Wolfe and Nix (2016) suggest that police administrators can accomplish the above functions by practicing **organizational justice** during management activities. Organizational justice is a leadership philosophy that focuses on three key issues.

- Managers ensure *procedural fairness* when dealing with employees. Their decisions do not unfairly favor one employee over another; the reasons for decisions are clearly explained to relevant parties; and employees are given a reasonable voice in the decision-making process.
- Managers must practice *distributive fairness*. They do this by ensuring that promotions, salary increases, and discipline are fairly distributed throughout the organization. Positive outcomes should not only fall on those with friends in high places. Likewise, negative outcomes should not manifest only among certain groups.
- Lastly, managers must strive for *interactional fairness*. Employees should be treated with respect and dignity. Supervisors should maintain an honest and open relationship with their subordinates.

Administrative Paradox

While the reform era police change agents sought to remove the influence of politics from policing, it is a fact that today police chief executives still serve at the pleasure of the mayor and/or city manager. As a result the chief executive's role is inherently political because he or she is appointed by the controlling governmental authority and represents the department to that authority and to the community (Cordner, 2013). However, the role of the executive also requires that the police chief balance external and internal environmental demand pressures that can be in conflict with the political expectations of his or her position. The external environment involves changing crime patterns, homeland security, numerous and variable demands for service, changing public safety conditions, demands for accountability, directives from the judicary and legislature, and state and federal mandated training. The internal environment involves the day-to-day task of managing the department, planning, setting direction, maintaining organizational integrity and transparency, creating goals, developing policies, ensuring fiscal accountability, supervison, workload efficency, and budget (Cordner, 2013). Police chiefs often find that the demands from these two environments are conflicting and difficult to address (Timoney, 2010). These issues have resulted in the police chief executives of Chicago, Illinois; Baltimore, Maryland; Fergurson, Missouri; Suffolk County, New York; and Cincinnati, Ohio, either resigning or being removed from their positions. One egregious act of misconduct by a police officer can lead to the firing of a police chief (Williams, 2015)

In the early years of the development of professional policing, organizational development was created by strong autocratic leaders such as London's Sir Richard Mayne (1796–1868) and Lieutenant Colonel Charles Rowan (1782–1852); Berkeley's August Vollmer (1876–1955); Boston's Stephen James O'Meara (1854–1918); Wichita and Chicago's O. W. Wilson (1900–1972); and LAPD's William Parker (1905–1966). During the last 20 years a shift has occurred in police organizational management from traditional autocratic systems to open strategic organizations that engage with the environments within which they operate. Through the emphasis on Community Policing and police legitimacy, police chief executives are now, more than ever, coming to understand the role that the community shares in police policy making. Traditional notions of command and managerial authority are no longer relevant to the day-to-day realities of today's police organization. They proved totally inadequate to prevent or respond to the 1992 riots that occurred in the city of Los Angeles (Domanick, 2015). Today's police executives are expected to be transformational leaders who can identify and understand the needs of the community, their agency, its political environment, and the motivations of each. To do so, many forward-thinking police executives seek to form a collaborative partnership model of policing. This model seeks to unite the police, the community, political and business leaders in a unified vision of police mandates and service.

In 1999, the International Association of Chiefs of Police held the organization's first President's Leadership Conference comprising carefully selected teams of nationally recognized and accomplished practitioners brought together to examine the roles of the contemporary police executive. The conferees sought to identify how the police executive role was changing and how police executives can manage current and changing community and organizational environments to satisfy the objectives of the many complex constituencies that police must serve. They concluded that police executives must possess an extraordinary range of capacities. At the core of the executive's role they identified the following areas of responsibility:

- The community.
- The governing body.
- The department and its workforce.
- The profession.

The chief executives' responsibilities to their community involves placing a high priority on communication, collaboration, partnership development as well as understanding and responsiveness to community needs. Less frequently cited by the conferees but identified as important were efficient service, freedom from fear, improved quality of life, equal protection and service, integrity of the police agency, and trust building. Responsibilities to the governing body involved demonstrating integrity, trust, truthfulness, candor, and commitment. Two sets of responsibilities to the department and the workforce demanded the highest priority. The first focused on inspiring and procreating leadership and the second providing a vision, a clear mission, goals and objectives, along with developing the department to successfully manage present and future workloads. The participants noted that the executive was obligated to advance the profession of policing by mentoring and developing new leadership, helping to develop a common body of leadership knowledge, and raising professional standards (IACP, 1999).

Recently, policing has been challenged by a growing protest movement accompanied with acts of civil disobedience after the deaths of several African Americans at the hands of police officers. In response to waves of protest and demands for reform on December 18, 2014, President Barack Obama issued an Executive Order appointing an 11-member Task Force on 21st Century Policing to respond to the number of serious incidents between law enforcement and the communities that have occurred. The president wanted a quick but thorough response that would begin the process of healing and restore community trust by identifying best practices and otherwise make recommendations on how policing practices can promote effective crime reduction while building public trust.

The task force noted that trust between law enforcement agencies and the people they protect and serve is essential in a democracy. It is key to the stability of our communities, the integrity of our criminal justice system, and the safe and effective delivery of policing services, as well as the foundational principle underlying their inquiry into the relations between law enforcement and the communities they serve (President's Task Force on 21st Century Policing, 2015). Today, building trust and nurturing legitimacy on both sides of the police/citizen divide has become a fundamental responsibility of all police executives and the basis upon which they are being evaluated.

Middle Management Level

Individuals at the *middle management level* in policing are majors, captains, lieutenants, watch commanders, or civilian managers in administrative positions. The primary responsibilities of their role varies with the department size but usually involves the oversight and direction of one or more of an agency's divisions or functional units responsible for Patrol, Investigations, Traffic, Communications, Personnel, or Special Operations. Administratively they command a budget, personnel, planning, internal affairs, training, or public information unit or serve in a senior staff position for the chief or other senior executives (Geller & Swanger, 1995). Their activities may range from actual operational work to largely administrative review.

Middle managers serve the critical function of aligning their department's mission, goals, and objectives with its operational accomplishments. They are primarily responsible for organizational effectiveness and efficiency. These managers interpret and operationalize departmental goals, objectives, policies and procedures into the day-to-day tasks of the units they command.

At their organizational level the chief executive's vision and direction is converted into operational reality. Stamper (1992, p. 153) claims that their responsibilities also involve keeping the promises made by higher-ups. What the chief or mayor, city manager or city council claims will occur, these managers ensure it will happen through their authority, planning, directional activities, and allocation of resources. As a result, they manage the day-to-day operations of police departments by standardizing and controlling both organizational procedures and officer performance. They strike a balance between what is desired and what must be done and the operational capability of the organization. Thus, they are the leading edge of centralized control over a department's internal environment and organizational operations (Kelling & Bratton, 1993, p. 9). In their capacity as interpreters of the chief executive's strategic decisions they can choose either to accept or to reject them. When they communicate their vision to employees, it can either be in a positive or a negative manner (Charrier, 2004). As a result, they have also been identified in the research as the major source of subversion, resistance, and sabotage of change efforts in policing. They are described as the lagging edge of resistance to innovation (Goldstein, 1990; Kelling & Bratton, 1993; Sherman, Milton, & Kelly, 1973; Sparrow, Moore, & Kennedy, 1990; Vito, Walsh, & Kunselman, 2005).

Middle managers accomplish their responsibilities by engaging in planning, organizing, commanding, coordinating, and controlling departmental resources and personnel (Fayol, 1992). In the exercise of these functions they activate the department's strategy and tactics by setting objectives, planning and implementing operations, and evaluating the performance of supervisors and units under their control. These managerial functions are activities engaged in by all managers, the time spent on each activity varies with each managerial level. They are critical middle-management activities because of the role they play in operationalizing the department's organizational direction and strategy.

Planning involves identifying the activities necessary for the operational translation of a department's mission, vision, and organizational goals into specific unit objectives and the identification of resources needed to accomplish these objectives. Since police departments exist in an ever-changing environment, middle managers must be aware of and monitor the changing demands created by the department's external and internal environments. Their planning activities involve setting of objectives, development of strategies, and identification of operational tactics for addressing these environmental demands (Kelly, 2015). Planning allows the manager to identify what should be done, when, by whom, and what needs to be accomplished. However, middle managers must also have the ability to implement their plans, communicate, and inspire the various units and personnel under their commad to achieve desired objectives. They also must be flexible and ready to change their plans when conditions change. All middle managers are held accountable for the quality of their plans, the quality of their efforts, their accomplishments, their managerial oversight of operations, and results obtained (Haneberg, 2005).

Organizing involves the structuring of an organization and deployment of resources necessary to establish accountability, workload and resource distribution, and a unified organizational effort. It involves the alignment of strategy, structure, process, information systems, reward systems, employees, and operational service delivery. Organizing takes into consideration the major purpose of a unit, the tasks required to fulfill this purpose, the nature and authority of the people involved, their geographical distribution and time constraints. A well-organized department acts as a unified team, supporting each other and the department's strategy, with a desire to achieve maximum effectiveness (More et al., 2012).

Police departments usually display their functional structure by a scalar chart. Organizational charts identify the department's chain of command, each managerial position, and the units commanded by each position. They also depict what each position is accountable for and whom each position is responsible to. These charts identify official lines of command, authority, and communication within the organization. However, they should not be etched in stone. Middle management problem solving and performance analysis will often result in repositioning units and personnel to align with the development of new strategic objectives.

Commanding involves setting direction through leadership, authority, motivation, and empowerment. The purpose of command is to achieve the optimum performance from all employees. Command success rests on a combination of personal qualities and a knowledge of general principles of management (Fayol, 1949, p. 97). Middle managers are accountable for achieving desired outcomes through the performance of the units under their command. The command function empowers managers with the authority to direct their units through the development of clear, effective operational strategies and tactics to achieve objectives. This is not a numbers game of achieving output statistics. Operational commanders have the authority but also must have the ability to implement their tactics and inspire their command to achieve desired objectives. They are accountable for the managerial oversight of their unit's operations and results obtained. Command is exercised through a thorough knowledge of personnel; by elimination of the incompetent; by balancing the interests of the organization and its employees through a "strong sense of duty and of equity" (Fayol, 1949, pp. 98–103). Successful commanding officers are capable of motivating employees and encouraging employees to take initiative. They engage in critical thinking, have integrity, communicate clearly, and base their decisions on regular evaluations and inspections. Their most important attribute is to be a complex problem solver.

Coordination is the process of achieving unity of action through the synchronization of the efforts of independent unit activities. Its purpose is the integration of several units into an orderly whole to achieve the mission of the organization. An ideal way of conceiving this principle of management is to think of the police department as comprising one large team, not individual power centers competing for resources and glory with each other. It requires that organizational managers engage in systems thinking, teamwork, and a breaking of traditional administrative barriers. Thus, middle managers should be proficient at networking and building relationships both within and without of the agency. They must think beyond their own areas of control and think of the department as an integrated team that works to support each other and the department's mission. Coordination is accomplished by the combined action of executive management which supervises the whole, plus middle managers whose efforts are directed toward the successful working of each particular part (Fayol, 1949, p. 106). Coordination is the essence of management and is implicit and inherent in all functions of management. It requires clear communication and good leadership.

Controlling involves all those activities undertaken to ensure that actual operations conform to the planned operations (David, 2014). All managers must fix accountability, set standards, compare actual performance with these standards, and then take corrective action where needed (Dessler, 2004). It is the managers' responsibility to know what is happening with both the technical and human resources entrusted to them by their organization. The essence of management thus involves the continual assessment of the performance and accomplishments. The control function involves the following activities:

1. Identifying goals and objectives,
2. Establishing and maintaining standards,
3. Continual communication with subordinates,
4. Monitoring individual and organizational performance,
5. Evaluating personnel by comparing actual to desired performance,
6. Rewarding when appropriate, and
7. Taking corrective action when necessary.

The primary objective of the control function is to certify that employee performance is at the desired level to accomplish organizational objectives and goals. However, managers must also ensure that their employees have the knowledge, skills, and ability to perform their duties at the desired level of performance. Organizational objectives will never be achieved if those responsible for task accomplishment are improperly informed, ill trained, or ignorant of the level of performance expected. Effective managers obtain, and share with their subordinates, the information needed to achieve operational progress. When conditions change, or when deviations from previously agreed-upon standards are identified, evaluation should identify what must be done and corrective action should be taken.

The five managerial functions just discussed are highly interrelated. They do not necessarily occur separately as listed but can happen at the same time. It is important to remember that performance of these functions is continually modified by any or all the following factors:

1. Changing environmental demands
2. Managerial knowledge and competence
3. Organizational level
4. Nature and type of activity
5. Knowledge, competence, and commitment of employees.

(More et al., 2012, p. 41)

Kelling and Bratton (1993), in their analysis of the administrative problems associated with implementing strategic change in policing, contend that middle managers became the main proponents of centralizing control during the reform era. Drucker (1998) asserts that the positional authority middle managers have provides them with the ability to slow the decisional process to a crawl and make the organization increasingly incapable of adapting to change. For example, failure to win middle management's support is cited as the primary contributor to the demise of team policing in the 1970s (Sherman et al., 1973). Geller and Swanger (1995) in their study of middle managers for the Police Executive Research Forum also identified this command level as the most daunting obstacle to efficient and meaningful organizational change.

Sparrow et al. (1990, pp. 213–214) identified several ways middle managers influence their organizations. First, middle managers operate at the boundary between knowledge and power in the department. Their positional authority empowers them with the responsibility for translating the executive's vision and direction into operational strategies. Second, middle managers largely control the nature of the department's professional environment. The processes they develop and the actions they take in dealing with subordinates define and reinforce the core cultural values of the department. These core values let the officers know what operational behavior is and is not acceptable. Third, middle managers are the ones who can determine how employees view the department's procedural manual—to justify strict bureaucratic discipline, or as a source of knowledge, guidance, and inspiration. Fourth, middle managers have the power to quash new ideas (and they have been routinely accused of doing so, especially ideas they believe challenge their authority). Fifth, middle managers can define work in a way that encourages their officers to tackle harder, broader problems: they can empower their officers by letting them know that the organization values their knowledge and expertise. Finally, middle managers control the extent to which the use of positive discretion, legitimacy, and procedural justice can be built explicitly into the department's value system and address the new leadership demands of the 21st century.

However, middle management's power to affect change can be harnessed in a positive way by including those managers in planning, acknowledging their legitimate self-interests, and motivating their investment in long-range solutions that enhance community safety and security (Travis, 1995). Geller and Swanger (1995) suggest that chief executives can engage middle managers in a positive way by providing them with support and authorization to devise strategies and modify systems and procedures to support strategic change. Such delegation of authority would entail involving middle managers in planning for change to increase their credibility with subordinates. Chief executives can maintain consultative relationships with middle managers to motivate ongoing thinking about effectively meeting strategic goals and objectives and developing a clear linkage of rewards to performance in implementing desired changes. Chief executives can make a serious commitment to training middle managers well in the skills they need in their adjusted roles. In summary, the middle managers' organizational position gives them the power to choose what they will do: passively resist, tolerate, or lend their support and lead in the reengineering of their organizations. Thus the skills and abilities of these managers are imperative to the department's successful service to the community.

Supervisory Level

Individuals serving at the supervisory level hold the rank of sergeant, corporal, or civilian supervisor except for integrated police-fire organizations, where supervisors hold the title of lieutenant. They are responsible for the achievement of departmental objectives through the direction and oversight of its operational activities. Supervisors are the department's first level of command authority and the primary contact officers have with their department's administration. They are accountable for their subordinate employees' performance on a day-to-day basis. Supervisors are the link between the department's executive and middle management levels and operations and a principal factor in the day-to-day control and accomplishments of the department. The quality of an officer's daily life and perception of their department depend heavily on how well the officer satisfies the expectations and demands of their supervisor (Goldstein, 1990).

Supervisors are accountable for ensuring that the department's employees perform according to law, departmental policy, procedures, and ethical values. Line supervisors in patrol and investigative units make important decisions regarding the utilization of their officers to meet workload demand and management of their subordinates (Cordner, 2013). Their decisions play a key role in converting mission and policy into day-to-day practice

(Willis, 2011). These decisions affect the quality and manner of police operations, the service provided to a community, and the commitment and competence of the employees who provide that service. Supervisors serve as a nexus of information gathering and distribution within the organization and serve as a point of legitimate contact for the community (Crank & Langworthy, 1992; Haberfeld, 2006). As the department's principal quality-control agents, supervisors have significant impact on the effectiveness and financial liability of the police organization (Walsh & Donovan, 1990). The ability to command depends on how effectively they build a positive relationship of mutual respect and trust within their work unit (More et al., 2012). However, they must also understand that their subordinate's performance is affected by their work group's dynamic, problem-solving process, and culture.

Individuals seeking to attain the position of supervisor must successfully complete a qualifying process set forth by the municipality's civil service regulations. Testing is usually established when supervisory vacancies exist or on a regular schedule basis. The promotional process normally requires that a period of time be established between the announcement and the test to give candidates time to prepare for the exam. These announcements usually contain the job classification, qualifications, dates and times of the process, location of each phase, description of assessment, if used, and the duties and responsibilities of the position. Each candidate is then given a bibliography, listing testing materials the examination process will cover. The testing weights, methods, time limits, and cut-off scores are also provided and will vary by department and civil service regulations. For example, to qualify to test for the position of Sergeant, in the Pinellas Park Police Department, Florida, candidates must:

1.   Be a currently employed full time Florida certified police officer
2.   Have three years with the Pinellas Park Police Department as of the testing date
3.   Have five years of total police experience
4.   The five years' experience must be within the last five years prior to the testing date
5.   Have an AA Degree from an accredited school

(PPPD Directive Manual, Standard Operating Procedure, Promotion SOP #32, 2006)

The process also may involve oral boards, chief's interview, in-basket exercises, and writing ability tests. Once it has been completed, a rank order list is created of the candidates. The chief of police, depending on the municipality, has the authority to select the candidate to be promoted from the top three or five on the list. The list will usually remain valid for a period of time established by local civil service regulations. Success in this process requires a great deal of preparation and commitment by the officer to achieve a high ranking on the candidates list. Thus, it serves as a valuable tool for enhancing officers' overall knowledge of their department's policy, procedures, and the law.

Newly promoted supervisors are usually required to complete a one-year probationary period in which their suitability to supervise officers is evaluated. In the majority of police departments the newly promoted supervisor will be assigned to uniform patrol and supervise officers on a patrol shift almost immediately. In most states, new supervisors are required to attend a mandatory basic supervision course within one year of their promotion. However, this course may only be available to them months after they have been functioning in their role. As a result, the primary way many supervisors learn the requirements of their position is through trial and error and/or mentoring by other supervisors. Unfortunately, this is not always adequate preparation for such an important and demanding role.

When an individual is promoted to supervisory rank they become for the first time part of the department's management team. They enter a new phase of their career requiring a transition to a different role and mindset (Van Maanen, 1984, More & Miller, 2014). This transition will necessitate a significant change in their operational philosophy and outlook. They will now be held accountable for the performance of their unit and their evaluation as a supervisor will be based upon their subordinates' accomplishments. On a day-to-day basis they must consider how organizational objectives and issues impact their and their officers' performance. This necessitates a personal and intellectual transformation that will change their organizational perspective, basic concepts of work, and relationships with others in the department. This transformational adjustment is further complicated by the fact that in many departments new supervisors are inadequately prepared for their role. They are often required to exert authority over individuals who are their social and professional colleagues. In the majority of medium to small police departments, new supervisors manage work units whose members represent a peer group whom they have befriended, identified with, and worked closely with for years. This is a challenging task.

One can easily conclude that the supervisor's position is a unique and a somewhat conflicting role. It intersects two different organizational worlds: administration and operations, management and the street (Reuss-Ianni, 1983). In some departments these two worlds view each other with hostility and animosity while in others there is mutual respect and cooperation. In departments where the organizational dynamics are negative, this places the supervisor in an in-between position that can be a continual source of conflict and stress. The differing expectations of the two sides, if not understood and responded to correctly, can develop into contradictory pressures that create conflict and role ambiguity for supervisors (More et al., 2012). To be effective supervisors must spend a significant amount of time identifying employee needs and expectations and using interpersonal techniques with their officers. They are required to develop skills and abilities that will allow them to manage the variety of people and performance challenges that occur daily in policing. They engage in directing, mentoring, training, coaching, and team-building and counseling to enhance their subordinates' knowledge, skills, and capabilities (More & Miller, 2014).

The department's executive and middle management levels expect supervisors to:

1. Manage day-to-day operations
2. Work for the attainment of organizational objectives
3. Maintain a well-trained, motivated work unit
4. Create a positive work environment
5. Use authority responsibly and legally
6. Adhere to and administer the department's policies and procedures
7. Keep superiors, employees, and peers informed
8. Prevent problems as well as solve them
9. Be creative, innovative and flexible
10. Provide leadership and use initiative
11. Be accountable.

(More et al., 2012, p. 48)

Employees will expect their supervisor to:

1. Be accessible
2. Be a role model
3. Assist them in attaining individual and organizational needs
4. Assist in integrating them into the organization
5. Create a work environment that provides for job satisfaction
6. Let them know what is expected
7. Use authority appropriately
8. Be fair in their personnel evaluations
9. Help in developing new skills
10. Identify and maximize their talents that result in growth
11. Providing information needed to accomplish tasks
12. Support in becoming a productive employee.

(More & Miller, 2014, p. 26)

Styles of Supervision

Styles of supervision refers to the different behavioral approaches used by supervisors to influence their employees' commitment and performance. It is the way by which supervisors manage and work with their subordinates. Some supervisors make the task of supervision look easy. They are efficient, competent, and respectful of their subordinates and motivate their officers to high levels of performance with minimum effort. While others constantly complain about the quality of their officers and the manner by which they perform the tasks they are given. They spend most of their time attempting to control their officer's work performance. However, their subordinates never seem to please them or accomplish what they expect. These are two different examples of supervisory styles.

The manner by which patrol officers perform their day-to-day operational tasks is the basis for the achievement of the department's mission and the community's cooperation with the department. It can also be the source of tension with the community, which can result in the dismissal of the police chief and civil unrest (Williams, 2015). Operationally, conflicts arise as police officers fail to fulfill the requests and orders of their supervisors. How proficiently an officer performs day-to-day tasks will be influenced by the interpersonal skills of his or her supervisor. How a supervisor interacts with subordinates, communicates responsibilities and expectations, motivates them, and gains their trust and respect determines the amount of influence and compliance they will achieve with their subordinates. The ability to influence subordinates is an important element of the supervisor's role because an integral part of the nature of the patrol officer's job involves autonomy. Unlike other organizational managers police supervisors are accountable for subordinates who work independently outside their immediate control (21st Century Policing, 2015). Officers are involved in countless situations on a daily basis that demand quick decisions and action without immediate supervisory direction. As a result, supervisors usually participate in an event after an officer has taken some type of action. They are often perceived by the officers they command as after-the-fact "Monday Morning Quarterbacks."

Thus, an officer's motivation to properly perform is directly affected by the manner in which they are supervised (Engel, 2003. The way in which supervisors interact with their officers and communicate their direction is a critical element in achieving willing compliance but can also create hostility and resistance. The development of successful and productive work teams is a function of the supervisor's ability to cultivate mutual respect, competence, and commitment in the officers they command. Research confirms that officers who feel respected by their supervisors and peers are more likely to accept departmental policies, understand decisions, and comply with them voluntarily (More & Miller, 2014).

Successful supervisory leadership occurs when their subordinates willingly comply with their direction. Supervisors must understand and be concerned with the impact they have on others if they truly wish to enhance their leadership ability. Their function is to accomplish tasks through the performance of their subordinates. Formal authority may be enough to effect limited changes in performance, but to gain commitment or lasting changes in attitude and behavior, supervisors must be able to influence others to perform willingly without using fear or coercion. This is the true essence of leadership. **Influence** is the process of altering, affecting, or changing others' attitudes, behaviors, values, and beliefs.

One way to convert positional authority into influence is for the supervisor to be willing to empower those whose performance they depend upon. **Empowerment** involves the sharing of leadership and is a sign of respect for others. It is more than a delegation task; it is an attempt to open and tap the creative power of the officers. Empowerment is based on the belief that organizations frequently underuse their employees' abilities. However, if given the chance and the responsibility, employees will contribute positively. Empowerment provides unit members with positional and personal sources of power so they can handle situations without always seeking supervisory approval. It helps to develop a sense of shared leadership and a sense of creative decision making. Empowerment develops a belief in unit members that they are all in it together and that their success depends on each team member's contribution.

Empowerment sends a message of trust from the supervisor to those they empower. This is an essential ingredient for teamwork to take place. Empowerment does not guarantee that others will or should exercise their influence in all circumstances; there may be matters that should be left to the officer's discretion. Thus, empowerment requires that supervisors through different behavioral actions establish boundaries within which the empowered employee has freedom to operate. These boundaries establish decisional guidelines and accountability. Supervisors can empower others by:

1. Letting others decide the methods they use for accomplishing tasks.
2. Creating an environment of cooperation, information sharing, discussion, and shared ownership of unit goals and objectives.
3. Encouraging their officers to take initiative, make decisions, and use their knowledge.
4. Letting others put their ideas and solutions into practice.
5. Building morale and confidence by recognizing successes and encouraging effectiveness.

Empowerment promotes trust and respect, which enhances a supervisor's ability to exercise influence. By sharing their power and not being critical or second-guessing their subordinates, supervisors can build relationships with their officers that will motivate and inspire them to pursue mutually agreed-upon goals. One of the authors on a visit to the Hungarian National Police observed a detective supervisor in a city of 65,000 people hold a by-weekly meeting with his seven subordinates. The agenda for the meeting was a review of the unit's unsolved cases. He encouraged the officers to make suggestions on how these cases should progress. These suggestions were analyzed by the group and the supervisor empowered his detectives to employ their suggestions. As a result they had an extremely high solvability rate. The meeting we observed displayed high officer commitment, mutual trust, respect for the contributions of each member, and a willingness to try new approaches. Instead of a power-based supervisory style, the unit's commander employed a team-centered approach that was grounded upon respect for each detective's contribution, talent, and commitment. It was a winning style of supervision that achieved a high solvability rate for the unit. Interestingly, the detectives all were older and had more police experience than their supervisor.

Factors Affecting Supervisory Style

Police supervisors by their role and occupational experience are task-oriented. They are required to respond to a variety of situations in which both their department and their subordinates expect them to take charge and handle. These factors reinforce the task orientation of the role. A supervisor's style of management also reflects their beliefs, values, and attitudes about what they think of their subordinates and how they think they should be managed. These psychological constructs contain the standards upon which supervisors judge themselves and others. Often they select a style of supervision because their mindset and on-the-job experiences tell them that this is the way supervisors should act. These factors raise the question of what style of supervision is appropriate for supervisors to use. How do supervisory styles influence officer behavior? Do successful supervisors have a personal outlook or vision that makes them successful leaders?

These questions were addressed by a study of data collected for the Project on Policing Neighborhoods, a systematic observational study of patrol officers and first-line supervisors in two metropolitan police departments in 1996 and 1997 (Engel, 2002, 2003). It examined the influence of 64 sergeants' supervisory styles on the behavior of 239 patrol officers, having identified the sergeant-supervisor of each officer. A review of prior research identified 10 attitudinal dimensions that potentially shape supervisors' styles: How they make decisions. How they distribute power. The extent to which they attempt or avoid exerting leadership. The priority they place on aggressive enforcement. The priority they attach to Community Policing and problem solving. How they view subordinates. Whether they engage in inspirational motivation. How task-oriented they are. Whether they focus on building friendships and mutual trust with subordinates. Whether they focus on protecting subordinates from unfair criticism and punishment. Factor analysis of these dimensions identified four distinct supervisory styles. These are traditional, innovative, supportive, and active supervisory styles. The influence of these different supervisory styles on patrol officer behaviors was assessed. The findings confirm that supervisory styles can influence patrol officer behavior when making arrests, issuing citations, using force, and engaging in Community Policing. The study's most important finding was that style or quality of field supervision can significantly influence patrol officer behavior, apart from quantity of supervision. Front-line supervision can influence patrol officer behavior, but the study found that this influence varies according to the style of supervision. None of the styles identifed by the study were found ideal because each has benefits and disadvantages (Engel, 2003).

Traditional supervisors are individuals who are direct, task-oriented, command and control supervisors. Their ultimate concern is to control subordinate behavior and achieve task completion. They expect their officers to produce measurable activity such as field interrogation reports, arrests, or citations along with the accompanying paperwork and documentation. They exert their authority in the majority of their encounters with officers by taking charge, making on-the-spot decisions, and telling their officers what to do. They are less likely to reward but more likely to punish subordinates. Their primary concern is task completion, not people. More than 60 percent of traditional supervisors in the study agree strongly that "enforcing the law is the patrol officer's most important responsibility." They strongly believe in the importance of the bureaucratic values such as adherence to the chain of command and the department's rules and regulations. These individuals are examples of the command and control authoritarian style of management that emerged during the reform era of policing in the 20th century. This supervisory style seeks to simplify the supervisor's control of their unit and enhance their authority over their officers, while leaving no room for independent thought on the part of the officers. There are some who believe that this supervisory style is required in the many emergency situations that demand strict control and rapid decision making. Unfortunately, it stifles employee initiative, development, and independent problem solving. These supervisors create dependents out of their subordinates because they restrict their officers' ability to innovate and use their intellect creatively.

Innovative supervisors are characterized by their tendency to form positive relationships with their officers, a low level of task orientation, and more positive views of their subordinates. They are considered innovative because they encourage their officers to support and use Community Policing and problem-solving strategies. They accomplish this through coaching, mentoring, and facilitating the use of these strategies. For example, Engel (2002) found that 96 percent of these supervisors agree strongly with the statement: "a good patrol officer will try to find out what residents think the neighborhood problems are" as compared to 48 percent of traditional supervisors, 68 percent of supportive supervisors, and 68 percent of active supervisors. They empower their subordinates by delegating decision making, refraining from telling officers how to handle a situation, and seldom intercede and take over an incident. They also spend more time per shift working with the public or other officers than supervisors using a different style of supervision.

This style represents a consensus-seeking approach to supervision. Supervisors who use it will make a decision after they obtain suggestions and advice from work unit members. The supervisor is still accountable for the final decision but it is arrived at after consulting his or her staff. This style of supervision requires an individual willing to be open and candid with their employees. However, it also requires work unit members who are competent and committed to the department's goals and objectives.

Supportive supervisors are characterized by their use of praise and encouragement to motivate subordinates, their willingness to be a personal counselor, and their desire to function as a protector of their subordinates from upper management's unfair discipline. They are less concerned with enforcing rules and regulations, and ensuring that officers produce. These supervisors are more likely to encourage their subordinates through praise and acknowledgment, counsel officers as needed, and consistently show a concern for subordinates. Just over two-thirds of these supervisors in the study believe that one of their most important functions is their duty to protect officers from unfair censure or punishment. Sometimes, supportive supervisors do not have strong ties or positive relationships with management. This working relationship results in the supervisor functioning as a protector rather than supporter. These supervisors have not completed their transition to the different role and mindset demanded by their supervisory position.

Active supervisors embrace a philosophy of leading by example. Their goal is to be heavily involved in the field alongside subordinates while controlling patrol officer behavior; they act both as street officer and supervisor. Almost all active supervisors (95 percent) report they often go on their own initiative to incidents that their officers are handling. Supervisors with an active style are characterized by directive decision making, a strong sense of supervisory power, and a relatively positive view of subordinates. Although active supervisors believe they have considerable influence over subordinates' decisions, they are less likely to encourage team building, coaching, or mentoring. The study proposes one possible explanation for this is that they are reluctant to become so involved that they alienate subordinate officers. A fine line separates an active supervisor from being seen as over-controlling or micromanaging.

In comparison with the other supervisory styles, the active supervisor appears to yield a great deal of influence over police officer actions. This is especially true, regardless of the style, when a supervisor is present at the scene of an incident, the more likely an officer will make an arrest. The longer the supervisor is present, the more likely there is to be an arrest. Also, patrol officers with active supervisors spend more time in proactive activities. However, patrol officers with an active supervisor are more likely to use force against a suspect. The study found that the mere presence of a supervisor had a significant influence on the use of force. One way active supervisors promote greater use of force and proactivity (which could expose the officer to greater risk if things go wrong) is by taking precisely the risks he or she wants the officer to take (Engel, 2003).

The study's findings identified the active style as more likely than the others to influence officer behavior. This influence can be positive or negative; for example, it can inspire subordinates to engage in more problem-solving activities, or it can result in more frequent use of force. The active supervisory style was also the most conducive to implementing Community Policing goals (Engle, 2001).

In another supervisory study, Willis (2011) used focus-group data from six police departments to analyze first-line supervisors' strategic decision making and how they operate within the context of Compstat and Community Policing. He noted that in the typical bureaucratic and reactive departments that existed before implementing these strategies, patrol supervisors were expected to exert internal control that was "essentially negative, relying primarily upon sanctions for non-compliance with police rules" (Engel, 2002, p. 52; Kelling & Moore, 1988; Weisburd & McElroy, 1988). A critical element of both strategic and Community Policing is the decentralization of decision-making authority to make police organizations more flexible and responsive to local conditions. Willis noted that the full implementation of these strategies would seem to require significant changes in how first-line supervisors learn about crime and disorder problems and exercise their judgment in ways most likely to produce desired results.

These studies disclose that the manner in which officers are supervised impacts their behavior. Unfortunately, styles of supervision are more likely to develop because of experiential learning rather than through the limited training offered by many police departments. Strategic policing properly implemented will change the role and decision making of operational supervisors (Willis, 2011).

To address the preparation of new supervisors, the Kentucky Department of Criminal Justice Training developed a three-week (120-hour) training program for newly promoted sergeants or officers on their agency's promotion lists. The course is specifically designed to assist in the understanding and development of styles of supervision by individuals who are taking a leadership position for the first time. The instruction emphasizes the importance of the sergeants' ability to identify their leadership strengths and style while maintaining a high standard of expectation both for themselves and those under their supervision. A central feature of this course is the Situational Leadership Model developed by Hersey and Blanchard (1993). This model is focused upon two central concepts: leadership style and the individual's or group's maturity level. Students are taught to adjust their leadership styles based upon the task they are confronting and the assessment of their subordinate's ability. In the course, students take part in classes focusing on the role of a supervisor, leadership, resolving conflict, managing diversity, monitoring officer performance, professional image, legal issues for supervisors, ethics, interpersonal communication, effective written communication, making decisions, solving problems, managing critical incidents, public speaking, emotional survival, budgeting, and media relations.

The above supervisory styles discovered by the research can serve as models for supervisors to measure themselves against. However, there remains the question whether there is one best way to supervise? Blake and Mouton (1994), developers of the "Managerial Grid," assert that there is and it is a supervisor who combines a high concern for employees and relationships with a high concern for task performance. Effective supervisors manage themselves and their unit's people so that both the organization and the employees have a meaningful experience when they work. Supervisors who are able to balance both concerns are more effective. However, this balance can only be achieved if the supervisors understand their own needs and the situational and human dimensions of the environment within which they are operating.

The Changing Nature of Police Management

Traditional methods of police administration, authority, and command are currently being challenged by substantial demands for change (PTF, 2015). Since the latter part of the 20th century, police departments have been restructuring their organizational strategies to respond more effectively to these demands. The emergence of Community Problem-Solving, Compstat, Intelligent-Led, Smart Policing, issues concerning police legitimacy, and Procedural Justice have resulted in the development of a new set of expectations for police managers at all levels of the organization. These efforts are challenging traditional beliefs about police administration, command, and authority. In this current climate of demand and change police managers are expected to be more effective by becoming strategic thinkers who engage in systematic problem solving while achieving desired operational outcomes through a variety of analytical and data-driven tactics and strategies instead of using traditional command and control processes based upon rules and procedures and statistical counting of outputs instead of outcomes.

Effective organizations are ones in which people work at their full potential to achieve the organization's mission (Drucker, 2004). Senge (1990) identified effective organizations as ones that are skilled at creating, acquiring, and transferring knowledge and at modifying their performance to reflect this new knowledge and insights. Organizations who do this are known as "**learning organizations**." Learning in these organizations reflects the willingness to question basic operating assumptions, using different tactical approaches, and experimenting with different strategies to achieve desired outcomes. Managers in these organizations are expected to be system thinkers and self-confident learners open to new information. They are concerned with how their current operational demands affect their department's ability to provide public safety to its community and how their tactics gain citizen respect and support.

The "learning organization" construct appropriately describes the **strategic management** process that is emerging as the new paradigm of police organizational management. A variety of departmental adaptations are taking place throughout policing in the United States, Canada, and Europe. Each of these involves the development of a strategic accountability system and philosophy of crime control that considers the identification and tracking of emerging crime or quality-of-life trends, and the dissemination of information to promote the development of a proactive, preventative approach to reduce crime and disorder. With goals to stimulate productivity, performance, and effectiveness, these police departments are using information technology and organized problem solving to turn police officers into problem solvers and to leverage their intellectual capital to preempt crime and neighborhood deterioration (Brown & Brudney, 2003).

This process requires that all levels of management support and develop best practices in crime trend evaluation and response. In these departments organizational strategy serves as the lynchpin that unites the decisions and actions of executives, operational commanders, line supervisors, and front-line officers into a coordinated and compatible pattern. As a result the **crafting,** implementation, and execution of operational strategies and tactics become critical managerial functions. Another critical management requirement in this type of organization is to develop, engage, and apply the intellect and skills of employees to strategic organizational activities (Walsh, 1998).

For strategic management to be successful and for police departments to become effective learning organizations, the empowerment of middle managers and line supervisors is critical. They must be empowered with the authority to develop clear, effective tactics to address crime and quality-of-life conditions in their operational areas. These managers must be ready to change their plans when crime conditions change or desired result are not achieved. They must also be held accountable for the quality of their plans, their efforts, and their oversight of operations and results obtained. Executives and middle managers must constantly follow up on what is being done and evaluate results. Evaluation makes it possible to assess the viability of particular tactical responses and to incorporate the knowledge gained into subsequent strategy development efforts. By knowing how well a particular tactic worked on a problem, and by knowing which specific elements of it worked most effectively, departments will be better able to construct and implement effective responses for similar problems. The follow-up and assessment process also permits the redeployment of resources to meet newly identified challenges once a problem has abated. Managers engaged in this process must receive training in critical thinking and problem solving and tactic development and implementation.

Strategic policing forces all managers at all levels of the department to be concerned with how they and their units are contributing to the department's mission and goals. This strategic redirection requires the development of a managerial skill set that involves information management and analysis, problem solving, planning, strategy development, measurement, and communication. Chief executives are the critical player of this process because they must both sponsor and champion this adaptation. The department's executive team must empower middle managers to develop strategies and tactics to meet objectives. The executive level must be able to accept failure and view it as an opportunity to create change. They must learn from failure and adjust by changing or replacing tactics rather than punishing for it. The ability and willingness to reallocate resources, support creative solutions to problems, track progress, and integrate functions within the agency require a strategic management orientation similar to that found in successful business organizations.

Conclusion

The majority of police departments in the United States are bureaucratic organizations with centralized managerial authority systems based on a logical hierarchical ordering of positions. This structural arrangement defines positional roles, departmental interdependences, and communication channels. It assigns authority, accountabilities, and responsibilities. It determines who makes decisions and the depth and extent of their authority and power. Managers use their authority to command and manage their organization's employees and assets. Command authority is structured through three distinct organizational levels, executive, middle management, and supervisory. The higher the administrative level, the greater the command responsibility, authority, and power. To understand the complexity of the relationship between organizational objectives, administrative levels, and employee performance requires a comprehension of the concepts of authority, power, and command.

Management is accorded legitimate authority and power to direct and control a group of employees assigned to accomplish specific tasks. Management develops the capacity to achieve its objectives by organizing and staffing, creating organizational structure, and identifying sets of job functions, staffing jobs with qualified people, delegating responsibility for carrying out strategy and tactics, and devising systems to monitor operations and accomplishments.

A new managerial era is emerging in policing because of the adaptation of different problem-solving, data-driven operational strategies. These strategies represent a significant change in the way the police conceive of their departments, manage, and respond to operational demand. Police executives using these strategies are proactively developing organizational processes that allow their departments to initiate and reshape their activities to meet changing public safety demand. They are transforming their departments into proactive strategically managed departments instead of reactive organizations (Wexler, Wycoff, & Fischer, 2007). Police departments that use strategic management techniques are aligning their external and internal environments through decisions based upon intelligence analysis. They are creating open-system adaptive-learning organizations. Crime and public safety are problems to be analyzed and resolved, not something to which to react.

This strategic transformation involves the restructuring of organizations and utilization of new outcome-based performance systems. Core functions, operational strategies, managerial accountability, distribution of power, and culture are being reorganized to achieve a more effective impact. A properly designed strategic management process should establish accountability at all managerial levels of the organization under the direction of the executive staff and focus the entire organization on the department's mission. Time will tell whether strategic policing is the appropriate model that police executives should adopt to govern their departments and provide public-safety services. Last, it should be remembered that in a democracy policing should always respond to the needs of the people. Policing is a work in progress shaped by the political, social, organizational, and economic trends of time and place.

KEY TERMS

Active supervisors	Coordination	Organizational structure
Administration	Empowerment	Organizing
Administrative functions	Executive strategic level	Planning
Administrative paradox	Influence	Strategic management
Authority	Innovative supervisors	Styles of supervision
Bureaucracy	Learning organizations	Supervisory level
Command levels	Managerial authority	Supportive supervisors
Commanding	Middle management level	Traditional supervisors
Controlling	Organizational justice	Voluntariness

References

Blake, R.R., & Mouton, J.S. (1994). *The managerial grid III: The key to leadership excellence.* Houston, TX: Gulf Pub.

Blanchard, K., & Johnson, S. (2003). *The one minute manager.* New York, NY: William Marrow.

Brown, M.M., & Brudney, J.L. (2003). Learning organizations in the public sector? A study of police agencies employing information and technology to advance knowledge. *Public Administration Review, 63*(1), 30–43.

Colvin, A. (2015, April). Mapping the future of policing: Developing capabilities and part- nerships. *The Police Chief,* 30–31.

Cordner, G.W. (2013). *Police administration,* 8th ed. New York: Elsevier.

Covey, S.R. (1997).The habits of effective organizations. In F. Hesselbein, & P.M. Cohen (Eds.), *Leader to leader* (pp. 215–216). San Francisco: Jossey-Bass.

Crank, J.P., & Langworthy, R. (1992). Institutional perspective on policing. *Journal of Crimi- nal Law & Criminology, 83,* 338–363.

Cunningham, M.R., Jones, J.W., & Behrens, G.M. (2011). Psychological assessment of chief of police candidates: Scientific and practice issues. *Journal of Police and Criminal Psy- chology, 26,* 77–86.

David, F.R. (2014). *Strategic management: A competitive advantage approach, concepts & cases.* Upper Saddle River, NJ: Prentice Hall.

Dessler, G. (2004). *Management: Principles and practices for tommorrow's leaders.* Upper Saddle River, NJ:Prentice Hall.

Dessler, G. (2012). *Human resource management.* Upper Saddle River, NJ:Prentice Hall.

Domanick, J (2015). *Blue: The LAPD and the battle to redeem American policing.* New York, NY: Simon & Schuster.

Drucker, P. (1998). *On the profession of management.* Boston, MA: Harvard Business Review.

Drucker, P. (2004). What makes an effective executive? *Harvard Business Review, 82*(6), 58–62.

Engel, R.S. (2001). Supervisory styles of patrol sergeants and lieutenants. *Journal of Criminal Justice, 29,* 341–355.

Engel, R.S. (2002). Patrol officer supervision in the community policing era. *Journal of Criminal Justice, 30,* 51–64.

Engel, R.S. (2003). *How police supervisory styles influence patrol officer behavior.* Washington, DC: National Institute of Justice.

Fayol, H. (1949). *General and industrial management.* London: Pitman.

Fayol, H. (1992). General principles of management. In J. Shafrits, & J. Ott (Eds.), *Classics of organizational theory.* Pacific Grove, CA: Brooks /Cole.

Fyfe, J.J., Greene, J.R., Walsh, W., Wilson, O., & McLaren, R. (1997). *Police administration.* New York: McGraw-Hill.

Geller, W.A., & Swanger, G. (1995). *Managing innovation in policing: The untapped potential of the middle manager.* Washington, DC: Police Executive Research Forum.

Goldstein, H. (1990). *Problem-oriented policing.* New York: McGraw Hill.

Haberfeld, M.R. (2006). *Police leadership.* Upper Saddle River, NJ: Prentice-Hall.

Haneberg, L. (2005). *High impact middle management.* Avon, MA: FW Publications.

Hersey, P., & Blanchard, K. (1993). *Management of organizational behavior—Utilizing human resources.* Englewood Cliffs, NJ: Prentice Hall.

International Association of Chiefs of Police. (1999). *Police leadership in the 21st century: Achieving and sustaining executive success.* Alexandria, VA: IACP.

Kelling, G.L., & Bratton, W.J. (1993). Implementing community policing: The administrative problem. *Perspectives on Policing, No. 14.* Washington, DC: National Institute of Justice.

Kelling, G.L., & Moore, M.H. (1988). From political to reform to community: The evolving strategy of police. In J.R. Greene, & S.D. Mastrofski (Eds.), *Community policing: Rhetoric or reality* (pp. 3–26). New York, NY: Praeger.

Kelly, R. (2015). *Vigilance: My life serving America and protecting its empire city.* New York: Hachette.

Moore, M.H., & Trojanowicz, R.C. (1988). Corporate strategy for policing. *Perspectives on Policing, No.6.* Washington, DC: National Institute of Justice.

More, H.W., & Miller, L.S. (2014). *Effective police supervision,* 7th ed. Burlington, MA: Elsevier.

More, H.W., Vito, G.F., & Walsh, W.F. (2012). *Organizational behavior and management in law enforcement.* Upper Saddle River, NJ: Prentice Hall.

Peak, K. (2012). *Policing America: Challenges and best practices.* Upper Saddle River, NJ: Prentice Hall.

Pinellas Park Police Department. (2006). *Directives manual, standard operating procedure, #32, promotions.* Pinellas Park, FL: Pinnellas Police Department.

President's Task Force on 21st Century Policing. (2015). *Final report of the President's task force on 21st century policing.* Washington, DC: Office of Community Oriented Policing Services.

Reiss, Jr., A.J. (1985). Shaping and serving the community: The role of the police chief executive. In W.A. Geller (Ed.), *Police leadership in America: Crisis and opportunity* (pp. 61–69). New York, NY: Prager.

Reuss-Ianni, E. (1983). *Two cultures of policing: Street cops and management cops.* New Brunswick, NJ: Transaction Books.

Senge, P. (1990). *The fifth discipline: The art & practice of the learning organization.* New York: Doubleday.

Sherman, L.W., Milton, C.H., & Kelly, T.V. (1973). *Team policing: Seven case studies.* Washington, DC: Police Foundation.

Sparrow, M.K., Moore, M., & Kennedy, D. (1990). *Beyond 911: A new era for policing.* New York, NY: Basic Books.

Stamper, N.H. (1992). *Removing managerial barriers to effective police leadership: A study of executive leadership and executive management in big-city police departments.* Washington, DC: Police Executive Research Forum.

Swanson, C.R., Territo, L.J., & Taylor, R.W. (2011). *Police administration: Structures, processes, and behavior.* Upper Saddle River, NJ: Prentice Hall.

Travis, J. (1995). Managing innovation in policing: The untapped potential of the middle manager. *Research in Brief.* Washington, DC: National Institute of Justice.

Timoney, John F. (2010). *Beat cop to top cop.* Philadelphia, PA: University of Pennsylvania Press.

Van Maanen, J. (1984). Making rank: Becoming an American police sergeant. *Urban Life, 13,* 155–176.

Vito, G.F., Walsh, W.F., & Kunselman, J. (2005). Community policing: The middle manager's perspective. *Police Quarterly, 8*(4), 490–511.

Walsh, W.F. (1998). Policing at the crossroads: Changing directions for the new millennium. *Policing: An International Journal of Police Science and Management, 1*(1), 17–25.

Walsh, W.F., & Donovan, E.J. (1990). *The supervision of police personnel: A performance-based approach.* Dubuque, IA: Kendall Hunt.

Weber, M. (1947). *The theory of social and economic organization.* New York, NY: The Free Press.

Weisburd, D., & McElroy, J. (1988). Enacting the CPO role: Findings from the New York City pilot program in community policing. In J.R. Greene, & S.D. Mastrofski (Eds.), *Community policing: Rhetoric or reality* (pp. 89–102). New York, NY: Praeger.

Wexler, C., Wycoff, M.A., & Fischer, C. (2007). *Good to great policing: Application of business management principles in the public sector.* Washington, DC: Department of Justice Office of Community Oriented Policing Services and Police Executive Research Forum.

Williams, T. (2015, December 9). Under fierce scrutiny police chiefs sift focus. *New York Times,* A23.

Willis, J.J. (2011). First-line supervision and strategic decision making under Compstat and community policing. *Criminal Justice Policy Review, 24*(2), 235–256.

Wolfe, S., & Nix, J. (2016). Managing police departments post-Ferguson. *Harvard Business Review,* https://hbr.org/ 9/13.

3 Police Leadership

The leader must lead from the front—exposing him or herself to the same dangers and hardships as the cops in the field while monitoring whether the department's tactics and strategies are being carried out and whether or not they're working.

Jack Maple, *The Crime Fighter* (1999, p. 244)

Learning Objectives

1.   To define leadership in policing.

2.   To identify the elements of leadership styles.

3.   To define the attributes of transformational leadership.

4.   To identify the elements of the Leadership Challenge Model.

5.   To identify the elements of servant leadership.

6.   To identify the elements of situational leadership.

Introduction

Leadership is the key force behind the creation of effective organizations. In policing, leadership can energize and become a dynamic force in the agency—invigorating change and sponsoring professionalization. Leadership motivates individuals to perform the tasks that can move the organization forward. Effective leaders motivate their followers to do what is best for the organization. They accomplish this by creating a sense of purpose that both motivates and directs followers so they voluntarily make meaningful contributions to the department. Thus a leader is a source of both guidance and inspiration. In this chapter, we will provide a review of relevant theories of leadership that apply to policing.

The elements of police leadership are a vital concern and provide a sign of what is important. Leadership is not found only at the executive/administrative level of the police organization. It can be exercised at any level of the department. For example, Haberfeld (2006, p. 3) defines police leadership as "the ability to make a split-second decision and take control of a potentially high-voltage situation that evolves on the street." She also asserts that line officers are "the true leaders on the streets, using their leadership skills in daily encounters with the community, and police executives and policy makers need to realize it" (Haberfeld, 2006, p. 3). Baker (2006, p. 41) contends that effective leadership is exercised by police managers in different ways, depending upon their rank in the department. Senior executive leadership should develop and share their vision for the organization, charting the path to the accomplishment of this vision by establishing strategic objectives and practicing collaboration and delegation of tasks. Police middle managers operationalize the vision through coordinating and planning, mentoring and coaching, building teams, and empowering and rewarding their subordinates. First-line supervisors who are the closest managers to department's employees provide leadership by example, supervising, training and developing teams while evaluating performance.

It is vital that all levels of the department are mobilized and involved to ensure successful police leadership. Coaching and mentoring of the people doing day-to-day operations ensures the leader's vision for the department is realized and that the organization will succeed. Leadership is most effective when it is aware of the need and expectations of subordinates. Villiers (2003, p. 33) notes that police leaders motivate their followers to:

- Transcend self-interest for the sake of organizational goals and values.
- Raise their need level up from security and safety to self-esteem or autonomy.
- Share with the leader a common vision of the importance of the leader's goals or values to the future of the organization.

Motivated followers can achieve more than they thought possible, strengthen their commitment to, and raise departmental performance.

There are three related ideas about administration that guide our definition of leadership. First, leadership is a process that cannot be conceptually separated from achieving organizational objectives. Second, leadership can be learned by people in administrative positions in organizations. Much of the leadership literature assumes that effective leadership can be taught. Third, the leadership process is a group process. To accomplish organizational objectives, leaders must identify and influence a significant number of people who must do the work necessary for success. According to Gladwell's (2006) Tipping Point Leadership theory, once the beliefs and energies of a critical mass of people are engaged, conversion to a new idea will spread, bringing about fundamental change quickly. The process of leadership must be examined in light of how leaders get people to achieve the tasks necessary for organizational existence and survival.

Effective leadership is grounded upon the direction and guidance provided by the leader through four styles of leadership. **Directive leadership** emphasizes the expectations of the leader and the tasks to be performed by subordinates. The leader emphasizes important organizational rules and regulations and their relationship to task performance. The leader provides guidance to subordinates and motivates them to accomplish the tasks required by the organization. **Supportive leadership** is an employee-centered process. Supportive leaders are approachable and friendly with their employees. Their primary concern is to accomplish the tasks of the organization while meeting the needs of their subordinates. **Participatory leadership** emphasizes collaboration between the leader and the subordinates. The leader seeks to involve subordinates in the decision-making process while assuring their importance in the organization. **Achievement-oriented leadership** is concerned with producing results. The leader expects that workers will attempt to do their best and is confident they will achieve stated goals. Each style can create an effective organization.

Studies of Police Leadership

The literature on police leadership reveals that distinct styles have been exercised in different ways. In an early study of 155 police managers, Kuykendall and Unsinger (1982) reported that "salesman" was the most commonly reported leadership style. The respondents noted that they viewed themselves as team managers who avoided "risky" styles. They avoided delegating high-level tasks to their subordinates. Apparently, these police managers lacked both trust and confidence in the abilities of their followers. However, in a similar study, Bruns and Shuman (1988) surveyed 365 law enforcement officers in 10 managerial training programs in Arizona from 1978–1982 and found that the respondents supported a highly participative management style for police leaders.

Girodo (1998) surveyed police chiefs from departments around the world, characterizing their leadership style under four categories. Transformational leaders were considerate, charismatic, and personable. Bureaucratic leaders identified with the management of a police organization structured by its rules. Social contract leaders felt that their approach was professional. Most of the police chief respondents identified with the Machiavellian model that stressed manipulating subordinates to achieve management ends. Girodo felt that the paramilitary structure of police departments helped create an authoritarian leadership style.

The bureaucratic structure of police departments is another major source of police organizational authoritarianism. Mayo (1985, p. 411) asserts that police chiefs spend too much of their time directing the daily operations of their departments because they have little faith in the talents and loyalties of their subordinates and fail to pay attention to long-term, strategic issues facing their departments. Archambeault and Weirman (1983) contend that the bureaucratic model of police departments results in a work environment that discourages productivity, initiative, and commitment among its workforce members. Bureaucracy also promotes the pursuit of individual self-interest and adversarial relationships between police managers and their employees, encouraging "game playing," resulting in an impersonal work climate.

The competency and background of police executives influences their leadership reputation. Krimmel and Lindemuth's (2001) analysis of 205 municipal managers in Pennsylvania revealed that these managers ranked the performance of police chiefs who managed a union shop, had some college credits, who were graduates of the FBI National Academy, and who were promoted from within consistently higher than those who did not possess these attributes. Similarly, Rowe's (2006) ethnography of British police officers determined that superiors who had direct experience with and maintained their ties with the street where "real police work" was done were considered the best leaders. Those management supervisors who moved up the ranks without such experience were viewed with suspicion and were less likely to be accepted.

Several studies have analyzed assessments of the leadership attributes and performance of police managers. For example, Stamper (1992) surveyed 52 police chiefs and 92 of their immediate assistants and found that their self-assessments and those of their subordinates revealed a discrepancy between belief and practice among these chiefs. The chiefs felt they placed a premium on sharing their vision of the future, practicing openness and honesty, fostering teamwork by helping their employees get the work done, and recognizing excellence in performance. Externally, these chiefs said that they promoted questioning of agency policies while working closely with the members of their community. They professed the adoption of an intuitive and creative approach to their work while taking a stand against discrimina-tory practices. The chiefs also believed that their leadership functions were most deserving of their time and attention on the job. However, their immediate assistants did not perceive that the behavior of the chiefs was consistent with their expressed beliefs about leadership. In their opinion, the chiefs were much more involved in the technical and procedural aspects of management than their leadership functions. These findings led Stamper to conclude that leadership had been "structured out" of police administration. Like Mayo, he surmised that police chiefs spent too much time and attention to management concerns and failed to lead their departments.

Recent studies assessing the state of police leadership have been more positive. Densten (2003) surveyed 480 Australian senior police officials. He reported that the effectiveness of a police leader was a function of leader reputation and followers' satisfaction with job perfor-mance of their leaders; impression management and image building by leaders; how depen-dent followers are on direction and resources from the leaders and how dependent leaders are upon the follower's completion of activities to achieve success (Densten, 2003, p. 412).

Similarly, interviews with 150 British officers revealed that they wanted leaders to make them feel proud of their work and their contributions. Effective leadership involved offer-ing high-quality service, maintaining high personal and professional standards, empowering staff, and possessing relevant knowledge and skills. The way officers feel about how they are treated by the organization affects both the quality of their performance and the service they provide to the community (Dobby, Anscombe, & Tuffin, 2004).

A case study examined the implementation of participatory management in a subur-ban police agency through the construction of a Leadership Team. The team established and enhanced collaborative relationships between all levels of the department and the community. Officers felt that the opportunity to take part in agency decisions increased and that their input and opinions were seriously considered. They noted increased pride in the agency—a zero officer turnover rate during the period in question. Noted empowerment factors included the participation of all ranks in the decision-making process, management seeking feedback from all levels of the department, and consistent and reliable support of employee decisions by management. Finally, the officers noted that they were motivated to implement Community Policing as they saw fit and they displayed greater motivation to engage in discretionary con-duct (Steinheider & Wuestewald, 2008). The study documents how participatory leadership can improve introducing innovations by increasing the motivation of workers at all levels of the department.

Fischer's (2009) interviews with 25 American police chiefs determined that police lead-ers must be both honest and transparent in their dealings with their subordinates, set a good example of performance and integrity, be a change agent that moves the agency forward, support and honor the performance of their charges. They should be "consensus builders" who should follow a democratic leadership approach (Fischer, 2009, p. 10). Results from Isenberg's (2010) survey of 26 American police chiefs mirrors these opinions. These chiefs also stressed the need for leaders to be optimistic role models who breed confidence in their agency and the community it serves. They should be unafraid to set goals that involve risk (Isenberg, 2010, p. 42). They recommended the use of a leadership style that is inclusive and seeks the support of all members of the organization (Isenberg, 2010, p. 44).

Support for the change to this police leadership style has grown. A survey of police managers attending the Southern Police Institute examined their attitudes concerning ideal leadership behavior. Andreescu and Vito (2010) found that gender and race played a significant role in structuring leadership preferences. Both males and females expressed a preference for task-centered and structured leadership. Yet, women and African Americans seemed to prefer transformational leaders who favored a democratic, work-oriented style and allowed subordinates freedom of action while responding to the concerns of followers.

Schafer (2010b) surveyed 1,000 police supervisors to determine their opinions regarding the traits, habits, and effective practices of police leaders. They ranked honesty and integrity as the most important characteristic. In addition they noted that personality and interpersonal skills (caring, communication, and work ethic) were more significant than technical aspects (decision making, competency, knowledge) in determining effective police leadership (Schafer, 2010b, p. 651; see also Schafer, 2013). While these officers considered the achievement of key goals as significant, they also gave weight to the "interpersonal dynamics of the workplace" including accessing the growth and development of subordinates, maintaining morale, and the leader's maintenance of positive standing within the agency (Schafer, 2010b, pp. 652–653). These mid-level managers also suggested that the best way to achieve police leadership development was through a mixture of education, practical application, and constructive feedback. Young officers should be exposed to leadership via mentoring and observation of positive role models (Schafer, 2009).

These studies illuminate the strong consensus that police leadership should be democratic. Officers want their leaders to be positive role models who seek their opinions and wish to foster their improvement and development. There is strong sentiment for the abandonment of the "command and control" model of police management and its replacement with an inclusive style of leadership. These empirical findings provide a basis for our review of three influential theories of leadership that have been applied to policing—Tipping Point, Transformational, and Servant Leadership.

Tipping Point Leadership

Tipping point leadership consists of a four-step process to bring about rapid, dramatic, and lasting change with limited resources. There are four "hurdles" that change agents must typically overcome in any organization (Kim & Mauborgne, 2003, p. 64). It can be applied to reveal the implementation problems that both Community Policing and Compstat have faced.

1. **The cognitive hurdle:** *Put managers face to face with problems and customers. Find new ways to communicate.*
   Community Policing faces a "model muddle." Hunter and Barker (1993, p. 157) define this muddle as layers of "BS" in that Community Policing "seeks to be all things to all people under the umbrella of community involvement." As a result, departments have great difficulty implementing the model because no one really knows whether it is a program, a philosophy, or both.
   In both New York and Los Angeles, Bratton perceived this as meaning that he had to get the department and its leadership to recognize that they were failing in their crime control mission and had been for several years.

2. **The resource hurdle:** *Focus on "hot spots" and bargain with partner organizations.*

    Departments implementing Community Policing have been hampered by resource limitations and the need to integrate handling high service demand resulting from calls for service with community problem solving (Kessler, 1993).

    As Bratton notes, the public sector has never had a vast surplus of resources. At the LAPD, he removed all personnel from special duties and placed them back on the street. In the Lowell (MA) Compstat implementation study, it was noted that flexibility in reassigning personnel was not accomplished due to the department's responsibility to be fair to its employees, respond to unpredictable situations, and be equitable to its citizens while meeting political demands of powerful constituents (Willis, Mastrofski, Weisburd, & Greenspan, 2004, p. 482).

3. **The motivational hurdle:** *Put the stage lights on and frame the challenge to match the organization's various levels.*

    Despite all the attention given to Community Policing, performance measures based upon its delivery have not been developed by police departments. By retaining traditional measures (like arrests and citations), departments implementing Community Policing have violated a fundamental maxim of organizational development: "*What gets measured, gets done!*"

    Bratton stresses that accountability is the key to Compstat. In particular, he feels that police officers must be controlled because of the vast power they hold over the citizenry. He also states that while he often must "lead from behind," he stresses inspiration and positive motivational techniques in his change efforts. Despite this description, one of the "urban legends" surrounding Compstat is that accountability becomes confrontational, personal, and ultimately, demeaning. Although they did not experience such treatment directly, Lowell line officers believed that Compstat sessions were forums where officers "had their balls ripped off," were "someone's punching bag," and were "sometimes kind of humiliated, or embarrassed in front of other people." Like Bratton, the Lowell chief noted that, while he did use Compstat sessions to reward or punish his officers, he was averse to humiliating them, preferring to ask questions and foster a supportive environment (Willis et al., 2004, pp. 477–478).

4. **The political hurdle:** *Identify and silence internal opponents; isolate external ones.*

    Although Community Policing typically enjoys support among political leaders and local officials who wish to appear progressive and responsive to the needs of citizens, Community Policing has been relegated to "innovation ghettos"—specialized units who provide services (see Toch & Grant, 1982). It has rarely been implemented on a departmental basis. In the meantime, the majority of the police department's service delivery strategy continues to be a response to citizen-generated calls for service and pressures brought by civic and political leaders.

    Bratton (1998) addressed this problem by downsizing one managerial level of NYPD between the executive staff and the operational precincts. He abolished divisional commands and placed the Inspectors and Deputy Inspectors assigned to these units in command of precincts. These are appointed ranks that serve at the pleasure of the Police Commissioner. If they failed to meet their outcome-based command leadership requirements, they could be demoted back to their civil service rank of

Captain and removed from command by order of the Commissioner. Internally, he recruited a top NYPD commander, John Timoney, to audit the responses of the top staff toward Bratton's concept of order maintenance-policing and identify those who would support and those who would oppose the premise. Externally, support was provided for this organizational direction by then Mayor Rudolph Giuliani who had considerable influence in the courts, district attorney's office, and jail due to his reputation as an effective federal prosecutor (Kim & Mauborgne, 2003, p. 69).

Bratton's use of the tipping leadership style described above energized the bureaucratic structure of police organizations he commanded. These organizations were changed through the introduction of an entrepreneurial spirit and the establishment of accountability measures that accurately determine levels of both production and performance. Instead of abandoning their citizen partners as in the past, they also recognized that citizens are partners in policing with responsibilities to their communities for assisting in the solving of crime and disorder problems (see Osborne & Gaebler, 1993; Osborne & Plastrik, 1997).

Transformational Leadership

Burns (1978) argues that individuals in an organization may be influenced and motivated by leaders via two methods: transformational and transactional leadership. Each of these types of leadership has different ways to influence attitudes and motivation. Transactional leadership relies on the reciprocal and deterministic relationship between a leader and their subordinates (Bass & Riggio, 2006). Here, leaders engage in a bargaining process with subordinates to motivate them. The leader regulates the bargaining process so that benefits may be issued and received to continue positively valued behavior. Officers are rewarded by their supervisors when they engage in and perform their duties in the manner prescribed by the rules and regulations of the organization.

Transactional leadership is characterized in multiple ways. First, a transactional leader uses contingent rewards (e.g., work for pay or time off) to underlie the arrangements for explicit or implicit agreement on goals to be reached to get the desired rewards or behavior. Second, the transactional leader monitors subordinate performance to ensure effectiveness. Third, transactional leaders are passive and only take action when a problem arises. It results in a mutually beneficial exchange that leads to goal achievement. Unfortunately, this exchange may only garner short-term commitment. Instead of creating a more sustainable performance change in officers, it creates reward-seeking behavior that ceases when the rewards end.

Transformational leaders seek to change the organizational status quo and take the organization on a new and effective path. Instead of maintaining traditional forms of command and control and reacting to crime, transformational police leaders develop a proactive strategic vision of their department's operational performance. They recognize the fluid context in which their departments operate. They also understand that there are forces to which police organizations must adapt and evolve to remain effective in a changing world. It is these forces that are creating new models for conducting the business of policing (Batts, Smoot, & Scrivner, 2012). The strategic policing methods they practice involve the effective use of intelligence and developing flexible strategies to meet public safety needs. They seek to instill in their departments a set of organizational values focused on effectiveness, crime prevention, community engagement, information management, organizational and managerial accountability, ethics, and the control of crime (Moore & Trojanowicz, 1988).

Transformational leaders are present in today's police organizations. In his assessment of leadership in the Los Angeles Police Department, Reese (2005, p. 132) identified Chief William Bratton as a transformational leader due to his intellectual vision, empathy for his officers and the community, his personal charisma and communication skills. Empirically, transformational leadership has been a focus of studies on police leadership. Murphy and Drodge (2004) interviewed 28 Royal Canadian Mounted Police officers on their views of police leadership within the framework of transformational leadership theory. They describe that at the center of transformational leadership theory is the "Four I's" (Murphy & Drodge, 2004, pp. 2–3):

1. *Idealized influence*: The leader stands for something that followers aspire to.
2. *Inspirational motivation*: A sense of collective identity inspired by the leader's vision.
3. *Intellectual stimulation*: challenges followers to examine ways to enhance their productivity.
4. *Individualized consideration* to followers.

The RCMP officers stressed that leaders can emerge at all levels of the organization and that leadership skills can be learned. They stressed the significance of the "Four I's" and how leaders must be genuinely concerned with the needs of followers.

The impact of transformational leadership was the subject of an ethnographic study of one department. Through interviews and observations, Murphy (2008) found that officers stressed that leadership was linked to shared values. Leaders must personify these values and demonstrate consistency, honesty, and fairness in their supervisory decisions. These officers felt an emotional attachment to leaders who inspired them by standing for their values, even when their attempts to implement change were blocked by upper management.

A study of German police officers found that transformational leaders exerted a direct, positive influence on shared leadership and an indirect, positive influence on follower job satisfaction through their capacity to clarify organizational goals (Masal, 2015).

In South Australia, Mazerolle, Darroch, and White (2013) examined the implementation of and outcomes from problem-oriented policing in South Australia. Using a time series design, they found that POP generated an overall drop in crimes per 100,000 population—particularly in property crime. These results were attributable to the transformational leadership style of Commissioner Mal Hyde who drove the innovation by supporting those who attempted to create new operational ideas. Through his top-down approach to implementation, Commissioner Hyde oversaw the POP agenda and changed the police culture.

Sarver and Miller (2014) surveyed 161 Texas police chiefs with scales designed to measure their leadership attitudes and aptitudes. They found that the chiefs were evenly split across several leadership styles: Transactional, Transformational, and Passive/Avoidant. Several attributes were identified as strongly related to the Transformational Leadership style as compared to the others, including extra effort, effectiveness, satisfaction, extraversion, openness, and conscientiousness. In terms of performance, chiefs who adopted the Transformational Leadership style were more successful in motivating their subordinates to make the extra effort on the job. Their followers were more satisfied with their leadership style than chiefs in the other groups. They also received fewer formal complaints than their counterparts.

However, several studies have noted the limitations of transformational leadership. Cockcroft (2014) suggests that transformational leadership is incongruent with the culture of policing where street-level and management cops possess different and sometimes opposing views of their world of work (see also Niederhoffer, 1969; Reuss-Ianni, 1983). He argues that much of police work relies upon "the transactional demands of command" and that one form of leadership will not be appropriate for every set of organizational relationships (Cockcroft, 2014, p. 12). Research by Swid (2014) shows that transformational and transactional leadership are not mutually exclusive and that both can be practiced by the same individual. Both are necessary for organizational growth and maintenance but subordinates preferred transformational leaders who provided opportunities for growth experiences (Swid, 2014, p. 590).

Yet, transformational leadership theory states that such leaders possess the ability to convey a sense of vision and mission in a way that transforms the follower's sense of the possible. Transformational leaders motivate their followers to:

- *Transcend self-interest for the sake of organizational goals and values.*
- *Raise their need level up from security and safety to self-esteem and autonomy.*
- *Share with the leader a common vision of the importance of the leader's goals or values to the future of the organization.*
- *Achieve more than they thought possible.*
- *Strengthen their commitment to the organization.*
- *Induce feelings of trust, admiration, loyalty and mutual respect.*

(Villiers, 2003, p. 33)

Transformational leaders are change agents who renovate the organization through the empowerment of their followers and getting their commitment to a new vision for the organization. In Chapter 5 we further discuss transformational leadership and the management of organizational change.

The Leadership Challenge Model

Transformational leadership serves as the basis for the Leadership Challenge Model (Kouzes & Posner, 2012). It comprises five practices that effective leaders demonstrate:

1. *Model the way* (setting a personal example).
2. *Inspire a shared vision* (envisioning, articulating, and sharing a new future).
3. *Challenge the process* (willingness to question and confront the status quo).
4. *Enable others to act* (nurture and empower the development of followers).
5. *Encourage the heart* (recognize and celebrate the accomplishments of followers).

Each of the Five Practices include Ten Committments that illustrate the performance of leaders in their accomplishment.

For example, under "Model the Way," Commitment 1 states that leaders find their voice by communicating their values. Leaders must express their values to empower and motivate others. Values are significant because they influence how leaders respond to followers. Genuine beliefs sponsor passion and strengthen moral principles among colleagues. Modeling the way is also linked to competence. Commitment 2 states that leaders must align their values with their actions. Successful leadership performance is tied to their ability to act upon their stated values. It enables them to both set an example and to build consensus among followers. To reinforce these values among their followers, leaders not only teach and tell stories but they give them life through their personal example. Murphy (2008, p. 176) directly observed that officers admired transformational leaders who "walked the talk" but saw they invoked fear and insecurity among upper management who constrained them from getting results when it meant breaking the rules.

Inspiring a shared vision involves a recognition of the challenges and opportunities facing the organization while working toward their realization. Thus, Commitment 3 finds that leaders envision the future by imagining exciting and enobling possibilities via positive messages. By articulating their vision, leaders enlist others to share it, finding a common ground with their followers by speaking from the heart (Commitment 4). There are three components of leadership vision: (1) The Past—where we have been, the tradition of the organization; (2) The Present—where we are now, colored by realistic optimism; and (3) The Future—Where we are going, the promise of success.

Leaders challenge the process and move their followers to action. They proactively seize the initiative to improve organizational effectiveness in the long term. Commitment 5 states that leaders find innovative ways to bring change about. They create meaningful challenges for their followers and invite them to seek ways to make changes effectively. Leaders experiment and take risks, creating small wins that generate enthusiasm and support among followers. Initiative is rewarded, not punished because mistakes are viewed as learning experiences that will help move the organization forward (Commitment 6).

Leaders enable others to collaborate and act through these practices. Collaboration is fostered by creating a climate of trust in the organization and ability and competence of its personnel (Bratton, & Tumin, 2012). They enable their employees by trusting in their ability to successfully complete assigned tasks. Such leaders are servants of the organization who assume their roles and responsibilities to meet the needs of others—not through seeking power and status. They encourage their officers to seize the initiative and feel the need to do so. In Commitment 7, leaders build collaboration by promoting cooperative goals and building trust. By sharing their power with their employees, leaders increase their own. They train and mentor their employees so they can solve problems and implement solutions, thus inspire confidence and build competence. Due to these actions, employees make ready to assume responsibility for their actions and performance. Leaders strengthen their followers in this fashion, sharing power and discretion with followers (Commitment 8).

Leaders encourage the hearts of followers by recognizing and celebrating their accomplishments. They promote high standards and holding followers accountable for their performance. Recognition is personalized when individual performance is commendable and outstanding. Rewards are creatively constructed, personalized, and recognized in a public setting. Commitment 9 finds leaders recognizing contributions by showing appreciation for individual excellence. Celebrating successful performance reaffirms values and creates a spirit of community within the organization (Commitment 10).

Kouzes and Posner (2012) assertatively conclude that leadership is a skill that can be learned through the study of these practices and commitments. They have been demonstrated in the past by effective leaders. Leaders who learn and practice them can make a positive difference in their organization, its members, and its clients. The Leadership Challenge Model is a construct that reflects the ideals and practices of transformational leadership (Carless, 2001). Transformational leaders make organizations more effective and successful by defining the values that embrace the enduring principles of a people. Transforming values lie at the heart of transformational leadership (Burns, 2008, p. 307).

Evidence of the Five Practices of the Leadership Challenge Model in policing is documented by Fischer's interviews with police chiefs. Under "Modelling the Way," Fischer's respondents advised new chiefs to keep in mind that actions speak louder than words when they are trying to gain the confidence of their officers (Fischer, 2009, p. 46). Chiefs must be open, honest, transparent, sincere, and have a strong work ethic. They should be accountable, and acknowledge the mistakes they make. "The measure of the character of a police chief is the ability to exercise constraint in the use of the awesome power we have" (Fischer, 2009, p. 18).

Transparency means being honest and open about both good and bad news in the police department. Accessability means having mechanisms in place to ensure that reporters can get answers to their questions in a timely way (Fischer, 2009, p. 97). Particularly, these chiefs value "Management by Walking Around" (MBWA): "You have to get off your butt, get out of your office, ride the streets, go to meetings, and see for yourself what the situation really is. This helps you identify problems before they occur" (Fischer, 2009, p. 84).

When "Inspiring a Shared Vision," Fischer's police chiefs noted that the vision itself is likely to be popular—who would object to visionary goals, such as making a city safer and providing a responsive, committed police department? But the decisions that a chief makes to *achieve* a vision can be controversial. Doing the right thing requires making difficult decisions that may be unpopular with politicians, the rank and file, or with the public (Fischer, 2009, p. 6). It is important that a good leader makes it clear what his or her vision is, and attracts those who believe in that vision to the leadership team (Fischer, 2009, p. 37). The chiefs also felt it was their job to sell their vision to their bosses. They advised that getting your bosses to buy into your vision for the department *before* you take the job is a key determinant in how you will fare as chief, and failing to get "buying in" should be a deal breaker when you are considering a job as chief (Fischer, 2009, p. 80).

To challenge the Process, the chiefs remind us that every chief is hired as a change agent. The test for a chief is to understand what changes to make, how much change is needed, and how much the department and elected officials can tolerate (Fischer, 2009, p. 5). They stressed the limited term of a police chief as cause for action: "You know the chief's job is not going to last forever. You have to be up for that kind of challenge. If survival is an issue, you shouldn't be chief. If you can't take the risks, get out of the business" (Fischer, 2009, p. 22). Be tough, confident, and decisive in your role as a change agent, and get moving on your plans for change early in your administration, when the department and the community are *expecting* changes to happen (Fischer, 2009, p. 120).

"Enable Others to Act" is concerned with the empowerment of subordinates. Most chiefs said that they were "consensus builders" and that they followed a democratic approach to leading their departments (Fischer, 2009, p. 10). "The real work is done by the young men and women who drive the radio cars, who answer the phone, who talk to the public. Our job is to make their job possible. It's not about you, it's about the officers who do the real work"

(Fischer, 2009, p. 13). The strategy for your vision "can't work unless the troops on the street do it" (Fischer, 2009, p. 39). "You can make mistakes here, but you can't lie, and you can't be dishonest. It's a tough job, but I want you to succeed, and you wouldn't be here if I didn't think you can succeed" (Fischer, 2009, p. 43). Chiefs have an obligation to consult with and empower their command staff; to give the members of the staff opportunities to show what they can do; and to help command staff members develop their leadership skills (Fischer, 2009, p. 51). "The chief needs to defend the department and its officers when they come under unwarranted criticism from elected officials. It sends a message to the other elected officials that the chief is not afraid to strike back" (Fischer, 2009, pp. 79–80).

Finally, these chiefs acknowledged the significance of "Encouraging the Hearts" of subordinates. "A chief's focus should always be to make folks as good as they can be, and then recognize them for their accomplishments" (Fischer, 2009, p. 24). "If you wanted everyone to like you, you should have been a circus clown, not a police supervisor. The job is about business" (Fischer, 2009, p. 35). Succession planning must include the encouragement of subordinates to undertake and successfully complete difficult assignments. They are the future of the department.

Servant Leadership

Servant leaders are those who provide direction, encourage participation, sponsor mutual respect between leaders and followers while fostering their independence (Gardner & Reece, 2012). This treatment leads to the achievement of high-quality organizational results. Servant leaders put the needs of their followers before and above their own concerns. They practice an ethical form of leadership that does not take advantage of followers. Jesus Christ is cited as the first teacher of the concept of servant leadership. He set the example by washing the feet of his disciples and taught that a leader's greatness is measured by a total commitment to serve fellow human beings (Sendjaya & Sarros, 2002, p. 59).

There are several distinct attributes attributed to servant leadership. For example, Greenleaf (1977) believed leaders should serve their followers and focus upon satisfying their needs. Servant leaders are less concerned with their personal power and devoted to leadership through providing service to others. Servant leaders put the needs of their followers above their own. It is an ethical style of leadership. The purpose of the organization is the welfare of its members, not to gratify the ego or reputation of the leader. The servant leader would never take advantage of followers.

Servant leadership is based upon five basic principles:

1. *Concern for people.*
2. *Stewardship of the organization.*
3. *Equity (or justice).*
4. *Indebtedness* (the Rights of Followers) including the right to: be needed and involved, a covenantal relationship, to understand (the organization and its goals and objectives), affect one's own destiny, be held accountable for performance, appeal decisions, and make a commitment to the organization.
5. *Self-understanding (or awareness)*: the creation of an ethical climate for others by questioning the motives of organizational leaders and members.

One of the most crucial attributes of servant leaders is *agape'*—an unconditional love of others without regard for their due or desert. It is a love of behavior and choice, not a romantic feeling. It is demonstrated by the servant leader through the following attributes:

- *Patience*: exercising self-control.
- *Kindness*: giving attention, appreciation and encouragement.
- *Humility*: authentic feelings without pretense or arrogance.
- *Respectfulness*: treating others as important.
- *Selflessness*: meeting the needs of others.
- *Forgiveness*: forgoing resentment when wronged.
- *Honesty*: freedom from resentment of others.
- *Commitment*: sticking to your choices and honoring your agreements.

(Hunter, 1998, p. 100)

As a result, the servant leader sets aside their own wants and needs and seeks the greatest good for others (see also Russell & Stone, 2002, pp. 145–147; Spears, 2002, pp. 27–29). The servant leader is committed to the growth of the organization and works to build community within them. In their research on police managers' attitudes toward leadership styles, Vito, Suresh, and Richards (2011) found that police managers attending the Administrative Officers Course at the University of Louisville's Southern Police Institute identified a marked preference for the principles of servant leadership.

Advice from the Dalai Lama

In his book, *The Leader's Way*, the Dalai Lama (2009) offers examples of servant leadership that are especially relevant to police leadership. His advice on decision making is pertinent to policing where the use of deadly force is an issue. For every decision, the goal of the leader is to take into account the interests of the organization and all of the people affected by it. The benchmark for the decision is that it must cause no harm to others or if harm is inevitable, to reduce the harm as much as possible. Leaders should question their motives and recognize how their actions can have an effect on other people—both within and outside the organization. They should serve the needs of the entire organization and those of individual workers.

The Dalai Lama lists his three stages of the decision-making process. First, make your initial decision and check whether there is harm to anyone and if there is none, proceed. If harm is present, apply your creativity to find another solution that eliminates the harm. If the harm is impossible to avoid, make certain that the harm is justified because it avoids a much greater harm or because it results in huge benefits to other people.

The Dalai Lama (2009, pp. 37–41) also lists "The Six Perfections" that mirror the attributes of servant leaders.

1. *Generosity*: A good leader is generous in giving credit where it is due.
2. *Ethical discipline*: Leaders must withstand temptation—greed, self-centeredness, lust, anger, hatred, fear, lack of self-confidence.
3. *Patience*: Must be cultivated. It makes it possible for the leader to deal with provocative circumstances (hostility, criticism, or disappointment) and improves judgment.

4.   *Enthusiastic effort*: Displays your belief in the importance of the goals and motivation to achieve them.
5.   *Concentration*: The ability to focus mental energy on one issue.
6.   *Wisdom*: The ability to see things as they are.

Cultivating the Six Perfections can reap several benefits for the servant leader. They increase the ability to deal with a crisis. They improve decision making and executing decisions. Other advantages are improved relationships with followers, heightened creativity, and increased enthusiasm for the job. Yet, the main theme is that the leader is a servant whose main concern is the welfare of others.

Good to Great

In *Good to Great*, Jim Collins (2001) led a team of researchers to examine 11 large companies that were particularly successful over a 15-year period.[1] Collins (2005) also took pains to show how these ideas could apply to the public sector in a second monograph—*Good to Great and the Social Sectors*. The Police Executive Research Forum showed how Collins's business model applied to police management in a monograph—*"Good to Great" Policing: Application of Business Management Principles in the Public Sector* (Wexler, Wycoff, & Fischer, 2007).

One major finding was that charismatic and transformational leaders were not the norm in the rise of these companies. Instead, they were led by persons who knew the business and rose up from the ranks. They were characterized as "Level 5" leaders—executives who built greatness that endured, blending personal humility with professional will. Specifically, Level 5 leaders:

- Were quiet, reserved, shy, gracious, mild-mannered and understanding.
- Were ambitious, but they put the needs of the organization first.
- Were modest, self-effacing, and understated in their personal style.
- Were driven by the need to produce sustainable results.
- Were concerned about the future of the organization and set up successors for effectiveness.

(Collins, 2001, pp. 30–31)

While they were exceptionally modest, Level 5 leaders were determined to do what was necessary to make the organization great. They were disinterested in setting themselves up as heroes. Typically, they were ordinary individuals who let their company's results speak for themselves. In the PERF monograph, Level 5 leaders in policing believed in maintaining a "command presence" during a "defining moment"—a crisis where the police chief must speak to the public to maintain credibility with both the community and members of the department (Wexler et al., 2007, p. 17). Level 5 leaders exhibited the attributes of servant leadership.

In particular, Level 5 leaders used the "Window and the Mirror" to achieve results. They maintained humility in times of success, attributing it to good fortune or factors outside their control. Yet they took direct responsibility for failure, taking stock of problems by looking within the organization. Leaders succeed by attracting and keeping the right employees by following three practical rules:

1. When in doubt, do not hire—keep looking. You need the right people to implement change.
2. Act on the need to change personnel. The best people need guidance, not management. They are self-motivated and are driven to produce the best results.
3. Put your best people to work on the biggest opportunities, not on the biggest problems. Opportunities allow people to become great.

(Collins, 2001, pp. 33–35)

Here, Collins uses the analogy of "getting the right people on the bus." The executives who ignited these transformations focused on getting the right personnel. The Good to Great leaders assembled their teams before deciding where the company should go. The PERF monograph recognized that this principle would be difficult to apply in policing because almost all of the personnel are inherited by the chief upon assumption of the office (Wexler et al., 2007, p. 20).

Truth telling is a major component of the *Good to Great* process. The Level 5 leader is particularly adept at "confronting the brutal facts"—any bad news (hazards) facing the organization (Collins, 2001, pp. 65–69). A primary task in taking a company from good to great is to create a culture wherein people have a tremendous opportunity to be heard. "Red flag" mechanisms and other tools are present that highlight information too perilous to be ignored. This leader takes care to tackle challenges without losing faith in the ability of the organization to overcome them. Here, the PERF monograph called attention to the Compstat process and problem-oriented policing (see Chapter 13) as examples of using data to confront the brutal facts in policing (Wexler et al., 2007, pp. 32–33).

The *Good to Great* companies were adept at determining just what they could be the best in the world at—what Collins termed "The Hedgehog Concept." Leaders must help organizations reflect on:

1. What the organization is passionate about. They did only those things that ignite the passion of organizational members, thus eliminating the need for motivation.
2. What the organization can be best in the world at. This recognition enables the organization to maintain a laser like focus on its core competencies and reason for being.
3. What drives the organization's economic engine? What element is crucial to maintaining economic efficiency?

(Collins, 2001, pp. 94–97)

The Hedgehog Concept simplifies the mission of the organization and provides a unifying principle to guide operations. The focus upon crime reduction was identified as an example of this principle at work in police administration (Wexler et al., 2007, pp. 36–37).

The *Good to Great* companies had a "culture of discipline" (Collins, 2001, p. 124). The focus upon implementing the Hedgehog Concept enabled employees to be diligent and intense in their thoughts and actions. Employees exercise self-discipline. They had greater freedom and responsibility to do their jobs. They were fanatical in the pursuit of excellence and greatness. Therefore, bureaucratic rules and tyrannical leadership, for the purpose of control, were unnecessary. Again, the PERF monograph urged police leaders to "take a long, hard look at the facts about the organization, and then act on those facts" (Wexler et al., 2007, p. 39).

Technological fixes were not essential to the rise of these companies. They were not the key to success. The lesson is that leaders should not seize on every technological fad out of fear of being left behind. Avoid the tendency to overreact in such a fashion. Rather, they should use technology selectively to speed up momentum that already exists and that is consistent with the Hedgehog Concept (Collins, 2001, pp. 152–153). In the PERF monograph, the use of a new data management tool in the Chicago Police Department (Citizen Law Enforcement Analysis and Reporting—CLEAR) is an example of how technology can speed up change (Wexler et al., 2007, p. 41).

Organizations should avoid the trap of the "Flywheel and Doom Loop" (Collins, 2001, pp. 174–180). There was no single defining action, no grand program, no one killer innovation, no solitary lucky break, no wrenching revolution or miracle that led to dramatic success. The *Good to Great* companies shunned the "Doom Loop"—the inconsistent and failed efforts resulting from chronic restructuring and management fads. Sustained momentum toward success was not the result of following an easy road. The PERF monograph described how crises in police agencies can become major catalysts for "widespread organizational change." This occurred in New Orleans in the mid-1990s when Chief Richard Pennington confronted severe and widespread corruption, implemented significant changes, established problem-oriented policing and Compstat programs (Wexler et al., 2007, p. 45).

Finally, the *Good to Great* companies aimed high in their goals. They set "big, hairy and audacious goals" (BHAGs). Their leaders exercised strategic thinking, setting goals that were extensive, comprehensive, and able to sustain long-term success for their organizations. BHAGs were clear, simple, and united to the core values of the organization (Collins, 2001, p. 203). In policing, Collins cited William Bratton's management of the New York City Police Department as an example of this concept—setting "audacious output goals, such as attaining double-digit annual declines in felony crime rates" via the Compstat process (Collins, 2005, p. 4). The PERF monograph noted that in public sector organizations "achieving greatness often is about 'overcoming obstacles'" (like the constraints imposed by budgets and labor agreements) (Wexler et al., 2007, p. 51). Taken together, the inclusive methods used by the "Good to Great" companies as identified by Collins and the attributes of methods practiced by Level 5 leaders support the premises of servant leadership.

Selecting a Leadership Style

The selection of a leadership style is affected by several factors. Tannenbaum and Schmidt (1958) developed a continuum of leadership that comprises seven different leadership styles, ranging from the full use of leadership authority to the allowance of complete freedom to subordinates to determine tasks and goals to follow. Under the first "autocratic" style, the leader makes a decision and announces it. In policing, this style is most appropriate when the leader wishes to maintain operational control such as in an emergency (Walsh, 1983). With the second style, the leader takes the additional step of "selling" the decision (such as a new organizational policy) to subordinates who now have minimal involvement.

In the middle of their continuum, Tannenbaum and Schmidt (1958) cover the participative approach to leadership. The leader acts after getting suggestions and advice from followers. The leader still makes the final decision but it is made in consultation with the staff. Through this interactive process, trust is built, providing that the leader informs subordinates of the reasons behind the decision and provides feedback on whether their input was utilized or not. If not, this style may be viewed as manipulation. Collaboration is another step toward the empowerment of subordinates. The leader maintains control over the decision-making process by defining the limits of the situation and asking the group to make the final decision. Thus, the consultative process does not give complete control to the group. The leader still is the decisive factor.

Using a participatory style is more likely when the leader requires the services of a qualified subordinate who possesses valuable knowledge and skills. For example, a police supervisor may seek the advice of line officers before establishing a new patrol method in their area (Walsh, 1983). The recognition they know their beat and the resulting consultation by the supervision is a morale builder. Such inclusion leads to support for the policy they helped to establish. Other beneficial attributes include sharing responsibility, development of mutual trust, personal commitment, and developing the potential of subordinates. However, the use of a participatory style requires mature subordinates and a leader willing to be honest and candid with followers.

The selection of a style is affected by three forces—those: (1) within the leader; (2) within the group; and (3) within the situation. The forces in the leader include their value system and the level of confidence they have in their subordinates. What are their leadership inclinations? Someone who feels they are the "Boss" is unlikely to engage in democratic leadership. What is their tolerance for ambiguity? Are you comfortable with turning decision-making power over to subordinates when you are unsure of what decision they will make? Overruling a democratic decision-making process after you gave permission to use it will have disastrous consequences.

The forces in the subordinates also help determine what type of style is in order. Participatory, democratic leadership is more likely when subordinates are independent, ready to assume responsibility for decision making, have their own "tolerance for ambiguity," are interested in the problem faced, have a high level of knowledge and experience, and expect to be consulted and involved in decision making.

The forces in the situation contribute to the selection of a leadership style in several ways. First, what is the type of organization under consideration? Police departments have typically been dominated by a "command and control" style that is not conducive to participatory leadership. In addition, what is the level of effectiveness of the group? A task force of experienced officers is more likely to be consulted than a group of newcomers to patrol. What is the nature of the problem itself and its level of complexity? Leaders seek help with complex problems. Subordinates are not interested in providing input to simple management decisions that do not affect their work life. Finally, the pressure of time itself is a crucial consideration. Consultation takes time. If a quick decision is required, the leader may not have the luxury of seeking time-rich consultation.

Tannenbaum and Schmidt (1958) conclude with the recognition that participatory, democratic leadership is a function of these factors and forces. It is not a matter of being strong or permissive—it is a matter of insight and flexibility. The successful leader knows the forces that are most relevant to decision making. They know and understand the competency and commitment of their people. They are ready to call upon the talents of their subordinates and sponsor their growth and development. They are flexible and analyze the situation to determine which style is most appropriate. If direction is in order, it is provided. If participatory management is called for, they can provide it.

Situational Leadership

Another variation on this question is provided by Hersey and Blanchard (1977) in their development of situational leadership. They describe leadership as composed of both a directive and a supportive dimension that should be applied appropriately in a given situation. To determine an appropriate style, the leader must evaluate subordinates and assess how competent and committed they are to perform a task. Leaders then adapt their style accordingly between directive or supportive methods to meet the changing needs of their subordinates. Leaders engage in directive behaviors by setting goals, establishing methods of evaluation, setting time lines, defining roles, and showing how goals should be met. Supportive behaviors are used to help subordinates feel comfortable about themselves, their colleagues, and their situation.

These methods are also presented along a continuum that parallels that provided by Tannenbaum and Schmidt that depends upon the talents and readiness of the followers along with the situation. Directing involves providing specific instructions and close supervision by the leader to achieve organizational goals. In the coaching mode, the leader explains his or her decision while providing the opportunity for questions about it to clarify meaning and purpose. Taking part gives subordinates control over decision making while the leader remains available to facilitate problem solving. In delegation, the leader turns decision making over to subordinates for implementing the solution and taking the responsibility to achieve it.

The abilities, willingness, and readiness of followers are also determining factors in the selection of a leadership style. Followers at Level 1 of readiness are unable or unwilling to engage in decision making. Often, they are new to the work and inexperienced. Level 2 followers have gained confidence but have lost some of their initial motivation for the work. At Level 3, followers have developed the skills to do the job but they are uncertain and lack the confidence to do the job on their own. Level 4 followers are fully developed, committed, and motivated to complete work successfully. Leaders must adapt their style to these levels to be effective.

Again, this theory illustrates that leaders cannot use the same style in all situations. Their choice is constrained by the competence level and experience of their subordinates and the situation they face. Therefore, leaders must show a great flexibility in their choice and adoption of their leadership style. No style is always relevant to meet the situation and the level of competence of both the leader and the followers.

Bad Leadership

Development of leadership ability can also benefit from negative examples—the mistakes that leaders make in temperament and execution. Kellerman (2004) offers seven ideal types of bad leadership. The first three are bad because they are ineffective while the last four are examples of unethical behavior.

The first ineffective behavior is incompetent leadership. The leader lacks the will or skill to be effective and fails to create positive change. With some leaders, their failure is due to absence of practical, academic, or emotional intelligence. Instead, ineffective leaders are often careless, dense, distracted, slothful, or they are easily undone by uncertainty and stress—unable to communicate, educate, or delegate.

The second category of ineffective leadership is rigid leadership. Here the problem is that the leader is stiff and unyielding. Although they may be competent, they are unable or unwilling to adapt to new ideas, new information, or changing times. They are "wooden headed" and will not be moved by facts or logic.

Intemperate leadership is the third form of ineffectiveness. Here, the leader lacks self-control and is aided and abetted by followers who are unwilling or unable to intervene. Intemperate leaders fail to control their impulses and fall victim to lust and drug and/or alcohol abuse.

The second group of ideal bad leadership types is characterized by their ethical lapses. The callous leader is uncaring or unkind. The needs, wants, and wishes of subordinates are ignored or discounted. Corrupt leadership is characterized by lying, cheating, or stealing and is typically motivated by power and greed. Unlike the servant leader, they put their self-interest ahead of the public interest. It features bribery, selling of favors, embezzlement, cutting corners, bending rules, and breaking the law.

The insular leader minimizes or disregards the health and welfare of both followers and persons that the organization serves. They ignore the needs of both groups. Evil leadership commits atrocities. Such leaders use pain as an instrument of power and commit acts of severe harm—physical, psychological, or both. Their intent is not only to terrorize but to prolong suffering.

Schafer's (2010a) analysis of police managers attending the FBI National Academy also identified the attributes of ineffective police leaders. They listed five acts of commission (conscious errors in leadership): (1) focus on self over others ("careerism"); (2) ego/arrogance; (3) closed-mindedness; (4) micromanagement (emphasizing autocratic control); and (5) capriousness. They also recognized five acts of omission (failing to take appropriate leadership actions): (1) poor work ethic (loss of enthusiasm for and commitment to the job); (2) failure to act (due to fear of the consequences of their decision); (3) ineffective communication (inability to engage in a two-way dialogue with subordinates, refusal to explain key decisions, failure to accept input and criticism); (4) lack of interpersonal skills (failure to establish human relationships with members of the department and the community); and (5) lack of integrity (past actions that led to the loss of trust and respect). Thus, bad leaders showed behaviors that undermined the followers' sense of trust, legitimacy, and confidence.

Schafer (2010b) raised the interesting question that policing may be responsible for the creation of ineffective leaders due to the constraints upon the organization and failing to develop and sponsor true leaders. The five largest commissions charged with investigating and solving problems in American policing from 1931–1973 noted the lack of strong leadership and effective administrative practices as contributing factors tied to corruption, abuse of authority, use of force, police crimes, and civil rights violations (Schafer, 2009, p. 239).

Conclusion

This review of leadership theories and research findings documents the promise and productivity of forms of democratic leadership. Autocratic leadership is ineffective and harmful to subordinates. The transformational and servant leadership styles are the wave of the future. The needs and wishes of subordinates must be met and their inclusion must be ensured to achieve organizational change.

In their literature review, Pearson-Goff and Herrington (2013, p. 17–18) reported research findings that listed the following attributes of police leaders:

1. Ethics: a sense of integrity and honesty.
2. Trust: generating a sense of trustworthiness among subordinates and with members of the community.
3. Legitimacy: the need for leaders to be seen as "good coppers" that the leader can pound a beat and do the job of a frontline officer.
4. Model the way: understanding their responsibility as a role model.
5. Communication: at all levels of the department, with the community, in government.
6. Competent decision making: be able to make decisions that lead to goal achievement. Involving subordinates in decision making.
7. Effective thinking ability: critical, strategic and creative.

This review also revealed that police leaders engaged in the following activities:

- **Create a shared vision**: creates a sense of purpose for followers.
- **Engendering organizational commitment**: providing support to subordinates, promoting collaboration, giving subordinates a voice in decision making.
- **Care for subordinates**: seek and provide opportunities for staff, take responsibility for their well-being, coaching and mentoring.
- **Driving and managing change**: managing the status quo while enacting change or reform.
- **Problem solving**: proactive and collaborative to address interdependent and unforeseen problems.

(Pearson-Goff & Herrington, 2013, p. 18)

These research findings are based upon officer perceptions rather than objective measures of police leadership performance.

A veteran police administrator and scholar, Robert Wasserman, has admonished police leaders to keep in touch with the lives of their subordinates, both on and off the job. They should be sought out—listen to what they say and think about their situation. Leaders must keep in touch with the needs of a changing workforce to understand their world and how they view it. Here, empathy will facilitate communication.

Wasserman also cautions police leaders (especially Chiefs and Sheriffs) to be aware and mindful of their political environment. When they first enter the job, they should be both thoughtful and careful—"listen and learn." They should pay attention to the "Issues of Complexity": race, homeland security, use of force, crime control strategy, ethics, public opinion and media, technology, and labor. They attempt to recognize and identify which of these issues will have "legs" and get out in front of certain key issues.

This advice and the leadership lessons provided in this chapter should help police leaders to be more effective. The autocratic, "command and control" methods of the past are not relevant to all aspects of police administration. Followers need to be empowered and a more inclusive style is necessary to practice strategic policing.

KEY TERMS

Achievement-oriented leadership	Motivational hurdle	Situational leadership
Cognitive hurdle	Participatory leadership	Supportive leadership
Directive leadership	Political hurdle	Tipping point leadership
Leadership Challenge Model	Resource hurdle	Transformational leadership
	Servant leadership	

Note

1. The 11 *Good to Great* companies were Abbott, Fannie Mae, Kimberly Clark, Nucor, Pitney Bowes, Wells Fargo, Circuit City, Gillette, Kroger, Phillip Morris, and Walgreens.

References

Andreescu, V., & Vito, G.F. (2010). An exploratory study on ideal leadership behaviour: The opinions of American police managers. *International Journal of Police Science and Management, 12*(4), 567–583.

Archambeault, W., & Weirman, C. (1983). Critically assessing the utility of police bureaucracies in the 1980s. *Journal of Police Science and Administration, 11*, 420–429.

Baker, T. (2006). *Effective police leadership: Moving beyond management.* Flushing, NY: Looseleaf Law Publications.

Bass, B., & Riggio, R. (2006). *Transformational leadership.* Mahwah, NJ: Lawrence Erlbaum Associates, Publishers.

Batts, A., Smoot, S., & Scrivner, E. (2006). *Police leadership challenges in a changing world. New Perspectives in Policing Bulletin.* Washington, DC: U.S. Department of Justice, National Institute of Justice.

Bratton, W. (1998). *Turnaround: How America's top cop reversed the crime epidemic.* New York: Random House.

Bratton, W., & Tumin, Z. (2012). *Collaborate or perish! Reaching across boundaries in a networked world.* New York: Random House.

Bruns, G., & Shuman, I. (1988). Police managers' perceptions of organizational leadership styles. *Public Personnel Management, 17*(2), 145–157.

Burns, J.M. (1978). *Leadership*. Mahwah, NJ: Lawrence Erlbaum.

Burns, J.M. (2008). The power and creativity of a transforming vision. In J. Gallos (Ed.), *Business leadership* (pp. 305–311). San Francisco: Jossey-Bass.

Carless, S.A. (2001). Assessing the discriminant validity of the leadership practices inventory. *Journal of Occupational and Organizational Psychology, 74,* 233–239.

Cockcroft, T. (2014). Police culture and transformational leadership: Outlining the contours of a troubled relationship. *Policing, 8*(1), 5–13.

Collins, J. (2001). *Good to great.* New York: Harper-Collins Books.

Collins, J. (2005). *Good to great and the social sectors.* New York: Harper-Collins Books.

Dalai Lama. (2009). *The leader's way.* New York: Broadway Books.

Densten, I. (2003). Senior police leadership: Does rank matter? *Policing, 26,* 400–418.

Dobby, J., Anscombe, J., & Tuffin, R. (2004). *Police leadership: Expectations and impact.* London, UK: The Home Office.

Fischer, C. (2009). *Leadership matters: Police chiefs talk about their careers.* Washington, DC: Police Executive Research Forum.

Gardner, B., & Reece, J. (2012, June). Revolutionizing policing through servant-leadership and quality management. *FBI Law Enforcement Bulletin,* 25–32.

Girodo, M. (1998). Machiavellian, bureaucratic, and transformational leadership styles in police managers: Preliminary findings of interpersonal ethics. *Perceptual and Motor Skills, 86,* 419–427.

Gladwell, M. (2006). *The tipping point: How little things can make a big difference.* New York: Little, Brown.

Greenleaf, R.K. (1977). *Servant leadership.* Mahwah, NJ: Paulist Press.

Haberfeld, M. (2006). *Police leadership.* Upper Saddle River, NJ: Pearson/Prentice Hall.

Hersey, P., & Blanchard, K. (1977). *Management of organizational behavior.* Englewood Cliffs, NJ: Prentice Hall.

Hunter, J. (1998). *The servant.* New York: Crown Books.

Hunter, R., & Barker, T. (1993). BS and buzzwords: The new police organizational style. *American Journal of Police, 12,* 157–168.

Isenberg, J. (2010). *Police leadership in a democracy: Conversations with America's police chiefs.* Boca Raton, FL: CRC Press.

Kellerman, B. (2004). Thinking about leadership: Warts and all. *Harvard Business Review,* 40–45.

Kessler, D. (1993). Integrating calls for service with community and problem oriented policing: A case study. *Crime & Delinquency, 39,* 485–508.

Kim, W., & Mauborgne, R. (2003, April). Tipping point leadership. *Harvard Business Review,* 60–69.

Kouzes, J., & Posner, B. (2012). *The leadership challenge.* San Francisco: Jossey-Bass.

Krimmel, J., & Lindemuth, P. (2001). Police chief performance and leadership styles. *Police Quarterly, 4,* 469–483.

Kuykendall, J., & Unsinger, P. (1982). The leadership styles of police managers. *Journal of Criminal Justice, 10*(4), 311–321.

Maple, J. (1999). *The crime fighter: Putting the bad guys out of business.* New York: Doubleday.

Masal, D. (2015). Shared and transformational leadership in the police. *Policing, 38*(1), 40–55.

Mayo, L. (1985). Leading blindly: An assessment of chiefs' information about police operations. In W. Geller (Ed.), *Police leadership in America* (pp. 397–417). New York: Praeger.

Mazerolle, L., Darroch, S., & White, G. (2013). Leadership in problem-oriented policing. *Policing, 36*(3), 543–560.

Moore, M.H., & Trojanowicz, R. (1988). *Perspectives on policing—Corporate strategies for policing.* Washington, DC: National Institute of Justice.

Murphy, S., & Drodge, E. (2004). The four I's of police leadership: A case study heuristic. *International Journal of Police Science and Management,* 1–15.

Murphy, S.A. (2008). The role of emotions and transformational leadership on police culture: An autoethnographic account. *International Journal of Police Science & Management, 10*(2), 165–178.Osborne, D., & Gaebler, T. (1993). *Reinventing government.* New York: Plume.

Osborne, D., & Plastrik, P. (1997). *Banishing bureaucracy: The five strategies for reinventing government.* New York: Addison-Wesley.

Niederhoffer, A. (1969). *Behind the shield: The police in urban society.* New York: Anchor.

Pearson-Goff, M., & Herrington, V. (2013). Police leadership: A systematic review of the literature. *Policing, 8*(1), 14–26.

Reese, R. (2005). *Leadership in the LAPD.* Durham, NC: Carolina Academic Press.

Ruess-Ianni, E. (1993). *Two cultures of policing: Streeg cops and management cops.* New Brunswick, NJ: Transaction Publishers.

Rowe, M. (2006). Following the leader: Frontline narratives on police leadership. *Policing, 29,* 757–767.

Russell, R., & Stone, A. (2002). A review of servant leadership attributes: Developing a practical model. *Leadership & Organizational Development, 23*(3), 145–157.

Sarver, M., & Miller, H. (2014). Police chief leadership: Styles and effectiveness. *Policing, 37*(1), 126–143.

Schafer, J. (2010a). The ineffective police leader: Acts of commission and omission. *Journal of Criminal Justice, 38,* 737–746.

Schafer, J.A. (2009). Developing effective leadership in policing: Perils, pitfalls and paths forward. *Policing, 32*(2), 238–260.

Schafer, J.A. (2010b). Effective leaders and leadership in policing: Traits, assessment, development and expansion. *Policing, 33*(4), 644–663.

Schafer, J.A. (2013). *Effective leadership in policing: Successful habits and traits.* Durham, NC: Carolina Academic Press.

Sendjaya, S., & Sarros, J. (2002). Servant leadership: Its origin, development, and application in organizations. *Journal of Leadership & Organizational Studies, 9,* 57–64.

Spears, L. (2002). Character and servant leadership: Ten characteristics of effective, caring leaders. *Journal of Virtues and Leadership, 1*(1), 25–30.

Stamper, N.H. (1992). *Removing management barriers to effective police leadership: A study of executive leadership and executive management in big-city police departments.* Washington, DC: Police Executive Research Forum.

Steinheider, B., & Wuestewald, T. (2008). From the bottom-up: sharing leadership in a police agency. *Police Practice and Research, 9*(2), 145–163.

Swid, A. (2014). Police members perception of their leaders' leadership style and its implications. *Policing, 37*(3), 579–595.

Tannenbaum, R., & Schmidt, W. (1958). How to choose a leadership pattern. *Harvard Business Review,* 1–12.

Toch, H., & Grant, J. (1982). *Reforming human services: Change through participation.* Beverly Hills, CA: Sage.

Villiers, P. (2003). Philosophy, doctrine and leadership: Some core beliefs. In R. Adlam, & P. Villiers (Ed.), *Police leadership in the twenty-first century: Philosophy, doctrine and developments* (pp. 15–33). Winchester, UK: Waterside Press.

Vito, G., Suresh, G., & Richards, G. (2011). Emphasizing the servant in public service: The opinions of police managers. *Policing, 34*(4), 674–686.

Walsh, W.F. (1983, November). Leadership: A police perspective. *The Police Chief,* 26–29.

Wexler, C., Wycoff, M.A., & Fischer, C. (2007). *"Good to Great" policing: Application of business management principles in the public sector.* Washington, DC: U.S. Department of Justice Office of Community Oriented Policing Services and Police Executive Research Forum.

Willis, J., Mastrofski, S., Weisburd, D., & Greenspan, R. (2003). *Compstat and organizational change in the Lowell police department.* Washington, DC: The Police Foundation.

4 Setting Strategic Direction

The New Professionalism can help police chiefs and commissioners keep their organizations focused on why they are doing what they do, what doing better might look like, and how they can prioritize the many competing demands of their time and resources.
Christopher Stone and Jeremy Travis, *Toward a New Professionalism in Policing* (2011, p. 2)

Learning Objectives

1. Identify the activities associated with setting organizational strategic direction.

2. Explain the difference between a reactive and proactive police organization.

3. Describe how to create an organizational strategy.

4. Explain the steps required to implement an organizational strategy.

5. Identify the issues relating to measuring the effectiveness of a strategy.

6. Understand what constitutes an effective police organization.

Introduction

The experiences of the past 20 years have emphasized that policing is constantly being challenged by ever-changing events. In this dynamic environment law enforcement organizations are attempting to become more adaptive and effective in meeting the demands of the complex public safety arena in which they exist. Today, innovation is essential for police agencies in the development of the strategies, tactics, and technologies they employ to prevent crimes and solve problems of public safety (Stone & Travis, 2011). Concerned police administrators are consistently seeking to reinvent their organizational strategies and discover better ways to manage and meet the changing and complex demands their organizations face. The operational strategies they are developing differ from those created in the past to address 19th- and 20th-century conditions. Operational tactics once dominated by random patrol, rapid response to calls for service, and past event investigation are being replaced by strategic policing, Compstat, predictive policing, and Intelligence-Led Policing. Departments who employ these strategies use data to inform their crime control and operational decisions (Ratcliffe, 2016). This process is transforming police departments from **reactive organizations** who respond to complaints after they have occurred to **proactive** ones that seek to prevent wrongdoings before they take place (Wexler et al., 2007). Proactive crime prevention is historically linked to the *Principles* of Sir Robert Peel, the founder of professional policing who believed that the true measure of police effectiveness is the absence of crime, not how it is responded to (Reith, 1956). Underlying the demand for innovation today is the belief that the traditional methods of policing are no longer effective and that police departments need to engage with and understand their environment and constituency base to appreciate their impacts on their work (Crank & Giacomazzi, 2009). As a result, a fundamental rethinking and questioning of the manner in which the police go about their day-to-day activities and accomplish their mission is occurring (Weisburd & Braga, 2006). This process involves the restructuring of police departments' direction, mission, values, and operational systems by changing core functions, methods, incentives, accountability, distribution of power, and culture to achieve more effective organizations. It is the premise of this discussion that this transformation is more in line with the concepts associated with the practice of strategic management in the business sector instead of those associated with bureaucratic public administration that emerged in policing during the reform era. A redefinition of what constitutes an effective police organization is taking place. This new definition defines an effective police organization as one that has developed the ability to initiate and reshape its operational service delivery in a variety of ways that allow it to more effectively fulfill its public safety mission and prevent crime while increasing its value and legitimacy in the eyes of the community it serves (More, Vito, & Walsh, 2012; Stone & Travis, 2011). Departments are doing this by acquiring, analyzing, and transferring and using information (communication processes/technology/analysis) about their environment to structure their operational responses. This transformation of information into intelligence allows organizational managers to plan, initiate, reshape, and evaluate their operational strategies in ways designed to increase their organization's effectiveness. As a result departments are transforming into learning organizations as they become skilled at creating, acquiring, and transferring information and modifying their operational tactics to reflect new knowledge and insights gained from the intelligence data they have developed. **Learning organizations** systematically identify and analyze the driving forces that are affecting them, evaluate their response to these forces, and adjust their operations based upon this evaluation (DiBella & Nevis, 1998). According to this new emerging paradigm, the role of organizational leadership and management is to develop the capacity for their organizations to interact, understand, and respond to the needs of their external environment with the internal resources and capabilities of their organization. It raises the following three specific challenges for police executives:

- Can their departments develop the capacity to obtain and analyze information and data about their environmental driving forces?
- Can their departments develop a flexible strategic response to these external driving forces?
- How do they accomplish this given their department's current resources and operational capability?

   Responding to these challenges requires organizations to develop:

- A shared sense of direction.
- A positive organizational culture.
- A culture of accountability.
- A desire for continuous improvement.

In this chapter we consider this perspective and identify what police executives should do to set this new direction to develop their department's strategic renewal, transformation, and effectiveness.

Strategic Direction

Strategic direction is defined by a department's vision, mission statement, values, operational strategies, tactics, accountability systems, and measurement of performance outcomes. Effective organizations are exemplified by a sense of direction (purpose) that is shared and supported throughout the entire organization. Their sense of direction is described in the organization's vision statement, is actively practiced by its employees, and serves as the foundation for the development of a strong positive organizational culture in which the performance of everyone in the organization is aligned. Organizational direction defines what the organization wishes to become and accomplish.

The chief executive and his or her management team must actively engage in the process of establishing a clear strategic direction for the department by implementing it as well as selling it to external and internal stakeholders. They also will need to empower their employees to fulfill it, while restructuring their organization to ensure that desired outcomes occur by intention not by chance. To develop a sense of direction that is believed in and shared by all members of the organization, the executive team must clarify and share the department's vison and mobilize their entire organization around it. A shared sense of direction will focus and develop a committed workforce, mission fulfillment, and community support. For example, the 3,000-employee Illinois State Police Department's vision and mission statement states that: "The Illinois State Police will strive for excellence in all we do—seeking to be one of the premier policing agencies in the country. The Illinois State Police will promote public safety to improve the quality of life in Illinois." (http://www.isp.state.il.us/aboutisp/ispvision.cfm) This statement is a concise description of what is expected to happen and what the department desires to achieve.

Effectiveness is a shared core cultural value in the strategic organization because employees believe in and know what is expected of them and what they should do to be effective. This knowledge assists them in taking accountability for their performance and supporting their department's strategic direction. Developing a sense of direction will depend on the ability of the department's leadership to create meaningful direction, implement it, and achieve the willingness of its employees to accept it. The strategic organization is organized and structured to employ its personnel and assets to a maximum affect.

Developing a shared sense of direction requires:

- Creation of a clear realistic strategic vision.
- Creation of an organizational strategy that operationalizes the vision, mission, and core functions into action.
- Mobilization of the employees to support the vision.
- Identification of outcome goals that relate to the organization's strategic functions.
- Fixing accountability for achieving outcome goals.
- Establishment of ongoing assessment of accomplishment. A willingness to adjust and redirect when it is necessary.

Vision

Creation of a realistic **vision** is the first step in setting the department's strategic direction. A department's vision should serve as the catalyst for building trust, collaboration, interdependence, motivation, and mutual responsibility for success (Blanchard, 2007, p. 22). It is the foundation for the development of an organizational **strategy** that will set desired performance goals, objectives, the quality of service desired, and the means to achieve it. It should identify where the organization is presently and define where it should be in the future. A strategic vision should present a challenge that motivates and energizes employees to give their best and gives meaning to what they do. It should answer the question, "What must the department do to enhance our present effectiveness and prepare for the future demands?" There is no standard formula for creating a vision; ideally, it should be created collaboratively. It has a greater chance of acceptance if it is developed through a process involving sworn and non-sworn personnel of all ranks, city leaders, other government agency partners, and a broad range of community representatives. It should define a sense of purpose that will be shared and accepted throughout the organization and the community. It should be an informed and forward-thinking statement of purpose that should serve as a guide for the organization in all it does. However, the long-term challenge to the vision's development is not "how" the vision is created but the extent to which the vision is accepted, understood, and correctly aligns the department's internal capacity and culture with its external demands (More et al., 2012, p. 408). Its purpose is to identify a direction for the organization that should be compatible with the basic function (mission) for which the organization exists.

An organizational vision statement should:

- Focus on the organization's mission.
- Link the present to the future.
- Establish a standard for excellence.
- Be a guide for unit action and accomplishments.
- Be a yardstick by which to measure organizational efforts.
- Be a standard for judging individual effort and behavior.
- Reflect the organization's core positive values.

(Blanchard, 2007, pp. 21–36)

For example, the vision statement of the 560-employee Glendale, Arizona, Police Department accomplishes these objectives by stating that:

> The men and women of the Glendale Police Department are committed to excellence and professionalism in delivering comprehensive law enforcement services. Our core responsibility is to prevent and reduce crime; we strive to create a community where everyone feels safe in their homes, businesses, schools and neighborhoods. We will be the model of an innovative, community-oriented police department. Using current and developing technologies, we are committed to research and innovation. Technology will enhance our highly skilled workforce in the investigation of crime and the analysis of trends. We will continually strive to develop the skills of our members and to efficiently and effectively manage our resources to deliver the highest level of

service to the public. Members of the Glendale Police Department will continue to form lasting and successful partnerships within the community as well as with law enforcement, government, faith-based and non-profit organizations. Everything we do, collectively or individually, will be done in accordance with our core values of Excellence, Integrity, Respect, Courage, Dedication, and Compassion.

(www.glendaleaz.com/police/VisionStatement.cfm)

Glendale's vison statement clearly identifies the department's core responsibility, and desired public safety outcomes, the means to achieve their vision, and core values to guide employee behavior.

It is important that when developing a department's direction its vision and mission be defined in terms of specific outcomes. This requires that the chief executive and his or her command staff clearly identify the performance outcomes that should be accomplished to achieve the department's vision. These outcomes should be communicated to those responsible for achieving them. This is the key activity by which the vision and mission are translated into operational terms. For example, the Idaho State Police (ISP) Strategic Plan (https://isp.idaho.gov/) identifies the following four focus areas as measurable outcomes for the department.

1.   Excellence in law enforcement services.
2.   Effective and efficient agency operations.
3.   Collaboration and partnerships.
4.   Workforce development.

During New York Police Commissioner William Bratton's first administration, the NYPD sought to maximize its potential for reducing crime and improving the quality of life by developing the following crime control and quality-of-life goals:

*   Getting guns off the streets.
*   Curbing youth violence in the schools and on the streets.
*   Driving drug dealers out of the city.
*   Breaking the cycle of domestic violence.
*   Reclaiming public spaces.
*   Reducing auto-related crime.
*   Bringing fugitives to justice.

(Henry, 2002, p. 227)

The establishment of these strategic outcomes clearly identified what the department expected of its officers. As a result the entire NYPD became focused on crime and disorder problems, deployment of resources, disruption of criminal enterprises, and obtaining information from each arrest they made that would lead to other criminals and arrests (Bratton, 1999).

Creating Organizational Strategy

The purpose of an organizational strategy is to shape in a coordinated manner the way by which the organization responds to the environmental demands challenging it. Strong directive leadership alone does not create an effective organization. The long-term challenge for the chief executive and the executive team is the extent to which their organizational vision is accepted, implemented, and correctly aligns the department's internal capacity with its external demands. Developing strategy requires that the department's leadership and decision makers understand the organization's external driving forces, demands, and its internal core values, resources, strengths, competencies, and weaknesses. The role of strategy is to set organizational direction by translating its vision, mission, tactics, and values into action (Daft, 2002). A strategy defines the process a department will use to achieve its goals. Strategy is the means or process that integrates an organization's vision, mission, policies, operational sequences (tactics), and people into a cohesive whole. In some departments, it also defines how the department relates to its employees, stakeholders, and customers. Thus, an organization's strategy defines a path for the agency to follow that will achieve its desired mission and vision (Moore and Trojanowicz, 1988). Moore (1995) has identified the following characteristics of a strategy:

1. It describes a purpose of value to the manager and the organization.
2. It is operationally feasible.
3. It takes advantage of the competencies and capabilities of the individuals involved.
4. It will attain the support of stakeholders.
5. It achieves its purpose.
6. It is ethical.

An organizational strategy should unite departmental operations, support units or operational unit members into a unified effort. It should identify how the community will be served and operational services delivered. It should address these questions:

1. What is the department's mission?
2. How will the department's mission be accomplished?
3. How will the department relate to the community?
4. How should the department be organized to achieve its mission?
5. How should the department structure its service delivery?
6. What core values should be adopted and supported?
7. What performance outcomes should be accomplished?
8. How will these outcomes be measured?
9. Who is accountable for achieving these outcomes?

Strategy development begins with the identification, analysis, and understanding of the public safety needs of the community and the department's present ability to fulfill these (Michaelson, 2001). On a daily basis police departments develop and record a wealth of data about every call for service, arrests, traffic stops, citations, crime complaints, and community safety conditions. Monitoring and analyzing the information in the department's data base on crime and public safety demand will provide the information necessary to complete this first step. The department's command team must also engage, interact, and dialogue with the community to understand its needs and the manner in which the department's core functions respond to these. This is the foundation upon which a positive and realistic understanding of what needs the organization must serve will rest. *The President's Task Force on 21st Century*

Policing Implementation Guide (2015, p. 18) recommends the following non-enforcement ways a police department and its community can engage and understand each other:

1. Conduct community surveys, forums and town hall meetings regularly, not just in crisis.
2. Encourage regular officer participation in neighborhood or school meetings.
3. Form community advisory groups (general or population specific).
4. Participate in positive interaction with the community that does not involve an enforcement action or investigation.
5. Involve community members in discussing policing tactics and designing problem-solving efforts to reduce crime and improve quality of life.
6. Adjust patrol schedules to allow time for interactions with the community.
7. Measure and reward non-enforcement community contacts.

An organizational-wide strategy should also respond to the critical leadership question: How does the department achieve desired outcomes in light of the organization's current situation and resources? Outcomes are the ends and strategy is the means for achieving them. However, a strategy is more than just a process developed in advance that contains a set of intended actions to be carried out. New circumstances always emerge and the future is not always what we expect it to be. Therefore, it is appropriate for us to think of a strategy as being both proactive (intended) and reactive (adaptive).

In this manner, strategy is best thought of as a combination of planned actions and on-the-spot adaptive reactions to developing information and circumstances. Strategy development is an interactive process that creates a game plan, or intended actions, and then adapts it as events unfold. A strategy is something managers must shape and reshape as new knowledge develops about events transpiring outside and inside the organization. This is why information analysis, monitoring work demand, creating feedback systems, and good communications within and without the department are important tools for the strategic manager. For example, a central part of the Compstat process is the crime strategy meeting. The communication process at these meetings is designed to access, evaluate, and adjust the use of organizational resources, strategy, and tactics. Strategy and tactics become defined when the best ways to use organizational assets to meet challenges or exploit opportunities in the environment are identified by the leadership team at these meetings.

For example, if the department holds a commanding officer accountable for a given geographical area, all other department units within and without this command that function within this area should be aligned operationally to support the commander's strategies and tactical initiatives. The commanding officer should hold strategy meetings involving all these units so that the different commanders can work closely with each other, provide timely intelligence, and take part in the analysis and tactical planning and evaluation process. Thus, all units assigned in the area operate as a strategy-focused team instead of competing units seeking to achieve their individual agendas.

In traditionally managed police departments executives often consider the question on how best to use their assets much more narrowly. They assume that basic purposes and operating objectives were set long ago and now remain fixed in policy and procedures. They see their job as optimizing performance regarding these objectives, not to consider new challenges within their organizations (Moore & Trojanowicz, 1988, p. 2). In these types of departments police managers also assume that in conducting their organization's functions, they are restricted to established policies and procedures. While they may institute a few innovative programs, however, these are rarely seen as part of a sustained effort to change the organization's basic methods of operating. This is a prime example of what Barker (1993) identifies as "***paradigm paralysis.***"

Paradigm paralysis develops over the life span of an organization as it encounters problems and resolves them. As more and more problems are resolved, the organization's leadership experiences a period of success. The success convinces organizational members that their way of "doing things" is correct, and a mindset develops whereby managers no longer solve new problems in any way other than what has worked in the past. Paradigm paralysis exists in police organizations that respond to the needs of a changing external environment with police methods created decades in the past to address different issues. Strategic policing suggests departments should develop the capacity to step back and place threats and risks into a holistic analytical perspective that will allow policing to prevent crime across a wide area rather than addressing a single event that has already occurred in the past (Goldstein, 1990; Ratcliffe, 2016, p. 6).

The above discussion indicates that strategy development is an exercise in **outside-in strategic thinking.** Thus, it is initially an externally driven activity. The challenge is for managers to keep their strategies closely matched to outside environmental driving forces such as crime, public safety threats, opportunities, work demand, and changing community demographics, and socio-economic needs. Indicators of these driving forces are identified by analyzing changing incidents of crime, social disorder, and the needs of specific communities, special events, and external political initiatives, shifting demographics, and projections of future community demands. This process requires an increase in proactive information gathering as an adjunct to traditional crime analysis (Ratcliffe, 2016, p. 176). "Crime analysis is the process of identifying patterns and relationships between crime data and other relevant data sources to prioritize and target police activity" (Cope, 2004, p. 340). It should summarize the data of crimes and public safety information, make it understandable for everybody, especially operational decision makers. One crime map, for example, can explain hundreds of pages of information. The essential functions for police crime analysis operations are:

1. to analyze the data of crimes in order to allocate resources and deploy personnel,
2. to discover crime and suspect relationships and provide information for investigations, and
3. to identify the reasons and conditions causing criminality,
4. to inform policymakers about the reasons and conditions requiring further policy development.

(Timothy, O'Shea, & Nicholls, 2003, p. 6)

An organization's strategy will never effectively meet the demands of its environment unless managers actively engage their organization's external environment and gain up-to-date information through intelligence gathering, data analysis, community surveys, and communication networks about it. This provides them with the knowledge to identify threats and opportunities that are and will affect the department and community public safety. Strategy development depends on the collection of accurate and timely information, data gathering and analysis, knowledge, and action. Ratcliffe (2016, p. 71) conceptualizes this process as a continuum that involves four critical elements, data, information, knowledge, and intelligence. He defines **data** as observations and measurements about crime, and **information** as data having greater relevance and purpose. **Knowledge** is data and information with a particular interpretation. **Intelligence** is knowledge that generates a strategist understanding and action. This continuum provides the basis for deciding what must be done, when, and by whom to achieve the department's vision and mission. It also allows for the identification of how the department responds to the driving forces that affect its public safety demand. This analysis should answer the following questions:

1.   What are the persistent patterns in our work demand?
2.   What treats and opportunities do these create?
3.   What are the critical areas we need to attend to now?
4.   What do we wish to accomplish?

The intelligence gained by this process can be used to identify prolific and serious offenders, crime and disorder hot spots, and link series of crimes and incidents (Ratcliffe, 2016). This data will allow operational commanders to develop tactical measures to reduce and prevent crime.

The use of information and the development of intelligence as a basis for the direction of operational resources is the **critical difference** between proactive and reactive policing. Strategic departments constantly analyze their external environment, acquire information from it to develop intelligence, and utilize this knowledge in their strategy and tactical development. Reactive managers seldom prepare for the future but instead focus on responding to the current crises with their standard operation procedures. As a result they become victims of the external driving forces they have failed to anticipate. The faster conditions change in a department's external environment, the more critical it becomes for that department to be proactive at gathering and diagnosing shifting external conditions and adjusting to these. This necessitates that, besides traditional crime analysis, departments should place high value on community engagement. Through building community relationships and collaborative partnerships departments can seek to obtain current information about their external environment. This will allow them to be knowledgeable about potential change in public safety issues and provide them with the information needed to respond to developing driving forces.

Creating strategy depends also upon **inside-out thinking** because a part of strategy development involves the planned use of internal resources and organizational strengths to respond to external conditions. Administrators must clearly understand their organization's strengths, capabilities, and weaknesses. Many traditional police executives try to improve organizational performance by pointing to the department's statistics and insist that their commanders achieve better ones, that is, more arrests and higher clearance rates. This is an example of what Goldstein (1979, 1990) identified as the "means over ends" syndrome. This syndrome places more emphasis on the department's operating methods and statistical counts of how they respond to crime rather than on the substantive outcome of their work. This condition developed during the 20th-century reform era with its concentration on managerial control and organization of police agencies. It is based upon that era's widely held assumption that improvements in the internal management of police departments will enable them to deal more effectively with community crime problems. In response to this paradigm Goldstein (1979, 1990) suggests that if the police desire to improve, they must concern themselves more directly with the end product of their efforts, not how they respond to the forces affecting them. These efforts are seldom successful and fail to produce more substantive outcomes.

Instead of relying on numerical increases or decreases, it is more productive if managers understand the forces that create their operational problems and develop tactics and solutions to address these issues through strategy development (Kim & Mauborgne, 2003). For this process to function correctly managers must understand and know how to use the core competencies and capabilities of their people and organization. Thus to implement an organizational strategy it may be necessary to adjust unit leadership, organizational structure, employee assignment, training, reward systems, accountability, budget allocations, policy and procedures. These decisions should be based upon an understanding of the department's current response to its work demand, how that demand is changing, and where improvement is needed. This requires knowledge of how the department presently handles these demands. It requires thinking and analysis about what steps must be taken operationally to put the department's strategic response in operation, execute it proficiently, and produce good results. Strategy developers must also know the danger of exclusively engaging in inside-out thinking.

Traditional managers cautious by nature usually focus most of their time and energy inward on internal problems only, improving organizational processes and procedures, and taking care of daily administrative duties. They are caught up in the day-to-day organizational management and the actions they decide to initiate are heavily dictated by policy and procedure considerations. Often, their organizational direction and strategy serves the purpose of accommodating their own fears, concerns, and desire for control. This style of management is referred to as "CYA management." It is a form of "paradigm paralysis" that will lock the organization into maintaining the status quo. How boldly managers recognize and meet the challenge of new strategic opportunities and champion actions to improve organizational performance and proficiency are good indicators of their leadership ability and value to the department. Good managers create strategic tactics by which they access, communicate, network, reinforce, or change the organization. They understand that if the organization suffers from paradigm paralysis then it will continue to do what it has always done and achieve what it always has.

McDonald (2002, p. 15) cites an old police adage: "What is counted is what is performed." This suggests that managers only do what is expected. Additionally, she claims that if police departments are serious about crime control and enhancing the quality of life in communities then police chief executives must focus on and reward their operational commanders for their ability to organize, create, implement, and execute strategies and tactics that successfully impact community crime and safety issues, not statistical counts of they response to crime incidents.

Implementing Strategic Direction

Implementing a department's strategic direction should be based upon a logical set of connected activities. Taken together they define where the organization is headed, identify performance targets and the operational tactics needed to achieve the department's transformation to the new direction. In order for a department to become a strategically focused organization, it must put strategy at the center of its management process. However, without a carefully planned approach to **strategy implementation**, strategic goals will not be attained and the strategy will never be institutionalized. A central part of implementing strategic direction is for each commanding officer to develop their unit's vision, objectives, strategy, and tactics based upon the overall department's direction.

One way of accomplishing this objective is for the department's executive team to conduct department-wide strategy meetings regularly with their operational commanders and support staff to achieve alignment between the department's operational demand, its mission, strategic objectives and tactics (Silverman, 1999).

The purposes of these meetings are to:

- Ensure that operational commanders are paying sufficient attention to crime and public safety issues in their geographical areas.
- Ensue that the strategies and tactics designed to resolve a problem are creative and varied.
- Follow up on events from the previous meeting to demonstrate consistency and stay focused on problems tied to the objectives.
- Ensure that all departmental and external resources that could be brought to bear on the problem are available and coordinated.
- Provide an ongoing teaching/learning situation in which those who attend can learn about developing strategies and assessing their impact.
- Review the impact of tactics and strategies that are developed and applied.

(McDonald, 2001)

In many departments these meetings are directed by the chief of police while in others it is the deputy chief of police or a designated member of the executive leadership team. It is important that throughout these sessions that top management provide strong and consistent support for the department's strategic direction. Redirection will rarely succeed without it. In some cases lack of executive support will result in implementation efforts being strongly resisted and chances for success severely crippled. The presence of the chief and/or top executives establishes commitment, accountability, and sets the tone for the organization and each commander's responsibility.

During these meeting each operational commander should report on their problem identification process and analysis, tactical response action plans, projected outcomes and results in responding to these issues. The executive conducting the meeting should ask specific, precise, and well-focused questions. Commanders should be held accountable and responsible for:

- Identification of crime and public safety problems and trends.
- The quality of their efforts toward crime prevention and problem reduction.
- The quality of their tactical plans.
- Their managerial oversight of operations (including evaluation and feedback).
- The results they obtain.

(Bratton & Knobler, 1998)

Commanders' problem identification and response activities should be evaluated by all commanders and administrators present. Commanders must be prepared to alter or eliminate failed tactics and continue successful ones. Reporting current intelligence, adapting tactics to changing conditions, and closely reviewing results should be a continual process at these meetings. This interchange serves as the bases for organizational learning about what is operationally successful and the detection and correction of error. Former NYPD Deputy Police Commissioner for Crime Control Strategies Jack Maple (Maple & Mitchell, 1999, p. 93) describes these meetings as a live audit of overall police performance that constitutes the **first step to crime reduction,** the gathering and analysis of accurate, timely intelligence quickened by the heat of accountability. When something goes wrong, an initial response is often to look for another strategy or tactic to correct the error. However, if chosen goals, values, use of personnel, plans and tactic implementation are not questioned, then *single-loop learning* occurs.

A more effective response is for the executives and operational commanders present to question these elements and to subject them to critical scrutiny. This sets the stage for double-loop learning. **Double-loop learning** occurs when error and/or problems are detected, analyzed, and corrected in ways that involve the modification of an organization's underlying norms, policies, strategic assumptions and objectives (Argyris & Schön, 1974, pp. 18–19). The meeting's discussion should contain a two-way give-and-take analytical communicative exchange in which all present can offer advice, support, and insightful analysis. It should be a dialogue involving the creative, free searching of complex issues and problem-solving techniques. Managers in a learning organization actively seek to expand their capacity to learn and adapt by consistently gathering and analyzing the information produced at these meetings. This knowledge assists them in creating problem-solving strategies that respond to changing environmental demands. These meetings should not consist of a blame game that embarrasses individuals but instead be a **diagnostic dialogue** that seeks to improve individual commanders, their operational capabilities and results.

A free flow of information is critical to the success of this process. It should be maintained so that a process of organizational assessment and learning takes place. If not, the goals and strategies formulated at the meetings or follow-up sessions will be diluted or diverted as they make their way down to the rank-and-file officers (Dabney, 2010). Operational commanders should identify the crime and quality-of-life problems they are focusing on, the tactical action plan they have developed, and the projected and actual results obtained from their past efforts. Successful tactics and results are shared with the other department managers present. Commanders should also be prepared to present alternative tactics to resolve the problem if their original strategy was unsuccessful. Failed tactics should be altered or eliminated and successful tactics continued and replicated. At the end of these meetings each commander should know what they have accomplished, what they must do to achieve their command objectives, and what their evaluation is by the department's executive staff (O'Connell & Straub, 2007, p. 62).

NYPD's Compstat strategy emerged out of that department's crime strategy meetings. These meetings were created by the department's executive team to focus their operational commanders' attention on the city's crime problems (Bratton & Knobler, 1998; Maple & Mitchell, 1999). Compstat evolved into a performance-based management accountability strategy that is radically different from the accepted concepts and practices that had guided police administration through most of its existence. The NYPD's department-wide strategy meetings became the vital link between information, intelligence development, strategic thinking, data-driven decision-making, command accountability, and double-loop assessment of the department's effectiveness. This process changed the department's flow of information, decision making, and organizational culture while creating one of the more successful police organizational strategies in the police profession (Silverman, 1999).

Strategy implementation should involve all levels of the organization. For example:

Executive leadership team: The department's chief executive and his or her leadership team are responsible for setting the department's strategic direction by framing a clear departmental vision and mission expressed in operational goals and objectives that define expected performance outcomes. This will establish priorities for the organization to address and measure. The chief executive must then empower operational commanders with the authority and resources to develop strategies and tactics to accomplish these objectives. This will establish who is accountable for what outcomes. Commanders must be supplied with accurate and timely intelligence upon which they can base their problem analysis and tactical plans. The operational commander's tactical plans and the results achieved become the basis for their evaluation at department-wide strategy assessment meetings. At these meetings tactical effectiveness and accomplishments are addressed and strategic adjustments are made where needed. Assessment is used to analyze, modify, or replace tactics rather than punishing staff (unless serious incompetence is evidenced). To assist operational commanders the executive team must reallocate resources, support creative solutions to problems, track progress, and integrate functions within the agency to support their commanders (Bratton & Knobler, 1998; More et al., 2012).

Subdivision commanders: Operational subdivision commanders should establish their command's vision, set direction, and develop performance objectives that link these units to the department's direction. They should hold their own strategy meetings in which they analyze and share intelligence and empower, interview, and assess their unit commanders regarding problem solving, plans, and desired outcomes. These meetings should develop teamwork, accountability, establish unity of command and implementation of the department's strategy. Working together the commanders' efforts should be focused in a synergistic way to achieve their objectives (Covey, 1989).

Unit commanders: Unit commanders should be accountable for the development of tactical action plans, the results they achieve, and the resources they use to achieve them. They should meet regularly with their line supervisors and officers, share intelligence and knowledge, set objectives, and empower individuals to accomplish objectives, develop action plans, and assess operational outcomes. A critical point of analysis at this level is the impact of the tactical deployment of resources to address specific conditions requiring attention in the areas for which the unit is accountable ((McDonald, 2001; More et al., 2012).

Line supervisor: The line supervisor and his or her team are the department's basic functional unit (Maple & Mitchell, 1999). These individuals operate at the strategic execution level. Therefore, it is the first-line supervisors and their units who ultimately decide the rate of organizational and tactical success. Line supervisors (sergeants) on a daily basis communicate and work with their officers to obtain and share intelligence, define, and implement street-level tactics and develop crime control measures for specific conditions. An important responsibility for these supervisors is the sharing of intelligence and analysis both down and up the organizational levels. This ensures that upper managers are constantly being informed of changing operational conditions at the point of service delivery. It is therefore critical that they be involved in this process because they are the individuals whose actions will produce the desired outcomes and maintain appropriate levels of organizational effectiveness.

The above-defined process serves as an operational mechanism designed to ensure that the strategic direction flows throughout the department. The intent is that this flow of information will develop a **critical mass** of creativity, innovation, communication, and dedication throughout the organization (Gladwell, 2002; Henry, 2002). The department-wide strategy meetings should spawn and spread effective improvement methods while developing the dynamics for command accountability at all levels of the organization. They serve as an arena for testing the ability of each manager and the capabilities of each unit. It provides the executive team with a means to match positions with commanders who have the skill, experience, expertise, and personality to manage proficiently. Organizational learning and strategic guidance should flow down to all areas of the department through this process, while successful tactics are disseminated upward and throughout the organization. Engaging in this process to develop and enact crime control strategies can help agencies of all sizes to address hot spots, crime patterns, and trends. However, in less hierarchical organizations this process can be adjusted to fit a smaller organizational structure.

Strategy implementation should develop an organizational culture that supports the strategic transformation of the department. Lastly, it should be institutionalized by incorporating it into:

- Organizational policy and procedures.
- Decision-making and problem-solving processes.
- Accountability systems.
- Measurement and follow-up systems.
- Reward and discipline systems.
- Managerial communication systems.
- Selection and advancement systems.
- Organizational training.

The following activities will help a department develop the effectiveness of its directional-setting process:

Reward the doers and performers by celebrating and rewarding those who achieve performance objectives.

Conduct strategy review meetings where honesty prevails. The integrity of this process is critical. Without a true analysis of the facts and the resultant learning, effectiveness and learning are jeopardized.

Clarify responsibility and accountability. Do not assume that everyone knows what they are supposed to do by when.

Controls require up-to-date information about performance. Crime control strategy cannot depend upon guesswork. Real-time data and analysis is a constant requirement for success and changes in strategy.

Leadership must play an active role and use performance analysis effectively, avoiding all-or-nothing objectives. They must demand total honesty and integrity from subordinates, and recognize and reward those who contribute to executional success.

Strategy review is the key to organizational effectiveness. A good review fosters discussion, clarifies strategy, helps set execution-related objectives, allows leaders to really understand their people, and facilitates learning and organizational change (Hrebiniak, 2005, p. 16).

Strategy implementation and execution are always the product of organizational learning. If it is developed unevenly or too quickly in some areas, then follow-up and assessment and ongoing searches for ways to continuously improve, as well as corrective adjustments, are necessary.

Measurement of Progress

It is the responsibility of the department's executive team to monitor the directional-setting process, in addition to deciding when things are going well and monitoring changing events. Indications and analysis of inadequate performance or too little progress, and important new external circumstances, are all part of the learning process and will require corrective action and adjustments. This may involve modifications in vision, long-term direction, creating more realistic objectives, strategy, or implementation in light of actual operational experience(s), changing conditions, new ideas, and new opportunities. This process should be managed and adjusted continuously because it will provide the executive team with ongoing assessment of command accountability and organizational accomplishments. Chapter 10 in this book provides a comprehensive discussion of measuring police performance.

As discussed earlier, the department's strategy meeting is an excellent management assessment tool because it matches quantitative information on crime events, their locations and times with police deployment tactics and community public safety information. Operational commander's tactics and accomplishments are reported on, considered, and evaluated at these meetings. This process involves traditional managerial oversight with strategic assessment, outcome measurement, and problem solving. A principal objective of these meetings should be the assessment of the department's reengineering efforts and the impact they have on the department's outcome measures. Continuous assessment is a central process needed to manage the department's strategic reengineering process. It creates information about the department's accomplishments and the data needed to improve performance. This enables the executive team to hold managers accountable and to introduce correction and/or consequences for performance (Osborne & Plastrik, 2000, p. 247).

Managers should always measure what they are trying to accomplish. Outcomes are achieved though the identification and accomplishment of specific performance objectives. These must be spelled out clearly and communicated to those responsible for achieving them. Feedback systems and measurable objectives should always be part of organizational plans. Establishing appropriate quantitative and qualitative performance measures will help link strategic redirection activities to specific outcomes. Hard data is necessary for evaluating managerial strategies and outcomes. Administrators should avoid setting expectations that are unrealistic and unattainable by developing a strategy that incorporates realistic and attainable goals as system elements. A **goal** is a general statement of purpose that should be related to the department's vision and mission. Goals and objectives (outcomes) should provide the manager with a way to measure progress, identify strategies that work, what are successful outcomes, and refocus resources as needed. Baseline measures that record conditions before change is implemented should be identified so that a before-and-after comparison of relevant changes can be made.

Valid and reliable evaluation of police organizational performance requires:

1. **Identification of measurable outcomes (goals).**
2. **Identification of measurable objectives (milestones, steps)** that will lead to the accomplishment of the desired outcomes.
3. A data **reporting system** for monitoring progress and maintaining **accountability.**
4. Assessment of actual accomplishments versus desired outcomes.

Lastly, all performance measures should relate to agency, program, and operational unit mission and goals. They should be both legitimate and fair. The design and implementation of performance evaluations depend upon the specific purpose they are intended to serve. Always measure what matters and what gives managers the information that they need. All else is a waste of time, budget, and organizational resources. According to McDonald (2002, p. 32) effectiveness comprises two types of measures.

Long-term measures are comprised of cumulative comparisons of data, such as annual comparisons of serious crime or some crimes of serious concern to the community such as youth homicides. Comprehensive measures might include location and frequency of disorder complaints and measures of citizen's fear.

Short-term measures are assessments of tactics or strategies during operations. For example, if a solution to a set of problems is being implemented, progress should be tracked carefully to alter parts of the strategy. If, ultimately, the strategy fails, analysis of how the solution was implemented, effects of the implementation and results obtained will assist in the design of a new approach. In this manner organizational learning takes place.

Strategy implementation is an action-oriented activity. It involves decision making, developing personnel competencies and capabilities, policy creation, motivating, culture building, and exerting the leadership necessary to achieve desired outcomes and objectives. A department's vision, objectives, strategy implementation, and execution are never final; evaluating performance, monitoring changes in the surrounding environment, and making adjustments are normal and necessary parts of the strategic management process. Proficient strategy execution is always the product of organizational learning. Follow-up and assessment, ongoing searches for ways to continuously improve, and corrective adjustments are thus normal and a necessary part of a learning organization. Ideally, assessment should focus on the effectiveness and efficiency of the strategy. It should answer the following questions:

1. Did the strategy impact the problems or conditions it was created to address?
2. To what extent was the impact (% decrease, increase)?
3. Was the process and service delivery consistent with strategy design specifications? Here a comparison is made between planned and actual events.

4.   What is the cost benefit analysis of expended resources to strategy outcomes?
5.   Were organizational resources used properly?
6.   Were targeted populations or neighborhood groups reached?
7.   How did the officers actually perform?

(More et al., 2012)

Assessing the effectiveness of the department's directional-setting efforts should be concerned with outcome goals rather than outputs. It is not just the numbers of calls for service responded to, arrest data, and crime rates alone but the condition of the community after implementing operational tactics. A primary concern should be whether the safety and security of the citizens in that community increased in a measurable way by the department's efforts. Performance measurement should not be an end but the pathway to a more effective service to the community. It is a feedback mechanism to help decision makers focus on goals, strategies, and resource allocation to accomplish the department mission.

Innovation Issues

Leading an organizational redirection is not without its difficulties. Public officials, community representatives, and department executives may be supportive of the new direction but internally members of the department may be against it because they wish to maintain the way things are now, the **status quo**. The department's internal environment comprises dynamic interrelationships among people who perform the functions and tasks necessary to implement organizational strategy and perform its day-to-day operations. Organizational reform will not be easily accepted by them. Executives seeking to establish a new direction for their organization must understand that they will face several formidable obstacles because of the difficulty of managing change in police agencies.

Based upon years of research in policing, Skogan (2008, p. 28) identified the following categories of resistance to transforming police organizations. These are:

• Resistance by mid-level and top managers.
• Resistance by front-line supervisors.
• Resistance by rank-and-file officers.
• Resistance by special units.
• Resistance by police unions.
• Competing demands and expectations.
• Inability to 'measure what matters'.
• Failure of interagency cooperation.
• Public unresponsiveness.
• Nasty misconduct diverting public and leadership attention.
• Reform may not survive leadership transition.

Ultimately, the department's successful redirection depends upon the ability of the executive team to anticipate, identify, and manage the redirectional process, overcome resistance, and the willingness of their employees to support their efforts. Police managers need to understand how their organizational redirection efforts will affect their people, be aware of the indicators that signal resistance, and be prepared to resolve any resistance they may encounter. Skogan's (2008) identification of top managers, mid-level, front-line supervisors, and rank-and-file officers reveals that the individuals needed to implement the department's new direction will resist this effort. This resistance can be overcome if the executive team develops a critical mass of internal supporters, a tipping point that will assist in overcoming the internal resistance as Bratton did in his 1994 reform of the NYPD (Henry, 2002; Kim & Mauborgne, 2003).

One way to accomplish this is to create dissatisfaction with the status quo and manage a process that coordinates events and changes in such a way that internal commitment is developed and resistance reduced. Dissatisfaction with the status quo is a critical motivator. In many turnarounds, the hardest battle is getting people to agree on the causes of current problems and the need for change. To overcome their resistance dissatisfaction with the current state of the organization must be sufficient for them to develop an urgent desire to do things differently (Kotter & Cohen, 2002). This can be accomplished by putting them face-to-face with operational problems at department-wide strategy meetings so they cannot evade the reality of the present state of the department. These meetings should be used to:

1. Communicate information about potential crises or threats to the organization and its members.
2. Provide employees with factual data about organizational performance: what they are really accomplishing as opposed to what they think they are.
3. Engage in frank discussion and dialogue about organizational problems and operational process.
4. Set realistic performance expectations that will create the desire to change.

It is not sufficient to just provide data or announce performance failures. There must be a real discussion and open communication about what is happening as opposed to what should or could be happening. The employees must develop an understanding of the need for the department to transform and a sense of urgency to bring about this redirection. Employee motivation should then be directed into a focused organizational improvement effort. The department's new direction must be communicated as a response to the present state of the organization. This process will function to spark motivation, keep changes aligned, provide a means to evaluate how the organization is doing, and provide a rationale for the changes the organization will need to make.

Beer (1988) asserts that the organization's response to dissatisfaction with the status quo must address needed performance changes structure and systems design that will make the organization more effective. It should communicate purpose, provide answers to employees' questions, and gain their support. Once people understand what is expected and why, they will often strive to achieve it.

Too often efforts to improve organizations specify only one or two elements such as structure and strategy, ignoring the behaviors and competencies required for change to take place. Ignoring the multiple elements of an organization is one of the primary reasons for failure. The directional-setting process will take time, and losing momentum and the onset of disappointment are real factors. However, developing a strategic redirection process cannot be developed in isolation. Those about to be affected by the change should have input into its implementation or as Skogan noted, they will be a primary source of resistance. Identifying and putting together a guiding coalition (critical mass) that is empowered to lead this effort is critical (Kotter, 1996). These individuals need to work together as a team to make the change happen. Obstacles to the change process must be identified and eliminated. This may mean changing strategies, structures, or people that will undermine the change effort. Visibly recognizing and rewarding people for their efforts to support the new direction sends a powerful message that supports the credibility of the redirection effort.

Goal Displacement

A persistent problem in assessing police performance is the difficulty in judging the outcomes resulting from the work of department. As a result police departments frequently evaluate their performance based on the numerical outputs they produce. Operational commanders are usually evaluated on the outputs they produce during a specific time period. Output measures such as numbers of calls for service responded to, time in responding, reported crime complaints, arrests, stop and frisk reports, cases cleared, and reduction in crime statistics are easier to measure. However, goal displacement occurs when these measures replace desired strategy outcomes, such as enhancing community safety, reduction of residents' fear levels, satisfaction with police services, development of problem-solving partnerships, and become ends in themselves. In many instances producing monthly increases in these numerical outputs emerge as the primary objectives for operational units. For example, a traffic unit is more concerned with producing increased numbers of citations and revenue from fines instead of addressing issues of traffic safety.

When a department's performance is evaluated in terms of numerical outputs, operational commanders have an incentive to maximize these outputs, regardless of whether maximizing outputs is the preferred strategy for achieving desired outcomes. This incentive to focus on statistical outputs can lead to organizational cheating, where unit commanders purposely manipulate output levels to portray their work in the best light possible. For example, in many traditionally managed departments using the Compstat strategy, crime strategy meetings have evolved into commander degradation ceremonies. Pressure on these commanders to produce desired numerical outputs is intense. This leads to a greater concentration on the production of output measures and transforms them into desirable ends-in-themselves. As a result goal displacement occurs.

A commonly used example of goal displacement involves the classification of crimes based upon how well crimes are solved rather than the level of public safety. Reports of burglaries and break-ins are labeled unfounded because they are difficult to solve rather than classifying them as real crimes. Whereas the probability of catching a burglar during or after the act is slight, the probability of catching drug dealers and prostitutes committing crimes is much greater. Thus, to ensure high clearance rates, a department may focus its attention toward crimes that are relatively easy to clear (Bohte & Meier, 2000). Another technique is to lower the value of stolen property so that a misdemeanor crime is reported instead of a felony. These examples suggest how incentive structures can generate goal displacement.

Recent research into the practice of manufacturing artificial crime statistics based on interviews with 2,000 retired police officers from the NYPD reveals pervasive, system-wide manipulation of these statistics. Eterno and Silverman (2012) claim that concern with the department's reputation for reducing crime, much more than with public safety, drives department policy. More evidence supporting this allegation has come forward because of several NYPD whistleblowers. Officers Adrian Schoolcraft, Craig Matthews, Frank Polestro, Adyl Polanco, and Vanessa Hicks have talked openly to the media about the routine downgrading of crimes and the use of illegal arrest quotas by the NYPD.

The research and the statements by the whistleblowers indicate that the manipulation of crime reports is a consequence of the misuse of Compstat. This innovative management accountability system was designed to reduce crime but has instead become a powerful mechanism to ensure that downgrading crime permeates the whole department. The researchers claim that their analysis found that there was a clear message emanating from the top commanders at police headquarters: make many stop and frisks, write many summonses, make many arrests for petty offenses, and downgrade serious crimes. These tactics have deeply alienated racial and ethnic minorities in New York City and revealed a broader dysfunction in the police department. The pressure on the officers to produce statistical output numbers and downgrade crime reports reflects the deterioration of effective management and goal displacement in that department. This unnecessary activity does not involve intelligence gathering, surveillance, or community involvement nor does it make good use of Compstat. It alienates communities and hurts the NYPD's ability to fight serious and violent crimes (Levine, Eterno, & Silverman, 2014).

Conclusion

Setting and implementing a new organizational strategic direction is an action-oriented activity. It involves decision making, developing personnel competencies and capabilities, policy creation, motivating, culture building, and exerting the leadership necessary to achieve desired outcomes and objectives. It is the executive team's responsibility to stay on top of the strategy development and implementation process, monitoring changing events, and deciding when things are going well. They must provide the leadership needed to drive the strategic direction forward and to keep monitoring on how the strategy is being executed. This entails assessing what it will take to make the strategy work and to reach the targeted goals and objectives on schedule. Success will depend upon the department's ability to uses its existing personnel and resources in an effective manner to produce favorable results. This is a critical step in strategy development, requiring the identification of who is accountable for what objectives and setting that accountability. This activity aligns the organization to the strategy. It involves the identification of who must achieve what, by when, using what resources. However, establishing accountability is only half the battle.

Outcome goals should be spelled out and communicated to those responsible for achieving them. Managers must be held accountable by the command staff for both their accomplishments and failures. Department-wide strategy meetings play a critical role because they provide information to reinforce execution methods, identify needed corrective mechanisms, and facilitate organizational learning and change. Corrective action and strategy adjustments are needed when assessments indicate inadequate performance or too little progress, and/or important new external circumstances have occurred.

The directional-setting process may involve modifications in vision, creation of goals and objectives that are more realistic, in light of actual experience, changing conditions, new ideas, and new opportunities. The executive team must think through operationally what must be done to put the strategy in operation, execute it proficiently, and produce good results. Outcomes are achieved through the identification and accomplishment of specific performance objectives. This is how strategy is translated into operational terms. Reengineering isn't just about redesigning the organization. It requires the translation of a new direction into reality. Departments that undertake this process with understanding, commitment, and strong executive leadership will succeed by doing the following:

- Identifying and focusing on core function(s).
- Identifying the outcome(s) that should be achieved by these functions.
- Analyzing the way these outcomes are presently achieved; (process).
- Identifying what you need to do to maximize the effectiveness of this process.
- Identifying and measuring everything that contributes to the outcome(s) desired.
- Designing the implementation process.
- Assessing and reassessing this process and its results.
- Making adjustments where needed.
- Linking the reward structure to the achievement of targeted results.

KEY TERMS

Accountability
Clarify
Conduct
Control
Crafting strategy
Critical difference
Critical mass
Data
Diagnostic dialogue
Double-loop learning
Executive leadership team
First step to crime reduction
Goal
Goal displacement
Identification of measurable objectives (milestones, steps)

Identification of measurable outcomes (goals)
Implementing strategy
Information
Inside-out thinking
Intelligence
KnowledgeLearning organization
Line supervisors
Long-term measures
Outside-in thinking
Paradigm paralysis
Proactive organization
Reactive organization
Reporting system
Reward

Short-term measures
Single-loop learning
Status quo
Strategic direction
Strategic tasks
Strategy
Strategy implementation
Strategy review
Subdivision commanders
Unit commanders
Vision

References

Argyris, M., & Schön, D. (1974). *Theory in practice: Increasing professional effectiveness.* San Francisco: Jossey-Bass.

Barker, J.A. (1993). *Paradigms: The business of discovering the future.* New York: Harper-Collins.

Beer, M. (1988). *Leading change.* Cambridge, MA: Harvard University Press.

Blanchard, K. (2007). *Leading at a higher level.* Upper Saddle River, NJ: FT Press.

Bohte, J., & Meier, K.J. (2000). Goal displacement: Assessing the motivation for organizational cheating. *Public Administration Review*, *60*(March/April), 173–182.

Bratton, W.J. (1999). Great expectations: How higher expectations for police departments can lead to a decrease in crime. In R.H. Langworthy (Ed.), *Measuring what matters: Proceedings from the policing research institute meetings*. Rockville, MD: National Institute of Justice.

Bratton, W.J., & Knobler, P. (1998). *Turnaround*. New York: Random House.

Charrier, K. (2004). Strategic management in policing: The role of the strategic manager. *The Police Chief*, *71*(6), 60–70.

Cope, N. (2004, March). Intelligence led policing or policing led intelligence? *The British Journal of Criminology*, 188–203.

Covey, S.R. (1989). *The seven habits of highly effective people*. New York: Free Press.

Crank, J.P., & Giacomazzi, A. (2009). A sheriffs' office as a learning organization. *Police Quarterly*, *12*(4), 351–369.

Dabney, D. (2010). Observations regarding key operational realities in a Compstat model of policing. *Justice Quarterly*, *27*(1), 28–51.

Daft, R.L. (2002). *The leadership experience*. New York: Harcourt.

Davenport, T.H. (1997). *Information ecology: Mastering the information and knowledge environment*. New York: Oxford University Press.

DiBella, A., & Nevis, E. (1998). *How organizations learn: An integrated strategy for building learning capacity*. San Francisco: Jossey-Bass.

Eterno, J., & Silverman, E.B. (2012). *The crime numbers game: Management by manipulation*. Boca Raton, FL: CRC Press.

Gladwell, M. (2002). *The tipping point: How little things make a big different*. New York: Hachett.

Glendale Police Department, www.glendaleaz.com/police/VisionStatement(2017).cfm.

Goldstein, H. (1979, April). Improving policing: A problem-oriented approach. *Crime & Delinquency*, *25*, 236–258.

Goldstein, H. (1990). *Problem-oriented policing*. New York: McGraw-Hill.

Henry, V.E. (2002). *The Compstat paradigm: Management accountability in policing*. New York: Looseleaf Press.

Hrebiniak, L.G. (2005). *Making strategy work: Leading effective execution and change*. Upper Saddle River: Pearson Education.

Kim, W., & Mauborgne, R. (2003, April). Tipping point leadership. *Harvard Business Review*, 60–69.

Kotter, J.P. (1996). *Leading change*. Boston: Harvard Business School Press.

Kotter, J.P., & Cohen, D.P. (2002). *The heart of change*. Boston: Harvard Business School Press.

Levine, J., Eterno, J.A., & Silverman, E.B. (2012, August 9). Manufacturing crime statistics at the NYPD: Reputation versus safety under Bloomberg and Kelly. *The Huffington Post*, www.huffingtonpost.com.

Maple, J., & Mitchell, C. (1999). *The crime fighter*. New York: Doubleday.

McDonald, P.P. (2002). *Managing police operations: Implementing the New York crime control model—Compstat*. Belmont, CA: Wadsworth.

Michaelson, G.A. (2001). *The art of war for managers: 50 strategic rules*. Avon, MA: Adams Media.

Moore, M.H. (1995) *Creating Public Value: Strategic Management in Government*. Cambridge, MA: Harvard University Press.

Moore, M.H., & Trojanowicz, R.C. (1988). *Corporate strategies for policing: Perspectives on policing*. Washington, DC: National Institute of Justice.

More, H.W., Vito, G.F., & Walsh, W.F. (2012). *Organizational behavior and management in law enforcement*. Upper Saddle River, NJ: Prentice Hall.

O'Connell, P.E., & Straub, F. (2007). *Performance-based management for police organizations*. Long Grove IL: Waveland.

Osborne, D., & Plastrik, P. (2000). *The Reinventor's' field book*. San Francisco: Jossey-Bass.

President's Task Force on 21st Century Policing. (2015). *Final report of president's task force on 21st century policing*. Washington, DC: Office of Community Oriented Policing Services.

Ratcliffe, J. (2016). *Intelligence-led policing*, 2nd ed. New York: Routledge.

Reith, C. (1956). *A new study of police history*. London: Oliver & Boyd.

Silverman, E. (1999). *NYPD battles crime: Innovative strategies in policing*. Boston: Northeastern University Press.

Skogan, W.G. (2008). Why reforms fail. *Policing & Society*, *18*(1), 23–34.

Stone, C., & Travis, J. (2011).Toward a new professionalism in policing. In *New perspectives on policing*. Washington, DC: National Institute of Justice.

Timothy, C., O'Shea, T.C., & Nicholls, K. (2003). Police crime analysis: A survey of US police departments with 100 or more sworn personnel. *Police Practice and Research*, 233–250.

Weisburd, D., & Braga, A.A. (Eds.) (2006). *Police innovation: Contrasting perspectives*. Cambridge: Cambridge University Press.

Wexler, C., Wycoff, M.A., & Fischer, C. (2007). *Good to great policing: Application of business management principles in the public sector*. Washington, DC: Department of Justice Office of Community Oriented Policing Services and Police Executive Research Forum.

5 Managing Change and Culture

Change can be brought about rapidly by the creation of and reaction to a "discernible crises" which leads to self-confrontation and requires both strategizing and action to correct.

William Bratton, *Turnaround: How America's top cop reversed the crime epidemic* (1998, p. 236)

Learning Objectives

1.	Define change and identify the different types of change.
2.	Understand the role and responsibilities of change agents.
3.	Differentiate between planned and unplanned change.
4.	Identify the characteristics of Transformational Leadership.
5.	Recognize the characteristics of a dysfunctional organization.
6.	Identify the sources of organizational change.
7.	Comprehend Lewin's three-stage process of planned change.
8.	Understand what is required to implement change.

Introduction

This chapter focuses on the process of managing organizational change and culture. Beginning with the Community Problem-Solving Policing Era in the 1980s and the emergence of strategic policing strategies in the 1990s change and innovation have become a continuous part of life in policing. Presently many police executives are reengineering their organizations with flexible and adaptive operational strategies. They are seeking to create more effective organizations by experimenting with public safety strategies that work and rejecting those that do not. As a result, understanding and implementing organizational change has emerged as an essential feature of police leadership and administration. Change is defined as any alteration that occurs in the structure, people, and practice of an organization (Zhao, 1996). It is a natural and inevitable factor in organizational life. Change is undertaken to improve an organization and prepare it for its future. Organizations that do not change become stagnant, unable to adjust to changing demands and subject to one crisis after another. One of the more important measures of an organization's strength is its ability to adapt to and manage change. Unfortunately many researchers have found that police departments can be highly resistant to change and police managers often have difficulty in implementing new programs (Weisburd & Braga, 2006). Leadership is about creating and managing change. Creating change involves the development of innovative approaches and putting them into practice. The development of organizational strategies such as Compstat, Intelligence-Led, and Evidence-Based Policing are examples of a creative change response to internal and external demands affecting police departments. They are also examples of a product of the acquisition of new knowledge obtained through systematic problem solving and experimenting with new tactical approaches. Sustainable change is earned by unlocking the forces of creativity and innovation through the management of an organization's culture and human capital (Schermerhorn, 2005). The end result organizationally is the transformation of a department to a more effective performance level by change that maintains and sustains itself. It sustains for a significant period of time. For example, the New York City Police Department developed Compstat in 1994 and it is still in use in that department today.

Change is constant, we create it, and we can control it. Organizational change typically affects processes, technology, positions, and culture in an organization. A significant change to even one of these areas requires leadership, analysis, and planning. Change is not a single occurrence that can be accomplished by the issuance of policy and procedural changes. It is a continuous process that must be clearly thought out with due consideration given to the people needed to support it and make it happen. It is about leadership that is open, honest, and willing to engage in frequent communication and exchange of information. Otherwise its impact will be cosmetic and short-lived.

For example, the change to Community Policing in the Tempe, Arizona, Police Department evolved in three phases: (1) the early planning phase, which began in the late 1980s; (2) the start-up phase, which encompassed a Beat experiment conducted in the early 1990s; and (3) a department-wide implementation, which was launched after the Beat project ended. During this change process the Tempe Police Department worked through a number of challenges. As a result the department evolved into a different and more responsive police organization in its service to Tempe's citizens. It changed from a reactive operational response mode to a proactive one centered on problem solving; from an entirely centralized operation to a decentralized operation; from a department with minimal contact with the public to outreach to the public; from decision making based on subjective judgment to decisions based on analysis; and from strict control of sworn personnel to flexibility and support for decision making. This transition took place over a 12-year period and is ongoing. The lesson learned from this effort is that changing police organizations requires time and patience because of the radical changes that it imposes on a police department previously accustomed to a professional reform style of policing (McEwen, 2002).

Individuals or groups who take responsibility for changing processes and organizations are known as change agents. These individuals are responsible for planning, coordinating, and developing the change process. They are the catalysts who make things happen. Change agents are proactive innovative managers who anticipate the need for change and take deliberate actions to initiate a program of planned change within their organization. They are alert for organizational performance gaps between desired and actual outcomes.

These individuals take responsibility for the analysis and resolution of problems or issues confronting their organization, coordinating the development of a planned response, and facilitating the collaboration of personnel involved in the change process.

However, the experience in policing is that organizational change has usually occurred as a reactive response, forced on many departments by external events or internal crises that demand change (Maguire et al., 2003). Policing today is facing difficult times involving crises of legitimacy in part to the ubiquitous presence of video cameras that have displayed before the American public the very best and worst of police conduct (Sparrow, 2016). Pressure from various sources such as the media, political structure, federal government consent decrees, changing crime conditions, community problems, civil disorder, political action groups, organizational crises, and/or other damaging events are all-too-familiar motivators for police organizational change. Henry (2002, pp. 31–32) claims that this pressure for change often results in an inadequate response by police administrators that he identified as "*cookie cutter management*." This is the tendency for police managers to find some policy or practice that another police department has successfully used and appropriate it. These administrators press the borrowed practice down on their department as if it were a cookie cutter or template. This practice is motivated by the subjective belief that "what works for others will work for us." Unfortunately, this activity is often devoid of systematic problem solving, planning, a careful implementation process, and/or assessment. Managers involved in this borrowing process fail to appreciate the differences between the originating department and their own. This approach is doomed to fail. If the factors that create the demand for change are not perceived and understood by the department's executive team and systematically analyzed, the change will become an externally imposed quick fix that underscores the leadership failure of the department's executive team.

Another aspect of externally imposed change is that administrators who are under pressure of the demand for organizational change respond by selecting the easiest way out of the stressful situation. Simon (1997) referred to this as *satisficing*. It occurs when an administrator feels pressured to appear decisive and does not take the time to fully identify and analyze the problem or issue generating the demand. These individuals seek to handle the demand quickly with a good enough solution that offers the least uncertainty and risk for themselves or their organization. Unfortunately, this type of decision making usually resolves day-to-day surface issues only and fails to consider the long-term impact on the department. Satisficing is a primary source of the managerial dictum that holds that "Yesterday's solutions are often the source of today's problems." It perpetuates organizational mediocrity and maintains the department's status quo.

A major source of resistance to change is often the department's culture. An *organization's culture* is a shared system of beliefs, attitudes, values, traditions, and modes of behavior held and practiced by organizational employees (Schein, 1990; Dessler, 2004, p. 38). It reflects what the department and its members believe in as an organization, and provides justification for what its employees do. Police culture teaches police officers what is acceptable behavior and the explanatory reasons why officers act the way they do (Sparrow, 2016, p. 36). In many departments culture maintains and perpetuates conformity to the established acceptable ways of doing things, the *status quo*. Status quo bias is often at the heart of resistance to change (Bratton & Tumin, 2012). People like to do exactly what they have always done. If a department's culture is not properly understood and managed, it will work against organizational change.

A police department's culture is displayed in its patterns of behavior such as ceremonial events, continuous behavioral activity, official and unofficial written and spoken ways of doing things. Organizational culture is reflected in the manner in which employees treat each other, what they brag about, the job-related stories they tell, what members wear, and the types of behavior in which they consistently engage. For example, the culture of a small 30-person municipal police department where most things are handled informally and formal ceremonies are non-existent is quite different from that of a large multilevel state police agency. In an address before a management class at the Southern Police Institute, a Florida police chief of a 38-employee police department defined his 38-person department as a team. He described his leadership style as one designed to foster teamwork, and mutual respect for all people who come in contact with his department and work in it. He claimed that he consistently seeks to shape the values that support positive internal as well as external departmental relationships. This is a different cultural perspective than that found in many multilevel bureaucratically administered agencies.

Types of Change

Organizational change results from either planned or unplanned efforts. **Planned change** occurs when administrators identify a problem or issue, diagnose it, develop a solution, and implement it. This should be a continuous process that occurs in all organizations as they endeavor to be more effective. Continuous improvement requires a commitment to organizational learning (Senge, 1990). This process is usually a series of planned steps that involves problem identification and analysis, solution development, an implementation process, and evaluation. Another type is **incremental change**. This type of change seeks to improve existing ways of doing thing by building upon existing organizational systems and practices to better align them with demands upon the organization. The objective is to achieve improved performance by making planned but limited change. Common incremental changes involve changing unit heads, developing new procedures, closing unit performance gaps, and improving outcome results.

Unplanned change occurs as a reaction to intense external pressure usually brought about by crises (Welsh & Harris, 2008). Pressure for change can come from both external and internal organizational forces. Police administrators need to be sensitive to the driving forces in their environments (crime, politics, the media, labor issues, economic events, and employee issues) that necessitate change. Organizations must be flexible enough to adjust to the need to change. A consistent event that creates change in policing is the replacement of the department's chief executive. This is a political decision that usually occurs after an election when the newly elected mayor wants to appoint a chief of his or her choosing. It can also occur if the department has been judged negatively and come under extreme pressure to change because of community unrest, excessive use of deadly force, officer misconduct, scandal, or other wrongdoing that led to dramatic incidents publicized by the media (Swanson, Territo, & Taylor, 2005). For example, the City of Baltimore's mayor fired the city's police commissioner, claiming that a recent spike in homicides weeks after an unarmed black man, Freddy Gray, died of injuries in police custody that resulted in civil disturbances and destruction of property required a change in leadership.

In the last two decades there has emerged in policing a form of leadership that is **transformational** in nature, focused on changing reactive departments to proactive ones. It involves an organizational reengineering process that is led from the top and designed to change operational strategies, tactics, and organizational effectiveness. Transformational police executives proactively create and implement the strategic redirection of their departments in order to effectively meet the changing demands of their operational environments. This leadership style is built around changing a department's vision, mission, values, goals, engagement, empowerment, accountability, outcomes, and evaluation. Transformational leaders seek to change their organizations from reactive organizations to open-system adaptive-learning organizations.

Transformational Process

James MacGregor Burns (1978) first defined the term **transformational leadership** as a process in which leaders and their followers help each other to rise to a higher level of morale and motivation. Leaders of **transformational change** model what they expect in others while appealing to higher ideals and values of their followers. They are change agents who take on the responsibility for revitalizing their organizations. They define the need for change, create new organizational visions, mobilize commitment to those visions, and ultimately transform their organization. Transforming an organization requires organizational change that involves new ways of thinking about strategy, structure, people, and outcomes. Transformational leaders start with the existing organization and redesign and reengineer it to achieve higher levels of accomplishment. The common characteristics of transformational leaders are:

They identify themselves as change agents. Their professional and personal image is to make a difference by transforming their organization.

They are courageous individuals. Courage is not stupidity. These are prudent risk takers, individuals who take a stand.

They believe in people. They are not dictators. They are powerful yet sensitive of other people and ultimately they work toward the empowerment of others.

They are value-driven. They are able to articulate a set of core values and exhibited behavior that was quite congruent with their value positions.

They are life long learners. They are able to talk about mistakes they had made and what they have learned from these.

They show an amazing appetite for continuous self-learning and development.

They modify their behavior to reflect new knowledge and insights.

They have the ability to deal with complexity, ambiguity and uncertainty.

They are able to cope with and frame problems in a complex, changing world. These individuals are capable of dealing with the cultural and political side of the organization, as well as the structural and human aspects. They are entranced by the world of ideas.

They are visionaries. They are able to dream and to translate those dreams and images so that other people could share them.

(Tichy & Devanna, 1990, pp. 271–280)

Transformational leaders reject the traditional view that police organizations operated in a stable and predictable environment that can be controlled through procedures and policy. They perceive of their organizations as open learning systems that exist in complex, demanding environments. They understand that as conditions in society, security, community inter-relationships, and people change, the need for modification in strategy, organizational structure, processes, and function increases. Their change efforts involve the effective use of information, analysis, problem solving, and the development of flexible operational strategies to meet public safety needs and align their organizations with the challenges they face. Police administrators who are transformational leaders seek to create learning organizations focused on effective performance, crime prevention, community engagement, information management, managerial accountability, ethics, and the control of crime in many police and sheriff departments across this nation. Learning organizations create, acquire, transfer, and apply knowledge to modify performance and achieve improved outcomes (Senge, 1990).

Successful transformational change is dependent upon the leader's ability to get others to not only see and understand a different organizational vision but also to commit to it. They seek to mobilize people within and without of the organization to accept and work toward achieving change. Lastly, they institutionalize these changes through a planned process so that they are sustained over time. The critical difference is that transformational leaders not only make major changes, they also evoke fundamental changes in the basic political and cultural systems of their organization (Tichy & Cohen, 1997). These police executives, instead of maintaining their organizations' status quo, seek to change it and direct their departments in the development of more effective ways to face the challenges of today and tomorrow. They are leading a change within policing that is emphasizing a greater focus on crime reduction, professionalization, developing a body of knowledge, and a move toward more data- and information-based problem solving (Ratcliffe, 2008, p. 187).

Dysfunctional Organization

Unfortunately, numerous organizations undertake change and commit substantial resources to the change effort but fail to create significant sustainable change (Kotter, 1996).

The history of police reform is filled with examples of highly publicized changes that promised much but failed to achieve lasting impact on police culture and value orientations. Recently the deaths of unarmed minority citizens at the hands of police have commanded national headlines and brought protesters and civil disorder to the streets in Baltimore, Ferguson, New York, and elsewhere (Walker, 2005). This should come as no surprise, given studies showing that police culture and value orientations changed little during this period (Cohen, 2017). These organizations often end up facing crises and become dysfunctional. By then, their ability to achieved desired change is greatly reduced, and even after heroic efforts, often decline into a crisis management mode. This is a bleak appraisal that has happened in many police departments whose efforts to implement organizational change have failed.

A **dysfunctional organization** is that who fails to serve the purpose for which it was created. Instead, it expends efforts and resources for the purpose of maintaining its existence (Balthazard Cooke, & Richard, 2006). Dysfunctional organizations eventually become victims of the driving forces in their environment. They respond and react to these forces moving from one crisis to another but never attempt to control or change their organization. A common development in dysfunctional organizations is administrative inattention to employee needs and effectiveness, which results in lower morale and employee accomplishment and disengagement. There are three stages through which organizations become dysfunctional. These stages and their contributing characteristics are:

STAGE ONE

1. The organization lacks a clear sense of direction.
2. The organization lacks vision, goals, objectives, or outcomes.
3. Performance expectations are unclear and variable.
4. The organization lacks intelligence gathering and analysis.
5. There is a lack of planning.
6. There is a lack of problem solving and innovation.
7. There is a failure to make important decisions.

STAGE TWO

1. There is a communication breakdown between administration and line operations.
2. There is a failure to focus on the department's primary mission.
3. There is low employee morale.
4. The department acts in a purely reactive mode.
5. There is high personnel turnover.

STAGE THREE

1. Management by crisis becomes the norm.
2. The organization is locked in to the status quo.
3. Resources are limited.
4. Officers are demotivated.
5. Powerful vested interests protect their turf causing internal conflict.
6. Employees have feelings of abandonment and disengagement.

It is not necessary that all of these characteristics exist at each stage. However, as the dysfunctional aspects of the organization become more pronounced, the department loses it sense of direction and its employees become demoralized and disengage. The absence of leadership in the dysfunctional organization generates a sense of abandonment in employees. Operationally people give up and only do what is necessary to get by. Everyone is worried about themselves and their unit to the overall detriment of the department. Employees are not team members but a group of people who show up and handle the day-to-day workload and crises. A common theme in the dysfunctional organization is management by crisis and there always is a crisis.

Sources of Change

Each organizational problem or issue, whether it is the result of factors in the external environment, such as an increase in incidents of violent crime, or internal pressure resulting from labor unrest or inadequate unit performance, has the potential to create the need for change. However, the most important challenge facing administrators is the degree to which the factor(s) necessitating change are recognized, understood, influenced, or resolved by managerial intervention. Some problems are easily resolved while others are much more complicated. As a result problem identification, analysis, and solution development and implementation are basic managerial elements in a planned change process. Yet, despite a disciplined and careful environmental scanning, police organizations still become victims of unplanned change. There are two basic sources of organizational change that are either external or internal to organizations.

External sources are factors outside an organization's control that have the power to affect the organization. The external environment is the context in which an organization operates. Police departments have had change imposed on them from the outside because of external forces such as legislation, court decisions, media pressure, political decisions, commissions of inquiry, the federal government, pressure groups, changing crime patterns, and high-profile incidents (Greenberg & Flynn, 2004). These external forces often trigger an unplanned response to the crises they create. Change implemented in response to crisis is highly risky but often occurs.

Organizations will find themselves victims of externally imposed change if they do not have subsystems designed to monitor key environmental indicators that will eventually influence them. Ongoing intelligence gathering, crime and incident data analysis, external relationship building, and stakeholder analysis (newspaper analysis, community surveys, call back programs, community dialogue meetings) can be used to identify areas and trends to which the department will need to respond. External indicators can serve as benchmarks for identifying the relative position and reputation of the police organization in the eyes of citizens.

It is the responsibility of the department's leadership to identify threats to the department's present and future status and then decide on what actions should be taken to neutralize or lessen their impact. Assessing the external environment includes monitoring the following:

Community crime and quality-of-life issues.
Special population or area needs.
Special events needs.
Potential crises areas.
Levels of community crime and violence.
Political impact issues.
Media relations.
Community support systems.
Probation and parole population.

Internal sources of change are factors found within the organization. Monitoring these is easier for administrators because they are under their control. Put simply, the internal environment of the organization is all that is within the organization. Organizations are composed of people, structure, patterns of behavior, and processes. People are an organization's most important asset because they perform all activities necessary for the department to fulfill its mission. A department can have the best structure and well-planned operational strategies, but without trained, proficient, and motivated people, it will not be able to accomplish anything. Thus, employees are the critical to the success of any change effort. Change will only succeed if an organization's employees are willing to change their work behavior and task accomplishment by more efficient and effective performance. Employee change is concerned primarily with values, attitudes, motivation, skills, competence, and on-the-job behavior.

Organizational structure is another internal area of concern. Structure is either formal or informal. **Formal structure** defines employee roles, organizational subdivisions, and their place in the organizational hierarchy of authority. It also contains rules and procedures that govern role behavior (Bolman & Deal, 1993). Over time, changes in organizational structure are needed to improve the effectiveness of the organization's response to changing demands. The **informal organization** is the interlocking social network of relationships that governs how people work together in practice. It is formed through the informal connections and relationships between organizational employees through which work is accomplished. It complements the formal organizational structure and processes. **Organizational processes** are all the activities required for the organization to function. In policing this involves administration, operations, and support services. The administrative process, for example, creates goals and objectives, policy and procedures, performance outcomes, and regulations and oversees operational performance. All of which can create the need for change and in some instances internal conflict. However, conflict created by change can be both functional and dysfunctional. **Functional conflict** is a positive factor that can energize people, lead to goal-oriented behavior, and create higher levels of achievement, awareness, and understanding. Under the right conditions, it has the potential to generate creative problem solving and produce adaptive change. **Dysfunctional conflict** is negative because it disrupts organizational performance and goal accomplishment. Problems occur in police organizations because many administrators do not recognize the interdependencies of their organizations' internal change areas (Barnett & Carroll, 1995). However, conflict created by change is not all bad. A certain amount of organizational conflict is normal and healthy. Under the right conditions, it can generate creative problem solving and produce adaptive change. Since change is both synergistic and cumulative, a change in one area often leads to changes in others. Common interrelated internal organizational targets for change include:

Tasks, elements of work required to achieve the organization's mission, objectives, and strategy and job designs of individuals and groups.

People, their commitment and competencies as well as the human resource system that supports them.

Culture, the organization's value and beliefs and the norms guiding individual and group behavior.

Technology, the operations and information technology used to support intelligence analysis, information distribution, work performance and outcome achievement.

Structure, the configuration of the organization, lines of authority, task responsibility and communication.

(Schermerhorn, 2005, p. 473)

The Process of Change

Effective change agents are problem solvers, strategic thinkers, and decision makers. How they think and make decisions is critical to their effectiveness. All organizational actions are contingent on decision making. Good managers develop their ability to perceive problems and create solutions to resolve them. This ability is based upon **strategic thinking**. Strategic thinkers are flexible decision makers who seek to understand the totality of the forces affecting the problems they are confronting while at the same time maintaining a focus on their mission and objectives. They are multidimensional thinkers who seek to understand the relationships existing in the whole organizational system rather than looking at the organization and its environmental relationships as the sum of its individual parts. Strategic thinking requires that managers examine the context, interrelationships, assumptions, and the potential impact of a situation or problem. This type of thinking enables change agents to develop an understanding of all sides of the complex issues involved in the organizational change process.

The capacity to think and analyze systematically is unquestionably a necessity for police managers. In order to make appropriate decisions in today's public safety environment, law enforcement managers need to possess a broad professional knowledge base, analytical skills, and the ability to make sound judgments. The ability to recognize organizational problems clearly and understand their potential meanings and relationships having to do with both persons and things is a critical managerial skill. It demands that managers must learn to see interrelationships rather than linear cause/effect sequences. This requires Diagnosis.

Diagnosis

The process of change begins by identifying what is known or suspected about a problem or issue or organization requiring change. The objective of diagnosis is to identify data, knowledge, and information about the problems and issues that are potential targets for change. A **diagnosis** should serve two critical functions. One, it begins the change process by identifying that a problem or issue does in fact exist. Two, it should clarify the problem or issue needing change and suggest what type of change is required. Accurate diagnosis ensures that managers have the information needed to develop intervention strategies based upon root causes rather than mere symptoms (More, Vito, & Walsh, 2012). Diagnosis sets the stage for the identification of the change target and the strategy required for its implementation. This information gathering and analysis should be guided by the following questions:

1.   What are the problems/issues?
2.   What is the evidence for clarifying these targets for change?
3.   What part(s) of the organization are affected?
4.   What type and level of change does the analysis suggest?

A diagnosis should draw information from a variety of sources such as: (1) performance observations, (2) crime and disorder information, (3) crime and place analysis, (4) employee interviews, (5) questionnaires, (6) critical incident reports, and (7) record analysis.

A proper diagnosis should identity conditions that require change, and suggest the appropriate strategy for implementing the change.

There are four stages to diagnosis:

1.   Problem identification.
2.   Isolation of primary and secondary causes of the problem.
3.   Identification of the current response to the issue.
4.   Development of a potential solution to the problem.

(Goldstein, 1990)

An excellent example of how to conduct a diagnosis has been an integral part of problem-oriented policing (POP) since its inception. POP is based on the belief that police organizations must develop systematic processes for examining and addressing problems. The POP approach to diagnosing and correcting problems uses a four-stage process called SARA (Scanning, Analysis, Response, and Assessment) that is an appropriate diagnostic technique:

1.   *Scanning* is the process of identifying a problem or issue.
2.   *Analysis* is the process of learning the problem's causes, scope, and effects.
3.   *Response* is the implementation of a planned action(s) to alleviate the problem and developing an appropriate and effective solution to the problem.
4.   *Assessment* is the determination of the effectiveness of the response.

(Scott, 2000, p. 15)

A successful diagnosis and change strategy will identify the areas of change, provide clear and realistic targets for measuring success, and appeal to the long-term interests of organizational stakeholders. The change process must address any and all changes that will make the organization more effective. It should communicate the need for these changes as well as their purpose. It should be designed to answer employee questions and gain their support. Once people understand why change is needed and what is expected, they will often strive to achieve it. The first step of the change process should clearly identify the direction in which the organization is going.

Too often efforts to improve an organization specify only one or two elements such as structure and unit command, ignoring performance changes and employee competencies required to take place. For example, in one police department several years ago a chief publicly declared that the agency was now engaging in Community Policing. Community Policing slogans were put on the side of patrol vehicles and a new community-oriented mission statement was developed. However, identification of duties, training, accountability, and procedural support for the change were never discussed or implemented. In fact, it was a change in name only that resulted in creating internal distrust, resistance, and friction in the department.

Police departments are organic organizations that are composed of dynamic inter-relationships among people performing various functions and tasks necessary to achieve the organization's mission. In order to anticipate and identify the need for change, police managers should continuously scan and understand their department's internal as well as external environment for factors calling for organizational change. They need to:

1. Recognize the indicators that signal the need for some type of planned change.
2. Plan and implement the required change via a planned strategy.
3. Regulate the change strategy implementation by monitoring, evaluating, and managing the process.

(More et al., 2012, p. 355)

Kurt Lewin (1947) developed a process of planned change that has three major elements. These are:

1. **Unfreezing the status quo** (Creating Dissatisfaction with the Status Quo and Acceptance of the Change Model).
2. **Changing to a new state** (Mobilization + Alignment Process).
3. **Refreezing the new state** (Institutionalization & Measurement).

    Unfreezing involves getting the organization ready for change by having its members confront the present reality in order to recognize the need and lessening their resistance to it. It involves creating dissatisfaction with the present state of the organization and a desire for a change to make things better. This is accomplished by confronting the inertia the organization's status quo has on the way the department functions and changing the existing culture that supports it. Unfreezing begins when support for current values and behavior is withdrawn, and old ways are seen as no longer desirable or acceptable. This requires the breaking down of the beliefs, values, customs, traditions, and culture that support the current ways of performing so the employees are ready to accept change (Schein, 1985). During the unfreezing stage it is necessary to overcome individual resistance and group conformity to the status quo. Good administrators utilize organizational analysis to scan the internal and external environments for potential problems and initiate planned change before a crisis occurs (Yukl, 2006).

    Changing occurs when the planned change process is implemented and the forces against it are overcome. The change process is designed to reduce or resolve the issue or problem it is targeting. It should introduce new performance behaviors and cultural outlook into the vacuum created during the unfreezing of the status quo. The change process is the responsibility of the department's executive team. Without top management sponsorship, implementation efforts will be strongly resisted and ineffective. Significant change takes place only when members of the organization identify with and accept new ideas, approaches, performance behaviors, and relationships. The mere introduction of change does not ensure its acceptance. The process must be carefully managed and evaluated in order for a successful implementation to take place (Hershey & Blanchard, 2012).

    Refreezing occurs when the new process of change is institutionalized in the organization and its employees. It becomes the new way or standard operating procedure for doing things. The change becomes stabilized when the forces for change overcome resistance. The mechanics of planned change are the same for organizations as for people, because changing people is the critical variable in changing the structure or function of any organization. Compstat is a good example of the planned-change process. Crime strategy meeting leaders facilitate the unfreezing process by inducing a certain amount of stress in unit commanders, to make them recognize their performance issues and why they should change their tactics. During these meetings through ongoing strategic diagnosis and dialogue, commanders are exposed to new ideas, values, skills, and tactics. Change begins when the commanders give credence to these ideas, values, and tactics and translate them into their problem-solving tactics. Once implementation of new ideas, values, skills, and behaviors elicit appropriate reinforcements (internal or external rewards and punishments), the refreezing process takes over when unit commanders accept, identify with, and internalize the change.

While there is great value in being aware of unfreezing-changing-refreezing theory and understanding the dynamics involved in it, good administrators know that using this knowledge effectively requires a tremendous amount of effort. It is not easily accomplished. Yet, the three-stage change process is applicable to small and medium-sized police departments as well as to large law enforcement agencies.

Implementing Change

In order for change to be adopted, it must be implemented. This will only happen after the desired change process is put into action, translated into reality, and the change into everyday practice. Implementation requires careful planning and development. One way to start this process is to begin by asking these simple planning questions:

1. Where are we going?   Defined by goals/objectives/outcomes
2. How do we get there?   Identified by strategy/tactics
3. What is our blueprint for action?   Created through an action plan
4. How do we know we are on track?   Planned controls/feedback
5. How do we know we did it?   Measurement of impact/outcomes

Step 1: Develop Goals, Objectives, and Outcomes

The first step in implementing a planned change process is describing what is to be accomplished through development and communication of the *goals, objectives, and outcomes* that everyone in the organization can understand, believe in, and strive to obtain. This should inform all members of the organization of what is expected to be accomplished as a result of the change process. This should guide the process and identify what is to be accomplished and provide the justification and approach for the entire change effort by answering the questions, "Where are we going? Why should we do it?" This step functions in many different ways: It defines what is expected to be achieved, helps spark motivation, keeps changes aligned, provides a basis to evaluate how the change process is doing, and it specifies a rationale for the changes the organization will have to make. In this manner a sense of purpose is established. It should build trust, collaboration, interdependence, motivation, and mutual responsibility for success (Stoner, Blanchard, & Zigarmi, 2007). Sir Robert Peel accomplished this with his first Principle of Law Enforcement for the newly created London Metropolitan Police in 1829 by stating, "The basic mission for which the police exist is to prevent crime and disorder, as an alternative to their repression by military force and severity of legal punishment" (Reith, 1956).

The long-term challenge to organizational revitalization is the extent to which the change process is accepted and implemented. Senior leadership must retain the responsibility for creating the change vision and strategy. Delegating all of the responsibility for this step is not desirable. Without top management sponsorship and oversight, implementation efforts can be strongly resisted and ineffective. Often, it is best for the chief or a small group of commanding officers to create the initial plan. From there, the management team and stakeholders can refine the process.

Recently a police chief was appointed to a department that had a long adversarial relationship with its community. Citizens saw the police officers as aloof, disrespectful, and quick to use force. The political structure and the community demanded that this change. In his first statements to his officers and the community, the new chief expressed his belief that "a safe community is a partnership effort and everyone has a role in it." In this manner, he was beginning to articulate a collaborative vision that all elements of the community as well as the police department were responsible for public safety. He was setting the direction for the community and the department to change the way they work together, support and respect each other. The chief executive's beginning statement help set the stage for the redirection of the department and the acceptance of the chief's efforts by the department's employees and community.

Step 2: Communicating the Change Process

Once the change process is developed, it must be communicated to the organization. This communication should be designed to inform organizational members of what the change is and why it is necessary. The need for change should be relatively easy to communicate and it should establish a clear direction for employees to follow. A useful rule of thumb is that if the reason(s) for the change cannot be communicated to someone in five minutes or less and get a reaction that signifies both understanding and interest, this part of the implementation is not yet completed (Galbraith & Lawler, 1993). During this process a sense of urgency must be created so that people start telling each other, "Let's go, we need to change things" (Kotter & Cohen, 2002). The basis for a sense of urgency is the creation of dissatisfaction with the organization's status quo. Kotter (1996) found that over half of the organizations he observed have never been able to create enough urgency to overcome resistance to change. He found that without a sense of dissatisfaction, people will not participate in the change effort and it will fail. Unfortunately, many managers often underestimate how hard it can be to drive people out of their comfort zones. During the 1990s, numerous police executives attempted to implement community and problem-solving policing in their departments but failed at changing their organizations. Many of these efforts were inadequately planned, disregarded the police officer culture, and met with mixed success because the officers involved were satisfied with the status quo and refused to change because they saw no need to change (McElroy, 1992; Sadd & Grinc, 1996).

The more successful change efforts begin with the leadership group facilitating a frank discussion of potentially unpleasant facts about the department and its performance results.

A primary objective of this discussion is to get employees to face the actual outcomes of their efforts and create a high urgency for change. This can be accomplished by:

1. Communicating information about potential crises or threats to the organization and its members.
2. Provide employees with factual data about organizational performance: what they are really accomplishing as opposed to what they say or think they are.
3. Engaging in frank discussion and dialogue about organizational problems, tactics, and strategy.
4. Setting realistic performance expectations that will create the desire to change.

All of the above elements evolved as part of the Compstat crime-strategy meetings that were begun in 1994 by then NYPD Commissioner William J. Bratton and his command staff (Henry, 2002). Compstat was created as a way to make NYPD's then 76 precinct commanders and their officers accountable for the city's crime rate. During the face-to-face communication at these meetings, collaboration between executive level, operational, and staff managers was established, real-time data on crime and community problems was presented and analyzed, consistent dialogue and diagnosis about tactics and strategy took place, and performance expectations were set. In these face-to-face meetings, a comprehensive, continuous analysis of crime, current crime conditions, and community problems became integral parts of the communication dialogue that consistently evaluated the department's performance as well as the identification of changes needed to strategy and tactics. These meetings focused the attention of the department's executive team and operational commanders on the development of crime prevention and control strategies. Compstat created an organizational climate in which change and collaboration were constant (Bratton & Knobler 1998; Bratton & Tumin, 2012; Maple, 1999).

Kim and Mauborgne (2003) in their analysis of Bratton's role as a change agent with many successful police organizational turnarounds identified this stage in the change process as the "**cognitive hurdle**." The objective is to get key organizational members such as unit commanders to confront their performance reality, create dissatisfaction, and achieve agreement on the causes of current organization's problems and the need for change. This can be accomplished by putting operational managers face-to-face with performance problems and issues to create dissatisfaction with inadequate performance. The dialogue that takes place during this activity should identify inadequate performance results, analyze them, and develop ways to address these problems through the collaborative efforts of the managerial group. It is also designed to identify successful performance results and identify how these were achieved. Kim and Mauborgne claim that Bratton's successful turnarounds of different police departments are textbook examples of "Tipping Point Leadership" (Kim & Mauborgne, 2003).

William J. Bratton Police Executive Career

- 1983 **Chief** of Massachusetts Bay Transit Authority Police.
- 1986 **Chief** of Massachusetts Metro District Community Police.
- 1990 **Chief** New York City Transit Police.
- 1993 **Commissioner** Boston Police Department.
- 1994 **Commissioner** NYPD.
- 2002 **Chief of Police** LAPD.
- 2014 **Police Commissioner** NYPD.

"**Tipping Point Leadership**" theorizes that in any organization, once the beliefs and energies of a <mark>critical mass</mark> of people are engaged, conversion to a new idea will spread like an epidemic, bringing about fundamental change very quickly. The theory suggests that such a movement can be unleashed only by change agents who are dissatisfied with the current state of affairs and who make unforgettable and unarguable calls for change. These leaders concentrate their efforts and resources on what really matters, and mobilize the commitment of the organization's key players, while silencing the most vocal naysayers (Gladwell, 2000). Kim and Mauborgne claim that Bratton did all of these things in each of his organizational turnarounds.

However, it is not sufficient just to provide data or identify performance failures. A real dialogue and analysis of what is happening as opposed to what should or could be happening must take place. All of these efforts must clearly establish in the employees a dissatisfaction with the organization's present reality and the need for change as well as a sense of urgency to bring about the change. Once this happens employee motivation can then be directed into a focused organizational improvement effort.

Step 3: Creating a Guiding Coalition

The next step in the implementation of the change is for the leader to identify a number of key organizational personnel that will be needed to successfully implement the new direction. These individuals must accept and believe in the change as well as make it happen. They constitute the change effort's <mark>guiding coalition</mark> because they have enough power to lead the change (Kotter, 1996). They are the organization's critical mass. This group should include both formal and informal stakeholders from all levels and units who need to be involved in the change process. A <mark>stakeholder</mark> is any person, group, or unit who has a legitimate interest in the problem or issue and its resolution. Some stakeholders will provide essential cooperation; others may provide potentially fatal opposition. If the change process is to be successful, it is important that the critical mass of relevant individuals, groups, and organizational elements be involved in the process. Otherwise, the project may run into insurmountable difficulties stemming from a lack of adequate information, resources, or cooperation. Police officers have a long history of using passive resistance and diversion to resist organizational change efforts. When identifying the critical mass, the following questions should be considered:

- Who are the individuals and groups that are vital to the change effort?
- How do we include these individual in the process?
- How can we develop a sense of ownership for the process in these individuals?
- What actions and results can be expected from this group?

A guiding coalition or critical mass consists of those employees that possess the vital skills, power, and influence that are needed for the implementation of the desired change. Once the beliefs and energies of this critical mass of people are engaged, conversion to a new idea will spread, bringing about fundamental change very quickly (Gladwell, 2000; Henry, 2002). It is the change agent's responsibility to identify these individuals and to get these individuals to accept the new direction and make it happen. If not, they will need to be neutralized or removed from hindering the process.

Leaders who wish to change their organizations must understand their people, the political context of their organization, and their organization's culture. As a result, change agents often find themselves in a continuous process of communication and negotiation with potential coalition members and employees in the attempt to win them over and motivate them to support the new organizational direction. It is important to remember that not all persons and groups are motivated in the same manner. People will differ as to how willingly they will be influenced and accept change. Membership in an organization's critical mass is not restricted to any one rank, position, or organization level. They are important because they are key stakeholders who are in a position to influence the support of the greater body of organizational employees. It should never be forgotten that there is also an external critical mass consisting of community stakeholders, political and elite powerbrokers, and the media that must be identified and won over to support the department's new direction.

A common approach for developing the guiding coalition is to start with a strong core of believers. At first, this core may be limited to a handful of people leading the effort. It then grows over time as respected, reputable individuals with the capacity to lead from various sectors within the organization are identified. Finding the right blend of strengths and interests pays great dividends toward future success. Coalition members should lead by example. They should embody the values of the vision for change and actively work to enhance the change process organizational-wide.

Step 4: Implementation of the Change

Implementing a change involves putting the change process into operation supported by the modification of the organization's policies, procedures, culture, performance regularities, values, and climate to enable the adoption of new practices and role behaviors required to complete the change (Stojkovic, Kalinich, & Klofas, 2012, p. 436). This entails designing and activating a set of activities that will have the best chance of achieving the desired change(s). It involves the identification of a planned sequence of behavioral actions that must be accomplished if the change is to achieve its goals and objective(s). The sequence of actions must be consistent with the goals, objectives, current information, resources, and needs of the change process. The sequencing of these action steps must be realistic, logical, and achievable. The monitoring of this process should be designed to provide feedback on progress and/or roadblocks. The change agent and guiding coalition can then adjust the implementation process to respond to the issues identified in the evaluation process. The successful implementation will require the emergence and reinforcement of a new culture that will support the leader's vision and the revitalization of the organization. At this stage a change in the employees' culture, attitudes, values, motivation, and patterns of behavior must take place. As we noted earlier, organizational culture is a system of shared beliefs, values, and meanings that develop within an organization and which guides the behavior of its members. It is a reflection of the basic values organizational members share and the way these values express themselves in their behavior (Dessler, 2004). Organizational culture theorists believe that formal rules, authority, and procedures designed to govern behavior do not restrain the personal preferences of employees (Kotter & Heskett, 1992). Instead, it is the organization's cultural norms, values, beliefs, and strongly held assumptions that control employee behavior (Lucas & Kline, 2008). Thus, culture is considered the hidden meaning behind behavior. Culture can function both as a help and/or hindrance to the implementation of change because it is the basis for the way organizational members perceive and feel about their organization, its leadership, and their work. It should be observed and understood by change agents if they want to implement change successfully.

The concept of culture is particularly important when attempting to manage organizational-wide change. Many of the organizational changes in policing have not been successful because they failed to address the organizational cultural norms of the employees involved. For example, during the early efforts to adapt to Community Policing there was strong resistance. This is one of the reasons why many strategic planners now place as much emphasis on identifying organizational values as they do mission and vision. In his first "turnaround" of the NYPD Police Commissioner William J. Bratton used a cultural diagnostic to identify the cultural assets, obstacles, operating culture, core identity, and values that must guide the revision of the department's key organizational systems to institutionalize a new high performance culture (Bratton & Knobler, 1998, p. 215).

Implementation and Organizational Culture

The implementation of change cannot be dealt with independently of organizational culture because the organization's culture will play an important role in shaping and reinforcing the employees' acceptance or resistance to the change. Management of an organization's culture during the implementation process involves establishing a clear direction for the change process and maintaining appropriate supporting values on a daily basis by the department's management team. In an organization with a strong culture, core values are intensely held, maintained, and widely shared among members. The more members who believe in and accept the organization's core values, the greater will be their commitment to those values and the stronger the culture. A strong culture will have a greater influence on the behavior of its members because it creates a climate of intense internal behavioral control. For example, World War II Japanese soldiers committed suicide rather than surrender and admit defeat. Surrender and defeat represented failure in their national duty and disgrace in their culture. An increasing body of research indicates that a strong positive organizational culture is associated with ethical organizations and successful organizational performance. However, a strong negative culture can serve the opposite goal and create an organization in which deviant behavior is condoned and protected (More et al., 2012).

Culture serves four basic organizational functions.

1. It provides a sense of identity to members and increases their commitment to the organization or their work group (a sense of belonging).
2. It provides a way for employees to interpret the meaning of organizational events and the external environment in which the organization exists (a way to make sense out of the demands of everyday life).
3. It reinforces the core values of the organization (Everybody knows what counts and the right way to behave.)
4. It serves as a behavioral control mechanism for organizational members (If they do not conform to the behavioral norms, they are an outsider or outcast.)

In order to understand or predict how organization members will behave during the change process the guiding coalition must know and understand the basic beliefs and values that form their organization's culture. One way to analyze organizational culture is to envision the organization as having two stages. One serves as its public front stage that contains the image its members want to portray to the outside world. This public image often represents an ideal state that the organization would like to achieve or would like others to think they have achieved. The other or inner stage contains the real organization, the internal world that is for organizational members only to see, never to be disclosed to outsiders. It is the arena of reality where things are done according to the pragmatic methods developed by workers to handle daily challenges, not the ideal procedural way. The closer these two stages correspond to each other, the more positive is the organizational culture. However, the wider apart they are, the more we can expect to find internal dissention, conflict, and deviant behavior. It is through culture maintenance and adjustment that managers keep their units focused on the mission and protect both the organization and the individual officer from liability.

Change agents should understand their organization's cultural system and the factors that create and sustain it. Value-based management actively identifies, develops, communicates, and enacts shared values. Organizational values serve a variety of purposes, including:

- Setting forth the department's philosophy of policing.
- Stating clearly what a department believes in.
- Identifies in broad terms the overall goals of a department.
- Serves as the basis for developing policies and procedures.
- Serves as the parameters for organizational flexibility.
- Provides the basis for operational strategies.
- Provides the framework for officer performance.
- Serves as a basis for which the department can be evaluated.

(USDJ, 2003)

Organizational values, reward systems, rules and policies should support a positive organizational culture. **Value-based management** has a major impact with respect to ethics and organizational integrity. All organizational managers are responsible for value-based management. How well the culture operates to support a change process and organizational performance objectives will depend upon the strength of the organization's core values and the manager's role in maintaining them. However, in some organizations, individual managers may claim they support certain values but their actions contradict these statements. When this occurs conflict, distrust, and unethical behavior can result.

Shared positive values promote loyalty, a willingness to change, feelings of personal effectiveness, consensus on goals, and sense of ownership for the organization and its people. They form the foundation for mobilization of commitment to the manager's vision. Thus, it is critical that all managers maintain a positive culture within their work units. Developing a strong ethical organizational culture is the primary responsibility of every manager. However, they must always model what they want in what they say and do. Employees watch and judge their managers every day. In addition to making clear the existence of positive core values, managers must continue to communicate and reinforce them through their observable actions.

Value-based management will assist in the development of the department's redirection and its institutionalization and sustainability. This can be accomplished through restructuring the following organizational elements to support the proposed change process:

- Selection and advancement systems.
- Managerial communication systems.
- Organizational policy and procedures.
- Decision-making and problem-solving processes.
- Accountability systems.
- Measurement and follow-up systems.
- Reward and discipline systems.

Step 5: Maintaining Dynamic Equilibrium

A well-managed change process must be able to adapt to and incorporate itself into the daily routine of the organization. However, the problem for most organizations is how to manage innovation and change while responding to the need for stability. Keeping these two opposing demands in balance is known as **dynamic equilibrium** (Smith & Lewis, 2011). This concept implies that administrators must maintain organizational stability, that is, perform the daily tasks of policing the community and providing public safety while creating change. They must strive to maintain a sense of order during the performance of day-to-day responsibilities while simultaneously initiating and managing the process of change. This requires that change be well managed. The basic elements of dynamic equilibrium are as follows:

Dimensions of Dynamic Equilibrium

1. Change agents must maintain enough **adaptability** so that the organization can react appropriately to external challenges as well as changing internal conditions.
2. At the same time **stability** must be maintained to facilitate the achievement of current performance levels, goals, and objectives. The organization must maintain its basic day-to-day processes.
3. Enough **cohesion** must be present to ensure an orderly change in either methods (means) or goals (ends).
4. Enough **innovation** must be permitted to allow the organization to be proactive in initiating change when conditions warrant it.

Step 6: Overcoming Resistance

Change is constantly accompanied by resistance. People often resist change because they fear what will happen to them and what they may lose. Change agents and administrators need to recognize and understand the causes of employee resistance so it can be dealt with in an effective manner. Resistance is a form of feedback that change agents can use to adjust the change process to fit situational needs and goals. Beer (1988) identified the following factors that form the basis for employee resistance when change occurs. He claims that employees fear a loss of:

1. **Power**—change involves the loss of power and control by some individuals in the organization.
2. **Competence**—change requires new competencies and skills that make the old ones obsolete. New ways of doing things create a loss of confidence. Employees often feel devalued by this and fearful of the new skills they must learn.
3. **Relationships**—changes in organizational arrangement typically will require new relationships and therefore make obsolete old networks.
4. **Rewards**—Major changes threaten the tangible and intangible rewards of some individuals. New ways demand that management align the reward and change structure.
5. **Identity**—Managers and employees for whom work is central to their concept of self are particularly subject to loss of self-esteem during a time of change. For example, many patrol officers believed that Community Policing lowered the self-esteem that they derived from the crime fighter role.

A principle of modern management holds that individuals closest to a situation should have the authority and discretion to make decisions regarding the management of the situations they are involved in. This concept is known as **empowerment**. It is the process of unleashing the power of people and focusing their knowledge, experience, and motivation to achieve positive outcomes (Randolph & Blanchard, 2007). During the change process executive managers should encourage line management decision making and command accountability while being tolerant of mistakes. Empowering this type of decision making and accountability will encourage participation and involvement in the change process. This in turn will create a broader acceptance and participation of organizational members.

Unfortunately, many law enforcement agencies have evolved into complex policy and procedural systems that are designed to protect the organization by controlling employee behavior and preventing mistakes. This is particularly true of traditionally managed organizations that have created a rule or policy each time a mistake or problem has occurred. However, those employees who fail to change and continue to resist cannot be ignored. Their immobilization must be analyzed and addressed. It may be that through training, communication, and participation they will become willing participants in the change process. If not, they will need to be disciplined or removed from their position. The action taken will depend upon the form and gravity of the resistance of the employee.

Step 7: Measurement of Progress

Lastly, leaders should always measure what they are trying to accomplish. How will they know if they have accomplished anything at all if they do not evaluate it? Establishing appropriate quantitative and qualitative performance measures will help link the change process to specific outcomes. Hard data is necessary for the assessment of managerial strategies and outcomes. Monitoring, measurement, and evaluation are keys to managerial success. They determine if you are accomplishing what you set out to do.

All elements of the change process should be conducted with evaluation in mind. Feedback systems and measurable objectives should always be part of organizational plans. Administrators should avoid setting expectations that are unrealistic and unattainable by developing a strategy that incorporates realistic and attainable objectives as system elements. Goals and objectives (outcomes) should be established to provide the change agent with a way to assess progress accurately, cite success, identify strategies that work, and refocus resources as needed. Appropriate baseline measures that record conditions before change is implemented should be identified so that a before-and-after comparison of relevant changes can be made.

Lastly, all performance measures should relate to agency, program, and operational unit mission and goals. The design and implementation of evaluations depend upon the specific purpose they are intended to serve. Always measure what matters and what gives you the information that you need. All else is a waste of time, budget, and organizational resources.

Attributes of Failed Change

There has been sufficient research in policing to tell us what contributes to failure in the change process.

- Lack of sustainable leadership.
- Change is imposed from the top or from outside without compelling reason or desire being established inside of the organization.
- Leaders think that announcing the change is the same as implementing it.
- Lack of planning involvement and understanding of the change process by those affected throughout the organization.
- A clear, concise vision that excites people about the future has not been developed or communicated. Vision is the primary ingredient for effective change leadership. It provides direction, alignment, and inspiration for people to create the change.
- No sense of urgency to overcome the status quo bias.
- Lack of employee support and union resistance.
- Mid-level managers and supervisors not included in planning, not prepared for role changes and not supportive.
- Organizational systems aren't aligned with the change.
- Supporting process and structural changes not considered or made.
- Organizational culture is non-supportive.
- New program introduced by a special unit, not integrated into the whole organization. This unit then becomes the organization's "Innovation Ghetto" (Grant & Toch, 2012).
- Overall effort is too much too fast.
- Change process is not measured, evaluated, or adjusted as needed.

Conclusion

Police administrators must be aware that in today's public safety environment change is a constant reality. They are expected to handle planned as well as unplanned change. Change agents should be future-oriented strategic thinkers. They must anticipate the need for change and be willing to do what is needed to bring it about. The success of any change initiative will depend on the desire and ability of the organization's leadership team to implement the change and the willingness of employees to accept the change. In order to be successful as change agents, administrators must understand the internal (organizational) as well as external (environmental) factors pushing for change. It is important to remember that people change what they do because they come to believe that it is the worthwhile thing to do. Creating the environment for change to take hold is a primary task of the department's leadership team.

The basic change process requires unfreezing the current organizational status quo, moving it to a new state, and refreezing the change to make it permanent. The dynamics of planned change involve pressure on, and arousal of, the leadership team to take action, diagnosis of the issue(s) or problem(s) involved, collection of data and identification of the real problem, development of a solution, implementation, and evaluation of the results.

Police administrators have a responsibility to assess the impact of a planned change. If the change effort proves beneficial, it should be institutionalized through positive reinforcement techniques using the organizational tools identified above. Police managers need to acquire an understanding of, and appreciation for, their role in the change process. One thing is certain: Now and in the future police administrators will be spending more of their time initiating, implementing, and managing planned change.

KEY TERMS

Adaptability	External sources of change	Relationships
Change	Formal structure	Rewards
Change agents	Functional conflict	Satisficing
Changing to a new state	Guiding coalition	Sources of change
Cognitive hurdle	Identity	Stability
Cohesion	Incremental change	Stakeholder
Communication	Informal organization	Status quo
Competence	Innovation	Strategic thinking
Cookie cutter management	Internal sources of change	Sustainable change
Critical mass	Lewin's three-stage process	Transformational change
Diagnosis	Organizational culture	Transformational leadership
Dynamic equilibrium	Organizational processes	Unfreezing the status quo
Dysfunctional conflict	Planned change	Unplanned change
Dysfunctional organization	Power	Value-based management
Empowerment	Refreezing the new state	

References

Balthazard, P., Cooke, R., & Potter, R.P. (2006). Dysfunctional culture, dysfunctional organization: Capturing the behavioral norms that form organizational culture and drive performance. *Journal of Managerial Psychology, 21*(8), 709–732.

Barnett, W.P., & Carroll, G.R. (1995). Modelling internal organizational change. *Annual Review of Sociology, 21*(1), 217–236.

Beer, M. (1988). *Leading change*. Cambridge, MA: Harvard University Press.

Bolman, L.G., & Deal, T.E. (1993). *Reframing organizations: Artistry, choice, and leadership*. San Francisco, CA: Jossey-Bass Inc.

Bratton, W., & Knobler, P. (1998). *Turnaround: How America's top cop reversed the crime epidemic*. New York: Random House.

Bratton, W., & Tumin, Z. (2012). *Collaborate or perish: Reaching across boundaries in a networked world*. New York: Crown Business.

Burns, J.M. (1978). *Leadership*. New York: Harper & Row.

Cohen, R. (2017). The force and the resistance: Why changing the police force is neither inevitable, nor impossible. *University of Pennsylvania Journal of Law and Social Change, 20*, 105.

Dessler, G. (2004). *Management: Principles and practices for tomorrow's leaders*. Upper Saddle River, NJ: Pearson.

Galbraith, J.R., & Lawler, E.E. (1993). *Organizing for the future: The new logic for managing complex organizations*. San Francisco CA: Jossey-Bass.

Gladwell, M. (2000). *The tipping point: How little things can make a big difference*. New York: Little Brown.

Goldstein, H. (1990). *Problem oriented policing*. New York: McGraw Hill.

Grant, J.D., & Toch, H. (2012). *Police as problem solvers*. New York: Springer Science & Business Media.

Greenberg, S., & Flynn, E.A. (2004). Leadership and managing change. In W.A. Geller, & D.W. Stephens (Eds.), *Local government police management* (pp. 67–84).Washington, DC: International City/County Management Association.

Henry, W. (2002). *The Compstat paradigm: Management accountability in policing*. New York: Looseleaf Press.

Hersey, P., & Blanchard, K. (2012). *The management of organizational behavior*. Engelwood Cliffs, NJ: Prentice Hall.

Kim, W.C., & Mauborgne, R. (2003). Tipping point leadership. *Harvard Business Review, 81*(4), 60–69, 122.

Kotter, J. (1996). *Leading change*. Boston: Harvard Business School Press.

Kotter, J., & Cohen, D.P. (2002). *The heart of change*. Boston: Harvard Business School Press.

Kotter, J., & Heskett, J.L. (1992). *Corporate culture and performance*. New York: Free Press.

Lewin, K. (1947). Frontiers in group dynamics: Concept, method, and reality in social science: Social equilibria and social change. *Human Relations, 1*(1), 5–41.

Lucas, C., & Kline, T. (2008). Understanding the influence of group dynamics on organizational change and learning. *The Learning Organization, 15*(3), 277–287.

Maguire, E.R., Zhao, J., Hassell, K. (2003). Structural change in large police agencies during the 1990s. *Policing: An International Journal of Police Strategies & Management, 26*(2), 251–275.

Maple, J. (1999). *The crime fighter*. New York: Doubleday.

McElroy, J.E. (1992, January 15). Judging community policing: Three views. *Law Enforcement News*.

McEwen, T. (2002). *Evaluation of community policing in Tempe, Arizona, Final Report*. Institute of Law and Justice, Washington DC: National Institute of Justice.

More, H.W., Vito, G.F., & Walsh, W.F. (2012). *Organizational behavior and management in law enforcement*. Upper Saddle River, NJ: Prentice Hall.

Randolph, A., & Blanchard, K. (2007). Empowerment is the key. In K. Blanchard (Ed.), *Leading at a higher level* (pp. 67–86). Upper Saddle River, NJ: FT Press.

Ratcliffe, J. (2008). *Intelligence-led policing*. Portland, OR: Willan.

Reith, C. (1956). *A new study of police history*. London: Oliver and Boyd.

Sadd, S., & Grinc, R. (1996, February). Implementation challenges in community policing: Innovative neighborhood-oriented policing in eight cities. *National Institute of Justice, Research in Brief*. Washington, DC: National Institute of Justice.

Schein, E.H. (1985). *Organizational culture and leadership: A dynamic view*. San Francisco: J Jossey-Bass.

Schein, E.H. (1990). Organizational culture. *American Psychologist, 45*, 109–119.

Schermerhorn, J.R. (2005). *Management*. Hoboken, NJ: John Wiley.

Scott, M.S. (2000). *Problem-oriented policing: Reflections of the first 20 years*. Washington, DC: DOJ, Office of Community Oriented Policing Services.

Senge, P. (1990). *The fifth discipline: The art & practice of the learning organization*. New York: Doubleday.

Simon, H.A. (1997). *Administrative behavior: A study of decision-making processes in administrative organizations*. New York: Free Press.

Smith, W.K., & Lewis, M.W. (2011). Toward a theory of paradox: A dynamic equilibrium model of organizing. *Academy of Management Review, 36*(2), 381–403.

Sparrow, M. (2016). *Handcuffed: What holds policing back, and the keys to reform*. Washington, DC: The Bookings Institution.

Stoner, J., Blanchard, K., & Zigarmi, D. (2007). The power of vision. In K. Blanchard (Ed.), *Leading at a higher level* (pp. 21–36). Upper Saddle River, NJ: FT Press.

Swanson, C.R., Territo, L., & Taylor, R.W. (2005). *Police administration: Structures, processes, and behavior*. Upper Saddle River, NJ: Prentice Hall.

Tansik, D.A., & Elliott, J.F. (1981). *Managing police organizations*. Belmont CA: Wadsworth.

Tichy, N.M., & Cohen, E. (1997). *The Leadership engine: How winning companies build leaders at every level*. New York: Harper Collins.

Tichy, N.M & Devanna, M.A. (1990). *The Transformational leader*. New York: Wiley.

USDJ. (2003). *Principles of good policing advoiding violence between police and citizens*. www.USDOJ.gov/CRS.

Walker, S. (2005). *The new world of police accountability*. Thousand Oaks, CA: Sage.

Welsh, W.N., & Harris, P.W. (2008). *Criminal justice policy and planning*. Newark, NJ: Lexis Nexis.

Weisburd, D., & Braga, A.A. (Eds.) (2006). *Police innovation: Contrasting perspectives*. Cambridge: Cambridge University Press.

Yukl, G. (2006). *Leadership in organizations*. Upper Saddle River, NJ: Prentice Hall.

Zhao, J. (1996). *Why police organizations change*. Washington, DC: Police Executive Research Forum.

6

Strategic Analysis

It is said that if you know others and know yourself, you will not be imperiled in a hundred battles; if you do not know others, but do know yourself, you win one and lose one; if you do not know others and do not know yourself, you will be imperiled in every single battle.

Sun Tzu, *The Art of War* (1994, p. 215)

Learning Objectives

1. Define strategic analysis.

2. List the elements of organizational direction.

3. Identify what is a SWOT analysis.

4. Describe what are threats and opportunities.

5. Describe what are strengths and weaknesses.

6. Define strategic management.

7. Identify organizational success factors.

8. Describe how to diagnose internal capability.

9. Explain how to use the Five Frames of Reference.

10. List the critical elements of each Frame of Reference.

Introduction

Strategic organizations have a clear sense of purpose that guides them in the utilization of their resources and capabilities in the fulfillment of their mission (Banner & Gagne, 1995). Their strategic direction is based upon accurate and timely intelligence that provides managers with the knowledge upon which they base their decisions. Setting operational priorities and deciding on strategy are intelligence-driven activities (Ratcliffe, 2016). In order to fulfill these responsibilities managers must have a clear understanding of the forces that affect their organization and its capacity to respond to these demands (Bryson, 2011). Police departments use crime analysis to identify patterns and relationships between crime data and other relevant data sources to prioritize and target their operational activity (Cope, 2004). This chapter will discuss the interdependence of the police organization and its environment.

Organizations are subjected to both internal and external environmental forces. Managers need to be sensitive to the driving forces that necessitate change in their resource utilization and operational strategies. They must be administratively flexible to adjust to the changing demands confronted by their organization. In order to accomplish this responsibility managers must become aware of, understand, and strategically analyze the forces that affect their ability to fulfill their mission.

Strategic Analysis

Strategic analysis begins with the continuous assessment of the department's external operational demand and internal response capabilities. It seeks to build a comprehensive and accurate picture of the department's efforts to serve the community by answering the following questions.

1. How effective is our present strategy and tactics?
2. What are our organization's strengths, weaknesses, opportunities, and threats?
3. How efficient are we?
4. What strategic issues does the department face?
5. What should the department do to respond to these issues?

A strategic analysis provides a structured way for gathering and analyzing relevant information to support strategic decisions (Henry, 2002). It makes sense that when managers act on timely information their organization's effectiveness will increase. A department's strategic analysis should analyze the forces that affect it, their underlying causes, and evaluate the manner in which these are responded to. It enables the department to view the entire organization and evaluate its relationship to its internal and external environments. It should provide the department with an overview of the current and long-term issues affecting or likely to affect it (Ratcliffe, 2016).

Strategic analysis involves the systematic process of collecting, analyzing, and disseminating timely and accurate information about crime and disorder problems, the conditions that generate them as well as organizational capability. It should also involve analysis of other police-related issues, including socio-demographic, spatial, and temporal factors that impact crime and disorder. This process serves three essential functions:

1. Analysis of crime data in order to allocate resources and deploy personnel.
2. Discovery of crime and suspect relationships as well as information for investigations.
3. To learn the reasons and conditions causing criminality, and to inform policymakers about these reasons and conditions for further policies.

(O'Shea, & Nicholls, 2003)

Knowledge obtained from this analysis is the basis upon which operational commanders develop strategies to apprehend criminals, reduce crime and disorder, and enhance crime prevention and evaluation (Boda, 2005; Ratcliffe, 2016). The department's command team should work closely with operational commanders to understand their informational needs and make intelligence gathering and its distribution effective. In strategic policing the process of gathering, analyzing, and acting upon timely intelligence develops the police department into a **learning organization** that assesses, evaluates, and adapts its operational responses to the demands of its environment (Senge, 1990; Walsh, 2001).

To obtain this information a department needs to create an information-gathering and processing system that will provide accurate and timely data (intelligence) about crime and community public safety issues. Data are observations and measurements about crime, disorder and alarms, persons, places, and events (Ratcliffe, 2016; Groff & Lockwood, 2014). What is needed is fluent and specific data about crime conditions and an adequate spatial analysis system which is capable of engaging and identifying local and global spatial factors that affect crime conditions (Adderley & Musgrove, 2001; Hillier, 2004). This information should be collected daily, analyzed, categorized, and mapped and disseminated to operational commanders in order to identify new or changing crime patterns or threats to public safety. All levels of the department should be involved in this process. Former Deputy Chief Jack Maple (1999, p. 97), one of the creators of NYPD's Compstat, asserts that the department's front-line officers are critical information gathers who should be trained to gather information beyond what is need to fill out reports. The ideal would be that every line officer in the department have information gathering at the forefront of his or her mind. The objective is for a department to develop enough information to provide operational commanders and administrators a clear understanding of the factors that affect current and future public safety issues and their ability to effectively respond to these driving forces.

Accurate and timely intelligence requires that administrators understand and be sensitive to the driving forces in their organizational environments (crime, politics, media, labor, economic events, employee capabilities, and issues) that impact the department and necessitate change. Strategically, they must be flexible enough to adjust organizational strategies, resource allocation, and tactics to respond to these driving forces. In order to accomplish this objective, departments need to develop the capability to gather and analyze a variety of information in order to understand the forces that affect them. The systematic gathering of information, its analysis, and evaluation of its relevance to the department's strategic objectives is the foundation of successful strategic policing. The United Kingdom's National Intelligence Model (NCPE, 2005) recommends that following analytical techniques as necessary for the basis for informed police decision making:

- *Crime pattern analysis*—trend identification and hot spot analysis.
- *Demographic/social trend analysis*—assessment of the impact of socio-economic and demographic changes on criminality as well as population shifts and homelessness.
- *Market profiles*—assessment of the criminal market for a commodity such as drugs or prostitution.
- *Criminal business profiles*—used to determine and understand the business model and techniques employed by offenders or organized crime groups.
- *Risk analysis*—accesses the scale of risks or threat posed by offenders or organizations to individual potential victims, police, and the public.
- *Target profiles analysis*—to understand the lifestyles, networks, criminal activities, and potential interdiction points in the life of a targeted offender.

- *Operational intelligence assessment*—evaluation of information collection to inform decision-making about existing operation.
- *Results analysis*—process used to evaluate the effectiveness of law enforcement activities.

One way to achieve this is for the department to continually monitor and analyze the department's operational demand, changing environment, and response capabilities. It makes sense that when police departments make decisions and act on relevant information and analysis, their organization's effectiveness will increase. Operational tactics developed through Compstat crime strategy meetings, for example, are based upon information that has been analyzed and integrated into a comprehensive format that can be used as the basis for police resource allocation and deployment. Strategic policing is based upon a structured way for gathering and analyzing relevant information to support operational decisions (Henry, 2002). This analysis should go beyond current situations and carefully assess the underlying causes of emerging public safety trends so that new and better ways to respond to these factors can be identified (Goldstein, 1990).

The department's analysis of its environment is a proactive instead of a reactive approach to organizational leadership. It is a process that leads to an understanding of the demands that are and will affect a department in the present and in the future. The driving forces that exist in a department's environment can affect a department's ability to achieve its mission, overcome performance problems, and be valued by the community it serves. These driving forces are often complex and usually are the result of a variety of factors. For example, the police shooting of 18-year-old Michael Brown in August 2014 in Ferguson, Missouri, generated clashes between the police and demonstrators that mirrored past, larger-scale riots in multiple U.S. cities. These demonstrations reflected long-held feelings of perceived racial injustice as well as strongly held views of policing and our justice system that transcended the incident and generated demands that were out of control of the local police department (Holland, 2014).

Defining the Environment

An organization's environment is defined as the internal and external elements that have the potential to affect all or part of the department's ability to fulfill its mission. Organizational leaders who have a clear understanding of their environment are better able to focus their department's resources on critical areas that demand its attention. This intelligence allows managers to align their department's internal capacity with its external demands. *Strategic alignment* is the linking of an organization's internal resources, capabilities, strategy, and tactics with the demands of its external environment. The goal is to achieve effectiveness and realization of desired outcomes through the strategic management of people, processes, and inputs (Kaplan & Norton, 2006). While some police managers may feel comfortable with their own subjective capacity to intuitively diagnose the agency's problems, a far more realistic and beneficial approach is for the leadership team to support their experiential insights with factual data obtained thorough systematic analysis.

Strategic alignment requires the development of data and analysis that enhances management's understanding of their department's operational capabilities, as well as its opportunities, and threats. A standard information-generating device used in strategic business

FIGURE 6.1 Strategic Management Process

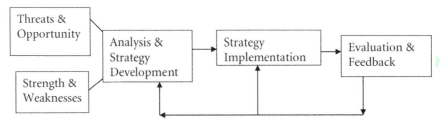

organizations is the **SWOT** assessment. It is an information-gathering technique conducted to provide information that will assist in identifying the organization's operational strengths and weaknesses as well as its opportunities and threats. Strengths and weaknesses are *internal factors* that constitute the capability of the organization to respond to its present and future demands. Opportunities and threats are *external factors* that increase demands for public safety and services that affect the value of the department to the community (Bryson, 2011). The purpose of this analysis is to identify those critical areas of service demand and potential problems that the department must respond to in order to maintain its effectiveness and efficiency.

Police departments do not function in isolation; they are affected by a variety of driving forces in their environment. These factors must be identified and understood so that a department's objectives, and tactics, can be assessed and revisited based on their relevance to changing demands. The task of evaluating strategic effectiveness and initiating corrective adjustments is both the end and the beginning of the strategic administration cycle (Thompson & Strickland, 1998). **Strategic management** is the process of formulating, implementing, and evaluating strategies that enable the organization to achieve its objectives (Schermerhorn, 2005). (See Figure 6.1.)

A properly conducted strategic assessment is similar to constructing a balance sheet where organizational strengths and opportunities represent assets and organizational weaknesses and threats represent liabilities. This activity is based upon the managerial principle that effective strategy making must aim at producing a good fit between a department's capability and its external demands. The department's leadership needs a clear understanding of its capabilities, its deficiencies, external opportunities, and threats they are facing. Otherwise, the task of conceiving strategy and setting direction becomes at best a chancy proposition based upon subjective guesswork and is doomed to fail.

Internal Capability

An organization's internal capability consists of key functions (**strengths**) a department does well or an organizational asset that provides enhanced ability to achieve objectives and mission fulfillment. Analyzing a department's capabilities will lead to the identification of the organization's **core competencies**. These are the areas that the department has or does exceptionally well. For example, they may include having close positive relationships with minority community leaders, motivated patrol officers, expertise in crime scene processing, good crime prevention tactics, crime analysis techniques, and investigative skill sets. These competencies are part of the department's knowledge base that has developed through experiential learning, training, education, and creation of employee skill sets. They are capabilities that are rare, difficult to develop, and are not easily replaced because of the advantage they give the organization (Prahalad & Hamel, 1990).

Organizational capabilities can take any of several forms such as:

- **Human capital**—The quality of a department's employees measured in terms of their knowledge, education, training, skills, expertise, and performance accomplishments. For example, the department is noted for having well-trained, committed, and motivated employees serving in key operational areas. Technological expertise and training enhances employees' ability to provide quality service to the community (Dessler, 2012). The department's investigators perform at a high level that is reflected in a very favorable clearance rate.

- **Physical assets**—A department's physical plant, equipment, vehicles, state-of-the-art computer hardware, and technology create a sense of organizational pride and assist the work process. Physical systems are evaluated, maintained, and updated on a regular basis.

- **Leadership**—Managerial knowledge, development, leadership skills, and/or the collective learning and expertise of the leadership team are all strengths. The department's mission and values are supported by all employees. Executive management mentors and develops employees who are identified as future leaders.

- **Valuable intangible assets**—The department's value as observed from the community's perspective. Value is assessed in terms of department's reputation, employee loyalty, positive work climate, community orientation, citizen support, cooperative managerial team, organizational culture, learning processes, and its ability to provide a safe community. The department has earned a high level of trust from the citizens it serves.

The capacity of a department to successfully respond to the demands of the external environment can take a variety of forms. They may be specific skills and/or expertise. For example, the ability of the command staff to create crime strategy meetings that bring a variety of internal resources together to engage in problem identification, analysis, and response. The regularity with which employees from different parts of the organization engage in teamwork; support each other; pool their knowledge, expertise, and skills in solving problems and achieving organizational performance goals are prime strengths. The effectiveness of this collaborative effort can create performance levels not otherwise achievable by a single unit. Taken together, a department's skills and expertise, its leadership, its collection of assets, its capabilities, and its achievements determine its ability to deliver services and respond to changing external demands.

When conducting a strategic assessment managers can evaluate a department's capabilities by observing them in action and measuring their impact. For example, the operational activities and tactics the department uses to achieve its goals and objectives should be monitored and evaluated as to their implementation and outcomes. Dedication and motivation of employees can be evaluated by observing the manner by which they perform their day-to-day work-related activities, noting how many employees are willing and able to achieve a high level of accomplishment in the performance of their duties. These assessments must be both objective and realistic. It is common for some managers to say, "Our employees are dedicated" or "Our community-based operations are the best" without offering any concrete evidence or data to support this assessment. In order for the strategic assessment to have validity, all evaluative statements should be backed up with hard evidence. Objective data speaks loud and clear as to what is actually happening.

Anything that detracts from the department's ability to perform its mission is a disadvantage (*weakness*) that must be addressed. Examples are inadequate management practices such as failing to hold employees accountable, lack of leadership development, failure to provide direction, poor decision making or problem solving, high turnover rate and poor morale. It may be something a department lacks like a crime analysis capability, does inadequately such as recruitment and training, or a condition that puts it at a disadvantage such as budget reductions, low wages, and a poor benefits package. Any one of these will have the potential to affect the department's ability to maintain effectiveness and fulfill its mission.

Once a department's internal capabilities are identified, they need to be carefully evaluated by the leadership team. The importance of each factor should be determined by its impact on the department's ability to respond to external demands and fulfill organizational priorities. Some weaknesses may prove fatal to the department over time if they are not addressed such as a failure to recruit quality employees. Employee quality directly affects the department's current and future capability to fulfill its mission and earn the community's support. Others may be easily corrected or offset by the department's strengths. For example, employee ability can be enhanced by a properly developed and conducted training program. The degree to which any of these factors affect a department's ability to fulfill its mission and delivery services determines its *criticality rating.* This rating is a numerical assessment with an assigned rating range from 1 (low criticality) to 5 (high criticality) for each factor based upon an evaluation of its organizational impact. Areas of high criticality need to be addressed quickly by the department's executive team.

External Demand

The purpose of an external assessment is to examine the environment outside the department and to identify the opportunities and threats that exist there. This assessment seeks to develop information that will identify factors in the external environment that affect the department's ability to serve the community. These factors involve crime, community, economic, political, legal, social-demographic, or technological issues. This information should be systematically complied, analyzed, collated, mapped, and disseminated to the department's administrative and operational commanders. This process is the basis for the creation of the intelligence data that will be the foundation for the development of operational strategies and tactics in strategic policing. Ratcliffe (2003) suggests that the application of information analysis should be used as a rigorous decision-making tool to facilitate crime reduction and prevention through effective policing strategies. It is an analytically driven objective process based upon hard data instead of the intuitive managerial feelings.

Identifying and paying attention to external demands coupled with ongoing intelligence gathering, external relationship building. and stakeholder analysis can identify areas and trends to which the department will need to respond. Stakeholder information can be obtained through newspaper analysis, community surveys, call back programs, and community dialogue meetings. This information can also be used to identify potential organizational success factors (Avinash & Nalebuff, 1991). It is important to remember that external factors are not under organizational control, while internal factors normally are.

Success factors are the things a department must do or the areas it must pay attention to for it to excel in addressing the demands of its external environment. These include such activities as assessment of crime conditions, crime control, identification of special population issues, planning for and management of special events, traffic control, crises and risk management, building public trust, obtaining political support for the department, relations with the courts and prosecutor's office, and media image. Paying attention to these factors and responding to them appropriately enhances the value of the department in the eyes of its community and stakeholders. Thus, external indicators can serve as benchmarks for identifying the relative position and reputation of the police organization in the eyes of citizens as well as the law enforcement profession (Moore et al., 2002).

An external environmental scan should always pay specific attention to "**stakeholders**." Stakeholders are persons who have a direct interest in what is done by the department (e.g., citizens of the community, community leaders and spokespersons, local government organizations, and elected officials). This definition should be considered in the broadest possible terms. The concept of stakeholders is not limited to those outside the department; all members of the police organization are also included in this definition because they have a direct interest in what the department does. Managers must decide who to involve, how to involve them, and how to solicit input from those who are not directly involved in daily contact with the department but are important to the mission of the department. Organizational executives must receive input from and consider the effect of their decisions and operations on their stakeholders. This is part of the political nature of the police executive's role (Osborne & Plastrik, 1997).

In addition to demand factors there are conditions, people, organizations, or situations in the external environment that can or will work to the department's benefit or advantage. Examples of these are positive political relationships, a supportive city manager, community partnerships, organizational partnerships, cooperative ventures, a good local employment pool, economy, and educational support systems. The factors most relevant to a department are those that offer support and aid toward mission fulfillment and organizational effectiveness. Those factors that can enable a department to advance beyond the limits of its internal constraints and achieve professional benefit must be identified and taken advantage of.

Corporate sponsorship of training scholarships for the development of department employees is one example. Annually, the International Association of Chiefs of Police awards the Michael Shanahan Award for Excellence in Public/Private Cooperation to recognize an agency's outstanding achievement in the development and implementation of public/private cooperation in public safety. Outreach and dialogue with representatives of new immigrant groups to promote mutual understanding is another example of developing information and knowledge about potential service demand.

Threat factors are external forces that threaten, or will threaten, the effectiveness and capability of the department. These can be in the form of increases in violent crime, potential crisis, competition from other police agencies for personnel, civil unrest, tax revenue shortfalls and community/political pressure groups, increased drug trafficking, political interference, community quality-of-life conditions, and organized criminal activity. External threats may pose no more than a moderate degree of hardship, or they may be so imposing as to make a department's capability and outlook quite weak. Management's task is to identify threats to the department's present and future status, prioritize these as to the criticality of their potential effect on the department, and then decide on what strategic actions should be taken to neutralize or lessen their impact.

Departments need to focus on external factors whose indicators exhibit they will become potential problems. These indicators need to be monitored. When patterns of criminal activity indicate an acceleration of incidences, appropriate response strategies must be developed and implemented. As part of its ongoing threat analysis function, police departments should have a crime analysis unit capable of providing an assessment of the broader patterns and ecology of community crime trends. Threat analysis requires that the department develop the capability to rapidly identify and understand the broader trends of criminal behavior in order to develop an effective crime control capability.

A basic premise of strategic police management is that a department should formulate strategies to take advantage of opportunities and strengths to overcome or reduce the impact of threats and weaknesses. For this reason, gathering intelligence, identifying, monitoring, and evaluating external opportunities and threats are essential to the success of the department's efforts.

A strategic analysis is therefore more than an exercise in making lists. In addition to identification of demand factors, it involves evaluating a department's response capabilities and drawing conclusions about how best to deploy its resources in light of the department's internal and external situation. Analysis of the above factors and prioritization of their impact on the department constitutes the beginning of both a strategic analysis and planning process.

Analyzing the Internal Environment

Diagnosing an organization's capacity to respond to its environmental demands requires that the executive team and all unit managers use their analytical skills to evaluate their organization's operational capability. Organizational performance issues are often complex, changing, and ambiguous. It is more advantageous to analyze organizational capacity by using different frames of reference as diagnostic tools. A frame of reference is an analytical tool that can be used by managers to evaluate an organizational element (Daft, 2002).

Described below are five frames of reference that managers can use to diagnose an organization's internal capacity (Bolmam & Deal, 1991). Each frame identifies a specific reference point and its core components. When these frames of reference are used together, they form an analytical framework that can be used to evaluate the organization or a specific performance problem as a whole. They provide the evaluator with a complete set of analytical perspectives that can be used to identify and evaluate the variety of factors that contribute to an understanding of internal organization.

Frames of Reference

Structural Frame

The Structural Frame's focus is the form and design of the organization. Its primary concern is how the organization and its subunits are structured, fit and synchronize their work to achieve the department's mission. Large-scale police departments are structurally complex because they combine a centralized authority system with a variety of specialized units. Smaller organizations tend to be more generalist in nature and thus less of a diverse structure. Structural analysis assesses the relationship between performance and organizational structural elements such as mission, goals, objectives, chain of command, span of control, unit size, formal roles, task specialization, job descriptions, unit outcome objectives and measures, policy and procedures. It should be remembered that organizational structure is a tool created to accomplish the mission, not blocks of unchanging granite once formed and never changed.

Organizational structures develop as the result of the need to accomplish a variety of tasks to fulfill the department's mission. It changes as police executives seek to find solutions to organizational problems through creation or disbanding of operational units. As the responsibilities of organizations and the external demands they confront become complex and grow, specialization increases and organizational divisions and subunits are created. This development can be haphazard and result in inefficient organizational structures, overlapping of responsibilities, and lack of strategic alignment if it is not periodically evaluated.

A common misconception of some administrators is their belief that the way to improve organizational performance is simply a matter of creating standardized operating procedures. This perspective perceives the organization as a rational, objective, orderly system that can be controlled exclusively through policy and procedures (Morgan, 1997). Departments of this type often evolve into command and control dominated organizations. Their internal structure becomes etched in stone and emerges as the primary organizational control mechanism. It is a serious matter if the chain of command is violated or procedures are challenged. Unfortunately, this is not realistic and hinders the way these organizations respond to the complex demands of their environment.

Today's law enforcement organizations face a fluid external environment that demands flexibility in organizational arrangement and strategy. A prime example of this new reality is the development of multijurisdictional task forces, cross-functional units, and special purpose units to address mutual public safety issues that cross jurisdictional boundaries.

Organizations that exist in a stable environment or have a singular purpose, with highly specific and measurable goals, are able to structure themselves tightly through written procedures and detailed check lists (e.g., McDonalds Corporation, prisons, and jails). The objective of this type of organizational structure is to control error and ensure a uniform product is produced. A Big Mac should be the same product in Akron, Ohio, as well as in Miami, Florida. However, the service area problems faced by police officers in these two cities are varied and diverse, demanding different strategies and tactics by their police departments. Environmental analysis, operational flexibility, and commander empowerment are essential for organizations to address changing conditions and threats. Unit structures will need to change over the life of an organization. Organizational leaders who fail to understand this run the risk of their organizations becoming stagnant and ineffective.

The use of the structural frame of reference as an analytical tool requires that managers seek to identify and analyze the structural factors that impact positively or negatively on the department's performance. If structural changes are required, these must be considered in relation to their impact on the organization's effectiveness and the other frames of reference. For example, a change in operational tactics may require employee input, retraining, a change of supervisors, and acceptable methods of performance.

It is a common practice when a crisis or a threatening incident occurs for some managers to call for reorganization, more rules, and centralization of decision making in order to restore their control. However, too much reliance on rules, procedures, and managerial control can create a rule-bound organization. In this type of organization, people do not engage in problem solving and creative decision making; they follow the rules. They continue to meet current operational problems with the standard operating procedures designed to resolve past issues. These organizations maintain their status quo and remain locked in the past.

Insufficient understanding of the structural factors can result in role confusion, duplication of effort, conflict, and costly mistakes. A balance must be achieved between the need for structure and the need for organizational flexibility. The manner in which a manager creates this balance is one of personal choice based upon need, experience, and analysis of the realities of the organizational situation. Remember organizations are not blocks of granite cemented together but tools to accomplish a mission (purpose). A way to address this problem is to start with the identification of what is to be accomplished and then restructure the organization to achieve this outcome. Below are a number of questions that will assist in conducting a structural analysis.

STRUCTURAL FRAME ANALYTICAL FACTORS CHECK LIST

Is the department (unit's) **Mission** clear and understood?
Have **Goals and Objectives** been **clearly** defined?
Are **Measures of Performance** defined and understood?
Does our current **Structure** contribute to mission accomplishment?
Has **Accountability** been clearly established in policy, job descriptions, and reality?
Are **Job Descriptions** clear and current?
Has **Position-Based Authority** been established?
Is the **Chain of Command** appropriate?
Is the **Span of Control** appropriate?
Is there a current **Policy** or does it need to be written?
Are the operating **Procedures** clear?
Are outcomes being **Measured and Evaluated?**

Human Resource Frame

The analytical focus of the **Human Resource Frame** is the department's management of its personnel resources and polices. This frame of reference is treated more in depth in Chapter 9 of this text. Human resource management is a critical factor in creating and maintaining organizational effectiveness. Police departments can do many things right, but if they hire the wrong people, do not prepare employees to perform properly or motivate them, they will not be effective employees. People produce results. The human resource perspective requires that a good fit be made between the organization's objectives and the people required to achieve them.

Today, there is a growing emphasis on "knowledge workers" and the importance of human capital. A **knowledge worker** is someone whose mind is a critical asset to the organization (Drucker, 1988). In strategic policing it signifies how officers think, use, analyze information, and engage in problem solving. Their performance is a product of how well they apply the core body of knowledge of policing in their daily tasks. **Human capital** refers to the quality of the knowledge, education, training, skills, and expertise of an organization's employees (Dessler, 2007). This is a qualitative assessment of the department's employees' skill set and intellectual abilities. On a regular basis strategic organizations actively modify their performance to reflect new knowledge, insights, and assessment of environmental driving forces (Senge 1990). These departments analyze the variety of situations they confront, encourage their employees to practice independent problem solving, and apply a diverse body of technical and analytical skills to resolve the driving forces that affect them. Organizations who seek to engage in strategic policing must actively develop the intellectual capabilities, information usage, and skill sets of their employees to accomplish their objectives. In strategic focused police organizations, effectiveness depends more on the intellectual capabilities of their employees than any other factor.

Police employees apply a complex body of knowledge in their work. This knowledge base is obtained through continuous education, training, occupational experience, and information analysis. Knowledge workers are self-starters who engage in continuous learning. They place a great emphasis on their competency and professional accomplishments (Schermerhorn, 2005). Thus, a critical executive skill is the ability to manage the human intellect and convert it into productive organizational activities (Walsh, 1998). A core belief of this frame of reference is that people who feel they are prepared to engage in meaningful work and are respected in the workplace will give their knowledge, talent, and commitment to their organization. This frame of reference focuses managerial attention to the **competency, commitment**, and **teamwork** of their people.

Leadership, management style, job analysis, employee selection, education, training, placement, empowerment, personnel and organizational development, networking, consultation, employee involvement, relationships, and self-managed work teams are analytical elements of this frame of reference. However, it should be remembered that employees are not the only source of organizational problems and/or solutions. Managers will often blame organizational problems on poor selection, employee motivation, lowered standards, or poor training. They fail to recognize that the human element is but one factor contributing to problematic conditions. The dominance of these beliefs can lead managers into believing that all their problems can be resolved through changing employees, discipline, or training. Unfortunately, it is never that easy.

Every organizational manager from the chief (CEO) to the sergeant (line management) is responsible for the competency, commitment, and development of their employees. Mentoring, counseling, training, and developing employees are basic managerial tasks. Management failure to address human resource needs can lead to incompetent employees, diminished creativity, little if any commitment, and communication breakdowns. Managers that treat their employees badly and with little regard will develop a conflicting or combative workforce that can make the lives of all involved miserable. Organizations that experience this form of conflict often break into warring camps that are divided into management versus operational personnel, them and us, line and staff (Reuss-Inanni, 1983). They become organizations in crisis.

A primary responsibility of a department's leadership team is to institute human resource policies and practices that produce employees with the competencies and commitment capable of achieving the department's goals and objectives. The following are several questions that will assist in a human resource analysis.

HUMAN RESOURCE FRAME ANALYTICAL FACTORS CHECK LIST

What kind of **leadership** style does this organization, and/or strategy need?
What type of **people** should be **selected** for this assignment?
What are our employee's **competency levels**?
How **committed** are our employees?
What type of **training and development** do our employees need?
How should our people **be developed** for the department's future needs?
How should individual performance be **evaluated?**
How should **unit performance** be evaluated?
How much **empowerment and discretion** should employees have?
How do our employees **communicate** between themselves and others?
What kind of **teamwork** exists in this organization?

Political Frame

Politics and conflict are a normal reality of organizational life. Different groups and individuals within organizations develop agendas to satisfy their own needs and wants. In many organizations powerful vested interests will resist any change that affects them. The more likely change becomes, the more fiercely and vocal these negative influencers will fight to protect their positions (Kim & Mauborgne, 2003). The political frame of reference identifies and analyzes conflicting groups and individuals who are competing with each other for power and control within and without a department. Its focus is the manner in which people use power, build alliances, and engage in conflict and either hinder or assist the department to achieve its mission.

This frame of reference emphasizes that managers should clearly understand the political context and power networks of their organizations. They need to identify the individuals internally and externally who hold positions that will affect the accomplishment of organizational goals and objectives and understand their impact on the organization. Managers need to know how to productively confront, use, and manage power and conflict. Conflict analysis, tactics of conflict creation and/or control and power are tools that can be used to resolve interpersonal and organizational problems. Organizational conflict must be managed before it involves the breakdown or disruption of normal operational activities to a point where individuals or groups experience real difficulty in working with one another (More, Vito, & Walsh, 2012).

Power is the ability to influence the behavior and attitudes of others (Luthans, 2002). Individuals hold power because of their positional authority, individual expertise, control of rewards and punishments, alliances and networks, control of organizational symbols, and personal attributes. Knowing how to use power is a skill that managers should develop if they wish to be successful. However, using power inappropriately can result in failure for both the organization and the manager.

Conflict is not always destructive and it does not always have to be resolved. Conflict can be used as a tool to force employees to face a situation or problem, deal with it, and develop innovative approaches to problem solving. It can be used to challenge the status quo and reduce complacency. If conflict is a normal organizational occurrence, then managers must understand it and learn to use it to their advantage Afzalur (2002).

It is also important to remember that one does not have to be in a position of authority to have power and influence over others. There are many individuals within and without organizations who possess different power bases that they use to affect the ability of others to achieve their goals. Individuals who understand and use power best will see their ideas implemented and their influence extend beyond their immediate area of control. Constructive use of power is necessary for the creation of effective organizations.

Managers who fail to understand the Political Frame of Reference will be ignoring an important aspect of organizational life. However, overuse of power as a management tool will increase conflict and prevent task accomplishment. It can lead people to feel they are being manipulated or devalued and result in their being cynical, pessimistic, and combative. Managers are often expected to balance and manage inevitable trade-offs and to equitably negotiate and integrate their organization's interests with those of others within and without the organization (Buchanan, 2008). Accomplishing this task requires expertise (technical knowledge), analytic ability (critical thinking), interpersonal and group dynamics skills (personal power). Network-building and team-building skills have become a necessity for managerial effectiveness because of the complexity of many contemporary organizations and the demands placed on them by stakeholders (Schermerhorn, 2005).

The first step in developing successful work relationships is to identify those individuals who hold power and resources inside and outside the organization. Next is to determine what differences and similarities exist between the people whose cooperation is needed by the manager; for example, differences in goals, values, position, pressure, and working styles. Then try to understand what the basis of these differences and similarities are so that the relationship with the person needed to accomplish objectives can be strengthened.

Effective managers consider those on whom they are dependent as potential allies, even when they may at first appear to be adversaries. Unofficial and informal networks evolve within organizations as employees develop methods to work together, achieve goals and objectives. These networks are often based upon the **exchange theory** that involves employees bargaining for assistance, resources, and information needed to accomplish their jobs and is the basis of this exchange. Thus, mutually beneficial alliances are developed between individuals by their identifying what each exchange member might have to offer that they need or want (Stojkovic et al., 2012). The basis for network building is the **law of reciprocity**; that is, that one good deed deserves another. The primary way managers extend their influence through networks is by providing resources, information, and services to others in exchange for resources, services, and information they require. The Political Frame check list below contains a number of questions that will assist with this analysis.

POLITICAL FRAME ANALYTICAL FACTORS CHECK LIST

How is power **distributed and used** in the organization?
Who are the **power holders** in this organization?

Who are the important **stakeholders outside** of the organization?
Whose **cooperation** is needed?
Whose **compliance** is needed?
What are the **conflict relationships** that exist within this organization?
What are the **sources of conflict**?
What **networks** should be developed?

Cultural Frame

An organization's shared values, beliefs, assumptions, perceptions, norms, artifacts, and accepted ways of behaving make up its culture (Ott, 1989). An organization's culture is passed from one generation of employees to another one through stories, rituals, myths, and day-today conversations. A department's history and traditions are the source of these stories, values, rituals, and myths. They form the basis of the department's belief system about how one should act as a member of the organization. The importance of an organization's culture is that it provides a sense of meaning and purpose for the way employees look at, attempt to understand, and work within their everyday world.

The critical point of analysis within this frame of reference is not the actual behavior of people but what the behavior means to the members of the organization involved. The reasons why people act in a specific manner can be found in their values and the meanings they attach to their behavior. These beliefs, values, and acceptable modes of behavior are learned through the process of organizational socialization and are often expressed as rationalizations for behavior.

Managers who understand the importance of culture appreciate the power of an organization's vision, values, rituals, ceremonies, and stories. They use these to create a set of shared beliefs that help to shape their department's self-image. Many police organizations have developed strong organizational cultures based on meaningful rituals, traditions, and visions of what is their actual function. Organizational symbols can also be used to camouflage or distort. The certified police officer may be incompetent because of a lack of training after the certification was originally achieved. The training officer may give out test questions and answers during mandatory training sessions. The organization that states "Our People Come First" in its value statement might actually treat their workers terribly. There may be one set of rules and behavioral boundaries for managers and another for employees. The "mission statement" on the wall may mean nothing at all. All of which can create a culture of distrust and conflict within an organization.

Organizations have been described as having two stages—one in front and one in the back of the curtain that divides them from the public (Goffman, 1959; Manning, 1997). The front stage projects the image the department wants to display to outsiders. They want outsiders to believe this is the real organization. However, only insiders, the organization's employees, get to see and know the real world hidden backstage—what the organization truly is and how it operates behind the front stage. In well-managed ethical organizations, there should be little difference between these two stages but in organizations that lack integrity and ethical accountability, there is a vast difference between the two.

For example, Sex Crimes and Special Victims Units are created by departments to handle the investigation of all rapes and attempted rapes, sexual batteries, and cases of a sexual nature. The Special Victims Section of the City of New Orleans Police Department consists of the Sex Crimes Unit, the Child Abuse Unit, and the Domestic Violence Unit. An investigation conducted by the City of New Orleans Office of Inspector General found that the department's investigators assigned to the Special Victims Section had questionable documentation for investigations. Detectives ignored reports of sex crimes, failed to follow up on reported sexual abuse cases, and routinely failed to provide documentation of sexual investigations, often writing up questionable case files. According to the report of the 1,290 sex crime incidents assigned to the unit's five detectives, from 2011 to 2013 only 179 (14%) included supplemental reports showing that they were properly pursued and investigated. In 450 cases with initial investigative reports filed by the detectives, 271 (60%) did not include documents showing that there was any additional follow-up (Quatrevaux, 2014). This report disclosed the huge discrepancy of what this unit was created to do and what it actually did.

For change to take place in an organization, managers must understand its cultural values and whether or not these could support behavior such as what was disclosed by the New Orleans Inspector General's report. However, this can be difficult for insiders to do because their organization's cultural system is very much a part of their psychological makeup. Organizational change agents must be able to stand outside of their organization's cultural value system, analyze it, and understand from without if their intervention is to succeed. Remember from a cultural perspective, what is real is real, whether in fact it is real or not.

CULTURAL FRAME ANALYTICAL FACTORS CHECK LIST

What is the true **vision of this organization** and its members?
What are the **values, beliefs, history, and traditions** of this organization?
What **image (front and back stage)** does the organization present?
How are **accountability and ethics maintained** in the organization?
What are the **acceptable modes of behavior** in the organization?
What **values drive employee performance**?
Is there a different **ethical standard** for managers and officers?

Technology Frame

This frame of reference's focus is the manner in which information is obtained and processed. Organizational technology refers to the tools or processes used by organizations to transform data and raw information into useful and actionable intelligence. This information becomes the basis for strategic decision making, strategy development, and the deployment of personnel and resources. Intelligence is not simply the collection of information; it is what is produced after the collected data is evaluated and analyzed (Peterson, 2005).

Operational managers, supervisors and officers, investigators and special unit officers should be trained to gather, receive, and disseminate time-sensitive and accurate crime and community problem information. This information is the foundation for crime analysis, strategy development, and outcome evaluation. The ability to make effective use of timely and accurate intelligence is linked to the department's technology systems that are used to collate, analyze, and present raw crime data. Teamwork and systems thinking should be employed between operational commanders, crime analysts, investigators, supervisors and officers. They must work together to make intelligence gathering and distribution effective. For example, the primary data component of NYPD's Compstat is a data base that contains daily crime counts, by precinct for seven major crimes. In order to gain timely information and intelligence about these crimes in New York City, the department's executive team required every precinct to create its own "crime information center" to collate information on crime events, their location, suspects and fugitives (Henry, 2002; Maple & Mitchell, 1999).

We exist in a technological age. Information gathering and processing is the lifeblood of an effective organization. Failure to engage the organization's environment in a structured manner to gain **accurate and timely intelligence** and to employ technology (tools/process, GIS systems) to process this information and to distribute it to those who need it will eventually victimize the organization and result in mission failure.

TECHNOLOGY FRAME ANALYTICAL FACTORS CHECK LISTS

What are our **information needs?**
Where do we obtain this **information? (Sources)**
How will this **information be processed?**
Who needs this information?
Who will be responsible for it?
When do they need it?
How will it be **distributed** to those who need it?
What do our **management information systems** tell us?
How is information used to **solve problems**?
What **technology** do we have and need?

Conclusion

Taken together the analytical tools described in this chapter can be employed by police administrators to analyze the environmental forces affecting their organization. Strategic analysis can provide timely information and differing perspectives and understanding of these forces. The subtlety is finding the right balance between the external and internal elements. Changes in one area inevitably reverberate through the other areas. Factors such as strengths or weakness that affect one frame of reference, if ignored, may distort or undermine the analysis. The process described above is an example of "**systems thinking**," because its focus is the whole organizational environment instead of its isolated parts (Senge, 1990). System thinkers strive to understand all the factors that affect their organization and how these relate to their problem-solving analysis as a whole. They are not fragmented thinkers but individuals who know and understand the interconnectivity of the many factors that affect their organization. In strategic policing all department managers should be system thinkers. The concept underlying this type of thinking is the understanding that nothing in the organization stands alone, it must always be considered part of a greater whole. Organizations are complex systems that involve a number of intertwined parts. The separate parts of the system do not exist nor function in isolation from each other. Managers need to understand the pattern of relationships that exist within and without their total organization and how these impact on their ability to function effectively (Banner & Gagne, 1995). An event in one part of the system can and often does have system-wide effects. Thus, managers must understand and learn to reinforce or change these relationships effectively. Unfortunately, managers usually focus on isolated parts of the organizational system instead and then wonder why their efforts at solving problems and effecting change fail.

KEY TERMS

Accurate and timely intelligence	Knowledge worker	Strategic management
Commitment	Law of reciprocity	Strength
Competency	Leadership	Structural Frame
Core competencies	Learning organization	Success factors
Cultural Frame	Physical assets	SWOT
Exchange theory	Political Frame	Systems thinking
Frames of Reference	Power	Teamwork
Human capital	Stakeholders	Technology Frame
Human Resource Frame	Strategic alignment	Threat factors
	Strategic analysis	Valuable intangible assets

References

Adderley, R.W., & Musgrove, P. (2001). Police crime recording and investigation systems. *Policing, 24*(1), 100–114.

Afzalur, R.M. (2002). Toward a theory of managing organizational conflict. *International Journal of Conflict Management, 13*(3), 206–235.

Avinash, D., & Nalebuff, B.J. (1991). *Thinking strategically: The competitive edge in business, politics, and everyday life.* New York: W.W. Norton & Co.

Banner, D.K., & Gagne, E.T. (1995). *Designing effective organizations: Traditional and transformational views.* Thousand Oaks, CA: Sage.

Boda, R. (2005). *Crime analysis and crime mapping.* Thousand Oaks, CA: Sage.

Bolmam, L.G., & Deal, T.E. (1991). *Reframing organizations: Artistry, choice, and leadership.* San Francisco, CA: Jossey-Bass Inc.

Bryson, J.M. (2011). *Strategic planning for public and nonprofit organizations: A guide to strengthening and sustaining organizational achievement,* 4th ed. San Francisco, CA: Jossey-Bass.

Buchanan, D.A. (2008). You stab my back, I'll stab yours: Management experience and perceptions of organization political behaviour. *British Journal of Management, 19*(1), 49–64.

Cope, N. (2004, March). Intelligence led policing or policing led intelligence? *The British Journal of Criminology, 44*(2), 188–203.

Daft, R.L. (2002). *The leadership experience*, 2nd ed. Orlando, FL: Harcourt.

Dessler, G. (2007). *Human resource management*, 11th ed. Upper Saddle River, NJ: Pearson Prentice Hall.

Dessler, G. (2012). *A framework for human resource management*, 7th ed. Upper Saddle River, NJ: Pearson Prentice Hall.

Drucker, P. (1988, January–February). The coming of the new organization. *Harvard Business Review*, 45–53.

Goffman, E. (1959). *The presentation of self in everyday life*. New York: Doubleday.

Goldstein, H. (1990). *Problem-oriented policing*. New York: McGraw Hill.

Groff, E.R., & Lockwood, B. (2014). Criminogenic facilities and crime across street segments in Philadelphia: Uncovering evidence about the spatial extent of facility influence. *Journal of Research in Crime and Delinquency, 51*(3), 277–314.

Henry, V.E. (2002). *The Compstat paradigm: Management accountability in policing*. New York: Looseleaf Law Pub.

Holland, S. (2014). *Obama on Ferguson: U.S. "has more work to do" on race relations*. Washington, DC, www.Reuters.org.

Hillier, B. (2004). Can streets be made safe? *Urban Design International, 9*(1), 31–45.

Kaplan, R., & Norton, D. (2006). *Alignment: Using the balanced scorecard to create corporate synergies*. Boston, MA: Harvard Business Press.

Kim, W.C., & Mauborgne, R. (2003, April). Tipping point leadership. *Harvard Business Review*, 60–69.

Luthans, F. (2002). *Organizational behavior*, 9th ed. New York: McGraw-Hill.

Manning, P.K. (1997). *Police work: The social organization of policing*, 2nd ed. Long Grove, IL: Waveland.

Maple, J., & Mitchell, C. (1999). *The crime fighter*. New York: Doubleday.

Moore, M., Thacher, D., Dodge, A., & Moore, T. (2002). *Recognizing value in policing: The challenge of measuring police performance*. Washington, DC: Police Executive Research Forum.

More, H.W., Vito, G.F., & Walsh, W.F. (2012). *Organizational behavior and management in law enforcement*. Upper Saddle River, NJ: Prentice Hall.

Morgan, G. (1997). *Images of organization*, 2nd ed. Thousand Oaks, CA: Sage.

NCPE. (2005). *Guidance on the national intelligence model*. Wyboston, UK: National Center for Policing Excellence on behalf of ACPO.

Osborne, D., & Plastrik, P. (1997). *Banishing bureaucracy: The five strategies for reinventing government*. Reading, MA: Addison-Wesley.

O'Shea, T., & Nicholls, K. (2003). Police crime analysis: A survey of US police departments with 100 or more sworn personnel. *Police Practice and Research, 4*(3), 233–250.

Ott, J.S. (1989). *The organizational culture perspective*. Pacific Grove, CA: Brooks Cole.

Peterson, M. (2005). *Intelligence-led policing: The new intelligence architecture*. Washington, DC: Bureau of Justice Assistance.

Prahalad, C.K., & Hamel, G. (1990, May–June). The core competencies of the corporation. *Harvard Business Review*, 79–91.

Quatrevaux, E.R. (2014). *A performance audit of the New Orleans police department's uniform crime reporting of forcible rapes*. Baton Rouge, LA: Office of Inspector General.

Ratcliffe, J. (2003). Intelligence-led policing. *Trends and Issues in Crime and Criminal Justice*, No. 248. Canberra: Australian Institute of Criminology, www.aic.gov.au/.

Ratcliffe, J. (2016). *Intelligence-led policing*, 2nd ed. New York: Routledge.

Reuss-Ianni, E. (1983). *Two cultures of policing: Street cops and management cops*. New Brunswick, NJ: Transaction Books.

Schermerhorn, J.R. (2005). *Management*, 8th ed. New York, NY: John Wiley.

Senge, P.M. (1990). *The fifth discipline: The art & practice of the learning organization*. New York: Doubleday.

Stojkovic, S., Kalinich, D., & Klofas, J. (2012). *Criminal justice organization: Administration and management*, 5th ed. Belmont, CA: Wadsworth.

Sun-Tzu (1994). *The art of war* (Trans. Ralph D. Sawyer). New York: Barnes & Noble, p. 215.

Thompson, Jr. A., & Strickland, A.J. (1998). *Strategic management concepts and cases*. New York: McGraw Hill.

Walsh, W. (1998). Policing at the crossroads: Changing directions for the new millennium. *International Journal of Police Science and Management, 1*(1), 17–25.

Walsh, W. (2001). Compstat: An analysis of an emerging police managerial paradigm. *Policing: An International Journal of Police Strategies & Management, 24*(3), 347–362.

7 Strategic Planning

Make no little plans. Make the biggest one you can think of, and spend the rest of your life carrying it out.

Harry S. Truman, 33rd President of the United States
(Axelrod, 2004, p. 30)

Learning Objectives

1. Define strategic planning.

2. List how strategic planning can be used in policing.

3. Identify the elements of the strategic planning process.

4. Describe the outcomes of strategic planning.

5. Define the limits of strategic planning.

6. Identify the elements of environmental analysis.

7. Describe how to implement a strategic plan.

Introduction

In recent years, the need for efficiency and effectiveness in the management of police agencies and their programs has increased. Pressures such as decreasing fiscal resources, increased demands for service, and citizen involvement have led to greater scrutiny of police operations. The development and implementation of a strategic plan can help police administrators address such concerns.

Through strategic planning, an organization attempts to anticipate future events and control its destiny. By analyzing its strengths and weaknesses, the organization can avoid future problems and ensure success in achieving its goals. Strategic planning represents a different way of managing police departments. It can serve as the basis for problem solving. Rather than responding to crises at the last moment, agencies can anticipate difficulties and develop plans to deal with them beforehand. To deal with a crime problem, agencies must have valid information about where and when it is occurring and then develop a response. Strategic planning can help police departments identify and mobilize available resources and apply them to community needs. It attempts to maximize opportunities and minimize threats to the organization.

Strategic planning has made a comeback in recent years. It is tied to participatory and **Total Quality Management** (TQM). (See Hoover, 1996; Manning, 1995; Couper & Lobitz, 1991, Kurz, 2006.) It is a way to mobilize the organization, recognize the importance and contributions of line staff personnel, and tap into the resources of the community. Strategic planning is also related to the "**Open Systems Model**" because it recognizes the crucial role played by both the internal and external environments in reaching organizational goals (Munro, 1971).

In policing, strategic planning is enjoying a renaissance for several reasons. One is the shift to Community Policing. Its title infers a partnership between the police and the people they serve. This partnership improves the quality of life in the community through introducing strategies designed to enhance neighborhood solidarity and safety (Trojanowicz & Bucqueroux, 1990). Community Policing requires that police departments initiate and adopt proactive strategies and tactics to repress crime, fear, and disorder within local neighborhoods. Citizens are expected take a proactive stance in helping the police and other government entities identify their public safety needs and policy. Agencies committed to community policing perform their traditional duties of law enforcement, order maintenance, and service and additionally solve community problems. Therefore officers and agencies must do more than just focus on crime control. They must anticipate social and law enforcement concerns before they become problems. Strategic planning is a tool to accomplish these tasks as well as revealing the road the organization should take to work with the community to achieve higher levels of satisfaction and safety.

In addition, Community Policing calls for a decentralized approach to policy development. The aim is to better protect citizens by allowing officers to adjust their responses to best serve the community. Decentralization forces the department to commit to partnering with citizens who are dealing with crime, disorder, and quality-of-life issues (Wasserman & Moore, 1988). It empowers both police officers and community members to take an active stance and become accountable and responsible for the crime problems that plague a community.

A second related change that supports strategic planning is problem-oriented policing. This policing strategy enables the police to develop a systematic process for examining and addressing the problems that the public expects them to handle. Problems are identified through a strategic process that engages in data analysis, identification, and assessment of the current police response, evaluating the adequacy of existing authority and resources, engaging in a broad exploration of alternative responses to the problem, weighing the merits of these alternatives, and choosing from among them. This planning process focuses on a problem in a long-term, comprehensive manner, rather than as a series of separate incidents to be resolved via arrest or other police action (Goldstein, 1990).

However, several impediments to the development of strategic planning in policing have been identified. These include:

1. Lack of up-front training in planning for operational managers.
2. Reluctance to "let go" of control by middle and senior managers.
3. Aspects of the processes for planning and evaluation did not match police skills, knowledge, and activities.
4. Good planning models (or exemplars of "best practice") were not readily available to operational police (Hann & Mortimer, 1994).

It has also been suggested that strategic planning is time-consuming and too demanding of human resources for many departments to undertake. Yet, these problems are not insurmountable. Strategic planning should be conducted because it is such a meaningful part of new policing strategies. For example, the Durham, New Hampshire, Police Department, a small agency with 19 sworn officers serving a fluctuating population comprising 8,700 full-time citizens and 12,000 students of the University of New Hampshire, found that the process benefitted their department in the following areas:

1. **Community perceptions and needs**. The Durham Police Department decided to treat its constituents as partners and customers. Like any business, it needed to identify its constituent's needs to know how to meet them. A Community Safety Survey was designed.
2. **Building community partners**. Community members often have questions about police services and how they're delivered. When constituents are familiar with police services, they are more likely to be supportive. The One-Day Community Planning Session has built strong community-police partnerships. Officers indicate the respect and cooperation they are receiving from the community has improved greatly since the strategic planning process was lunched several years ago.
3. **Internal agency improvements**. Officers' responses to the agency's Internal Survey informed the chief more effectively about his officers' views and needs so that he could adequately respond (Kurz, 2006).

Elements of Strategic Planning

Planning is a primary step in the process of management. It attempts to mobilize organizational members and its resources toward the achievement of stated goals. An effective strategic plan answers the basic question, "What is the purpose of our organization?" Planning sets goals for the organization and maps out the methods to achieve them. It helps determine how to obtain resources and commit them to goal attainment. It directs organization members and channels their activities in the right direction. Their progress toward meeting organizational goals can be measured. As a result, they can be rewarded or changes can be made to correct and direct their efforts in a constructive fashion.

Strategic planning requires a focus on what is important for the organization. This can be developed through discussions among key decision makers and followed by implementing these decisions through specific decisions and actions. It has three basic goals:

1. To build teamwork: People should not only be productive but would enjoy their work and understand their role in the organization.
2. To strengthen communication and empower each staff member to help shape the culture and values of the organization.
3. To identify the tools that people need to do the job, including resources, but also training, development, and recognition.

(Denhardt, 2000, p. 206)

Strategic planning does not just result in a document; it helps build the organization and develop teamwork.

The Process of Strategic Planning

As a process, strategic planning requires that the leader of the organization be inclusive. Members of both the organization and the community are asked to take part. Their joint input is vital and important to creating the plan. The *process* involves a systematic examination of the organization and its environment by those who have a stake in its success (Gordon, 2005, pp. 3–4).

Internally, strategic planning requires democratic, participatory management. It brings the members of an organization together to discuss the strengths and weaknesses of their organization, where they would like to go, and how best to get there. It cannot function in an authoritarian organizational structure. Thus, the process of goal construction also promotes reaching a consensus.

It is not always a smooth process. Consensus must be built. It cannot be achieved through coercion. Strategic planning recognizes that conflicts exist within organizations. The process attempts to promote compromise by bringing disagreements into the open. As Gordon notes, "It is better to invite and resolve conflict early in the discussion and decision making stages than to confront it while trying to implement the final plan" (Gordon, 2005, p. 10). For example, the Louisville Police Department completed a strategic planning process to implement Community Policing that included "Citizens Against Police Abuse"—a group that formed in response to several civilian shootings by officers. The inclusion of groups critical of police operations is recognition they are present and have a voice to be heard. They cannot be ignored, cowed into submission, or co-opted. Inclusion of the community in a meaningful way in the strategic planning process provides an agency with an avenue for establishing, regaining, or increasing police legitimacy (Aden, 2013).

The strategic planning process must have the support of partners—both internal to and external from the police department. These partners should include:

INTERNAL

- **Department and city leaders**. Organizational change cannot be achieved without strong support from the top. The police chief and the mayor must support the plan. So should other political and civic leaders.
- **Departmental personnel**. The plan must be developed with the full involvement of the people who will be most responsible for implementing it: supervisors, officers, and unsworn personnel—all members of the department. There must be consensus on the mission and objectives among those who will carry out the plan.

EXTERNAL

- **Active community leaders**. The plan must be developed in partnership with the community it serves.
- **Interagency partners**. They include active community members and staff from other government agencies.

(Gordon, 2005, pp. 18–20)

Thus, the strategic planning process requires that these partners be brought together for consultation to construct, implement, and change the plan.

The Outcomes of Strategic Planning

As a document, the strategic plan provides a long-term guiding vision and steps for practical, short-term action.

- **One outcome is a document that specifies the actions required to achieve future goals based upon the information generated during the planning process.** It can build a bridge between the community and law enforcement agencies and help them to understand and work with each other. It creates an outline that all parties have agreed to and thus clears the way for action.
- **It builds upon identifying the police agency's current strengths and weaknesses—** What works and what doesn't work within an agency, with intra-governmental relations, and within the community.
- **It offers a strong, central, guiding vision.** Without it, an organization will lack the ability to adjust when change demands it. The mission statement is used to develop new strategies and show when it is time to discontinue old ones.
- **Success is gauged and progress toward it is measured.** The goals and objectives define direction from the beginning of the program. They provide standards against which budgeting, work plans, hiring, promotion, deployment, organizational structure, and all other implementation elements are tested. They are used to keep both the community and the law enforcement agency on track and to ensure effectiveness and efficiency.
- **It provides a vehicle to build consensus within an organization.** Strategic planning is a democratic process. It provides a method to establish and build consensus, both within and outside of the organization. Strategic planning has become a crucial part of the "empowerment model." It urges organizations to be more open in their deliberations and welcome input.
- **It offers specific strategies for near-term completion of tasks.** The manager can engage in strategic planning at all levels of the organization. It applies to the organization as a whole and to specific programs and policies. It is a management tool to guide operational strategies throughout the organization.
- **It assigns specific responsibilities for tasks and results.** It builds in an accountability process that determines whether tasks are being undertaken and whether the desired outcomes are achieved. Evaluation is a key component of strategic planning. Valid measures of outcome must be established along with a computerized information system to capture data in regular, routine fashion. These data must be analyzed and serve as a feedback loop for operational performance. When data are used, reports become valuable and valued. Personnel are more likely to capture information when they see it is used.

With all these positive elements in mind, it is necessary to also consider the limitations of strategic planning.

What Strategic Planning Is Not

Gordon identifies some of these limitations (Gordon, 2005, pp. 10–11):

- **It is not a substitute for leadership**. It cannot prescribe specific courses of action that ensure success. The leader can use strategic planning to make change by building and mobilizing support for initiatives. But these initiatives must reflect consensus. Strategic planning is democratic. It is the hallmark of participatory management. A strategic plan with attainable goals coupled with a realistic strategy provides the membership of an organization with a clear vision of the leader's charted course. Developed with representation throughout the organization, it promotes the allegiance of the members of the organization.
- **It is not a panacea for resolving organizational or community conflicts**. Strategic planning can structure and routinize community input. However, problems must be resolved through active participation of department and community members.
- **It cannot increase scarce resources**. But it can promote sharing of resources to accomplish organizational goals and thus build unity across the organization. It can break down the tendency of organizational subunits to go their own way. It calls for a flexible approach to managing organizational resources.
- **It is not a one-time endeavor**. To maintain flexibility, an organization must analyze the past, scrutinize the present, and prepare for the future. It is an ongoing process.
- **The final plan is not an endpoint**. It must be disseminated to local interest groups, explained, and promoted if it is to be embraced and supported by those who are expected to implement it and those who affected by it. Failure to get commitment at all levels of the organization will doom the strategic plan to failure. Input must be sought and obtained from all levels of the organization since they will be responsible for implementation of the plan.
- **The final plan is a tool, not a task**. Strategic planning will develop the organization's future, but it does not stop there. It moves on to a series of action steps that will guide future activities (Denhardt, 2000, p. 37).
- **The final plan is not unalterable or carved in "stone."** Assumptions must be continually questioned if the plan is to be flexible and accurate.

The strategic plan is meant to be used, not saluted or placed on a shelf and forgotten. It is a guide for action and a directive for the entire organization. It should change to meet the changing conditions that the organization will face in the future.

Strategic Planning Methodology

In recent years, many different strategic planning models have been developed. Each is unique in its own right but all contain the same primary element of management-for-results orientation. Here is an example of a basic approach (see Garner, 2005; Bryson & Alston, 2011).

1. Determine the Problems Facing the Organization

Determine the scope of the planning effort:

A. **Time frame**: What is the period for which the plan is being developed?
B. **Focus**: What are your objectives? How can they be prioritized?
C. **Geographic area**: What geographic area is your organization responsible for?

It is important to have a common understanding of what is expected as the plan develops. A budget and a fairly detailed work plan should be prepared. The work plan will help to keep the project on schedule.

2. Scan the Environment

(S.W.O.T.—"Strengths, Weaknesses, Opportunities, and Threats")

The SWOT analysis identifies a "tension field" that acts as a lens that brings together opposing developments, focuses their effects, and offers direction to the organization (Seagrave, 1993).

It should consider such questions as (Garner, 2005, p. 15):

A. **Past, present, and future**: What has happened in the past? Where is the organization now? What is likely to happen during the time frame of the plan?
B. **Comparative information**: What is happening nationally? Internationally? Within the state or region?
C. **Opportunities and constraints**: What advantages and obstacles to the goals of the plan exist in the immediate environment?

What must the department do in response to the issues it faces?

The stages in the process follow this pattern, leading from the SWOT to the development of the strategic plan:

1. *The search for information and ideas*: Assess the immediate situation in terms of strengths and weaknesses and future opportunities and threats.
2. *Synthesis*: Find generalizations and patterns. This leads to an agenda of strategic issues to be managed.
3. *Selection*: Set priorities for action by assessing the options in terms of stakeholders affected and resources required and then implement the selected strategies.

Nutt and Backoff stress that this process should focus on key stakeholders, not just senior managers within the organization (Nutt & Backoff, 1992, p. 157). In Greensboro, NC, Chief Aden personally invited citizen stakeholder groups that had not traditionally worked with each other or collaborated with the police department, including the Chamber of Commerce, East Carolina University (students and administrators), the Vidant Medical Center, Neighborhood Association boards, the Greenville Property Management Association, the NAACP, the Southern Christian Leadership Council, the Human Relations Council, and several non-profit organizations (Aden, 2013, pp. 29–30).

Typically, the environmental scan takes the form of a "needs assessment." A needs assessment pays specific attention to "stakeholders." Stakeholders are persons who have a direct interest in what is done by the organization (e.g., the community, local government organizations, and local elected officials). This definition must be interpreted in the broadest possible terms. Strategic planners must decide who to involve, how to involve them, and how to solicit input from those who are not directly involved. Planners must receive input from and consider the effect on their stakeholders.

Needs assessment focuses on collecting information from various sources and analyzing the data to determine what problems the organization should address. It asks and answers the question, "What must be done?" Potential sources of information for police departments include community residents, the business community, city and county governments, other law enforcement agencies, the judicial system, health care providers, schools, and churches. Surveys and questionnaires distributed to these various groups can produce valuable information. Another excellent source of information is community meetings. Here, citizens can voice their concerns and provide ideas they may or may not state on a survey or questionnaire. Both sources should be used.

This analysis involves scanning the organization's environment for signs of change. Strategic planning enables an organization to cope better with change and to take maximum advantage of it. It also includes an internal scan of the strengths and weaknesses of the organization. With Community Policing, a citizen attitude survey of the police and problems in the community is a usual starting point.

The environmental scan should be both external and internal to the organization. Strengths and weaknesses are addressed in the Internal Analysis. Opportunities and threats are examined in the External Analysis.

- **The internal analysis** is a "resource audit"—an evaluation of the strengths and weaknesses regarding each strategic issue. They are subject to influence and change. To ensure a complete listing, make a direct comparison to other cities and counties.

Here, the strengths and weaknesses of the organization are evaluated. The resources that the organization can bring to bear on the issues identified in the external analysis are evaluated. The key question is: "What are we able to do and what do we do well?"

Creating key performance indicators is a crucial element in this. Here are some examples of information that may be useful to an organization's internal assessment (Zurcher & Hudak, 1987):

- Number of police per capita.
- Non-sworn employees as a percentage of total.
- Number of calls for service.
- Response time.
- Number of crimes against persons.
- Number of hazardous traffic violation citations/arrests.
- Number of driving while intoxicated arrests.
- Population density.
- Number of neighborhood watch programs.

The information compiled will identify what the organization can use to solve the selected problem.

Warren (2012, p. 39) identifies several symptoms of organizational problems that should be considered including:

- Poor business practices.
- Lack of written or conflicting policies and standard operating procedures.
- Lack of required skill sets in the employee workforce.
- Redundancy of effort.
- Areas of undue risks experienced.
- Ethical transgressions and violations of rules and regulations.
- Morale issues.
- Mission creep.
- Major personality conflicts.
- Areas of disruptive or aggressive internal competition.
- Poor individual or team performance levels.

These issues must be addressed to unite and bring together members of the organization in support of the strategic plan.

The line officers on the street are another valuable source of information that should not be overlooked. Officers acutely know of the problems and needs existing on their beat. Soliciting information from the line officer also provides a secondary benefit. It allows the officer to be an integral and active participant in the strategic planning process. When the time comes for implementation, consulted officers will have a sense of ownership and be more likely to support any transition (Durivage, Barrette, Montcalm, & Laberge, 1992; Toch, 1980).

In his internal scanning effort, Bratton hired a management firm to conduct a "cultural diagnostic" of the NYPD. This tool determines the cultural factors impeding performance and the corrective values that must be used as principles for organizational change. The method defines the cultural assets, obstacles to change, inherited core identity, projected core identity, and the values that must guide revising key organizational systems to institutionalize a new, high-performance culture. They surveyed nearly 8,000 police officers and found:

- At its highest levels, the basic aim of the NYPD was not to bring down crime but to avoid criticism from the media, politicians, and the public. "Nobody ever lost a command because crime went up. You lose a command because the loudest voices in the community don't like you, or because of a bad newspaper story, or because of corruption."
- The greater the distance from headquarters, the lesser the trust from one rank to the next. Exclusion was the rule. Creativity was actively discouraged. "I have 300 assassins in my unit."
- Police officers believed the department had not backed them up, even when their actions were warranted.
- The department was structured to protect its good name (and the careers of its senior executives) rather than to achieve crime-fighting goals.
- The Internal Affairs Bureau was intent on tripping up officers for minor infractions rather than rooting out real corruption.
- The mayor and commissioner had voiced strong support for the Department but officers were waiting to see what they would both do.

- They found a wide disparity between statements by the bosses and what the officers believed the bosses wanted.
- Officers felt they were in a "twilight zone" where staying out of trouble (and thus keeping their bosses out of trouble) was more important than reducing crime rates.

(Bratton & Knobler, 1998, pp. 215–216)

BOX 7.1:   NYPD Internal Scan

CONSIDERED BY OFFICERS AS MOST IMPORTANT TO THE

DEPARTMENT

1. Write summonses.
2. Hold down overtime.
3. Stay out of trouble.
4. Clear backlog of radio runs.
5. Report police corruption.
6. Treat bosses with deference.
7. Reduce crime, disorder, and fear.

CONSIDERED BY OFFICERS AS MOST IMPORTANT TO

THEMSELVES

1. Reduce crime, disorder, and fear.
2. Make gun arrests.
3. Provide police services to people who request them.
4. Gain public confidence in police integrity.
5. Arrest drug dealers.
6. Correct quality-of-life conditions.
7. Stay out of trouble.

The internal analysis is thus structured to tap the opinions and perceptions of the departmental staff. In the Durham, New Hampshire, Police Department, officers rated each of the agency's functions (administration, first-line supervision, patrol, vehicle and equipment maintenance, computerization, and accreditation). The officers also rated each component's effectiveness, philosophy, leadership, policy development, and support to other components. They wrote responses to open questions such as:

1. What would you change about this function if you were the chief of police?
2. What challenges does this function currently face and what challenges will it face in the future?

In this manner, the internal analysis provides valuable information while sponsoring a sense of ownership and belonging among department staff. Their opinions are solicited and treated with respect.

- **The external analysis** pinpoints key threats and opportunities posed by the external environment. It forces the organization to remedy the tendency to look at internal forces while planning. External indicators can serve as benchmarks for identifying the relative position of the organization. Trends that are occurring elsewhere could affect the organization in the future. External factors are usually uncontrollable. They include such items as national and international trends (social, political, demographic changes), actions of other governmental bodies, and technological change. This analysis should have a future (rather than past) orientation.

Cohen and Brand have identified four aspects of the external environment of public agencies:

1. **The political environment**: the legislative branch, the executive branch, the judicial branch, interest groups, and the political views of the broad public and the various politically active elites.
2. **The economic environment**.
3. **The social environment**: the sphere of interaction between the organization and the community at large.
4. **The technological environment**: the technologies used or produced by the agency. In police work, they include things like automatic weapons, improved communications, and DNA evidence.

(Cohen & Brand, 1993, pp. 61–66)

Regarding police departments, it is useful to identify and get information on crime trends:

1. What is the trend?
2. What is its background?
3. What is the probability of the trend occurring?
4. What will be the magnitude of its impact?
5. Does it provide an opportunity or pose a threat to the organization?

(Zurcher & Hudak, 1987, p. 27)

Once this information is obtained, the trend must be interpreted in terms of its magnitude and the probability it will occur. Armed with this information, high-impact/high-probability trends will receive the greatest scrutiny. With information from the needs assessment, it will provide the basis for the action plan to be addressed later in the strategic planning process.

3. Develop a Mission and a Vision Statement

The mission statement of an organization reflects its essential purpose. It should seldom change. Such statements should be concise but encompassing enough to withstand the changes wrought by time and the environment. It reflects the central purpose of the law enforcement agency.

The mission statement communicates the organization's purpose to a variety of audiences and forms the basis for goals, objectives, and strategies (implementation plans) (Gordon, 2005, p. 26). These statements describe what the strategic plan should do for the organization and the community. It also describes the target population and outlines the general approaches used to bring about change.

• A mission statement should convey, articulate, and reinforce the long-term view of where the law enforcement agency and the community want it to be. It creates a desired future that can serve as the basis for developing goals, objectives, and strategies.

The mission statement is a concise account of what is expected to happen because of strategy development and implementation. It is a prelude to developing goals, objectives, and strategies. For example, here is a mission statement from the Greenville (NC) Police Department:

The Greenville Police Department exists to enhance public safety and quality of life, in partnership with ALL people in OUR community, by preventing crime with honor and integrity.

(Aden, 2013, p. 31)

The mission statement provides a focus for the strategic planning enterprise. It is a brief statement of the agency's long-range plan.

Values are also an important part of this process. They are the defining characteristics of the culture of an organization that foster the mission statement. They ensure that persons within the organization will respond to issues in an appropriate fashion.

Values are the defining principles that embody the philosophy of the law enforcement agency that guide its operation. They represent enduring beliefs about what is right, good, and desirable. They are standards of conduct that members of the department believe in. They guide behavior since they communicate standards of conduct to all members of the organization (Community Policing Consortium, 1998, p. 1).

A values statement should:

• Set high standards for excellence
• Reflect high ideals
• Be based upon sound philosophy
• Inspire commitment
• Be proactive and positive
• Be communicated clearly
• Integrate the unique qualities and competencies of the organization.

(Community Policing Consortium, 1998, p. 2)

For example, consider the values statement from the Boston Metropolitan Police shown in Box 7.2.

BOX 7.2:   Boston Metropolitan Police Values

- The Metropolitan Police Department exists to protect and serve the public.
- The Department and its members will maintain the highest ethical standards of conduct.
- We will treat all citizens with dignity, respect, and courtesy.
- We will safeguard each citizen's rights to free expression, movement, and constitutional liberty while within the Metropolitan District Commission jurisdiction.
- We will use only minimum necessary force when performing our lawful duties.
- In applying the law, we will exercise discretion with consistency and equitableness.
- We are committed to giving each employee the authority to make decisions and to hold them accountable for their actions.
- The Department is committed to creating an environment that is productive and satisfying and of which its members can be proud.

Source: Bratton & Knobler (1998, p. 137)

4. Develop Goals, Objectives, and Strategies

Goals and objectives are used interchangeably. Both are statements about intended future affairs—how you intend things to be. However, goals and objectives are inherently different. Goals are broad, vague statements intended to provide organizational direction. Objectives are detailed, results-oriented, measurable, and time-specific. Strategies are the steps in the action plan—who must do what and when to implement the designed changes. They also identify resources needed to carry out the plan, step by step.

Goals

Goals are generalized statements of where an organization wants to be at some future time. They define the major directives of the strategic plan. They are broad, visionary, projected outcomes viewed from a long-term perspective. Goals should be based upon the external and internal analyses. They should build upon strength while negating a weakness. Goals are few in number, concise yet not specific, and non-quantitative. Law enforcement goals address societal problems unlikely to be solved in the immediate future. They tend to be permanent (Community Policing Consortium, 1998, pp. 1–2).

Law enforcement goals include four major desired outcomes:

1.   A reduction in the incidence of crime.
2.   The repression of criminal activity.
3.   The regulation of non-criminal conduct.
4.   The provision of services.

Under community policing, departmental goals include:

1.   A reduction in the fear of crime.
2.   A reduction in social and physical disorder.

3. Strengthening of community involvement.
4. The empowerment of employees and citizens.

Goals should be attainable yet ambitious to make an organization and its people grow. *Stretch goals* are a part of the motivational technique known as Strategic Intent. It calls for the leader of the organization to create unattainable, "stretch" goals and then challenges everyone in the organization to develop methods to attain them. Stretch goals challenge organizations to forego incremental change in favor of "reinventing" the standard ways of doing business. They require that we do more than maintain the current rate of progress. They call for us to improve upon it. Yet, they should be realistic (based upon trend data and research findings) and plausible. There should be a reasonable probability that, with integrated effort and commitment, they can be achieved. Stretch goals are objectives or performance targets used to evaluate the effectiveness of program strategies.

At the NYPD, Bratton said that they would take back the city "block by block." Over a two-year period, Bratton proposed to achieve a dramatic decrease in crime ("Ten percent the first year. Fifteen the next. Twenty-five percent in two years"). Several chiefs responded, "Can't be done." They thought they were already doing everything they could to bring down crime, and anything more was out of the question. "Dramatic? No. You can have decreases. Crime goes down 2 to 4 percent a year, and we can continue that trend. But 10 percent? No chance." Bratton wanted people who were "not only going to think differently, but who were willing to go through walls to do it" (Bratton & Knobler, 1998, pp. 201–202).

The issue surrounding the use of stretch goals is whether to use the goal as a motivational tool or as a valid standard for performance measurement. Garner (2005, p. 18) suggests the use of *SMARTER goals*. Well-defined goals should be:

*   **Specific**: Goals must be clear and specific. They should represent what the program is trying to accomplish and accurately measure successful operations.
*   **Measureable**: If the goal is not measurable, there is no way to gauge progress.
*   **Acceptable (or attainable)**: Again, goals must be realistic. Some effort and stretching is always in order but goals should neither be too high or too low so they become meaningless.
*   **Realistic (or relevant)**: The goals should represent and mirror the vision and mission of the program.
*   **Timely**: Goals must have starting and end points and the duration of the measurement should be stated clearly.
*   **Extend** the capabilities of those working to achieve them.
*   **Rewarding** for the organization and its members.

To be useful in planning, goals must have a basis in fact and have a reasonable expectation of occurrence. They should represent the desired impacts of the program or policy. Cohen and Eimicke do not favor setting numerical performance targets. They find it "more useful to work on improving the day-to-day performance of work processes" (Cohen & Eimicke, 1995, p. 165).

However, it is impossible to implement all of the goals established in a strategic planning process. Since so many actors are present at the table, several alternatives are likely to be proposed. The goals that are generated must be prioritized according to their feasibility. It may be impossible to implement some goals because they are politically impossible and/or they require more resources than are possible to commit at the present time. Choices must be made concerning the methods of solving a particular crime problem.

Objectives

Once goals are established, they need to be further defined and quantified into objectives. Objectives set performance targets to be accomplished over time and act as "benchmarks" that aid decision making and to evaluate progress. They are the specific, measurable targets set for each goal. They define the actions needed to achieve each goal. They must be stated as succinctly as possible and immediately understandable. Objectives are outcome-oriented statements of what a program intends to achieve for the community.

Objectives should be:

- Action-oriented: It starts with "to" followed by an action verb.
- Specific: states a particular result to be accomplished.
- Time-limited: Specifies a defined time frame for completion.
- Quantifiable: Presents a measurable standard of achievement.
- Realistic: Designates a feasible, attainable outcome.

Objectives should be cost-effective and consistent with available resources. They should provide a return on the investment of time, funding, facilities, and people. All stakeholders should support them (Community Policing Consortium, 1998, p. 1).

Strategies

Strategies are the step-by-step means by which an organization reaches its goals. They are programs, events, operations, and projects for the organization to accomplish its objectives. They are the "action steps" that help managers assign tasks and allocate resources to be successful. A strategy can be assigned to someone to be carried out. They represent specific approaches and help define what is to be accomplished. An effort should be made to include some innovative or original ideas, as long as they are likely to be effective.

The following information should be obtained for each proposed strategy:

- Cost.
- Personnel requirements.
- Agencies and organizations involved.
- Time frame.
- Impact.
- Legal implications.

Development of this information will lead to the listing and elimination of strategies. Here, feasibility is the key—figuring out which strategies have a chance of being implemented.

Contingency plans should also be considered. They are fallback positions that are used if the initial strategy is unsuccessful or if the environment shifts.

Strategies bridge the gap between results and the specific tasks required to accomplish them. Implementing a specific strategy is less important than meeting the greater aim or goal. You should leave room for them to be changed or dropped, or for different ones to be implemented.

Here is a brief example of how strategies can be developed. These elements are used in Community Policing when the goal is to reduce crime and the fear of it. When designing strategies for objectives, you should consider the steps that can be taken by every level of the organization and strategies to strengthen the response of the community and outside agencies.

STRATEGIES FOR REDUCING CRIME AND THE FEAR OF CRIME

- **Crime response**. This includes everything concerning a specific crime (i.e., prioritization of calls for service, backup response, report-taking, criminal investigations, warrants and arrests, district attorney prioritization/caseload, incarceration policies, probation and parole management, etc.).
- **Problem solving to reduce crime**. Methods for addressing chronic crime problems that are not addressed through the traditional, incident-based approach. Problem solving addresses the specific elements that allow crimes to occur and aims to prevent crime by eliminating root causes. Examples: Hot Spot analysis and response; civil action against owners of crack houses; prioritization/use of information received through drug hotlines; intervention by code enforcement at sites where environmental factors lead to crime; development of new ordinances to help address chronic problems.
- **Crime prevention**. Crime prevention removes the opportunity for crime to occur. One method often promoted here is Crime Prevention Through Environmental Design (CPTED). CPTED encourages involvement by citizens and changing the physical environment. They take responsibility for public places and watch over them.
- **Early intervention**. This approach entails the sponsorship and development of long-range approaches aimed at reducing the conditions that breed crime (i.e., root causes, including domestic violence, reaching youth at-risk for delinquency and drug abuse, etc.). Familiar approaches include the Police Athletic League (PAL), Drug Abuse Resistance Education (DARE), and Gang Resistance Education (GREAT). With such direct involvement by police departments, partnerships should be established with other governmental and civic agencies, schools, and churches.

The goals, objectives, and strategies provide the organization with an outline of programs, services, facilities, and staff to be funded over the period of the plan—a blueprint for the budgeting process.

5. Develop an Action Plan

This plan shows who is responsible for carrying out the strategies, when it should be done, and how it will be paid for (if direct costs are involved). The action plan will serve as a basis for monitoring implementation but it must be flexible. It can include a month-by-month calendar showing what is to happen at each point in the implementation process. It can list all the strategic actions (relating to several issues and objectives) for which each key actor is responsible. It can include an overall budget for the implementation effort.

The implementation plan takes the strategic planning process to the level of individuals. It assigns specific responsibilities for programs and strategies. Individuals and groups within the organization are drawn into the plan. It forms the basis for personnel assignments and performance measures. They are lengthy. They often list the strategies and then list the corresponding official or agency with the primary responsibility for that effort.

The plan moves toward the vision or mission and is translated into practice in a way that everyone can understand what will be done, at what cost, and how the success of the project will be measured.

An integral part of the implementation plan is a time line that breaks down each action into interim steps for completion. This permits easier tracking of progress toward achieving goals and objectives. Outlining interim steps also facilitates making mid-course adjustments that might be necessary in response to changing conditions or information.

The implementation plan should also identify who will be responsible for overseeing, coordinating, and evaluating progress toward achieving goals and objectives. It should also include provisions for gathering and incorporating public input from area residents and businesses to determine whether actions taken are producing the desired effect within the community.

Costs should be presented in detail. Costs are a significant element of a strategic plan that must be presented. Even if no new personnel or equipment are required, the "in-kind" costs of such elements should be listed.

6. Implementation

The key to strategic planning is that it is action-oriented, rather than planning-oriented. It allocates scarce resources to solve critical issues. Thus, the implementation phase is crucial. It depends upon the process of constructing the strategic plan. If this process has gone well, there should be a broad consensus about what the key issues are, how the external environment will affect the community in the future, and what the key strengths and weaknesses are. New coalitions of business, government, and community members will be formed with a commitment to specific strategies. Much of the success of the strategic plan comes from the process that developed it. Coalitions can develop to guide the implementation process. However, there must be a direct link between implementing the strategic plan and the budget cycle to ensure that funds are available to carry it out.

Once the plan of action is in place, it must be merged into the programs, policies, and daily operations of the organization. The best plan will be of no use to the organization unless it is carried out effectively.

Implementation can be made much easier by involving employees in the planning process as much as possible. The strategic planning process can pull an organization together and give it a common purpose if all employees feel involved. If done properly, employees will know what is expected of them. They will understand what the organization is trying to achieve and how their work fits into the overall picture. By being actively involved in the process, communications between management and employees will improve, and team building will occur. Employees will develop a sense of ownership in the plan that translates into enthusiasm and support.

7. Monitoring and Updating

Successful strategic planning requires continuing review of actual accomplishments in comparison with the plan. Responsibility for monitoring must be given to a specific individual or organization. The monitoring system should track time and other resources expended versus resources allocated. It should keep track of changes in key actors and their assignments. Monitoring keeps the plan on target by accommodating adjustments as circumstances and the environment change. The environment should continue to be scanned to assure that unforeseen developments do not sabotage the adopted plan or that emerging opportunities are not overlooked. This effort continuously renews the Strategic Plan so it continues to develop and does not become static. New strategies should be developed periodically to ensure that the plan adjusts to changing conditions. The process for developing new strategies should include substantial involvement by the original stakeholders.

As implementation proceeds, managers must check progress periodically. Here, the key questions are: (1) "Is the plan being implemented as designed?" and (2) "Is the plan achieving the intended results?" To accomplish this step, supervisors will monitor and evaluate the plan's success based upon how well the objectives are being met as measured against the established performance criteria. If the results are as intended, the process continues. However, if the process is not producing the intended results, then corrective action must be taken. The manager should also document what changes were made and for what reason. Flexibility is paramount. Documenting such alterations will allow the planning and evaluation process to continue.

8. Evaluation

The impact of the plan must be evaluated. The evaluation is a research design that focuses on program outcomes (see Vito & Higgins, 2015). Plans should provide personnel with a clear definition of the desired outcomes and allow as much discretion as possible to achieve them. Also, outcomes should not be confused with process. Again, partnership, problem solving, arrest, and investigation are all processes that can achieve outcomes, but they are not outcomes in themselves.

Evaluation assesses the effectiveness of the plan. For example, in order for the changes introduced with Community Policing to become permanent, it is necessary to recognize and reward new aspects of organizational performance. The criteria for recruitment, performance evaluation (both individual and departmental), management, and training must be developed.

9. Dissemination

The plan must be widely disseminated. The plan should be made available throughout the organization and to leaders of the community and other agencies. The plan can be promoted in the media.

An examination of strategic planning in American law enforcement agencies revealed how this method was implemented. This research was based on a telephone interview survey of 289 and site visits to seven law enforcement agencies (Zhao, Thurman, & Ren, 2008). As a result, a model of four types of strategic planning in police departments was constructed along a grid.

Model 1 was an in-depth one with limited application—rank involvement was high but the extent of application was low. It was characterized by an efficient use of limited resources and experimentation with change in a few selected divisions. Their objectives reflected the needs of the department and was thus designed to gain the support of employees. Measures of effectiveness were easier to develop (Zhao et al., 2008, p. 21).

In the second model, top administration was in firm control of the planning process. Dissemination of information about the plan was restricted, making it difficult for employees to gain knowledge about it. This model fails to achieve the consensus-building effort that is the very heart of strategic planning. Employees do not support implementing such a model (Zhao et al., 2008, p. 22).

Top administration in the third model included divisions in the planning process and developed specific goals and measures to assess effectiveness. Yet, line officers were still uninformed about the plan. It created consensus among division commanders and demonstrated departmental priorities to the external community (Zhao et al., 2008, p. 23).

The fourth model contained the elements of true strategic planning. Implementation of the plan was department-wide and all employees were held accountable for it. It became the agency's daily plan for operations and represented a proactive, inclusive approach to implementation. Consensus about the direction of the department spread across all levels of the department (Zhao et al., 2008, p. 23).

Example: United Kingdom's National Policing Plan, 2003–2006

Following the passage of Britain's Police Reform Act of 2002, the first annual National Policing Plan was published. It was developed in consultation with a number of internal (the Association of Police Officers, the Association of Police Authorities) and external (members of the National Policing Forum) stakeholders.

It was designed to provide a single place where the government's priorities, plans, and performance indicators could be found. It provided a sense of strategic direction for the police service as shared by the police and all its key stakeholders—in and outside of government. The plan contains priorities for police service plus performance indicators to test the success of police actions.

Overall priorities were established for the period 2003 to 2006:

- Tackling anti-social behavior and disorder.
- Reducing the volume of street, drug-related, violent and gun crime in line with local and national targets.
- Combating serious and organized crime operating across force boundaries.
- Increasing the number of offences brought to justice.

The National Policing Plan uses a strategic planning format similar to that presented in this chapter. This plan provides an overall framework for local British police agencies to follow. As we see in Box 7.3, both goals and objectives are set forth by the plan. The goals are broad and set direction while the objectives are more narrow, specific, and measurable. The objectives set the benchmarks by which police performance can be measured and to determine the effectiveness of crime-reduction methods.

: Setting Goals and Objectives—Thames Valley Policing Authority (UK)

GOAL: REDUCING CRIME

This means working with our partners, including our local communities to prevent crime, including drug-related crime by addressing the causes of crime as well as actual incidents of crime.

OBJECTIVES:

Domestic burglary: Achieve a 14.5% reduction in the level of offences compared to 2002/2003 by 2004–2006.
Vehicle crime: Achieve a 17% reduction in the level of offences compared to 2002/2003 by 2004–2006.
Robbery: Achieve a 27% reduction in the level of offences compared to 2002/2003 by 2004–2006.

Source: *Thames Valley Police Authority Strategic Plan, 2003–2006*, pp. 11–12, www.thamesvalley.police.uk

Conclusion

Strategic planning is a proactive management approach that can help an agency determine whether its services respond to the needs of the citizens. It can shape the delivery of services. It is also a means of facilitating participation, communication, and systematic decision making within the organization.

We have reviewed a general framework to develop a strategic plan. Its preparation requires a commitment by the organization and its employees to engage in participatory management.

Strategic planning makes it possible for the organization to respond to change. Will the organization let change control it, or will it attempt to control its destiny? Strategic planning offers a tool to gain a semblance of control over future direction.

KEY TERMS

External Scan
Goals
Internal Scan
Mission Statement

Objectives
Open Systems Model
SMARTER Goals
Strategies

Stretch Goals
S.W.O.T. Analysis
Total Quality Management
Values Statement

References

Aden, H. (2013, October). Inviting the community into the police strategic planning process. *The Police Chief*, 28–31.

Axelrod, A. (2004). *When the Buck stops with you: Harry S. Truman on leadership*. New York: Portfolio.

Bratton, W., & Knobler, P. (1998). *Turnaround: How America's top cop reversed the crime epidemic*. New York: Random House.

Bryson, J., & Alston, F. (2011). *Creating your strategic plan*. San Francisco: Jossey-Bass.

Cohen, S., & Brand, R. (1993). *Total quality management in government*. San Francisco: Jossey-Bass Publishers.

Cohen, S., & Eimicke, W. (1995). *The new effective public manager: Achieving success in a changing government*. San Francisco: Jossey-Bass Publishers.

Community Policing Consortium. (1998). *A staircase to strategic planning*. Washington, DC: Community Policing Consortium.

Couper, D.C., & Lobitz, S.H. (1991). *Quality policing: The Madison experience*. Washington, DC: Police Executive Research Forum.

Denhardt, R.B. (2000). *The pursuit of significance: Strategies for managerial success in public organizations*. Prospect Heights, IL: Waveland Press.

Durivage, A., Barrette, J., Montcalm, L., & Laberge, M. (1992). Analysis of organizational culture: A key to strategic planning. *Canadian Police College Journal, 16*, 94–134.

Garner, R. (2005, November). "SWOT" tactics—Basics for strategic planning. *FBI Law Enforcement Bulletin*, 17–19.

Goldstein, H. (1990). *Problem oriented policing*. New York: McGraw-Hill.

Gordon, G.L. (2005). *Strategic planning for local government*. Washington, DC: International City Management Association.

Hann, J., & Mortimer, B. (1994). Strategic planning and performance evaluation for operational policing. *Criminal Justice Planning & Coordination Conference Proceedings*.

Hoover, L.T. (1996). Translating total quality management from private sector to policing. In L.T. Hoover (Ed.), *Quantifying quality in policing* (pp. 1–22). Washington, DC: Police Executive Research Forum.

Kurz, D.L. (2006). *Strategic planning: Building strong police-community partnerships in small towns*. Alexandria, VA: IACP.

Manning, P.K. (1995). TQM and the future of policing. *Police Forum, 5*, 1–5.

Munro, J.L. (1971, November/December). Towards a theory of criminal justice administration: A general systems perspective. *Public Administration Review*, 621–631.

Nutt, P.C., & Backoff, R.W. (1992). *Strategic management of public and third sector organizations: A handbook for leaders*. San Francisco: Jossey-Bass.

Seagrave, J. (1993). Obtaining information for the corporate strategy: The Vancouver police department telephone survey. *Police Studies, 16*, 147–156.

Toch, H. (1980). Mobilizing police expertise. *Annals of the American Academy of Political and Social Science, 45*, 53–62.

Trojanowicz, R., & Bucqueroux. (1990). *Community policing: A contemporary perspective*. Cincinnati: Anderson.

Vito, G.F., & Higgins, G.E. (2015). *Practical program evaluation for criminal justice*. New York: Taylor & Francis.

Warren, G.A. (2012, March). Is your agency an integrated strategic management system? *The Police Chief*, 38–41.

Wasserman, R., & Moore, M.H. (1988). *Values in policing*. Washington, DC: National Institute of Justice.

Zhao, J., Thurman, Q., & Ren, L. (2008). An examination of strategic planning in American Law enforcement agencies. *Police Quarterly, 11*(1), 3–26.

Zurcher, J., & Hudak, D. (1987). How to build a crystal ball: Strategic planning for police agencies. *The Police Chief,* 24–31.

8

Strategic Operations

One can seek to define the mission of a police department by trying to discover the unchanging essence of policing, or by thinking through the question of how particular police departments, embodying particular kinds of competencies and capabilities, might make the greatest contributions to the quality of life in the communities in which they operate.

Mark H. Moore and Darrel W. Stephens, *Beyond Command and Control* (1991, p. 29)

Learning Objectives

1.	Describe Strategic Policing.
2.	Identify how to conduct community needs to determine accountability.
3.	Identify the steps in the strategic management process.
4.	Analyze and review the implementation and effectiveness of Community Policing (COP).
5.	Analyze and review the implementation and effectiveness of Problem-Oriented Policing (POP).
6.	Analyze and review the implementation and effectiveness of Compstat.
7.	Analyze and review the implementation and effectiveness of Intelligence-Led Policing (ILP).
8.	Analyze and review the implementation and effectiveness of Smart Policing.

Introduction

Many law enforcement organizations are struggling to become more adaptive to the demanding, complex, and external environment in which they exist. Police agencies are balancing consistency and predictability with adaptation and change. Most police leaders recognize the fluid context in which their departments operate (Batts, Smoot, & Scrivner, 2012). They are developing organizational strategies to meet these challenges that are different than the patrol-dominated ones created to address 19th- and early 20th-century conditions. As a result, there is occurring a fundamental rethinking of the manner in which the police are operationalizing their response to the complex crime and disorder needs of the communities they serve. These current changes represent a strategic shift in the basic "business" of policing (Kelling & Bratton, 1993).

The present challenge for police leadership during this era requires police executives to think, manage, and lead in a strategic fashion. Strategic management is

> the continuous process of determining the mission and goals of an organization within the context of its external environment and its internal strengths and weaknesses, formulating and implementing strategies and exerting strategic control to ensure that the organization's strategies are successful in attaining its goals.
>
> (Parnell, 2014, p. 14)

Police organizational reforms such as Community-Oriented Policing, Problem-Oriented Policing, Compstat, Intelligence-Led, and Smart Policing have led to reconsideration about how police operational services are delivered. As a result, concerned police administrators are consistently seeking to discover better ways to manage their organizational resources and reinvent their organizations. This process involves systematic searching for and testing of new methods of police operations to serve communities. Police organizations are restructuring by changing their goals and objectives, core functions, incentives, accountability, distribution of power, and cultures to achieve a more effective public safety impact. The long-term result of these efforts is a redefinition of organizational effectiveness. Effectiveness is now measured in outcomes instead of statistical outputs that focus on tasks performed instead of results achieved. It is hoped that this process will lead to improved ways to create community security and safety, also that operational services will be better managed and problem solving will emerge as an important operational technology. Strategic management will test the intellectual skill set of all police employees to its full capacity as creativity emerges as a primary organizational asset. This transformation demands that police executives meet these challenges by actively engaging the process of designing effective organizations to ensure that it occurs by intention, not by chance.

This redefinition of policing holds that an effective organization initiates and reshapes its operational service delivery in ways that will facilitate the fulfilment of its primary mission while increasing public value (Moore, 1995). It accomplishes its mission by understanding and adapting to the demands of its environment through the creation, acquisition, and transformation of information. This transformation of information creates intelligence data that serves as the basis for police managers to successfully plan, initiate, reshape, and evaluate their operational strategies in ways that promote effectiveness (Tilley, 2003).

This constitutes a strategic shift in policing. According to this new operational paradigm, the primary function of police administration and leadership is to actively engage, analyze, and respond to the needs of the external environment with the internal resources and capabilities of the organization. If we consider this new perspective valid, then we need to identify the operational processes currently being developed and employed by policing to enhance its effectiveness.

The Strategic Policing Process

Strategic policing is built upon four interrelated elements: (1) a Shared Sense of Direction, (2) Creativity, (3) Commitment, and (4) Accountability. Successful strategically managed organizations have a shared sense of direction present throughout the organization. This direction is defined by the organization's vision and mission statements, values, operational objectives, and performance. A vision that is actively practiced and shared by organizational members creates excellence, commitment, and effectiveness by focusing the entire organization on what must be accomplished. These are the desired outcomes the department wishes to achieve. In this manner effectiveness becomes a core value in the high-performance agency. In this type of organization, operations are structured to maximize the use of organizational assets. Through constant managerial communication and teamwork, people know what is expected of them and what they must do to be effective. Lastly, they are held accountable for their effectiveness. A critical success factor is managerial commitment to the development and maintenance of a positive organizational culture that values both creativity and accountability.

New ideas come from within or outside the police organization. Whatever their source, the purpose for developing new operational tactics is improved performance. Ideas on their own cannot create an effective organization. Without accompanying changes in the way information is disseminated, problems are identified and solved, employees are empowered, projects created and problem-solving teams develop strategies and plan, only the potential for improvement exists. If the department's leadership wishes to encourage creativity, they must ask themselves this basic question: "How do we utilize the intellectual capacity and experience of our people?" It must be remembered that creativity is the basis for effective tactics.

People are the organization. Without their commitment to the mission and goals of the department, nothing will ever be accomplished. However, not everyone will agree with the organization's dominant or proposed new strategy. Fortunately, total agreement among all members of an organization is not required to change its direction. As we noted earlier in Chapter 4, the individuals who are needed are the organization's *critical mass*. The critical mass comprises individuals who because of their positions, personal charisma, skill set, and leadership ability exert the most power and influence over the other employees and organization.

For example, middle managers and supervisors define and shape a department's operational reality. They have the responsibility and power to convert the executive's vision and the organizational mission into operational behavior, performance, and outcomes. The true measure of their leadership is influence. They need to be made full partners in the development of the new organizational vision and believe in the direction it is setting. They are the managers who translate the department's mission, plans, objectives, policy, and procedures into day-to-day operations and outcomes. A critical number of these individuals constitute the department's critical mass. They are needed to commit to the organization's direction so that the strategies and operational tactics necessary are developed and implemented.

Architects of the strategic transformation must build on such time-tested strengths of middle management as these: close relationships with beat officers; breadth of organizational vision (vis-à-vis first-line officers and sergeants); knowledge of departmental culture (including agency strengths, weaknesses, and receptivity to innovation); the know-how to get things done without undermining resource commitments to preexisting programs; and attention to detail (Travis, 1995).

However, a major problem for strategic leaders seeking to create more effective organizations is this: What should they do with managers who either do not support the new direction or are incapable of learning new skills? Judgments about who is working for the success of the organization and what works must be objective and grounded in data, not subjective feelings. This is why follow-up, feedback, assessment, and evaluation that occurs at crime strategy meetings are critical factors in effective strategic management. Empowering managers and holding them accountable for achieving results is one way to create the means to assess effectiveness and to identify and remove incompetent ones. Middle managers and supervisors must be involved in the planning process and be provided with a clear mandate, authority, and responsibility to create and implement operational tactics. They should be prepared and trained for their new roles. While they must be held accountable for desired outcomes and provided with performance feedback, mistakes made in the attempt to advance organizational performance should be tolerated, not punished. A balance must be maintained between the use of elimination and retraining of individuals who fail to perform well (see Kelling & Bratton, 1993; Oliver, 2000; Vito, Walsh, & Kunselman, 2004).

We noted earlier in this text that organizational culture is the hidden energy that moves people to act. It provides meaning for what people do and why they do it. Effective organizations promote shared values, beliefs, assumptions, perceptions, norms, and patterns of behavior that support quality and effectiveness of performance. All members of the organization share a strong organizational culture. It is promoted by example. Managerial behavior must model the behavior desired by the organization as it attempts to introduce new ideas. Reward systems must be based upon supporting positive norms and behaviors. Policies and procedures must hold individuals accountable for performance.

Leaders can affect organizational culture in several ways. They communicate the vision of the organization—where it has been (past), where it is now (present), and where it is going (future). Through their day-to-day actions they can reinforce the values the organization considers important. They model the actions they wish to see subordinates exhibit. These values are important to the achievement of the operational strategies promoted by the leader (Yukl, 2013, p. 287).

Accountability is established through an internal assessment process that gives managers the authority but also assesses the effectiveness of their strategies and tactics developed to address operational problems and conditions. In this manner the department responds to the environmental conditions that spawn crime and disorder. External monitoring should consider such issues as the following (see Yukl, 2013, p. 297):

1. What do the citizens of the community need and want?
2. What is the reaction of citizens to the department's current practices and services?
3. How will the department be affected by changing population demographics (e.g., aging, diversity) among the citizenry?
4. How will the department be affected by national and international events?

The answers to these questions will provide the information necessary to assist mangers with their strategy formulation.

Strategic managers must also consider how to achieve performance objectives in light of the situation they face and the organizational resources that are available to them. The department's organizational strategy should unite managerial and employee decision making and actions into a coordinated and compatible pattern. Strategies can be both proactive (intended) and reactive (adaptive)—a combination of planned actions or "on-the-spot" reactions to changing and unanticipated conditions. Strategic managers must be flexible—shape and alter their tactics as events transpire and operational demands change.

The following elements of the strategic management process must be completed before a strategy is formulated (Parnell, 2014, p. 2; Yukl, 2013, p. 299):

1. *External Analysis*: Requires an analysis of both the opportunities and threats present in the external environment.
2. *Internal Analysis*: Determination of the organization's strengths and weaknesses in its internal environment. Identify the "core competencies" (the technical expertise and application talents) of the department.
3. *Strategy Formulation*: The strategy should be developed by matching the organization's strengths and weaknesses with the opportunities and threats provided by the external environment. Evaluate the need for a major change in strategy and identify promising strategies to deal with the problems ascertained. Anticipate the likely outcomes of potential stratgies.
4. *Strategy Execution*: Implementing the strategy developed.
5. *Strategic Control*: Assess performance and make adjustments if the strategy is not achieving the desired outcome.

It must also be stressed that a strategy can be altered to meet changing conditions. Flexibility to meet changes in the external environment is crucial.

The strategic decisions made by the department's executive (chief, director, or sheriff) and their command staff should follow the steps listed above accompanied with a thorough consideration of the internal and external factors facing the police organization. While a strategy should be based upon knowledge of the past and present, it must also attempt to anticipate future conditions and concerns. It should take advantage of the opportunities presented and balance them against the threats posed by the external environment. The process involves choice and trade-offs between immediate and long-term outcomes (see Parnell, 2014, p. 10).

New strategies and tactics developing in policing have been created in response to the failure of the "standard model of police practices" (National Academy of Sciences, 2004, p. 223). This model consists of a "one-size-fits-all" approach, of reactive methods to deal with crime by:

- Increasing the size of police agencies.
- Random patrol across all parts of the community.
- Rapid response to calls for service.
- Generally applied follow-up investigations.
- Generally applied intensive enforcement and arrest policies.

(National Academy of Sciences, 2004, p. 224)

In sum, this was the standard model developed during the early 20th-century's professional reform movement. Its primary focus is on the tasks of policing rather than strategies and tactics designed to identify and solve the problems that lead to crime (Goldstein, 1990). In response to the shortcomings of the standard model, several new strategies have been developed under the strategic policing process: (1) Community Policing, (2) Problem-Oriented Policing, (3) Compstat, (4) Intelligence-Led Policing, and (5) Smart Policing. You were introduced to most of these strategies in Chapter 1. Here, we will briefly define each model and focus on the research on their implementation and effectiveness.

Community Policing

As introduced in Chapter 1, Community Policing constitutes the first attempt to challenge the organizational tactical orthodoxy that emerged during the reform era. It attempts to increase the interaction between police and the community through a process of collaboration and consultation leading to partnerships between the police and community residents. Community is recognized as a required, crucial partner and participant in the production of public safety that policing needs to be successful. The hope is that the quality of life in the community will improve due to the introduction of collaborative strategies designed to enhance neighborhood safety. The police and community citizens are expected to work together to address problems of disorder and crime.

Typically, Community Policing features the provision of identifiable officers who know their assigned patrol area and its residents. The assumption is that a mutually supportive bond will develop between the community and its patrol officers. They are encouraged to get close to citizens on their beats and better understand their needs and desires. It is hoped that the officers will develop a sense of territorial responsibility for their patrol beat and partnership with its residents. Due to this close collaboration, officers can truly relate to the communities they serve and better understand and identify local problems. It is hoped that this will feed their creativity and make it possible for them to solve problems before they become major criminal incidents. Under Community Policing, the police are not supposed to be insular, self-contained or otherwise cut off from the communities they serve and from where their true power resides (Skolnick, 1999). Measures of success in Community Policing include:

- Improved community quality of life.
- Problem solving.
- Resident fear reduction.
- Decreased incidents of disorder.
- Increased resident satisfaction with police services.
- Increased crime prevention.

Community Policing also assumes that because of their development of a collaborative relationship with their communities, police departments will adopt proactive strategies that will repress crime, fear of crime, and disorder within neighborhoods. In addition, it assumes that citizens in a community who partner with their police officers will take a proactive role and help the police set and implement these strategies. Through this exchange process, citizens have input into the determination of police priorities. As a result, every community should be policed in accordance with neighborhood needs and values (see Trojanowicz & Bucqueroux, 1994; Kelling & Coles, 1996). Community Policing rejects the traditional, bureaucratic, policing model that promotes one service delivery strategy for all communities. Instead, it features a decentralized approach designed to provide citizens with tailor-made protection to meet the needs of diverse communities (see Reiss, 1992). Strategically, it attempts to align police operations and community needs.

This decentralization process also seeks to give the line officer a greater role in decision making. Thus, it promotes a change in organizational operations away from the "top down" approach typical in law enforcement organizations. Community Policing is thus more flexible, decentralized, and (hopefully) more humane due to the input sought from community members and line officers. It requires officers and the department to commit to collaborative problem-solving partnerships with citizens (Wasserman & Moore, 1988, p. 5). Police officers and citizens in the community are empowered to take an active stance and become both responsible and accountable for community problems.

Community Policing shifts the focus of police work from answering random calls for service to the identification, responding to, and resolving of community problems (Peak & Glensor, 2002). Departments thus have the responsibility to perform traditional duties of law enforcement, order maintenance, and service in addition to engaging in community problem solving (see Rosenbaum, 1998). Police tactics include establishing a proactive response to maintaining order and dealing with quality-of-life offenses in communities (see Goldstein, 1993). Under Community Policing, operational officers are viewed as intelligent agents able to intellectually and analytically react to citizen concerns. Operational officers are expected to engage community citizens and anticipate their social and law enforcement concerns before they become community problems.

Through its emphasis upon the police/community partnerships, Community Policing restores the legitimacy of the police in the public's esteem. By making operations transparent and visible to the public, police accountability and procedural justice is stressed. It is a social service approach to fuel community safety and security. The assumption is that getting to know a community and its citizens and solving its problems will be more effective than traditional, reactive, single-incident, call for service–driven law enforcement. The ultimate goal is for both the police and the community to solve problems before they become crimes. Community Policing officers are expected to directly engage in true, proactive crime prevention.

Implementing Community Policing

Evaluations of Community Policing programs have focused upon the impact of specific programs limited to certain areas. Research on Community Policing has examined the internal effects of these programs on the operations of departments, including the job satisfaction and related attitudes of police officers working in Community Policing programs. The strengths and weaknesses concerning Community Policing have been documented by this research. In most cities, Community Policing has been developed as a program or project rather than a full-blown, department-wide strategy (Skolnick & Bayley, 1988).

Research on the Innovative Neighborhood Oriented Policing Project (INOP) revealed the strengths and weaknesses of Community Policing. For example, in the city of Louisville, Kentucky, site interviews revealed that police administrators and officers believed their INOP project had been very effective in reducing fear in the target areas. However, community residents were less certain about these accomplishments. Across all eight Louisville sites, the authors uncovered several suggestions for departments seeking to establish Community Policing. For example, they noted that before implementation of Community Policing there is a need for extensive training. Patrol officers in all eight INOP sites had little understanding of the goals of the INOP projects or Community Policing that their police departments were seeking to accomplish (Sadd & Grinc, 1994, p. 31). Officers resisted Community Policing because it redefined the role of the patrol officer from crime-fighter to problem solver (Sadd & Grinc, 1994, pp. 40–41). The need for training was also evident for community residents so they understood what the department was doing and trying to accomplish in the community. In all eight INOP sites, community leaders and residents complained that the police did not adequately inform or educate them about the goals and objectives of Community Policing. They also stressed the vital need for interagency involvement so that Community Policing is not an isolated change within city government.

These results mirror the findings of other studies of Community Policing. In their literature review on Community Policing, Lurgio and Rosenbaum consolidated research findings over an 18-year period covering 11 cities (Lurgio & Rosenbaum, 1994). They concluded Community Policing has exerted a positive influence on both the police and on citizens' views of the police. Police reported increases in job satisfaction and motivation, a broadening of the police role, improved relationships with co-workers and citizens, and greater expectations regarding community participation in crime prevention efforts. Citizens felt that Community Policing officers were more visible, helpful, polite, and effective on a variety of job activities (see Greene, 1989; Hayeslip & Cordner, 1987). In Madison, Wisconsin, Wycoff and Skogan (1994) found that even senior officers supported Community Policing. Madison officers also reported that increased contacts with citizens led to an increase in citizen requests for assistance. Wycoff (1988) also reported that four Community Policing strategies tested in Houston and Newark, NJ, appeared to reduce citizen fear of crime, improve citizens' views of crime and disorder problems in their neighborhoods, and improved evaluations of the police.

As previously noted, Community Policing recognizes the role of public and private institutions and organizations in combatting crime in partnership with the police. This proposed change proved difficult to achieve. In 1989, a representative survey of police chiefs in cities of more than 25,000 revealed that 67 percent had implemented Community Policing programs in the last 3 years. However, Zhao, Thurman, and Lovrich (1995, p. 20) found that the departments with the greatest interest in training and education were more likely to implement Community Policing programs. Their factor analysis of the responses revealed three types of impediments to implementing Community Policing (organizational, community, and transitional). The mean ratings revealed that police agencies were more concerned with internal organizational barriers than obstacles in their community. The dominant factors were resistance from middle management and line officers. Departments with high correlations on these factors were less likely to implement Community Policing. In another analysis, these authors discovered that, between 1993 and 1996, interest in Community Policing had risen and impediments to implementation had been identified. However, they concluded that the institutionalization of Community Policing was far from certain (Zhao et al., 1999).

An assessment of the implementation of Community Policing in several U.S. cities revealed that cities that received federal funding under the Crime Control Act of 1994 (that also established the Office of Community Policing Services) and that had city manager forms of government were mostly likely to implement Community Policing (He, Zhao, & Lovrich, 2005). However, further analysis of this data set determined that police chiefs largely maintained their operational priorities within the dictates of the professional model of policing (emphasizing crime fighting) over those of Community Policing. As local crime rates increased, police agencies emphasized crime fighting over the provision of services and order maintenance (Zhao, He, & Lovrich, 2003, pp. 715–716).

Walsh's (1994) survey of Northeastern first-line police supervisors revealed problems in the implementation of Community Policing. Notable was a lack of support and understanding from patrol supervisors and officers assigned to traditional patrol operations separated from the Community Policing unit. In addition, group discussion sessions revealed that these supervisors felt that operational personnel considered community-oriented policing as "soft-policing" or not "real" police work and that Community Policing lacked legitimacy because the purpose of the program, personnel authority, and duties were not clearly specified nor training adequately provided. As a result, the feeling among the supervisors was that the program was temporary and would be disbanded when the funding ended.

However, a small portion of this sample offered a different perspective of their programs. These supervisors said that their chief's leadership is the driving force behind the shift to Community Policing. They claimed that Community Policing has reduced service calls and has gained significant support throughout the department and community. In each of these departments, the chief established external political and community support for the program prior to establishing it. They also worked closely with the program supervisors to ensure it became established properly. Many of these supervisors were having problems balancing their traditional control orientation with the autonomy needs of their officers. Although administrators voiced support for team building and employee participation, their actual behavior was control-oriented. For example, they expressed fear that the officers' familiarity with community members and operational freedom may lead to deviations from their department's standards of behavior and give management an excuse to end the program.

Similarly, police managers enrolled at the Southern Police Institute were asked to identify obstacles to the implementation of Community Policing, whether they could be overcome, and would Community Policing help solve the problems facing their department. Overall, their responses indicated that they had "adopted the philosophy of community policing but were unwilling to make the organizational changes necessary to support it" (Vito, Walsh, & Kunselman, 2005, p. 18). They identified community involvement as the greatest hindrance to the adoption of Community Policing but also offered methods such as strategic planning and new forms of performance evaluation to deal with implementation issues. They were particularly hopeful about the potential that Community Policing held for the line officer. However, they were reluctant to accept their role in the implementation process and assert the development of Community Policing as something other than a specialized unit in their departments.

Similarly, Bradstreet's (1997) interviews with a group of 20 patrol sergeants from the Austin Police Department (in Texas) led to several recommendations concerning the implementation of Community Policing. To ensure its acceptance, these sergeants advocated working in teams, the freedom to choose and tailor projects to fit officers' styles, tying Community Policing to police traditions, and working directly with citizens.

Finally, Gianakis and Davis (1998) conducted a survey of Florida law enforcement agencies and found that Community Policing took a variety of forms. They discovered that all of the agencies employed some variety of Community Policing but, even when structural change occurred, the impact on existing policies and systems was minimal. The majority of the organizations in this survey instituted Community Policing by changing the officers' role rather than the organization. The most common variant used was restructuring of patrol operations through the creation of decentralized substations (Gianakis & Davis, 1998, p. 489).

Yet, research on Community Policing programs in six cities revealed that resistance to change may be an overrated threat (Weisel & Eck, 1994). Here, at least two-thirds of all officers felt that Community Policing is here to stay. A positive view of Community Policing held regardless of years of service, education, race, sex, and experience in fixed beat areas. Several organizational approaches were common across the Community Policing sites, including the use of participatory management, seeking input from line-level staff, changing promotional practices to reinforce officer involvement, changing performance evaluation systems to support Community Policing, and providing formal training for personnel. An interview-based study with Cleveland, Ohio, officers engaged in Community Policing determined that they had positive views toward the program and the communities it served. They specifically noted that there were "good people" living in the neighborhood who wanted something done about crime. The study also found "no ascertainable pattern" between the race of the officer, their attitudes toward the Community Policing program, and the racial composition of the neighborhood (Ammar, Kessler, & Kratcoski, 2007, p. 319).

A study of attitudes toward Community Policing in a small Southern city between 2002 and 2005 found that, while the police built neighborhood partnerships, there were no significant changes in the fear of crime or satisfaction with the police expressed by the citizenry. However, citizens who had direct contact with the police had higher levels of satisfaction and a lesser fear of crime (Lord, Kuhns, & Friday, 2009). Burruss and Giblin (2014) found that centrist forces in organizations (publications, the professionalization of law enforcement, and other law enforcement agencies) aided the implementation of Community Policing. They help an organization become familiar with the nature of an innovation.

Overall, these findings suggest that researchers of Community Policing programs must closely examine how community police units are integrated into the organizational structure of the department and how the culture of the department contributes to or hinders this operational reform. Community Policing must not lead to creation of what Toch and Grant (1991, p. 65) termed "innovation ghettos" that isolate the people in them and minimize the service they provide. However, evidence is lacking that Community Policing was ever implemented in a way that actually promoted structural changes in police departments (Maguire, 1997; Maguire & Katz, 2002).

Several issues raised by these studies serve notice to departments who are planning a move to Community Policing. First, there is a clear need to conduct training sessions for both police officers and citizens on the meaning and nature of Community Policing. The nature of the process and the benefits to be gained should be fully specified and recognized. Similarly, a clearly defined relationship should be established between police departments and other agencies to address the community problems that are related to crime but know no jurisdictional boundaries. Finally, the most crucial element is a working relationship with the community. Community leaders must be identified, their support obtained, and partnerships maintained if Community Policing is to achieve its potential for meaningful change.

Effectiveness of Community Policing

In their review of research on the effectiveness of policing methods, the Committee to Review Research on Police Policy and Practices (National Academy of Sciences, 2004, p. 234) noted that Community Policing lowers the fear of crime in communities when the level of interaction between citizens and officers is increased. Direct community involvement was increased through the use of police community stations and citizen contact patrols. However, the reduction in the fear of crime was not evident across all socio-economic groups. The research also determined that if the police evidenced respect toward citizens, they were more likely to obtain compliance for their requests (National Academy of Sciences, 2004, p. 235).

These research findings were upheld by studies that followed this report. In the most comprehensive evaluation of a Community Policing program, Skogan (2006) reviewed 12 years of data on Chicago's Community Policing program (**Chicago Alternative Policing Strategy**—CAPS). Unlike other departments, Chicago implemented Community Policing on a city-wide basis, dividing the city into beats. The CAPS program attempted to mobilize community members to partner with the police to prevent crime. In Chicago, Community Policing allowed residents to address crime and disorder problems by securing ties to both the police and public officials (Lombardo & Lough, 2007, p. 132). Skogan (2006) specifically analyzes data from two aspects of CAPS, one effective (beat meetings—open forums for neighborhood residents and officers assigned to it) and one less so (district advisory committees comprising selected community leaders and police officials). In particular, Skogan's (2006) analysis reveals that there was a differential effect for CAPS by race. African Americans were most involved in the program and their neighborhoods benefitted from it most of all, while White residents did not seem to need it at all. Latino neighborhoods suffered from a lack of participation due to language and economic barriers (Latino households were too involved in work to take part). Skogan notes (2006, p. 317) that beat officers "adopted very traditional problem-solving strategies, including high-visibility patrol, aggressive stops and field interrogations, and undercover operations." They also made referrals to other city agencies in 63 percent of the beats in the study.

In their reanalysis of data from the CAPS evaluation, Lombardo Olson, and Staton (2010) determined that residents in areas served by the program had higher opinions of the ability of the police to fight crime than residents in matched comparison group neighborhoods. Overall, the CAPS experience documents that police departments need to tailor their approaches and responses to specific communities regarding their socio-economic background to be effective in implementing Community Policing.

An analysis of the effect of Community Policing on crime showed that one jurisdiction registered a significant decline in the level of violent and property crimes in the area served by the program (Connell, Miggans, & McGloin, 2008). The research also determined that the officers working under this program were committed to implementing Community Policing. Also, the Community Policing program was implemented within a single unit, not adopted by the entire department. A similar study determined that Community Policing had an indirect effect on crime (Xu, Fiedler, & Flaming, 2005). It also found that citizens' fear of crime and perceived quality of life were significant predictors of the level of citizens' satisfaction with police performance.

These goals are a key part of the Community Policing strategy—meeting the demands of citizens for police services and promoting feelings of safety in the community. The core idea of Community Policing encourages individual agencies to adapt it to meet the circumstances they face. Thus,

> community policing is a philosophy that promotes organizational strategies which support the systematic use of partnerships and problem solving techniques to proactively address the immediate conditions that give rise to public safety issues such as crime, social disorder, and fear of crime.
>
> (Scheider, Chapman, & Schapiro, 2009, pp. 697–698)

In this chapter, we will also review how Community Policing was combined with other strategic policing strategies.

Problem-Oriented Policing

Many departments use Community Policing within a framework of Problem-Oriented Policing (POP) to enact it. Problem-Oriented Policing recognizes that the role of the police as law enforcers is overrated. Noted police scholar Herman Goldstein (1990) has suggested that if the police are serious about controlling crime they need to analyze the problems they are called to address on a daily basis. Problem-Oriented Policing requires that the police develop a systematic process for identifying, examining, and addressing the problems that the public expects them to handle. It requires identifying these problems in more precise terms, researching each problem, documenting the current police response, assessing its adequacy and the adequacy of existing authority and resources, engaging in a broad exploration of alternatives to present responses, weighing the merits of these alternatives, and choosing from among them (Goldstein, 1979).

The heart of Problem-Oriented Policing is the **SARA model**. It directs police officers to engage in the following four basic steps in the problem-solving process (Goldstein, 1990):

- *Scanning*: Identify recurring problems and how they affect community safety.
- *Analysis*: Determine the causes of the problem.
- *Response*: Seeking out, selecting and implementing activities to solve the problem.
- *Assessment:* Determine if the response was effective or identify new strategies.

This method encourages the police to adopt operational tactics to reduce or eliminate the problem that is the major contributor to the crime in question. As defined in San Diego (Capowich & Roehl, 1994, pp. 127–128), Problem-Oriented Policing:

> POP emphasizes identifying and analyzing problems (criminal, civil, or public nuisance) and implementing solutions to resolve the underlying causes of the problem. It emphasizes proactive intervention rather than reactive responses to calls for service, resolution of root causes rather than symptoms, and use of multiparty, community-based problem solving rather than a unilateral police response. POP focuses on a problem in a long- term, comprehensive manner, rather than handling the problem as a series of separate incidents to be resolved via arrest or other police action.

In San Diego, the police focused upon street robberies. Research determined that calls for service did not decrease over the one-year period. Yet, the indicators revealed that the POP approach improved the circumstances for those who use the Community Policing stations and reduced the police workload at these stations. However, the role played by citizen groups in this project was limited.

Cordner and Biebel (2005) interviewed officers engaging in Problem-Oriented Policing in San Diego, CA—a department that has been devoted to the approach. Their analysis gives insight to implementation issues associated with the process. They determined that the officers tackled small-scale problems—particularly drug and disorder problems. In terms of the SARA model, POP initiatives flowed from observations and complaints, rather than data analysis or a sophisticated scanning process. Analysis was informal and limited, originating from small-scale, reactive, incident-oriented problem-solving approaches. Officers did not expect that analysis would lead to effective responses to problems. Officers focused upon the response aspect of POP but relied upon their personal experience and the advice of fellow officers rather than developing imaginative responses through consultation with research results. As a result, they used such traditional responses as targeted enforcement by uniformed patrol officers and directed or saturation patrol tactics. These officers explained that their lack of creativity was tied to their reliance on their experience with traditional responses and time pressures to develop a response. They were too busy answering calls to brainstorm about creative responses. However, these officers reported that their efforts were successful with over half of the problems eliminated and 83 percent showing that the problem was reduced in severity (Cordner & Biebel, 2005, p. 170). They felt that POP was a good way to respond to community concerns. To improve the process, they suggested that: (1) supervisors needed to be more supportive of POP efforts, (2) the use of more group meetings to do brainstorming, (3) more direct POP mentoring in the field, and (4) more POP support from crime analysts (Cordner & Biebel, 2005, p. 173).

A study of POP implementation in Colorado Springs, CO, also revealed several implementation problems and issues. First, the external partners of this department did not appear to play a central and collaborative role in problem identification. Second, record-keeping was inconsistent and made it difficult to identify effective responses. Third, assessment of the effectiveness of the responses was negligible. Officers typically did no assessment or just a shallow one (Macguire, Uchida, & Hassell, 2015, p. 87). Finally, as with COP, POP is a function of specialty units rather something routinely practiced by all officers. Although POP has registered success in several instances, these findings highlight that ideal implementation of this reform has been difficult to achieve, possibily due to a lack of resources and proper training.

Elsewhere, research on POP reports positive results. In both Newport News (VA) and Baltimore County (MD), officers concentrated on underlying causes of crime. They collected information and enlisted the support of public and private agencies. As a result, both crime and fear of crime were substantially reduced in both areas (Eck & Spelman, 1987). In a systematic review of POP research findings, Weisburd and his colleagues (2010) conducted a meta-analysis of more than 5,500 articles and reports (resulting in finding 10 methodologically rigorous studies) and concluded that POP had an overall modest but statistically significant impact upon crime and disorder. The overall percent change in crime and disorder recorded by the studies was over 44 percent (Weisburd, Telep, Hinkle, & Eck, 2010, p. 162).

Hot Spot Policing

Another tactic of strategic policing that has been extensively researched is known as Hot Spot and/or place-based policing. A hot spot is defined as a small geographic location where the rate of crimes per square foot is higher than that of the areas surrounding it. Thus the hot spot is a useful way to determine where police should focus their efforts to solve a crime problem. This tactic represents a shift from person-based policing to place-based policing. It has emerged as a central feature of cutting-edge law enforcement (Weisburd & Lum, 2005). While evolutionary, it demands radical changes in data collection, in the organization of police activities, and in the overall worldview of the police that see their primary task as catching criminals (Weisburd, 2008).

Crime hot spots are also examined to determine the day of the week, time of day and hours when crime calls are concentrated (Sherman, 2009, pp. 157–158). Besides the clustering of crime events, Hot Spot Policing analyses consider such variables as facilities (bars, churches, apartment buildings), site features (lack of guardianship, inept or improper management, presence of valuable items), offender mobility (factors influencing target selection by offenders—gender, race, age, experience, crime type), and target location (places that present acceptable risks and gains) (Braga, 2005, p. 319). A *hot spot* is a "micro" place that can be seen in its entirety by the human eye at one location on the ground (Sherman, 2009, p. 158).

In the 1980s, policing researchers narrowed the geographical area focus of their analysis to small high-crime areas within particular neighborhoods. The best-known study was conducted by Sherman and Weisburd in Minneapolis (Sherman & Weisburd, 1995). This study examined data on over 300,000 calls to Minneapolis police city-wide over a year and found that a few hot spots accounted for nearly all calls to the police. These areas, some as small as street intersections, were especially high in predatory crimes such as robbery, rape, and auto theft. These findings suggest certain locales are more susceptible to crime. Presumably, further examination of these areas might provide tips on how to prevent offenses from occurring. If risks at these locations are stable, community problem-solving techniques may reduce crime and disorder substantially. If locations run high risks only temporarily, such strategies may not work.

Reviews of studies of the effectiveness of Hot Spot Policing are encouraging. A meta-analysis of five Hot Spot Policing experiments published between 1989 and 1995 determined that these interventions reduced calls for service in the target areas (particularly for disorder offenses) but treatment effects for property and violence calls were small and not statistically significant (Braga, 2005, pp. 333–335). Similarly, Weisburd and Braga (2006, pp. 232–233) reviewed nine prominent studies of Hot Spot Policing (published from 1989–1999) and determined that "noteworthy crime reductions" were reported in seven of these analyses. The results also showed that, rather than a displacement of crime, there was a "diffusion of crime control benefits." The areas that were not served by the experiment also improved in terms of crime prevention and reduction.

Recent research results on Hot Spot Policing are also positive. In Lowell, MA, a randomized controlled trial of Hot Spot Policing registered strong results. The identified Lowell hot spots accounted for over 23 percent of the total calls for crime and disorder in 2004 (Braga & Bond, 2008, p. 583). The police interventions resulted in a 14 percent reduction in disorder/nuisance calls, a 29.4 increase in misdemeanor offenses, and an 21.5 percent reduction in calls for service compared to the control areas. Social disorder was eased at 14 out of 17 of the treatment areas (Braga & Bond, 2008, pp. 594–596). It was also noted that Lowell police commanders were continuously held accountable for results in the treatment areas via a Compstat-like system.

In Philadelphia, a hot spot study constituted as part of Operation Safe Streets examined the impact of placing officers at 214 of the highest drug activity locations in the city—24 hours/day, 7 days/week (Lawton, Taylor, & Luongo, 2005). The research findings determined that the police crackdown failed to have a significant impact upon homicides, violent crime, or drug crimes on a city-wide basis. However, localized analyses determined that it impacted violent and drug crime and a spatial diffusion of benefits rather than displacement of crime (Lawton et al., 2005, p. 447). In fact, a meta-analysis of Hot Spot Policing studies determined that diffusion of benefits was a much more likely outcome than crime displacement (Bowers, Johnson, Guerette, Summers, & Poyton, 2011). The authors cautioned that crackdowns, especially for drug crimes, may have a short-lived effect and do not constitute a long-term solution.

A second Philadelphia-based study examined the impact of the placement of 200 foot patrol officers upon 60 violent crime hot spots in the summer of 2009 through the use of an experimental design. The violent crime hot spots were foot patrolled for up to 90 hours per week and benefitted from a net effect of 53 fewer violent offenses during the experiment, outperforming the control areas by 23 percent (Ratcliffe, Taniguchi, Groff, & Wood, 2011, p. 818). This experiment reveals the potential of foot patrol as an effective element of a problem-oriented place-based policing strategy to reduce violent crime. Further study on this experiment revealed a complementary relationship between foot and car patrol in these areas. Overall, the research findings indicated that car patrol officers could concentrate on serious violent crime incidents while foot patrol officers concentrated on order-maintenance activities (Groff, Johnson, Ratcliffe, & Wood, 2013, p. 136). Therefore, both types of patrol should be possible operational tactics in a violent crime prevention strategy.

There are other issues surrounding the use of crime hot spots. First is dosage. How long should the police patrol the hot spot? Reanalyzing data from the Minnesota Preventive Patrol Experiment, Koper (1995) attempted to determine the optimum time that officers should spend in a hot spot to obtain the maximum deterrent effect upon crime. He found that a "dosage effect" existed. Police stops were most effective when they were 13 to 15 minutes long and that the impact deteriorated after that point and must be of some quality, not just driving by (Koper, 1995, p. 663). Therefore, there is a saturation point for Hot Spot Policing that ultimately weakens any deterrent impact. The policy recommendation from this study, known as the "Koper Curve" theory, is that "police could maximize crime and disorder reduction at hot spots by making proactive, medium-length stops" and reduce the unnecessary time spent at these locations (Koper, 1995, p. 668). But if this patrol is effective, a paradox may occur, the more crime police prevent, the more boring they may find patrol to be. Yet, even if this happens, patrolling hot spots puts officers in an improved position to respond to emergency calls in these high call producing areas when they come in. The "Koper Curve" demonstrates that the common practice of sitting on a hot spot for 8 to 24 hours a day is wasteful (Sherman, 2009, p. 159). The effectiveness of Hot Spot Policing following the Koper Curve recommendations was supported by an experiment conducted in Sacramento, CA. The results showed that 15-minute, randomized visits to crime hot spots significantly reduced Part I crimes and calls for service (Telep,

Mitchell, & Weisburd, 2014). Increased police presence of medium length and randomly timed may be the most effective dosage for Hot Spot Policing.

Second, what is the effect of Hot Spot Policing methods on community residents? A study of the effect of police focus on crime hot spots determined that order maintenance methods promulgated under the Broken Windows theory may have unanticipated effects. Hinkle and Weisburd (2008) found that in Jersey City, NJ, fear of crime expressed by citizens increased even though crackdowns had lowered the crime rate. The increased presence of police in the area negatively impacted residents' perception of the safety of the area. This finding underscores the necessity that the police communicate with citizens and explain their methods to mitigate their fear and be effective (Hinkle & Weisburd, 2008, p. 510).

In addition, results from a telephone interview survey with respondents from two southeastern U.S. cities found that physical disorder, rather than social disorder, affected their opinions about the quality of life in their neighborhoods. These findings suggest that police efforts to reduce social disorder may not have an effect on the quality of life in areas (Chappell, Monk-Turner, & Payne, 2011). Similarly, data from Jersey City, NJ, from a telephone survey of residents and an observational study of blocks determined that evidence of physical disorder affected their notions of social disorder in neighborhoods. Therefore, the police may wish to include methods to reduce physical disorder (like graffiti removal) when conducting Broken Windows Policing (Hinkle & Yang, 2014). Finally, an analysis of survey data from Washington State also determined that people have difficulty discerning their perceptions of physical disorder and crime. People who felt that their neighborhood was disorderly were more likely to make distinctions between disorder and crime (Gau & Pratt, 2010). However, one Hot Spot Policing study that considered community attitudes toward operations found no significant impacts on fear of crime, police legitimacy, collective efficacy, or perceptions of crime and disorder (Weisburd, Hinkle, Famega, & Ready, 2011).

Third, which patrolling strategy is most effective in policing hot spots? An experiment focusing upon 83 hot spots in Jacksonville, FL, used a Problem-Oriented Policing strategy and directed, saturation patrol as the treatments over a 90-day period. Both of the treatments resulted in higher levels of self-initiated police activity and field stops when compared with the control group area. The main finding was that the problem-solving intervention was associated with a 33 percent reduction in violent street crime. No statistically significant differences were registered for property and other violent crimes but they were also declining in the problem-solving intervention areas (Taylor, Koper, & Woods, 2011, pp. 172–173). These findings show that the intervention strategy adopted for hot spots can make a difference.

Lawrence Sherman maintains that the concentration of crime in hot spots is more intense than it is among individual repeat offenders (Sherman, 1995). Such places have characteristics like those considered in the criminal careers of persons: onset, continuance, specialization, and desistance. The development of computerized geographical information systems (GIS) has made the identification of hot spots routine among police departments. Like individuals with a long "rap sheet," high-crime locations have become targets of policing initiatives.

Hot Spot Policing has demonstrated great promise. In their review of the effectiveness of recent police strategies, Eck and Weisburd (2004, p. 57) determined that such focused policing efforts had the strongest evidence of success. A meta-analysis of Hot Spot Policing studies was conducted on studies published on or before 2010 on police-led crime control efforts. The overall conclusion was that Hot Spot Policing generated small, but noteworthy reductions in crime that also spread to other areas surrounding the targeted area. Problem-oriented tactics were especially effective. Studies that considered resident attitudes reported positive reactions to hot spot methods (Braga, Papachristos, & Hureau, 2014).

However, it is also evident that the police must do more than put "cops on the dots" and create strategies that can change conditions in the hot spot locations (Casady, 2011, p. 2). Koper (2014) surveyed 305 agencies led by general members of the Police Executive Research Forum in 2008 on Hot Spot Policing. The respondents indicated that they focused on larger areas as hot spots rather than the prescribed focus on micro-places. However, their efforts in these areas were still determined to be effective. Koper (2014, p. 137) suggests that police could focus on micro-places within a broader context of areas and neighborhoods to be optimally effective. In addition, the survey results suggested that police efforts could be more effective by focusing attention on hot spots over longer periods of time such as giving them daily attention. Here, Koper (2014, p. 137) recommends the creation of "place-based data systems" to track crime trends, actors, social and physical features, and interventions at hot spots over time. The police respondents relied upon traditional methods to handle hot spots (patrol, enforcement, targeting offenders) rather than adopting situational crime prevention methods. Only one half of the respondents stated that they regularly briefed patrol officers and detectives on hot spot operations and only one third engaged in communicating with problem groups in the hot spot area. While police agencies have adopted Hot Spot Policing as an operational tactic, some fine tuning is required to determine the proper methods and dosage of patrolling. Still to be determined are such questions as how Hot Spot Policing operations affect perceptions of police legitimacy, if it will be effective in smaller cities and rural counties, and what the long-term impact of Hot Spot Policing upon crime rates will be (Weisburd & Telep, 2014).

Compstat

Developed and implemented by the New York City Police Department, Compstat is a managerial accountability system that focused the department on proactive crime control. It is a goal-oriented, strategic management process that aims to control crime by holding police operational commanders accountable for organizational performance. It has been recognized as a revolutionary strategic police management paradigm that has been adopted by departments throughout the world (Henry, 2002; McDonald, 2002; Walsh, 2001).

Compstat is a product of the innovative strategies and the dynamic management processes developed in 1994 under then New York City Police Commissioner William Bratton and continued by his successors Howard Safir, Bernard Kerik, and Raymond Kelly and Bratton again (Bratton & Knobler, 1998; Giuliani, 2002, pp. 87–88; Henry, 2002; Maple, 1999; Safir, 1997; Silverman 1999). Compstat evolved from the New York City Police Department's weekly Crime Control Strategy meetings that began in January 1994. These meetings increased the flow of crime information between the agency's executives and the commanders of operational units. William Bratton and his command staff created these Compstat meetings as a way to make his 76 precinct commanders and their officers accountable for the crime rate (Silverman, 1999). From 1993 through September 2014, using the Compstat process, seven felony crimes in New York City (Murder, Rape, Robbery, Felony Assault, Burglary, Grand Larceny, and Grand Larceny Auto) have declined by about 77.8 percent (www.nyc.gov/html/nypd/downloads/pdf/crime_statistics/cscity.pdf).

Bratton challenged the New York City Police Department to "Take Back the City, Block by Block" and reduce crime. During his tenure as the head of New York City's Transit Police, he made Wilson and Kelling's Broken Windows theory the centerpiece of his operational tactics. Zero tolerance for graffiti, aggressive panhandling, fare beating, and public urination led to a literal and figurative cleanup of the crime-ridden subway system. He also used it as his "lynch-pin strategy" to "Reclaim the Public Spaces of New York" as NYPD Commissioner. Instead of concentrating on felony offenses, quality-of-life crimes (or "incivilities") became the primary target for law enforcement. Bratton thus publicly and passionately embraced crime reduction as the primary mission of the department.

Compstat promoted and enforced administrative responsibility. Basically, it comprises a four-step process:

1. **Accurate and timely intelligence**: To reduce crime, you must know about it.
   - What type of crime is it (i.e., drug sales, robbery, burglary)?
   - Where is the crime occurring (i.e., areas, types of location)?
   - When is the crime happening (i.e., day of week, hour of day)?
   - Why is the crime happening (motive, i.e., drug-related shootings)?
2. **Rapid deployment**: Compstat's provision of weekly crime statistics provides data that allows operational commanders to assess crime conditions and quality-of-life trends in their geographical area of responsibility. Commanders can then decide how they will use and deploy their resources as rapidly as possible to address these conditions.
3. **Effective tactics**: Commanders have the discretion to use a variety operational tactics to address specific problems. What they develop, how and what are the results are an important part of the evaluation process that takes place at crime strategy meetings.
4. **Relentless follow-up and assessment**: The first three steps are only effective if commanders constantly follow up on what is being done, and assess their results. If results are not what they should be, something needs to change. Compstat requires this activity of all operational commanders at all levels of the department.

The centerpiece of the Compstat process is the briefing. The briefings are a strictly New York–style melding of Total Quality Management (in this case, directly opening lines of communication between executive leaders and staff and precinct commanders and their staff) and Theory X (with the "boss" calling subordinates on the carpet in a most aggressive fashion). Compstat transformed the NYPD into a "learning organization" that used up-to-date crime information, processed it quickly, and acted upon it (O'Connell & Straub, 2007, p. 55). Compstat briefings played a crucial role in this transformation by "improving the flow of useful information across NYPD's large and traditionally opaque bureaucracy" (Sugarman, 2010, p. 172).

Bratton stressed accountability. He also gave precinct commanders increased discretionary power and resources to focus on departmental goals, rather than maintaining their own commands.

There are four levels of Compstat. Bratton created a system in which the police commissioner, with his executive core, first empowers and then interrogates the precinct commander, forcing him or her to come up with a plan to attack crime. But it should not stop there. At the next level down, it should be the precinct commander,

> taking the same role as the commissioner, empowering and interrogating the platoon commander. Then, at the third level, the platoon commander should be asking his or her sergeants, "What are we doing to deploy resources on this tour to address these conditions?" And finally, the sergeant at roll call should be doing the same thing. This process then flows throughout the department until everyone in the department is empowered and motivated, engaged and assessed and successful. It can work in all organizations, whether it's 38,000 New York cops or Mayberry.
>
> (Bratton & Knobler, 1998, p. 239)

This is a major point. All too often, other departments and police experts dismiss innovations in New York Police Department. They are considered untranslatable due to the size of the city and the resources of the NYPD. This misperception often leads to the fatal error of not examining and considering the Compstat process. Yet, departments of all sizes have reviewed these principles and have adopted Compstat-like management processes.

Under Compstat operational managers are empowered to focus, manage, and direct their unit's problem-solving process. They are held accountable for addressing the crime and disorder issues and trends associated with the Compstat data for their areas. Traditional, Community and Problem-Oriented Policing strategies are integral parts of their operational tactics. A principal aim of the Compstat process is not to just displace crime but to reduce it and create a permanent change in the community. Compstat is not just about crime statistics but crime control (Safir, 1997).

The underlying concept of Compstat is that police officers and police agencies can have a substantial positive impact on crime and quality-of-life problems facing the communities they serve if managed strategically. It presents police executives and managers with a new way of looking at police organizations and police activities. It is radically different from the accepted concepts and practices that have guided police administration through most of its existence and it points to new methods and strategies similar to those used by business managers that police agencies can use to fulfill their mission (Henry, 2002). Compstat emphasizes the vital link between information, operational decision making, and crime control objectives (McDonald, 2002). However, as a management tool, its impact extends way beyond crime fighting and can apply to any organizational setting. Its strength is that it is a contingency management process that is flexible enough to adapt to constantly changing conditions. It is strategic policing at its best.

Again, the vital heart of the process is the Compstat briefing. Besides analyzing crime information, the Compstat briefing provides four functions. First, it is the "master classroom for on-the-job training and coaching" with supervision provided by top-level administrators who officers may never see on such a regular basis. Second, it is a place for "peer learning among middle managers" who can learn from the experience and thus spread the benefits of successful crime-fighting methods. Third, senior managers obtain a "regular overview of all operations and problems needing special attention" rather than a piecemeal approach. Finally, it gives "top brass a bully pulpit and a megaphone to send edicts across agency and a stage to recognize and honor outstanding performers at any rank" (Sugarman, 2010, p. 173).

In Baltimore, in December 1999, Mayor Martin O'Malley established CitiStat, a program modeled on NYPD's Compstat paradigm. Unlike Compstat, CitiStat was aimed at improving the performance of all governmental agencies, not just the police department. Every two weeks, agency administrators were expected to present findings on key performance and human resource indicators for review by the Mayor's staff and at meetings with the Mayor's Office. While accounting for their performance, agency heads were also provided with the support to improve their operational performance (Henderson, 2003, p. 6). The process was established because of Mayor O'Malley's belief that the Compstat strategy could be used to make government agencies more efficient and effective. While improving agency performance and accountability, CitiStat also aimed to increase efficiency in the use of resources and improve the quality and quantity of services provided to the citizens of Baltimore (Henderson, 2003, p. 12).

Behn has extensively examined the factors influencing the implementation and execution of the CitiStat process. Specifically, he lists six core drivers of CitiStat:

1. The active engagement of the city's top executives;
2. The breadth, depth, disaggregation and "nowness" of the data plus the thoroughness of the analyses of these data;
3. The perserverance of the questioning, feedback, and follow-up (which is more persistent than relentless);
4. The consequences for both good, poor and improved performance;
5. The focus on problem solving, continuous experimentation, and learning; and
6. The institutional memory of the city's top executives.

(Behn, 2005, p. 301)

Behn believes that, individually, none of the drivers suffices to make CitiStat effective and also that none of them are required. Behn notes that maps were a key for CitiStat analysis in the Baltimore Police Department. They summarize crime patterns and consider such questions as: "How many burglaries occurred on a block during any given month or week?" or "How many robberies occurred at an intersection between 2:00 and 5:00 a.m. on the last five Saturdays?" (Behn, 2005, pp. 298–299).

Potential Problems in Compstat Systems

Behn also diagnoses the "seven big errors of PerformanceStat"—an assessment of implementation and operational difficulties with a process like Compstat. These errors are:

1. **No clear purpose:** What results are we trying to produce? What would better performance look like? How might we know if we made some improvements?
2. **No one has specific responsibilities:** Requires the conversion of clear purposes into specific responsibilities, like reaching specific performance targets.
3. **Meetings are held irregularly, infrequently, or randomly**.
4. **No one person is authorized to run meetings**.
5. **No dedicated analytic staff**. When dealing with crime, the following questions should be considered:
   a. What crimes were committed? Where? When? By Whom?
   b. What have we done about them?
   c. What patterns can we detect?
   d. What strategies should we employ in the future in response to these patterns?

6. **No follow up:** Did today's meeting build upon the problems identified, solutions analyzed, and commitments made at the previous meeting?
7. **No difference between the brutal and the bland:**
    a. *The Brutal ("Gotcha")*: NYPD's Compstat meetings were infamous for being tough, uncompromising with poor performers, unsentimental affairs—aggressively demanding and sarcastically demeaning. O'Connell and Straub (2007, p. 88) assert that Compstat-like systems "can devolve into a forum for negative reinforcement, whereby field commanders can be subjected to embarrassing or harassing questioning."
    b. *The Bland*: Mostly "show & tell", a series of PowerPoint slides, presenting another glowing picture of the unit's latest accomplishments.

(Behn, 2008, pp. 3–6)

Behn also recommends that "PerformanceStat" meetings maintain open avenues of communication and that the system be interactive and supportive.

A source of the perception that Compstat can affect homicide rates is that homicides dropped sharply (84.3%) between 1993 and 2014 in New York City. Within Compstat, this result is attributed to the NYPD's "Quality of Life" initiative, Street Crimes Unit, and stop-and-frisk program that attempted "to remove guns from the street and to prosecute petty offenders with the hope of connecting them to more significant crimes" (Joanes, 1999–2000, p. 275). However, this decline began in New York City before Compstat was implemented. Comparing homicide trends in other U.S. cities during this time period, Eck and Maguire (2000, p. 232) concluded that the claim that Compstat accelerated the homicide decline was not supported by the data (see also Joanes,[1] 1999–2000, p. 292). Yet, these authors also cautioned that it was possible "given the complexity of homicide patterns, that the Compstat process had a subtle and meaningful but difficult-to-detect effect on violent crime in New York" (Eck & Maguire, 2000, p. 235).

Compstat meetings should be strategy sessions where data is analyzed to determine the nature of the problem to develop operational methods to deal with it effectively. It should be a collaborative process. It is not the setting of crime rate targets that is the problem. The issue is how these targets are used to motivate individuals and hold them accountable for performing operations as directed. Sample (2000, p. 27) reminds us that "under certain conditions the process of measurement can affect the outcome of a measurement in unpredictable ways"—the act of asking the question can dramatically skew the answer. Similarly, Tenbrunsel (2011, p. 61) describes how setting specific performance targets can affect how employees conduct the process of measurement. Such goals can lead them to neglect other areas, take undesirable "ends justify the means" risks, be dishonest in their reporting, or engage in unethical behavior they would not otherwise do.

Eterno and Silverman (2006) believe that NYPD's Compstat process fell prey to some of these evils. Based upon their research and observation of Compstat in action, they identifed several flaws. The most notable problem is that Compstat's focus on crime reduction can lead police to ignore their "most fundamental goal"—protecting legal principles and democratic rights (Eterno & Silverman, 2006, p. 221). In addition, this focus promoted the perception that Compstat was a numbers game that used fear to drive the process. Berated by high-level NYPD command officers, commanders feared presenting their crime information at Compstat meetings and "would do almost anything to escape the embarrassment of crime statistics going up" (Eterno & Silverman, 2006, p. 223). The commanders then used fear to drive their charges to make arrests and generate statistics to promote crime reduction. Thus, the rank and file typically viewed Compstat as a numbers game where they were required to make more arrests and issue more summonses. They were not motivated by the process to fight crime, unless they were members of specialized crime units designed to address a particular problem, like drugs. In such an atmosphere, reducing crime at any cost can be an outcome.

In a survey and interview study of over 500 NYPD officers (at the rank of captain or above), Eterno and Silverman (2010) examined whether the Compstat process exuded pressure upon officers to record crime statistics in favorable ways—specifically, pressure to downgrade index crimes. The research group included officers who served both before and after Compstat was initiated by Comissioner Bratton. The retirees from the Compstat era reported that they felt significant pressure to decrease index crime (Eterno & Silverman, 2010, p. 434). They also noted that the demand for integrity in crime statistics was significantly less in the Compstat era and that promotions were more likely to be related to demonstrated decreases in the crime rate (Eterno & Silverman, 2010, p. 442). Thus, pressure and fear may lead subordinates to cheat on statistics, rather than develop inventive ways to reach performance targets. This possibility must always be considered in any management strategy that is focused on performance-based outcomes. Departments can manage this tendency, however, by using management systems designed to prevent falsifying performance outcomes.

Compstat Effectiveness

Research by Braga and Weisburd (2011, p. 4) provides empirical evidence that "police can control crime hot spots without displacing crime problems to other places" by utilizing Problem-Oriented Policing and situational crime prevention techniques to address the "dynamics, situations and characteristics" of the location. To effectively implement and manage a Hot Spot Policing program, they recommend that police departments use a "Compstat-like accountability system that puts a premium on problem oriented policing and community policing" (Braga & Weisburd, 2010, p. 243).

An examination of the impact of Compstat operations on homicide rates in New York City between 1990 and 1999 also considered the effect of cocaine use during the time period. The analysis found that misdemeanor arrests were negatively related to gun-related homicides. This effect was statistically significant, even when related factors (socio-demographic characteristics, changing levels of police manpower, and changes in felony arrests) were controlled for. In addition, declining cocaine use was related to declining gun-related homicide rates. These two trends, including the NYPD's initiative to "take guns off the street," impacted gun-related homicides in the city (Messner et al., 2007, pp. 405–407).

The impact of order-maintenance policing on homicide rates in New York City is supported by research by Fagan, Zimring, and Kim (1998). They examined the city's homicide rates from 1950 to 1996 and determined that the decline in gun-related homicides during the period could not be completely explained by mean regression. Order-maintenance policing could be responsible for this decrease but exactly to what extent was open to question (Faganet al., 1998, p. 1322).

Rosenfeld, Fornango, and Rengifo (2007) examined the impact of order-maintenance policing upon New York City homicide and robbery rates between 1988 and 2001. Using a multivariate design that controlled for other pertinent factors, they reported a modest impact for order-maintenance policing on these crimes. However, they also concluded that these declines would likely have occurred without order-maintenance policing. Control measures such as socio-economic disadvantage, racial composition, and immigrant population concentration were also significantly related to homicide and robbery declines (Rosenfeld et al., 2007, pp. 377–379). Yet, there is some noted impact that shows the effectiveness of order-maintenance policing under Compstat.

An exhaustive analysis of the effectiveness of the Compstat program by Zimring (2012, p. 134) reveals that New York City experienced a decline in seven major crime categories (Homicide, Rape, Robbery, Assault, Burglary, Larceny, Auto Theft) that was greater than the nine other largest U.S. cities during the period 1990–2009. For these crimes, the average decline in New York was 63 percent during the 1990s and 45 percent after 2000 (Zimring, 2012, p. 139). Specifically, Zimring (2012, p. 147) attributes this crime drop to the effective use of hot spots emphases and tactics—"the most important of these is a data driven crime mapping and control strategy management program with many of the elements of Compstat."

The use of a Compstat system in the White Plains, New York, Police Department between 2002 and 2005 led to a 69 percent increase in arrests that resulted in a 32 percent decrease in crimes against the person and a 33 percent decrease in property crime. In addition, vehicle and traffic summonses rose by 81 percent and there was a 6.4 percent reduction in motor vehicle accidents (despite an increase in traffic flow) (O'Connell & Straub, 2007, p. 19).

Other studies of Compstat have been less conclusive. Harcourt and Ludwig (2006) analyzed crime data from New York and five other cities where a social experiment (MTO— Moving to Opportunity) had taken place to consider if violent crime was related to disorder (as noted by the Broken Windows hypothesis). They concluded that the crime rate reduction noted by Kelling and Sousa could be attributed to mean regression. The precincts that received intensive order-maintenance policing were also the ones with the largest increases and levels of crime during the city's crack epidemic (Harcourt & Ludwig, 2006, p. 315). The results of the MTO analysis found that disorder led to crime rate decline when people moved to more advantageous neighborhoods. Examining county crime data from California, Worrall (2006) found a significant relationship between Broken Windows Policing and burglary rates. However, there was no evident impact upon larceny-theft crimes in these areas. An analysis of Texas crime data from 1990–2004 on the 35 largest municipal police agencies found that Broken Windows Policing raised clearance rates for burglaries and auto thefts (less significant) but decreased clearance rates for larceny-theft (Jang, Hoover, & Lawton, 2008). An evaluation of the impact of Compstat policing on crime rates in Fort Worth, TX, found an impact upon property and total index crime rates but violent crime rates did not decrease. It was recommended that the police focus on a particular crime when using a Compstat approach (Jang, Hoover, & Lawton, 2010).

The Committee to Review Research on Police Policy and Practices (National Academy of Sciences, 2004, p. 185) noted in their literature review that the effectiveness of Compstat would be difficult to scientifically ascertain. Recent research on the impact of Compstat and its strategies in New York City have been mixed and qualified in its assessment of effectiveness (Rosenfeld & Fornango, 2014; Weisburd, Telep, & Lawton, 2014). In the NYPD, Compstat remains in place despite a change in mayors (from Giuliani to de Blasio). All police commissioners who have followed Bratton to date have retained the Compstat process as NYPD organizational strategy. In addition, it is a process that was manufactured and defined by police administrators with little guidance from academic intelligensia and absolutely no governmental grant dollar support.

One lesson for administrators that has evolved out of the current development of strategic policing is that the use of technology is not enough. The technology must be used in a strategic fashion that assists commanders to respond to current and future problems in innovative ways. This response should be built upon collaboration and support between units of the organization to achieve commonly held goals. Technology can structure and analyze information. It then must be transformed into intelligence that can drive the development of tactics that effectively address community crime and public safety. However, it is the operational commander who must have the leadership ability and training to use this intelligence to its maximum advantage.

Intelligence-Led Policing and Focused Deterrence

Intelligence-Led Policing (ILP) empathizes the use of information to guide police operations, especially to anticipate future risks and influence decision makers to take action to prevent crime (Ratcliffe & Guidetti, 2008). Ratcliffe (2009, p. 176) defines Intelligence-Led Policing as:

> a law enforcement operational strategy that sought to reduce crime through the combined use of crime analysis and criminal intelligence in order to determine crime reduction tactics that concentrate on the enforcement and prevention of criminal offender activity with a focus on active and recidivist offenders. This approach emphasizes information gathering through the extensive use of confidential informants, offender interviews, analysis of recorded crime and calls for service, surveillance of suspects and community sources of information.

Originally used to identify crime prevention targets, Intelligence-Led Policing has become a management philosophy that can lead to collaborative and strategic solutions to provide public safety. ILP began in the United Kingdom in response to official reports that the police were not spending enough time targeting offenders to prevent crime. The generation of reliable crime information is the key to this approach. Ratcliffe (2014) offers two "laws of intelligence":

1. *The most reliable indication of future criminal activity is current criminal activity.* Offenders will continue to exploit a criminal opportunity until they are stopped (Ratcliffe, 2014, p. 2).
2. *Intelligence that does not influence the thinking of a decision-maker is not intelligence.* Intelligence must guide meaningful action against crime (Ratcliffe, 2014, p. 3). Crime analysis can tell a decision-maker *what* is going on, and criminal intelligence can tell them *why* it is going on.

The basis of ILP is the creation of "**actionable intelligence**." This is the generation of useful information that can inform and guide operations to drive operational responses and for strategic planning against threats (Carter & Carter, 2009, p. 318). One example of actionable intelligence is the creation of operational information to combat international terrorist attacks and attacks from far right, domestic extremists (McGarrell, Frelich, & Chermak, 2007, p. 149).

To summarize, ILP:

- Is designed to be a model for the business of policing.
- Aims to achieve crime and harm reduction and prevention and disruption of offender activity.
- Focuses on crime hotspots, prolific offenders, repeat victims and active criminal groups.
- Employs a top-down management approach.
- Merges crime analysis and criminal intelligence to objectively direct police resources.
- Aids police resource prioritization decisions.

(Ratcliffe, 2016, p. 65)

Thus, ILP is a managerial model of evidence-based, police resource allocation decisions featuring the prioritization of problems. ILP methods use investigation to determine the existence and management of linked series of crime incidents (hot spots), the targeting of specific offenders, and the application of preventative measures to combat the crime problem. Ratcliffe has studied the implementation of ILP in police departments and identified several areas of concern. For example, in New Zealand, he found that the police had difficulty recording crimes other than burglary and vehicle crime in their computer system. More time was spent on data entry than on data analysis (Ratcliffe, 2005, p. 442). Another common problem was a reliance upon line staff to use information to guide operations. The difficulty here, that plagues other police innovations, is that line officers are typically limited in their ability and opportunity to engage in proactive policing methods because they are spending the bulk of their time responding to calls for service (Ratcliffe, 2005, p. 443). Besides performing data entry, crime analysts spent time on generating administrative statistics like performance appraisals rather than developing tactical intelligence. Executive decision makers failed to make the development of criminal intelligence a priority. When intelligence reports were provided, they were "rarely read and even more scarcely acted upon" (Ratcliffe, 2005, p. 448). In New Jersey, the state police adopted a more positive approach to ILP. Using a strategic, state-wide approach to gang problems led to the arrest of nearly 100 Bloods gang members on charges of racketeering, conspiracy, and drug distribution (Ratcliffe & Guidetti, 2008, p. 119). Darroch and Mazerolle's (2013) ILP implementation study underscored the importance of leadership in the adoption of this process. They conducted an analysis of the organizational factors that constrained or facilitated the adoption of Intelligence-Led Policing principles in New Zealand police departments. Tactical operations under ILP included directed patrols at hot spot areas, bail checks of active offenders, and targeting the routine activities of prolific offenders. They determined that successful implementation of ILP was related to several factors including evidence of a transformational leadership style in the area—including the celebration of crime reduction as a goal, the existence of a "can do" organizational culture, support for partnerships and problem solving, tolerance for experimentation and trial of novel approaches, openness to learning, a willingness to sponsor improvement and engage in innovation. The areas that promoted and sponsored ILP were distinguished by an open management style where officers felt closer to their managers, were comfortable taking independent action and felt they could influence their job in a team environment. The implementation and development of ILP in these New Zealand departments was not driven by top-level administrators but led by individual commanders at the area and district levels who focused upon crime reduction within their local area. These local-area and district-level commanders represent the critical mass for change in their organization.

In the United States, Intelligence-Led Policing activities have been implemented in several cities. David Kennedy (2011) and his colleagues have helped police departments in Boston, Cincinnati, and other cities create and evaluate programs designed to deter specific criminal activity (e.g., gang violence, drug markets) without alienating the law-abiding residents in those areas. This program, now operating under the name National Network for Safe Communities, was adopted effectively in Boston (**Operation Ceasefire**—the Boston "Miracle"), Minneapolis, Stockton (CA), Indianapolis, Memphis, New Haven, Portland, Baltimore, High Point (NC), and Cincinnati.

Consistent with the premises of deterrence theory, drug market operators and juvenile gang members are viewed as rational actors who will respond to the threat of imminent punishment. For example, the carrying of guns by these offenders is a rational response to their sense of fear they will be shot. This approach applies a variety of "levers" that selects a target group of offenders, announcement of potential heavy and swift enforcement ahead of time to the group, showing the offenders they are under police surveillance, and showing the prison terms given to their convicted peers while asserting the necessity of punishment that is immediate and forthcoming (through the use of federal enforcement and sentencing). It is a strategy of "**focused deterrence**" directed at one problem, aimed at stopping the violence associated with the illegal drug trade.

In Cincinnati, the use of focused deterrence resulted in the decline of homicides by almost 20 percent overall, and 36 percent among Black males using handguns (University of Cincinnati Policing Institute, 2009). While previous crackdowns in Cincinnati had resulted in a backlash from law-abiding residents who felt harassed by police, this targeted crackdown was praised by community members. In High Point, NC, an evaluation of the drug market policing strategy in that city found a statistically significant reduction in violent crime within the targeted neighborhoods compared to other High Point neighborhoods, although the violent crime rate actually increased after the interventions were implemented (Corsaro, Hunt, Hipple, & McGarrell, 2012).

Other programs designed to reduce violence have produced mixed results. In seven areas of the city, Chicago's CeaseFire program effectively reduced shootings (declines ranged from -16% to -27%), violence in hot spot areas (declines ranged from -15% to -40%), and gang homicides were reduced in six of the seven city locations (Skogan, Hartnett, Bump, & DuBois, 2008). An evaluation of the Phoenix TRUCE project (a program modeled after Chicago's CeaseFire) uncovered mixed findings. Shootings increased during the program but assaults and other formsW of violent crime declined as the program served more gang-involved clients, were recent victims of violence, or were released from prison (Fox, Katz, Choate, & Hedberg, 2014). In Pittsburgh, PA, the One Vision program failed to reduce violence. It had no effect upon homicide rates and aggravated and gun assaults increased in the three service areas (Wilson & Chermak, 2010). An evaluation of a pulling levers drug market intervention strategy in Peoria, IL, produced negative results (Corsaro & Brunson, 2013). There was no evidence of an impact on violent, property, drug, and disorder offenses or in total calls for service in the targeted areas. A survey of residents showed that the majority of them had no knowledge that the program was in operation.

However, a review of crime reduction programs in Chicago, Tampa, Topeka, and El Monte (CA), reported positive results. These programs had several common elements:

1. Significant attention on building strong partnerships with other components of the criminal justice system, local government, the business community, neighborhood groups and residents by fostering shared information between members.
2. Each community had established regular processes for analyzing crime, feeding crime information to officers and managers, building accountability for crime prevention and control into the mission of the department.
3. Each department had decentralized policing services to focus on specific neighborhoods and reporting districts.
4. Clear leadership in each jurisdiction that continually emphasized the expectation that the police (working in concert with community partners) were responsible for preventing and controlling violent crime.

Overall, these programs featured working coalitions, a focus on local problems and resources, data-driven problem solving, and interventions that featured focused deterrence (Hipple, McGarrell, Klofas, Corsaro, & Perez, 2010, pp. 79–81).

New Orleans developed a focused deterrence approach (the Group Violence Reduction Strategy—GVRS) to address the homicide problem. The GVRS targeted gang violence in hot spots identified by researchers throughout the city for a "pulling levers" approach—targeting 158 individuals from 54 gangs (Corsaro & Engel, 2015, p. 479). Findings from an interrupted time series design revealed significant reductions in overall homicides (-17%), gang member involved homicides (-32%), homicides with Black male victims (-26%), and both lethal and non-lethal firearms violence (-16%) (Corsaro & Engel, 2015, p. 496). The research showed that street-level outreach workers were not responsible for this decline in violence, but it was greatly enhanced by the level of cooperation evidenced by political and police officials in New Orleans and that "maintaining a clear focus on problem identification (gangs and groups) is vital to sustained success" (Corsaro & Engel, 2015, pp. 497–498).

A similar approach in Chicago determined that gang members who attended a violence reduction strategy (VRS) call-in evidenced cooperation. The purpose of a VRS is to send a deterrent message to gang members about the violence raging in the city and "tell them, in no uncertain terms, to put down the guns" (Papachristos & Kirk, 2015, p. 526). Using propensity score matching techniques to make relevant comparisons between groups, the research revealed a VRS treatment effect—a 23 percent reduction in overall shooting behavior and a 32 percent reduction in gunshot victimization (Papachristos & Kirk, 2015, p. 551).

McGarrell et al. (2007, p. 154) suggest that police departments could adopt ILP in the following manner. Focus on the greatest threat facing the community. Establish a multiunit, multiagency task force to meet regularly and be held accountable for effectively addressing the issue. Use the intelligence process to develop information to guide and assess operations, efficiently deploy resources, and evaluate performance to enforce accountability. Implemented in this fashion, ILP has the potential to disrupt, enforce, and prevent crime problems previously believed to be intractable. Yet, it is most important that the police avoid the use of "institutional bullying" and make certain that programs like focused deterrence promote less biased and blanket discriminatory policing practices (Griffiths & Christian, 2015, p. 7).

Smart Policing

Another initiative that seems to meld police strategies is known as Smart Policing. The website for this approach (www.smartpolicinginitiative.com/) states the goal of Smart Policing is to build "evidence-based, data-driven law enforcement tactics and strategies that are effective, efficient and economical." The Bureau of Justice Assistance has sponsored several Smart Policing Initiatives (SPI) in several cities. These initiatives feature approaches based upon Hot Spot Policing and focused deterrence, offender-based strategies (Coldren, Huntoon, & Medaris, 2013, p. 281). Several forecasting techniques have been used by policing experts (Perry, McInnis, Price, Smith, & Hollywood, 2013, p. xiv) that are features of Smart Policing. They include:

1. Methods for identifying locations with an increased risk for crime.
2. Methods for identifying individuals at risk for future offending.
3. Methods to match likely offenders with specific past crimes.
4. Methods for predicting victims of crime.

Making predictions is only the beginning of the process. The next step is the creation of initiatives aimed at crime prevention. The entire process is dependent upon the collection and maintenance of accurate data. Finally, again the assessment process (evaluation of the effectiveness of the implemented interventions) is recommended.

Several strategies have been determined to be effective. For example, a problem-oriented approach to convenience store crime in Glendale, Arizona, resulted in a 42 percent decrease in crime at targeted stores (White & Katz, 2013, p. 305). In Boston, Safe Street Teams identified and targeted hot spots of violent crime resulting in a 17 percent reduction in violent crimes—particularly robbery and aggravated assault (Braga & Schnell, 2013, p. 351). In Lowell, MA, the police indentified hot spots of property crime. Increased survellience of these areas resulted in decreases in motor vehicle theft (61%), larceny (43% and 50%) and shoplifting (42% and 41%) (Bond & Hajjar, 2013, pp. 332–333). The LAPD targeted repeat violent offenders and gang members (Operation LASER) in its Newton Division—a hot spot of gun and gang-related, violent crime. The removal of the targeted offenders resulted in a 5.2 percent decrease in gun crime per month in the hot spot area (Uchida & Swatt, 2013, p. 297). In sum, these Smart Policing Initiatives have showed that evidence-based strategies can effectively reduce crime in areas that have had long-term crime problems (Joyce, Ramsey, & Stewart, 2013, pp. 366–367).

Targeting of gun violence in nine cities funded by the Smart Policing Initative featured the following strategies:

*   Targeting persistent gun violence hot spots.
*   Targeting prolific offenders in persistent hot spots.
*   Employing new technologies and advanced crime analysis.

- Engaging a wide range of collaborative partners.
- Conducting advanced problem analysis.

The results of the LASER program in Los Angeles were listed above. Efforts in other cities were also effective. In Boston, a problem-oriented strategy focused on micro-level hot spots was able to reduce aggravated assaults by more than 15 percent, violent crime by more than 17 percent, and robberies by more than 19 percent. Target enforcement of crime hot spots in Baltimore reduced homicides by 27 percent. In addition, a related focused deterrence intervention reduced non-fatal shootings in one neighborhood by 40 percent and a gun offender registry reduced gun-related reoffending risks among participants by 92 percent (Braga, Webster, White, & Saizow, 2014, pp. ii–iii).

Conclusion

What do these strategies have in common and how do they differ? First, they use information to develop strategy and tactics to guide operations and meet the true purpose of policing, to prevent and respond to crime. Second, they also follow up to evaluate and assess the effectiveness of these operations to determine whether they have been effective and if not, how to alter operations so they can improve. Third, they seek the support of and input from the community and recognize that citizens are in partnership with the police in crime prevention efforts. Fourth, they hold the police accountable for their performance.

They are not mutually exclusive and can be blended together. For example, Willis, Mastrofski, and Kochel (2010) examined how police departments faced implementing both Compstat and Community Policing in their departments. They conducted surveys and visited five police departments to make observations. They addressed the problem of co-implementation by comparing Compstat and Community Policing operations on seven elements or aspects: (1) Mission, (2) Internal Accountability, (3) Decentralization of Decision Making, (4) Organizational Flexibility, (5) Data-driven Problem Identification and Assessment, (6) Innovative Problem Solving, and (7) External Accountability. They concluded that there was no level of integration between the two concepts regarding all aspects except decentralization of decision making and organizational flexibility. These last two concepts were considered as achieving a low integration. In their study, Community Policing achieved some level of decentralization of decision making to the neighborhood level but not to sergeants or beat officers. Compstat led to a territorial focus at the district level by delegating decision making authority to district commanders (Willis et al., 2010, p. 976). Across the board, the two organizational reforms appeared to have an "additive effect." One compensated for the other by helping the organization respond more comprehensively to the diverse demands confronted in its environment (Willis et al., 2010, p. 977). Although officers viewed these reforms as complementary, they seemed to respond to different problems in the organizational external environment.

Willis (2013) also addressed the co-implementation issue by examining how the decision making of first-line supervisors operated under Compstat and Community Policing. He examined data from focus groups conducted with 34 participants. Under Compstat, sergeants could address crime problems as they saw fit, with no specific directives from above—just do something about crime. The sergeants used Compstat crime data to determine where and when to focus patrol resources—particularly in the identification of crime hot spots. Beyond this, their ability to engage in problem solving was limited. Community Policing tended to be the province of a specialized unit rather than implemented through permanent beat teams. Both reforms were hindered by the department's focus on handling 911 calls (Willis, 2013, p. 248).

Two particular management issues appear to affect the implementation of all of the strategic initiatves covered in this chapter. The first is loose coupling. Coupling refers to the degree to which organizational elements are linked, connected, related, or inter-dependent. Loose coupling is the problem when organizational elements are minimally connected (Maguire & Katz, 2002, p. 504). To ensure the success of any of the strategies discussed in this chapter, all levels of the police organization must be both informed and involved. The typical problem here is that the line staff (patrol officers) are not con-sulted and trained in the nuances of the chosen method. The result is that they do not implement the initiative correctly when left to their own devices. Their performance is the key to implementing any initiative and their input can help prevent errors. Detec-tives serving the area must also be informed. Area residents and organized groups must be aware of police operations to secure their support and to establish legitimacy. A Hot Spot Policing effort in the Trinidad and Tobago Police Service used "scaling up" (from specific hot spot locations to a district-wide focus) and "feeding back" (telling constables what they have done and its effect) to overcome the problem of loose coupling. Every two weeks a district-level "COPstat" meeting was held with the officers doing the patrols (Sherman et al., 2014).

Second, community involvement is a crucial element of these approaches. The police must recognize that effective crime prevention is tied to the support of the community. Their eyes and ears are always present and they naturally have a key stake and interest in the safety of their neighborhood and its surroundings. Like the beat officers, they must be kept informed about police operations in their area so they can contribute to their success. They also act as a barometer of the legitimacy of such operations and provide feedback on their appropriateness.

Third, the 911 issue is a particular hindrance to the establishment of these methods across the board. In order to prevent crime, police departments must find a way to divest themselves of their 911 burden. The citizenry have come to expect responses to 911 calls and the response affects citizens' attitudes toward the police. However, to truly focus on crime problems, manpower must be made readily available to implement these different strategies. They are evidence-based and their effectiveness is supported by recent research. Strategic policing is the wave of the future.

Elements of these paradigms are summarized and presented in Table 8.1.

It is paramount that law enforcement agencies evaluate and consider the impact upon public trust when proposing and implementing crime control strategies. The obligation is not only to reduce crime but to do so fairly in a way that protects the rights of citizens. The absence of crime is not the sole or final goal of law enforcement. The promotion and pro-tection of public safety must be balanced with the dignity and rights of all (*President's Task Force on 21st Century Policing*, 2015, p. 13). Establishing and maintaining this balance is the hallmark of police professionalism.

TABLE 8.1 Strategic Policing Strategies

Paradigm	Focus	Strategy	Implementation Issues	Effectiveness
Community Policing (COP)	Community partnerships to deal with problems of crime and disorder.	Decentralized approach. Use of beat patrol, substations and "beat meetings" to get close to citizens and obtain their input.	Lack of support among police administrators and officers. Tendency toward partial implementation in specialized units and creation of "innovation ghettos."	Improved relations and appreciation of citizens (by the police) and police (by citizens). Reduction in the fear of crime among some community residents. Some evidence that COP lowers the crime rate.
Problem-Oriented Policing (POP)	Police are required to develop a systematic process to identify the nature and causes of crime problems, review, analyze and select a response, and determine the effectiveness of the chosen response and/or select new strategies.	Police should focus on identifying and solving problems. Proactive intervention is required such as the use of "Hot Spot" Policing.	Police tend to engage in "shallow" problem solving and use traditional methods of policing rather than develop innovations.	Hot Spot Policing has been found to result in crime reduction (with violent and drug offenses) with a diffusion of crime control benefits to neighboring communities. Reduction in calls for service.
Compstat	Operational managers are held accountable for addressing the crime and disorder issues and trends from crime data and are empowered to focus, manage, and direct their unit's problem-solving process.	Four step process: 1. Accurate & Timely Intelligence. 2. Rapid Deployment. 3. Effective Tactics. 4. Relentless Follow-Up & Assessment.	1. Lack of a clear purpose. 2. No one has specific responsibilities. 3. Meetings held irregularly, infrequently, or randomly. 4. No one person is authorized to run meetings. 5. No dedicated analytic staff. 6. No follow-up. 7. No difference between "the brutal and the bland". 8. Fear and pressure lead to data manipulation and falsification.	Seven major crime categories (homicide, rape, robbery, assault, burglary, larceny, auto theft) that was greater than the nine other largest U.S. cities during the period 1990–2009. For these crimes, the average decline in New York was 63 percent during the 1990s and 45 percent after 2000.

Intelligence-Led Policing (ILP)	ILP focuses upon the ability of information to guide police operations—especially in terms of anticipating future risks and influencing decision makers to take action to prevent crime.	Reduce crime through the combined use of crime analysis and criminal intelligence in order to determine crime reduction tactics that concentrate on the enforcement and prevention of criminal offender activity with a focus on active and recidivist offenders. Emphasizes information gathering through the extensive use of confidential informants, offender interviews, analysis of recorded crime and calls for service, surveillance of suspects, and community sources of information.	More time spent on data entry than data analysis and crime analysts spent time on administrative statistics like performance appraisals rather than developing tactical intelligence. Intelligence rarely read and even more scarcely acted upon.	Focus deterrence programs have proven to be effective. Involve Heavy enforcement announced ahead of time, showing the offenders that they are under police surveillance, and demonstrating the prison terms given to their convicted peers while asserting the necessity of punishment that is immediate and forthcoming. Reduction in gun crimes and drug activity.
Smart Policing	Use of evidence-based, data-driven law enforcement tactics and strategies that are effective, efficient and economical.	Initiatives feature approaches based upon Hot Spot Policing and focused deterrence, and offender based strategies.	Requires performance measurement and research partnerships. Must manage organizational change. Make better use of intelligence and other data and information systems.	Across several cities, Hot Spot Policing resulted in reductions in violent and property, gang-related crime.

KEY TERMS

Accountability
Actionable Intelligence
Chicago Alternative Policing
Strategy (CAPS)
Community Policing

Compstat
Critical mass
Focused deterrence
Hot Spot Policing
Intelligence-Led Policing

Operation Ceasefire
Problem-Oriented Policing
SARA Model
Smart Policing
Strategic Planning Process

Note

1. Joanes (1999–2000, p. 298) determined that the decrease in NYC's homicide rate was "well within the range of decreases observed in half of the seventeen largest U.S. cities" following the 1991 peak in NYC homicides.

References

Ammar, N., Kessler, D., & Kratcoski, P. (2007). The interaction between a neighborhood's racial composition and officer race in community policing: A case study from the residential area policing programme (RAPP), Cleveland, Ohio. *International Journal of Police Science and Management, 10*(3), 313–325.

Batts, A., Smoot, S., & Scrivner, E. (2006). *Police leadership challenges in a changing world. New Perspectives in Policing Bulletin.* Washington, DC: U.S. Department of Justice, National Institute of Justice.

Behn, R.D. (2005). The core drivers of CitiStat: It's not just about the meetings and the maps. *International Public Management Journal,* 295–319.

Behn, R.D. (2008). *The seven big errors of PerformanceStat.* Boston: Harvard University John F. Kennedy School of Goverment.

Bond, B.J., & Hajjar, L.M. (2013). Measuring congruence between property crime problems and response strategies: Enhancing the problem-solving process. *Police Quarterly, 16*(3), 323–338.

Bowers, K., Johnson, S., Guerette, R., Summers, L., & Poyton, S. (2011). Spatial displacement and diffusion of benefits among geographically focused policing initiatives. *Campbell Systematic Reviews.* doi: 10.4073./csr.2011.3.

Bradstreet, R. (1997). Policing: The patrol sergeant's perspective. *Journal of Police and Criminal Psychology, 12,* 1–6.

Braga, A.A. (2005). Hot spots policing and crime prevention: A systematic review of randomized control trials. *Journal of Experimental Criminology, 1,* 317–342.

Braga, A.A., & Bond, B.J. (2008). Policing crime and disorder hot spots: A randomized controlled trial. *Criminology, 46*(3), 577–607.

Braga, A.A., Papachristos, A.V., & Hureau, D.M. (2014). The effects of hot spot policing on crime: An updated systematic review and meta-analysis. *Justice Quarterly, 31*(4), 633–663.

Braga, A.A., & Schnell, C. (2013). Evaluating place-based strategies: Lessons learned from the smart policing initiative in Boston. *Police Quarterly, 16*(3), 339–357.

Braga, A.A., Webster, D.W., White, M.D., & Saizow, H. (2014). *SMART approaches to reducing gun violence: Smart policing initiative spotlight on evidence-based strategies and impacts.* Washington, DC: Bureau of Justice Assistance.

Braga, A.A., & Weisburd, D.L. (2010). *Policing problem places: Crime hot spots and effective prevention.* New York: Oxford University Press.

Bratton, W., & Knobler, P. (1998). *Turnaround: How America's top cop reversed the crime epidemic.* New York: Random House.

Burruss, G., & Giblin, M. (2009). Modeling isomorphism on policing innovation: The role of institutional pressures in adopting community-oriented policing. *Crime & Delinquency, 60*(3), 331–355.

Capowich, G.E., & Roehl, J.A. (1994). Problem-oriented policing: Actions and effectiveness in San Diego. In D. Rosenbaum (Ed.), *The challenge of community policing: Testing the promises* (pp. 127–128). Thousand Oaks, CA: Sage.

Carter, D., & Carter, J. (2009). Intelligence-led policing: Conceptual considerations for public policy. *Criminal Justice Policy Review, 20*(3), 310–325.

Casady, T. (2011). Police legitimacy and predictive policing. *Geography & Public Safety, 2*(4), 1–2.

Chappell, A.T., Monk-Turner, E., & Payne, B. (2010). Broken windows or window breakers: The influence of physical and social disorder on quality of life. *Justice Quarterly, 28*(3), 522–540.

Coldren, J.R., Huntoon, A., & Medaris, M. (2013). Introducing smart policing: Foundations, principles, and practice. *Police Quarterly, 16*(3), 275–286.

Committee to Review Research on Police Policy and Practices. (2004). *Fairness and effectiveness in policing: The evidence.* Washington DC: The National Academies Press.

Connell, N., Miggans, K., & McGloin, J. (2008). Can a community policing initiative reduce serious crime?: A local evaluation. *Police Quarterly, 11*(2), 127–150.

Cordner, G., & Biebel, E.P. (2005). Problem-oriented policing in practice. *Criminology & Public Policy, 4*(2), 155–180.

Corsaro, N., & Brunson, R.K. (2013). Are suppression and deterrence mechanisms enough? Examining the "pulling levers" drug market intervention strategy in Peoria, Illinois, USA. *International Journal of Drug Policy, 24*, 115–121.

Corsaro, N., & Engel, R.S. (2015). Most challenging of contexts: Assessing the impact of focused deterrence on serious violence in New Orleans. *Criminology & Public Policy, 14*(3), 471–505.

Corsaro, N., Hunt, E.D., Hipple, N.K., & McGarrell, E.F. (2012). The impact of drug market pulling levers on neighborhood violence. *Criminology & Public Policy, 11*(2), 167–199.

Darroch, S., & Mazerolle, L. (2013). Intelligence-led policing: A comparative analysis of organizational factors influencing innovation uptake. *Police Quarterly, 16*(1), 3–37.

Eck, J., & Maguire, E. (2000). Have changes in policing reduced violent crime? An assessment of the evidence. In A. Blumstein, & J. Wallman (Eds.), *The crime drop in America* (pp. 207–265). New York: Cambridge University Press.

Eck, J.C., & Spelman, W. (1987). Who ya gonna call? The police as problem-busters. *Crime & Delinquency, 33*, 31–52.

Eck, J.E., & Weisburd, D. (2004). What police can do to reduce crime, disorder and fear. *Annals, AAPSS, 593*, 42–65.

Eterno, J.A., & Silverman, E.B. (2006). The New York City police department's Compstat: Dream or nightmare? *International Journal of Police Science & Management*, 218–231.

Eterno, J.A., & Silverman, E.B. (2010). The NYPD's Compstat: Compare statistics or compose statistics? *International Journal of Police Science & Management*, 426–449.

Gau, J.M., & Pratt, T.C. (2010). Revisiting broken windows theory: Examining the sources of the discriminant validity of perceived disorder and crime. *Journal of Criminal Justice*, *38*(4), 758–766.

Gianakis, G., & Davis, G. (1998). Reinventing or repackaging public Services? The case of community policing. *Public Administration Review, 58*.

Giuliani, R. (2002). *Leadership*. New York: Hyperion Books.

Goldstein, H. (1979). Improving policing: A problem-oriented approach. *Crime & Delinquency, 25*, 236–258.

Goldstein, H. (1990). *Problem-oriented policing*. New York: McGraw Hill.

Goldstein, H. (1993). *The new policing: Confronting complexity*. Washington, DC: National Institute of Justice.

Greene, J.R. (1989). Police officer job satisfaction and community perceptions: Implications for community-oriented policing. *Journal of Research in Crime and Delinquency, 26*(2), 168–183.

Griffiths, E., & Christian, J. (2015). Considering focused deterrence in the age of Ferguson, Baltimore, North Charleston and beyond. *Criminology & Public Police, 14*(3), 1–9.

Groff, E.R., Johnson, L., Ratcliffe, J.H., & Wood, J. (2013). Exploring the relationship between foot and car patrol in violent crime areas. *Policing, 36*(1), 119–139.

Fagan, J., Zimring, F.E., & Kim, J. (1998). Declining homicide in New York City: A tale of two trends. *Journal of Criminal Law and Criminology, 88*(4), 1277–1323.

Fox, A.M., Katz, C.M., Choate, D.E., & Hedberg, E.C. (2014). Evaluation of the Phoenix TRUCE project: A replication of Chicago Ceasefire. *Justice Quarterly, 32*(1), 85–115.

Harcourt, B.E., & Ludwig, J. (2006). Broken windows: New evidence from New York City and a five-city social experiment. *The University of Chicago Law Review, 73*(1), 271–320.

Hayeslip, D.W., & Cordner, G. (1987). Effects of community-oriented patrol on police officer attitudes. *American Journal of Police, 6*(1), 95–119.

He, N., Zhao, J., & Lovrich, N. (2005). Community policing: A preliminary assessment of environmental impact with panel data on program implementation in U.S. cities. *Crime & Delinquency, 51*(3), 295–317.

Henderson, L.J. (2003). *The Baltimore CitiSAtat program: Performance and accountability*. Baltimore: University of Baltimore.

Henry, W. (2002). *The Compstat paradigm: Management accountability in policing*. New York: Looseleaf Press.

Hinkle, J., & Weisburd, D. (2008). The irony of broken windows policing: A micro-place study of the relationship between disorder, focused police crackdowns and fear of crime. *Journal of Criminal Justice, 36*, 503–512.

Hinkle, J., & Yang, S. (2014). A new look at broken windows: What shapes individuals' perceptions of disorder? *Journal of Criminal Justice, 42*(1), 26–35.

Hipple, N., McGarrell, E., Klofas, J., Corsaro, N., & Perez, H. (2010). Identifying effective policing strategies for reducing crime. In J. Klofas, N. Hipple, & E. McGarrell (Eds.), *The new criminal justice: American communities and the changing world of crime control* (pp. 69–82). New York: Routledge.

Jang, H., Hoover, L.T., & Joo, H-J. (2010). An evaluation of compstat's effect on crime: The Fort Worth experience. *Police Quarterly*, 13(4), 387–412.

Jang, H., Hoover, L.T., & Lawton. B.A. (2008). The effect of broken windows enforcement on clearance rates. *Journal of Criminal Justice*, 36(6), 529–538.

Joanes, A. (1999–2000). Does the New York City police department deserve credit for the decline in New York City's homicide Rates? A cross-city comparison of policing strategies and homicide rates. *Columbia Journal of Law and Social Problems*, 265–311.

Joyce, N.M., Ramsey, C.H., & Stewart, J.K. (2013). Commentary on smart policing. *Police Quarterly, 16*(3), 358–368.

Kelling, G.L., & Bratton, W.J. (1993). *Implementing community policing: The administrative problem*. Washington, DC: National Institute of Justice.

Kelling, G., & Coles, C. (1996). *Fixing broken windows: Restoring order and reducing crime in our communities*. New York: The Free Press.

Kennedy, D.M. (2011). *Don't shoot: One man, a street fellowship and the end of violence in inner-city America*. New York: Bloomsbury.

Koper, C.S. (2014). Assessing the practice of hot spots policing: Survey results from a national convenience sample of local police agencies. *Journal of Contemporary Criminal Justice, 30*(2), 123–146.

Koper, C.S. (1995). Just enough police presence: Reducing crime and disorderly behavior by optimizing patrol time in crime hot spots. *Justice Quarterly, 12*(4), 649–672.

Lawton, B.A., Taylor, R.B., & Luongo, A.J. (2005). Police officers on drug corners in Philadelphia, Drug crime, and violent crime: Intended diffusion, and displacement Impacts. *Justice Quarterly, 22*(4), 427–451.

Lombardo R., Olson, D., Staton, M. (2010) The Chicago Alternative Policing Strategy: A reassessment of the CAPS program, *Policing: An International Journal*, 33 (4), 586–606.

Lombardo, R., & Lough, T. (2007). Community policing: Broken windows, community building, and satisfaction with the police. *The Police Journal, 80*(2), 117–140.

Lord, V., Kuhns, J., & Friday, P. (2009). Small city community policing and citizen satisfaction. *Policing: An international journal, 32*(4), 574–594.

Lurgio, A., & Rosenbaum, D. (1994). The impact of community policing on police personnel: A review of the literature. In D. Rosenbaum (Ed.), *The challenge of community policing: Testing the promises* (pp. 147–163). Thousand Oaks, CA: Sage.

Maguire, E.R. (1997). Structural change in large municipal police organizations During the community policing era. *Justice Quarterly, 14*(3), 547–576.

Maguire, E.R., & Katz, C.M. (2002). Community policing, loose coupling and sensemaking in American police agencies. *Justice Quarterly, 19*(3), 503–536.

Macguire, E.R., Uchida, C.D., & Hassell, K.D. (2015). Problem-oriented policing in Colorado Springs: A content analysis of 753 cases. *Crime & Delinquency, 61*(1), 71–95.

Maple, J. (1999). *The crime fighter: How to you can make your community crime free*. New York: Broadway Books.

McDonald, P.P. (2002). *Managing police operations: Implementing the New York Crime control model—CompStat*. Stamford, CT: Thomson.

McGarrell, E.F., Frelich, J.D., & Chermak, S. (2007). Intelligence-led policing as a framework for responding to terrorism. *Journal of Contemporary Criminal Justice, 23*(2), 142–158.

Messner, S.F., Galea, S., Tardiff, K.J., Tracy, M., Buccarelli, A., Piper, T.M., Frye, V., & Vlahov, D. (2007). Policing, drugs, and the homicide decline in New York City in the 1990s. *Criminology, 45*(2), 385–414.

Moore, M. (1995). *Creating public value: Strategic management in government.* Cambridge, MA: Harvard University Press.

Moore, M., & Stephens, D. (1991). *Beyond command and control: The strategic management of police departments.* Washington, DC: Police Executive Research Forum.

National Academy of Sciences. (2004). *Fairness and effectiveness in policing.* (W. Skogan & K. Frydll, Eds.). Washington, DC: The National Academies Press.

O'Connell, P.E., & Straub, F. (2007). *Performance-based management for police organizations.* Long Grove, IL: Waveland Press.

Oliver, W.M. (2000). The third generation of community policing moving through innovation, diffusion, and institutionalization. *Police Quarterly, 3,* 365–388.

Papachristos, A.V., & Kirk, D.S. (2015). Changing the street dynamic: Evaluating Chicago's group violence reduction strategy. *Criminology and Public Policy, 14*(3), 525–558.

Parnell, J.A. (2014). *Strategic management.* Thousand Oaks, CA: Sage.

Peak, K., & Glensor, R. (2002). *Community policing & problem solving: Strategies and practices.* Upper Saddle River NJ: Prentice Hall.

Perry, W.L., McInnis, B., Price, C.C., Smith, S.C., & Hollywood, J.S. (2013). *Predictive policing: The role of crime forecasting in law enforcement operations.* Santa Monica, CA: The RAND Corporation.

President's Task Force on 21st Century Policing. (2015). *Interim report of the President's task force on 21st century policing.* Washington, DC: Office of Community Oriented Police Services.

Ratcliffe, J. (2005). The effectiveness of police Intelligence management: A New Zealand case study. *Police Practice and Research, 6*(5), 435–451.

Ratcliffe, J. (2016). *Intelligence led policing,* 2nd ed. New York: Routledge.

Ratcliffe, J.H. (2009). Intelligence-led policing. In A. Wakefield, & J. Fleming (Eds.), *The Sage dictionary of policing* (pp. 176–179). London: Sage.

Ratcliffe, J.H. (2014, March 14). Retrieved from Jerry Ratcliffe: Policing, criminal intelligence, and crime science, www.jratcliffe.net/papers.

Ratcliffe, J.H., & Guidetti, R. (2008). State investigative structure and the adoption of intelligence-led policing. *Policing, 31*(1), 109–128.

Ratcliffe, J.H., Taniguchi, T., Groff, E.R., & Wood, J.D. (2011). The Philadelphia foot patrol experiment: A Randomized controlled trial of police patrol effectiveness in violent crime hotspots. *Criminology, 49*(3), 795–831.

Reiss, A.J. (1992). Police organizations in the twentieth century. In M. Tonry, & N. Morris (Eds.), *Modern policing* (pp. 51–97). Chicago: University of Chicago Press.

Rosenbaum, D.P. (1998). The changing role of the police: Assessing the current transition to community policing. In J. Brodeur (Ed.), *How to recognize good policing* (pp. 3–29). Thousand Oaks, CA: Sage.

Rosenfeld, R., & Fornango, R. (2014). The impact of police stops on precinct robbery and burglary rates in New York City, 2003–2010. *Justice Quarterly, 31*(1), 96–122.

Rosenfeld, R., Fornango, R., & Rengifo, A.F. (2007). The impact of order-maintenance policing on New York City homicide and robbery rates: 1998-2001. *Criminology, 45*(2), 355–384.

Sadd, S., & Grinc, R. (1994). Innovative neighborhood oriented policing: An evaluation of community policing in eight cities. In D. Rosenbaum (Ed.), *The challenge of community policing: Testing the promises* (pp. 27–52). Thousand Oaks, CA: Sage.

Safir, H. (1997, December). Goal-oriented community policing: The NYPD approach. *The Police Chief*, 31–58.

Sample, S.B. (2002). *The contrarian's guide to leadership*. San Francisco: Jossey Bass.

Scheider, M., Chapman, R., & Schapiro, A. (2009). Towards the unification of policing innovations under community policing. *Policing: An International Journal, 32*(4), 694–718.

Sherman, L.W. (1995). Hot spots of crime and criminal careers of places. In J.E. Eck, & D. Weisburd (Eds.), *Crime and place—Crime prevention studies, volume 4* (pp. 35–52). Monsey, NY: Criminal Justice Press.

Sherman, L.W. (2009). Hot spots. In A. Wakefield, & J. Fleming (Eds.), *The Sage dictionary of policing* (pp. 157–160). London: Sage.

Sherman, L.W., Williams, S., Ariel, B., Strang, L.R., Wain, N., Slothower, M., & Norton, A. (2014). An integrated theory of hot spots patrol strategy: Implementing prevention by scaling up and feeding back. *Journal of Contemporary Criminal Justice, 30*(2), 95–122.

Sherman, L.W., & Weisburd, D. (1995). General deterrence effects of police patrol in crime "hot spots": A randomized control trial. *Justice Quarterly, 12*(4), 625–648.

Silverman, E.B. (1999). *NYPD battles crime: Innovative strategies in policing*. Boston: Northeastern University Pre.

Skogan, W.G. (1994). The impact of community policing on neighborhood residents: A cross-site analysis. In D. Rosenbaum (Ed.), *The challenge of community policing: Testing the promises* (pp. 167–181). Thousand Oaks, CA: Sage.

Skogan, W. (2006). *Police and community policing in Chicago: A tale of three cities*. New York: Oxford University Press.

Skogan, W.G., Harnett, S.M., Bump, N., & Dubois, J. (2008). *Evaluation of casefire-Chicago*. Washington, DC: U.S. Department of Justice, Office of Justice Program, National Institute of Justice.

Skolnick, J.H. (1999). *On democratic policing*. Washington, DC: The Police Foundation.

Skolnick, J.H., & Bayley, D. (1988). *Community policing: Issues and practices around the world*. Washington, DC: National Institute of Justice.

Sugarman, B. (2010). Organizational learning and reform at the New York City police department. *The Journal of Applied Behavioral Science*, 157–185.

Taylor, B., Koper, C.S., & Woods, D.J. (2011). A randomized controlled trial of different policing strategies at hot spots of violent crime. *Journal of Experimental Criminology, 7*, 149–181.

Telep, C.W., Mitchell, R.J., & Weisburd, D. (2012). How much time should the police spend at crime hot spots? Answers from a police agency directed randomized field trial in Sacramento, California. *Justice Quarterly, 31*(5), 905–933.

Tenbrunsel, A.E. (2011, April). Ethical breakdowns. *Harvard Business Review*, 58–67.

Tilley, N. (2003). Community policing, problem-oriented policing and intelligence-led policing. In T. Newburn (Ed.), *Handbook of policing* (pp. 311–339). Cullompton, UK: Willian.

Toch, H., & Grant, J. (1991). *Police as problem solvers*. New York: Plenum Press.

Travis, J. (1995). *Managing innovation in policing the untapped potential of middle managers: Research in brief*. Washington, DC: National Institute of Justice.

Trojanowicz, R., & Bucqueroux, B. (1994). *Community policing: How to get started*. Cincinnati: Anderson.

Uchida, C.D., & Swatt, M.L. (2013). Operation LASER and the effectiveness of hotspot patrol: A panel analysis. *Police Quarterly, 16*(3), 287–304.

University of Cincinnati Policing Institute. (2009). *Implementation of the Cincinnati initative to reduce violence (CIRV): Year 2 report*. Cincinnati, OH: University of Cincinnati.

Vito, G., Walsh, W., & Kunselman, J. (2004). Community policing: The middle manager's perspective. *Police Quarterly, 8*, 490–511.

Vito, G., Walsh, W., & Kunselman, J. (2005). Community policing: The middle manager's perspective. *Police Quarterly, 8*(4), 490–511.

Walsh, W. (2001). Compstat: An analysis of an emerging police managerial paradigm. *Policing, 24*(3), 347–362.

Walsh, W.F. (1994). Community policing: Analysis of the supervisor's role. In P.C. Kratcoski (Ed.), *Community policing* (pp. 141–152). Cincinnati: Anderson.

Wasserman, R., & Moore, M.H. (1988). *Values in policing*. Washington, DC: National Institute of Justice.

Weisburd, D. (2008). *Place-based policing: Ideas in American policing series*. Washington, DC: Police Foundation.

Weisburd, D., & Braga, A. (2006). Hot spots policing as a model for police innovation. In D. Weisburd, & A. Braga (Eds.), *Police innovation: Contrasting perspectives* (pp. 225–244). Cambridge, UK: Cambridge University Press.

Weisburd, D., Hinkle, J.C., Famega, C., & Ready, J. (2011). The possible "backfire" effects of hot spots policing: an experimental assessment of impacts on legitimacy, fear and collective efficacy. *Journal of Experimental Criminology, 7*(4), 297–320.

Weisburd, D., & Lum, C. (2005). The diffusion of computerized crime mapping in policing: Linking research and practice. *Police Practice and Research, 6*, 419–434.

Weisburd, D., & Telep, C.W. (2014). Hot spots policing: What we know and what we need to know. *Journal of Contemporary Criminal Justice, 30*(2), 200–220.

Weisburd, D., Telep, C.W., Hinkle, J.C., & Eck, J.E. (2010). Is problem-oriented policing effective in reducing crime and disorder? *Criminology & Public Policy, 9*(1), 139–172.

Weisburd, D., Telep, C.W., & Lawton, B.A. (2014). Could Innovations in policing have contributed to the New York City crime drop even in a period of declining police strength?: The case of stop, question and frisk as a policing strategy. *Justice Quarterly, 31*(1), 129–153.

Weisel, D.L., & Eck, J.E. (1994). Toward a practical approach to organizational change: Community policing initiatives in six cities. In D. Rosenbaum (Ed.), *The challenge of community policing: Testing the promises* (pp. 53–72). Thousand Oaks, CA: Sage.

White, M.D., & Katz, C.M. (2013). Policing convenience store crime: Lessons from the Glendale, Arizona Smart Policing Initiative. *Police Quarterly, 16*(3), 305–322.

Willis, J.J. (2013). First-line supervision and strategic decision making under Compstat and community policing. *Criminal Justice Policy Review, 24*(2), 235–256.

Willis, J.J., Mastrofski, S.D., & Kochel, T.R. (2010). The co-implementation of Compstat and community policing. *Journal of Criminal Justice, 38*, 969–980.

Worrall, J.L. (2006). Does targeting minor offenses reduce serious crime? A provisional, affirmative answer based on an analysis of county-level data. *Police Quarterly, 9*, 47–72.

Wilson, J.M., & Chermak, S. (2011). Community driven violence reduction programs. *Criminology & Public Policy, 10,* 993–1027.

Wycoff, M.A. (1988). Benefits of community policing: Evidence and conjecture. In J.R. Greene, & S. Mastrofski (Eds.), *Community policing: Rhetoric or reality?* (pp. 103–120). New York: Praeger.

Wycoff, M.A., & Skogan, W. (1994). Community policing in Madison: An analysis of implementation and impact. In D. Rosenbaum (Ed.), *The challenge of communiity policing: Testing the promises* (pp. 75–91). Thousand Oaks, CA: Sage.

Xu, Y., Fiedler, M.L., & Flaming, K. (2005). Discovering the impact of community policing: The broken windows thesis, collective efficacy, and citizens' judgment. *Journal of Research in Crime and Delinquency, 42*(2), 147–186.

Yukl, G. (2013). *Leadership in organizations.* Upper Saddle River, NJ: Prentice Hall.

Zhao, J., He, N., & Lovrich, N. (2006). Community policing: Did it change the basic functions of policing in the 1990s? *Justice Quarterly, 20*(4), 679–724.

Zhao, J., Lovrich, N., & Thurman, Q. (1999). The status of community policing in American cities. *Policing, 22,* 74–92.

Zhao, J., Thurman, Q., & Lovrich, N. (1995). Community-oriented policng across the U.S.: Facilitators and impediments to implementation. *American Journal of Police, 14,* 11–28.

Zimring, F.E. (2012). *The city that became safe: New York's lessons for urban crime and its control.* New York: Oxford University Press.

9 Human Resource Management

Of all the decisions an executive makes, none are more important as the decisions about people because they determine the performance capacity of the organization.

Peter Drucker, *On the Profession of Management* (Drucker, 1998, p. 24)

Learning Objectives

1. Describe and define Human Resource Management in Policing.
2. Identify and define the historical and institutional context of police human resource management.
3. Explain the beliefs supporting Strategic Human Resource Management.
4. Describe the relationship between human resource management and the law.
5. Identify the steps in the Recruitment process.
6. Analyze the Police Selection process.
7. Identify the steps in the training and development of recruit police officers.
8. Understand the Discipline process in Human Resource Management.
9. Identify the difference between negative and positive discipline in policing.
10. Analyze the issues associated with implementation of police discipline.
11. Identify the steps required to create a positive work environment.

Introduction

This chapter identifies and explains the concepts, techniques, issues, and problems associated with human resource management function in policing. The term **human resource management** (HRM) refers to the functions, policies, and activities a police department employs to manage the effective utilization of its human resources now and in the future. Policing is a labor-intensive endeavor. A department's most important and valuable resource is its employees, both sworn and non-sworn (***personnel***), who do police work (Nowicki, 2003). The ability of a police department to fulfill its mission and provide effective services is directly related to the quality of its personnel and the manner in which they are recruited, selected, developed, and managed. This presents organizational administrators with the following challenges:

How should these critical resources be recruited, selected, trained, developed, and managed?

What are effective policies and practices for managing human resources?

How should the department manage its human resources that will ensure organizational effectiveness?

The goal of human resource management is to maximize both employee and organizational potential. The term "human resource management" has the same meaning that personnel administration did many years ago. The different titles reflect the changing mindset of today's organizational leadership and their understanding of the strategic role of this function (Dessler, 2013). Recruitment, selection, training, development, and management of personnel are critical human resource functions. However, a department's human resource process does not exist in a vacuum. The law, both federal and state, local charters and ordinances, political motives, jurisdictional size, community values, budgets, and the department's culture influence the administration of its human resources.

A unique problem police departments face in formulating human resource management policy and strategies is that they are not fully in control of their human resource function. Authority over this function is divided between the department's chief executive and the following:

The mayor or city manager.

Personnel administrator.

Personnel department.

City council.

Civil service commission.

Department's staff.

As the above list indicates, there is a variety of individuals and functional subdivisions involved in the administration of police human resources. In many municipalities, there is a Human Resource Department under the jurisdiction's chief executive, city manager, mayor, or chief administrative officer, or it may be a civil service commission, independent of any administrative office. The Human Resource administrative function is usually the responsibility of a separate bureau or division in large police agencies. In most departments it is a sub-unit of administrative services. Normally, a department does not have final decision-making authority in the selection of police officers and/or promotional candidates. These decisions by law are assigned to the department's political subdivision's (Township, City, County, or State) administrative body responsible for human resources. Because of this many state legislatures have created police officer standards and training commissions or POSTs that are empowered to establish state-wide minimum personnel training certification standards that all police departments within the state must follow. These factors contribute to a view held by some police managers that they are not responsible for the HRM function. Nothing is further from the truth. Managers have a responsibility to understand and interpret the political subdivision's and department's personnel policies and procedures, create and maintain a qualified workforce as well as the develop the skills and abilities of their officers. This is a critical responsibility because as Drucker noted in the quotation heading this chapter the decisions about people determine the performance capacity of an organization.

Historical Development

Human Resource Management (HRM) has evolved from an administrative function concerned only with the needs of the organization to one that emphasizes both the needs of the employees of the organization and its strategic direction. In the early part of the 20th century, **Scientific Management** concepts developed by Frederick W. Taylor (1856–1915) dominated managerial philosophy. He advocated that managers should take a scientific and objective approach to how a person would perform a job. Taylor believed that organizational productivity could be improved by the use of scientific methods to analyze workflow and structure it into easily performed tasks. He was convinced that the one best way to do a job was to break it down to its smallest parts, specialize it, and train the worker to perform these tasks without thinking. This concept is known as "task specialization" and it is designed to leave little opportunity for error because the worker was not required to make decisions, think, and use judgment or discretion. This was a production-oriented process grounded in bureaucratic structural control and the employee was considered just another factor in the production effort (Taylor, 1911). Taylor's influence is present today in the use of a job task analysis to analyze jobs, create job descriptions, and establish the validity of hiring decisions, testing, and performance appraisal standards for police departments. It is also reflected in the task specialization structure of many large urban police departments.

A shift to the importance of the employee's impact on organizational effectiveness emerged out of the **Hawthorne Studies** conducted by Elton Mayo and F. J. Roethlisberger during the 1920s to the 1940s. They discovered that employee productivity was affected not only by the way a job is designed and structured but also by human, social, and psychological factors. Employees' feelings, emotions, and sentiments were strongly affected by their work conditions such as group relationships, leadership styles, and support from management. These feelings could have significant impact on productivity and organizational effectiveness. The findings of Mayo and Roethlisberger disclosed the individual's critical role within the organization and the impact of group dynamics on employee performance. Out of their research developed the **Human Relations School** of human resource management. This approach to management emphasized a shift in focus to the most vital of all organizational resources, the employee, and to a more supportive approach to the treatment of employees. It held that most employees desired to have a job that was worth doing and meaningful to them. Workers also desired safe and secure work conditions, adequate pay and benefits, job security, competent supervision, performance feedback, recognition for their efforts, advancement on merit, and fair treatment by the organization.

Building on the lessons of the past, **Human Resource Management** emerged during the period from the 1960s to the 1980s. It held that organizational goals and human needs are mutual and compatible and that one need not be treated at the expense of the other.

It hypothesized that if organizations wish to maximize employee performance, they need to consider culture, morale, and the psychological environment as important variables that affect their employees and their performance. These factors should be managed to have a positive impact on both the organization and its employees. Today, human resource management involves designing, planning, and implementing policies and systems to improve these factors.

Police departments today find themselves in a challenging and changing environment consisting of workforce diversity, technology, developing legal trends, community expectations, and new employee value systems that necessitated that organizations take a strategic approach to employee management. As a result **Strategic Human Resource Management** has emerged as the prevailing approach to achieve effective organizations (Dessler, 2013). Strategic human resource management is the art and science of linking a department's personnel management with its strategic goals and objectives to improve organizational performance and develop a culture that fosters commitment, learning, innovation, and flexibility. The department administrative leadership has the responsibility to create human resource policy and practices that are intended to produce employee competencies and behaviors needed to achieve its strategic objectives and enhance its human capital. The department's executive leadership team fulfills this responsibility by creating the strategic human resource process through the development of an organizational philosophy and management practices that support the department's strategic direction. The department's strategic direction provides the framework that guides the design of specific human resource activities such as recruitment, training, development, and discipline. In this manner an integrated framework should systematically link human resource activities with strategic need. This means getting everybody in the department from the top of the organization to the bottom doing what is necessary to implement activities to enhance organizational effectiveness (Schuler, 1992).

Strategic human resource management links the organizational effectiveness to the development and management of its people. It considers employees as organizational assets who when effectively recruited, selected, trained, developed, and managed will provide long-term commitment and service to the organization. This perspective holds that the management of human resources should be in perfect fit with the strategic management of the organization. In this way, employee behavior and skill sets form the bridge between the department's strategic direction and the effectiveness of its performance. It seeks to create a work environment in which employees are encouraged to develop and use their skills and abilities to the maximum extent. Thus, how an organization goes about organizing its human resource functions has significant consequences on what it can actually accomplish. This process involves answering the following key questions:

- What is our fundamental purpose? (mission).
- How do we accomplish this purpose? (identifying strategy and functions).
- What type of resources do we need? (human/budgetary/technological).
- What Knowledge, Skills, and Abilities are required? (job analysis/learning systems).
- How do we acquire individuals with these KSAs (recruitment and selection).
- How do we prepare these people for their roles? (training, development, and management).

HR Management and the Law

A fundamental value of our society is that there be equality of opportunity and fairness of treatment for all individuals in the workplace. The broad goal of this perspective is to provide all Americans, regardless of race, age, gender, religion, national origin, or disability, an equal opportunity to compete for jobs for which they are qualified. Civil rights legislation has been passed at the federal and state levels to provide remedies for job applicants or employees who feel they have been victims of unfair discrimination. It is critical from a personal, organizational, and managerial perspective that police administrators understand the rights and the obligations of employers, job candidates, and employees. Ignorance of the law in this area has resulted in lawsuits and claims of personal liability against police departments and their administrators. Briefly described below is important **equal employment legislation.**

EQUAL EMPLOYMENT LEGISLATION

1. **5th Amendment (1791)**—"no person shall. . . . Be deprived of life, liberty, or property, **without due process of the law**." This means that the government has to follow rules and established procedures in everything it does.
2. **13th Amendment (1865)** outlawed slavery and has been held by the courts to bar racial discrimination. Under this amendment any form of discrimination may be considered an incident of slavery or involuntary servitude.
3. **14th Amendment (1868)** makes it illegal for any state to "make or enforce any law which abridges the privileges and immunities of citizens of the United States." This amendment guarantees equal protection of the law for all citizens and bars discrimination on the basis of sex, race, or national origin.
   Both the 13th and 14th Amendments are the source of constitutional power that all subsequent civil rights legislation originates from because they granted to Congress the constitutional power to enact legislation to enforce their provisions.
4. **Civil Rights Act of 1866** gives all persons the right to make and enforce contracts and benefit from the laws of the land.
5. **Civil Rights Act of 1871** granted all citizens the right to sue in federal court if they feel they have been deprived of any rights or privileges guaranteed by the Constitution and laws.
6. **Equal Pay Act of 1963 (as amended 1972)** requires equal pay for equal work, regardless of sex; pay differences may be based on a seniority system, a merit system, a system that measures earnings by quantity or quality of production, or a differential based on any factor other than sex.
7. **Title VII of the 1964 Civil Rights Act,** as amended, prohibits employment discrimination based upon race, color, religion, sex, or national origin. This Act covers all public and private employers of 15 or more persons. Title VII is the most important federal EEO law because it contains the broadest coverage, prohibitions, and remedies. This Act created the Equal Employment Opportunity Commission (EEOC) to ensure that employers comply with its provisions.
8. **Age Discrimination in Employment Act of 1967**, as amended in 1986, prohibits discrimination and specifically protects individuals over 40 years old unless an employer can demonstrate that age is a BFOQ (bona fide occupational qualification) for the job in question.

Although the Act serves to protect older employees, it does not require an employer to hire or retain an individual who is not qualified. Police officers are involved with public safety, job fitness is a principal concern; age, therefore, is asserted as a BFOQ in this profession. Fitness for the job, rather than age, is the employment criterion and focus of the BFOQ analysis. If age is to be a reason for discharge or refusal to hire, it should be supported by empirical data which validates a BFOQ. This data can be provided only by assessment of the police officer's job-related abilities as they are impacted objectively by the age factor.

9. **Equal Employment Opportunity Act of 1972**, amended Title VII of the 1964 Civil Rights Act and instituted the **Equal Employment Opportunity Commission (EEOC)**. The EEOC is responsible for receiving and investigating complaints of job discrimination from aggrieved individuals. When it finds reasonable cause that the complaint is justified, it attempts to eliminate the discrimination through conciliation. If this fails the EEOC has the power to go to court to enforce the law.

10. **Pregnancy Discrimination Act of 1978** prohibits sex discrimination based on "Pregnancy, childbirth, or related medical conditions" and establishes that if an employer offers disability coverage, pregnancy and childbirth must be treated like any other disability.

11. **The Americans with Disabilities Act 1990** prohibits discrimination against a "qualified individual with a disability" with regard to applications, hiring, compensation, advancement, training, or other terms, conditions, or privileges of employment. A qualified individual is one able to perform the "essential" functions of a job with or without accommodation.

12. **The Civil Rights of 1991** is an amendment to Title VII that holds that a violation exists when an employee demonstrates that race, color, religion, sex, or national origin was a motivating factor in an employment action. Eliminated is the defense that the employer would have reached the same decision without considering these forbidden factors. It also added compensatory and punitive damages to the remedies available to plaintiffs.

    This act directly impacts police department entry-level physical testing procedures. It was a common practice for these tests to adjust for differences in upper-body strength between men and women. This act makes it unlawful "to adjust the scores of, use different cutoff scores for, or otherwise alter results of employment related test on the basis of race, color, religion, sex, or national origin."

13. **Sexual Harassment.** Title VII of the Civil Rights Act of 1964 42 U.S. Code Section 703 states that harassment on the basis of sex violates the act.

    Sexual Harassment is any repeated and/or unwelcome verbal or physical sexual advances, request for sexual favors, sexually explicit derogatory statements, or sexually discriminatory remarks made by someone in the workplace, which is offensive or humiliating or which interferes with the recipient's job performance. Or when

    1. Submission to such conduct is made either explicitly or implicitly a term or condition of an individual's employment.
    2. Submission to or rejection of such conduct by an individual is used as the basis for employment decisions affecting such individual, or
    3. Such conduct has the purpose or effect of reasonably interfering with an individual's work performance or creating an intimidating, hostile, or offensive working environment.

    There are two ways in which sexual harassment can be proved.

    Quid Pro Quo is when submission to or rejection of sexual harassment is used for employment decisions.

Hostile Work Environment is when the sexual harassment unreasonably interferes with an employee's work or creates an intimating or offensive workplace. A hostile work environment can by created by supervisors, co-workers, or non-employees (Freyss, 2004, p. 126).

In *Meritor Savings Bank, FSB v. Vinson (109 S.Ct. 2399, 1986)* the Supreme Court endorsed broadly the EEOC's position on sexual harassment and indicated that employers should establish meaningful complaint procedures and head off charges of sexual harassment before they occur. In 1998, the Supreme Court in *Oncale v. Sundowner Offshore Services (523 S.Ct. 75)* held that Title VII's protection against workplace discrimination "because of . . . sex" applied to harassment in the workplace between members of the same sex.

14. **Family and Medical Leave Act of 1993 (FMLA)**
    This Act requires employers to provide up to 12 weeks of unpaid job-protected leave to "eligible" employees for certain family and medical reasons. Eligible employees must have worked for the employer for at least one year, and for 1,250 hours over the previous 12 months.
    Leave must be granted for the following reasons:

    1. To care for the employee's child after birth, or placement for adoption or foster care.
    2. To care for the employee's spouse, son, daughter, or parent who has a serious health condition.
    3. From a serious health condition that makes the employee unable to perform the employee's job.

    At the employee or employer's option, paid leave may be substituted for unpaid leave. Employee must provide 30 days' advance notice of request whenever the reasons for the leave are "foreseeable."
    Employers have the right to:

    1. Require medical certification to support family leave made because of serious health consideration.
    2. Require second and third opinions at the employer's expense.
    3. Require a fitness for duty report prior to the employee's return to work.

    During family leave, the employer must maintain the employee's health coverage under any group plan. Upon return employees must be restored to their original or equivalent position with equivalent pay, benefits, and other employment terms.

15. The **Fair Labor Standards Act** (FLSA) establishes minimum wage, overtime pay, recordkeeping, and child labor standards affecting full-time and part-time workers in the private sector and in federal, state, and local governments. Employees that hold positions covered under the mandatory overtime provisions of the FLSA must be compensated with overtime pay or compensatory time for all hours worked over 40 in a single workweek. Special rules apply to state and local government employment involving fire protection and law enforcement activities, volunteer services, and compensatory time off instead of cash overtime pay.

Recruitment

Recruitment is the first step in the process of selecting individuals to become police officers. It is considered an extremely important human resource function because the quality of a police department is directly linked to the quality of its employees (Berman, Bowman, West, & Van Wart, 2013). The primary goal of the recruitment process is to generate a large pool of applicants from which the department can select the best-qualified individuals, not merely eliminate the least qualified. A qualified candidate is a person who possesses or can acquire through entry-level training the skills, knowledge, abilities, and job behaviors needed to perform the tasks and duties of a police officer (Nowicki, 2003). The Commission on Accreditation for Law Enforcement Agencies (2006, pp. 31) identifies the benefits of effective recruitment and selection for a department as lower rate of personnel turnover, fewer disciplinary problems, higher morale, better community relations, and more efficient and effective services. Recruitment of qualified individuals is a challenging and competitive task. Recruiting and staffing shortfalls that plagued law enforcement agencies across the United States during the late 1990s have continued into the 21st century (Beres, 2009). During last third of the 20th century, the labor market benefitted from 76 million Baby Boomers in the workforce. Applicants were plentiful and police departments recruited sufficient qualified candidates with a minimum effort on their part. However, as more and more Baby Boomers retire, there are 10 million fewer Gen-Xers to replace them (Robbins & Judge, 2013). Military call-ups, Homeland Security obligations, retirements, and increased competition with business organizations and between departments at the local, state, and federal level, for qualified applicants have created a highly competitive recruiting environment. Greater than half of the police agencies serving populations fewer than 50,000 report they have difficulty in filling open positions because of a lack of qualified applicants (Koper, 2004). The numbers of qualified applicants have also diminished because of changes among today's youth. They have high levels of indebtedness, poor physical fitness, with higher obesity rates, and drug use (Raymond, Hickman, Miller & Wong, 2005). All of which has resulted in police departments facing a continual challenge to recruit qualified candidates known as the "*cop crunch*" (Taylor et al., 2006).

Recruitment begins by a department specifying its human resource requirements (numbers, skills mix, knowledge, abilities), through a job task analysis and human resource planning activities. A **job task analysis** is a systematic detailed study of the content of a job so that one can develop an accurate description of what the job entails, the conditions under which the job is performed, and the knowledge, skills, and abilities needed to perform the job (*Segar v. Civilliti 25 FEP 1425, 1981*). The U.S. Supreme Court established that without a job analysis to define the knowledge, skills, or behavior required on the job and a description of how the appraisal system or instrument samples critical and/or frequent components of the job a claim of validity cannot be sustained (*Albemarle Paper Co v. Moody 95 S.Ct. 2362, 1975*). A job task analysis benefits an organization by:

- Providing data for recruitment and selection planning.
- Forming the basis for the development of a performance evaluation system.
- Establishing the link between evaluation criteria and job content.
- Providing information on current performance responsibilities.
- Providing information on workload demand and distribution.
- Serving as a basis for assessing training needs.

In 1972, the U.S. Congress enacted the Equal Employment Opportunity Act in an effort to eliminate discriminatory practices in hiring. The Act requires that police departments have policies and engage in practices that ensure equal opportunities and treatment for employment of minorities and women. Departments must meet the requirements of federal, state, and local regulations that prohibit discrimination. In many municipalities, the recruitment process is controlled by a governmental civil service system. Today the recruitment of a diverse workforce reflective of the community served is both an ethical and a management necessity. Recruitment should seek to address this issue by attracting qualified candidates across the range of race, ethnicity, gender, age, and sexual orientation. The goal is for a police department to reflect the diversity of the community it serves. A lack of African American police officers became an issue during the civil unrest in the St. Louis suburb of Ferguson, Missouri, after a White police officer killed an unarmed Black teenager. Two-thirds of Ferguson's residents are African American. All but three of the department's 53 officers were White (Rice & Rizzo, 2014).

Recent studies have noted that during the first half of this century the White labor force is projected to increase less than 15 percent, whereas the African American labor force is expected to grow by nearly 29 percent, and the Hispanic labor force by more than 74 percent. Women will account for about 64 percent of the net increase in the labor force during this same period (Dickerson, 2003). In 2008, in the United States general-purpose state and local law enforcement agencies employed 705,000 full-time sworn personnel. These agencies hired about 61,000 officers, but lost about 51,000 through resignations (54%), non-medical retirements (23%), dismissals (10%), probationary rejections (5%), and medical or disability retirements (5%) (Reaves, 2012).

Maintaining a diverse workforce that reflects the community served requires targeting special populations for recruitment. This should be carefully thought out and planned. One of the more effective strategies to attract diverse applicants is to specifically target them for recruitment (Roberg, Novak, Cordner, & Smith, 2012). It is also important that a police department be recognized for having a positive relationship with minority communities as well as being compatible with diversity through its promotional processes and organization culture. These factors necessitate that attracting special populations be part of the department's planning. A **special population recruitment plan** should contain these elements:

1. Statement of desired measurable goals and objectives.
2. Identification of key stakeholders to assist in this effort.
3. Specific time-sequenced steps to reach targeted populations.
4. Appropriate budgetary and human resources to achieve goals and objectives.
5. Specific actions to address issues related to past inequities.
6. Procedures to periodically evaluate the progress toward targeted goals and objectives and revise the plan if needed.
7. Special population awareness training for recruiters.

However, because of the estrangement of minority groups with policing the ability of many police departments to recruit qualified candidates that reflect the diversity of their communities represents a continuing challenge. Recruitment planning is a process with several interlocking stages. It begins by forecasting positions that either will become open or will need to be added to the organization for it to meet the needs of the community served. The factors involved in personnel forecasting include analysis of:

1. Workload demand (present and estimated future projections).
2. Current organizational strength and weaknesses.
3. Quality of current personnel in relation to department objectives and their changing requirements of knowledge, skills, and abilities.
4. Projected turnovers, resignations, terminations, retirements.

Once this analysis is conducted, a **recruitment plan** can be developed. This plan should comprise the following elements:

1. Goals and objectives stated in quantitative terms.
2. Key activities timetable that list steps recruiters must take to fulfill this plan.
3. An itemized recruitment budget.
4. Outline of procedures to follow in seeking assistance from community leaders and organizations.
5. Reporting procedures.
6. Evaluation criteria and process.

In developing recruitment plans departments must take into consideration the nature of their labor market. What sorts of potential employees are available? How do we find qualified people? A **labor market** consists of a geographical area in which the forces of supply (people looking for work) and demand (organizations looking for people to hire) interact. The maintenance of a police department at full staff with highly trained officers is a significant, ongoing challenge for department administrators. Many organizations are competing for the same labor supply. There are numerous factors that affect an individual's decision to seek police employment. Following are some examples.

Starting salaries for entry-level police officers are important. Organizational salary levels will either enhance or decrease a police department's ability to attract qualified employees. Job seekers and well-qualified individuals searching for jobs in policing will seek out the departments with the best salaries and benefit packages. **Organizational image** is another factor in recruitment. Smaller applicant pools have been attributed to negative media imagery and poor relationships with minority communities, competition of new jobs in the security sector created by the war on terror, and millennials' aversion to strict regulations in the workplace. In some areas of the country, departments maintain a very positive professional image and close relationship with the diverse population they serve. This is a positive factor that attracts people seeking police careers. However, many other departments because of low wages, lack of professional image, and their general negative demeanor toward citizens, especially minorities, have trouble recruiting and keeping qualified applicants. As a result, departments have experimented with relaxing certain criteria for recruits in order to expand the applicant pool. However, lowering employment standards comes with its own repercussions. For example, some departments have eased their residency requirements, but this results in recruits who are not familiar with the community and its residents. Other departments have become more tolerant regarding past drug use, poor credit history, or minor arrests, but this may weaken the community's trust in the police force. In 2015, the New Orleans Police Department eliminated its requirement that new officers without two years of military service have at least 60 college credits, and Louisville Metro Police Department reduced its education requirement as well. These changes are reflecting the desire for more applicants but research suggests that the more college education an officer has, the less likely he or she is to be physically or verbally abusive and involved in unethical behavior (Rydberg & Terrill, 2010).

Another critical factor is the individual or individuals responsible for recruiting, the **recruiter**. Smaller police departments do not have the available personnel to assign an officer to a full-time recruitment position. The chief of police often fulfills this responsibility in these departments. However, the larger agencies that do have recruiter assignments sometimes select the wrong people. Whatever the department size, individuals selected for these positions should represent the image the agency is seeking to project to the potential candidate and they should be trained for their position.

Training should provide recruiters with the knowledge and understanding of:

1. Agency's recruitment needs and commitments to candidates.
2. Career opportunities, salaries, benefits, and training requirements.
3. Federal, state, municipal compliance guidelines.
4. Community demographic data, organizations and educational institutions that are potential sources of candidates.
5. Cultural awareness orientation.
6. Procedures for candidate tracking.
7. Agency selection process.
8. Characteristics that disqualify candidates.
9. Candidate medical requirements.

Recruiters armed with the above information are qualified to answer potential applicant's questions. They possess the knowledge to become salespersons for their agency. Everything about them, dress, image, knowledge, communicating skills, and general demeanor will attract or turn away potential candidates.

Most small and medium-sized police departments rely on posting of job announcements as their major source of recruitment. Many municipal civil service systems require positing in a minimum number of public outlets. These can include in-house bulletins, newspapers, agency websites, and job placement websites. The most common recruitment methods include:

1. Advertisement, through brochures, newspapers, television, radio, mass mailings and journals
2. Request to special interest groups, such as neighborhood, social, political, and minority groups
3. Public-service announcements on television and radio
4. Request to university career planning and placement officers
5. Referrals from current employees

(Roberg, Kuykendall, & Novak, 2002, p. 236)

The *Law Enforcement Recruitment Toolkit* published by the U.S. Department of Justice (2009) to assist local police departments with their recruitment efforts suggests the following strategies for departments who wish to improve their recruitment process:

Collaborate with other police agencies.
Engage the community.
Improve relations with external human resources and elected officials.
Streamline your recruitment and selection process.
Involve everyone in the department in recruitment.
Put someone in charge of recruiting.
Tell the police story.
Enhance web outreach.
Enlist the support of the media.
Reach out to the young.
Hire younger—and older.
Hire transitional workers.
Mentor applicants through the process.

A common practice by many large police and federal law enforcement agencies is personal contact recruitment. This technique involves recruiters or other agency representatives attending job fairs, conducting on-campus recruiting, or individually contacting top candidates for positions. Recruitment is the beginning step to a long, often time-consuming process of obtaining a position in a police department. Next, we will discuss the process of selection and testing of the recruited candidates.

Selection

The next step in the human resource management process is selection. Selection is the process of making a final employment decision to "hire" or "not hire" each applicant (Gomez-Mejia, Balkin, & Cardy, 2012). The goal is to select the best-qualified candidates from the recruitment pool who can be trained to do the job for which they are being hired. Jurisdictions differ in the variety of ways they conduct personnel selection. The process may be handled entirely by the police department, a merit board, civil service, or human resource department of the governmental jurisdiction that the agency serves. The standards used to evaluate candidates must conform to legally administrative practices and procedures. They must also be statistically valid as predictors of success in the position and job-related. Validity must be established through a job task analysis. The nature of police work is such that a department should not take chances with a questionable candidate. All doubts about a candidate's fitness for policing should be resolved in favor of the agency and the public its members have sworn to protect (Fyfe, Greene, Walsh, Wilson, & McLaren, 1997, p. 290).

The components and procedures of the selection process are often referred to as the **multiple hurdle process**. It begins with evaluation of the candidates based upon pre-established standards that include age, residency, education, medical condition, height and weight, vision, physical ability, and psychological condition. This process usually starts with the least expensive element first, the application, and ends with the successful completion of a probationary period. Each level acts as a screening device designed to eliminate candidates who fail to possess or achieve a certain standard. The following are elements of this process:

Application.
Written examination.
Physical test/examination.
Polygraph.
Assessment center.
Drug testing.
Psychological examination.
Background investigation.
Oral interview.
Police academy training.
Field training program.
Probationary period.

Police departments vary in their use of the above selection elements. Most jurisdictions begin with an application and written civil service exam. However, the order in which the candidates take the remaining parts of the process is much less standardized. The selection process depends also upon several professionally and legally accepted administrative practices and procedures, which include:

- Written directives that describe all elements and activities of the selection process.
- Informing candidates of all parts of the selection process at the time of formal application.
- Maintaining written procedures governing lateral entry and reapplication of unsuccessful, retesting, and reevaluation of unsuccessful candidates.
- Timely notification of candidates about their status at all critical points in the process, and
- All elements of the selection process must be administered, scored and evaluated in a uniform manner.

(CALEA, 2006, p. 32)

Police departments must be able to prove that their selection criteria is valid based on its relationship to success or failure on the job and that it does not discriminate against either minority or other protected classes. EEOC guidelines and laws apply to screening or selection devices, including interviews, application, and references. **Validity** is established when the selection criteria is constructed from job-related criteria that measure traits or characteristics of the position for which the candidates are being selected. *Griggs v. Duke Power Co. (401 U.S. 424, 1971)* upheld this standard when it ruled that any and all employment criteria used to evaluate an *individual* must be job-related. Job-relatedness is established through a job task analysis that validates the selection mechanism as a predictor of future job success. The issue here is **validity**, which means that there is evidence that the criteria being used actually measures what it is supposed to measure. It is a valid predictor of subsequent performance on the job. The Uniform Guidelines on Employee Selection Procedures (Equal Employment Opportunity Commission, 1978) identify three types of **validity standards**: content, construct, and criterion.

- **Content validity** requires demonstrating that a direct relationship exists between the test and the actual job duties or responsibilities for the position.
- **Criterion validity** means that a significant correlation exists between candidate test scores (predictor) with good job performance (criterion).
- **Construct validity** documents whether the criterion measures what it claims to measure. Abstract personal traits and characteristics for job performance.

Negligent hiring is a critical issue for police departments. This factor and research that indicates that past performance is often an indicator of future performance emphasizes the importance of background investigation as a tool in policing hiring (Freyss, 2004). A complete background investigation should include:

- Verification of candidates' qualifying credentials.
- Criminal records check.
- Driving records check.
- Verification of the character of the candidate with at least three (3) personal reference interviews.
- A home visit with candidate and his or her family.
- Interviews of the candidate's neighbors.

The Commission on Accreditation for Law Enforcement Agencies (CALEA, 2006, 32.2.1) recommends that background investigations be conducted in person, though telephone and mail inquiries are considered appropriate in obtaining criminal history and driving records. During this process, a candidate usually will complete a background questionnaire covering a breadth of data, including all places of residence, level of education, identities of family members and friends, and personal references. The questionnaire will ask an applicant to provide an employment record, credit history, criminal history, and any alcohol or other drug use. This document then serves as a basis for the investigation (Decicco, 2000). The actual investigation should involve a home visit with the candidate and his or her family and interviews with neighbors. CALEA recommends that personnel used to conduct these investigations should be trained to collect this information and that the record of the investigation is maintained on file with the agency for at least three years. To avoid violation of a job candidate's privacy rights, departments must obtain written consent before contacting educational institutions for transcripts, previous employers for references, or credit-reporting firms for credit reports.

Another important and frequently used selection device is the oral interview. It allows assessors to directly observe the candidates' attributes and evaluate their suitability for the department. It also is used to clear up inconsistencies that may have developed during the earlier stages of the selection process (Roberg et al., 2012). A recruitment survey conducted by the Academy of Criminal Justice Sciences found that interviews explore such areas as common sense, verbal communication skills, motivation, appearance, quick thinking, racism, compassion, sexism, and patience (Langworthy, Hughes, & Sanders, 1995). However, research on selection interviews gives them mixed reviews for reliability and validity (*City of Canton v. Harris, 109 St.C. 1197, 1989*; Macan, 2009, Posthuma et al., 2002). Structured interviews in which candidates are asked how they would respond in a job-related situation seem to be the most useful for predicting job performance (Dessler, 2006). The key to a useful interview depends upon how it is administered.

A good interview takes preparation, knowledge of the position, and awareness of the various interviewer mistakes that may occur. Some of these common mistakes are interviewers making snap judgments, having a negative bias, limited position knowledge, and influence of a candidate's non-verbal behavior. To overcome the negative influence of these factors interviewers should receive training. A properly conducted interview should be a standardized process based upon a job analysis. It should comprise a set of uniform, objective, behaviorally oriented questions that is asked of all candidates. A uniform rating scale should be used and evaluations should be recorded on a standardized form. Each candidate should be evaluated for a defined set of personal attributes that relate to the position. All questions raised by the applicant should be answered and clarified.

It is important to remember that the multiple hurdle process is not foolproof. The period between the initial application and appointment process can be very lengthy and time-consuming in many municipalities. As a result, it sometimes has a negative impact on candidates who will seek employment elsewhere because they are tired of waiting to be called for appointment. In addition, a hiring process does not shield agencies from hiring employees who later turn out to be problem employees.

Last, the department should have a probationary period of at least a minimum of six months prior to the final selection decision. The probationary period should be used to ensure that the applicant selected is qualified to perform the job. During this period, the employee's performance and general suitability as a police officer should be carefully evaluated. This evaluation should be based upon established performance expectations and objectives, observations of the employee, and their responsiveness to feedback. The components of the systematic selection approach have changed over the years. When each element lends positive results, the multiple hurdle approach will produce individuals qualified to be police officers.

Training and Development

Providing public safety to a community is a complex task that is governed by constantly changing federal, state, and local laws, case law, established professional standards, policy and procedures. In day-to-day decisions the complexity of the police officers' role is reflected in their need to balance conflicting values, laws, and rights, demands for effectiveness while protecting individual rights, the need for public order without excessively restricting liberty, the application of force without abuse, and adhering to professional and legal standards simultaneously (Marenin, 2004, p. 108). Since a department's effectiveness depends on the skills, abilities, and intellectual capabilities of its employees more than any other factor, employee training and development have become important continuous management functions.

Today all police departments offer some form of training for their officers. It may be provided within the department or by outside organizations such as state-accredited training institutes, community colleges, consultants, regional academies, other police departments, and professional associations like the International Association of Chiefs of Police. The good news is that the knowledge, skills, and abilities needed to ensure organizational effectiveness are teachable (Vosburgh, 2006).

Training is the activity undertaken to increase the knowledge, skills, and abilities of an organization's employees and managers (Berman et al., 2013). Its focus is on improving the employee's ability to perform a particular task or function and improving their performance in their present assignment. **Development** is designed to improve future performance by providing skills and knowledge to be used in a subsequent assignment. It increases employee potential by ensuring that they have the relevant skills to meet present challenges as well as being prepared for future advancement or reassignment. For example, many police departments assign individuals who are about to be promoted to sergeant to a first-line supervisors course or assign officers designated for advancement to attend managerial training programs. These programs provide participants with training in the knowledge, skills, and abilities (KSA) they will need to know in order to fulfill their future role. Training and development are critical factors in the enhancement of employee knowledge, intellectual capacity, and a department's effectiveness. Training serves three broad purposes. First, well-trained officers are generally better prepared to act decisively and correctly in a broad spectrum of situations. Second, training results in greater productivity and effectiveness. Third, training fosters cooperation and unity of propose (CALEA, 2006, p. 33).

Training and development play an important role in the strategic development of a department because it can:

1. Assist new employees to become current on the procedures, equipment or standards of the department;
2. Help existing staff to adapt new tasks as a result of promotion, restructuring or reassignments;
3. Ensure that employees are aware of new laws, procedures, or knowledge pertinent to the department, its strategic direction and their environment;
4. Validate that personnel in critical positions perform in satisfactory ways.
5. Use training and development as a tool to ensure that employees and managers stay current and committed to the department; and
6. Ensure that everyone has the knowledge, skills and abilities consistent with what is needed to effectively perform today and tomorrow
                                        (Berman, Bowman, West, & Van Wart, 2006, p. 222)

Police departments are also legally accountable for the actions of their officers resulting from their failure to provide training. The U.S. Supreme Court in *City of Canton v. Harris (109 S.Ct. 1197, 1989)* held that a municipality (or county) could, under very limited circumstances, be held liable for constitutional violations resulting from the municipality's failure to train its employees. This case holds that a municipality is liable when there is sufficient evidence to establish that the city's failure to train its employees caused the violation of a federally protected right and that the inadequate training of employees resulted from a deliberate indifference to constitutional rights. Since this finding several municipalities have been found liable for failure to train because of the actions of their employees. However, the United States Supreme Court has held that a municipality may be held liable under § 1983 for violations of rights guaranteed by the U.S. Constitution, resulting from the municipality's failure to adequately train its employees, only if that failure reflects a **deliberate indifference** on the part of the municipality. It should be noted that failure to train cases can be established in two ways. The first involves a lack of training in an area where there is a patently obvious need for training, for example, an officer who is untrained in deadly force unreasonably shoots someone. The second method of establishing a failure to train by an agency is to establish a pattern of conduct by officers that would put the final policy maker on notice and the policy maker failed to respond with training. Research by Alpert and Smith (1991) and Ross (2000) found that because of *Canton* police operational training has exploded.

Types of police training include such activities as:

- Pre-employment.
- Entry level training.
- Field training—orientation and socialization.
- Roll call training.
- In-service training.
- Certification training.
- Managerial training—supervisory, middle management, command level.
- Special unit training.
- Self-development.

Entry-Level Training

A Bureau of Justice Statistics survey of police training in 2006 found that 648 state and local academies provide entry-level training to police recruits in the United States (Reaves, 2009). Entry-level training teaches the basic skills and knowledge required to perform the job of a police officer. It is the foundation upon which the development of a proficient and competent police officer is based. Recruit officers experience this training in either a pre-service academy, agency-managed academy, regional or college-sponsored academy.

Besides basic recruit training, 87 percent of academies provide in-service training for active-duty officers and for officers in specialized units such as K-9 or special weapons and tactics (SWAT) units. A majority also provided training for first-line or higher supervisors (57%), and field training instructors (54%). The report found that an estimated 57,000 recruits entered basic training programs during 2005. On average these programs included 761 hours of classroom training. A third of academies have an additional mandatory field training component with an average length of 453 hours. About six in seven recruits completed their basic training program and graduated from the academy (Reaves, 2009).

Pre-employment academies train people who have not been hired by a police department. The trainee pays his or her way through the academy and receives certification as a police officer upon graduation. However, these individuals are not guaranteed police employment. They are allowed to seek police employment within the state in which they are certified for a specific period. This process is utilized as a source of employees by many smaller police agencies that wish to hire new officers but cannot afford the cost of recruitment and entry-level training.

Agency-managed academies are found in large municipal and state and highway police departments. New recruits receive training in basic police tasks, procedures, and skills required by their agency. Regional police academies handle the training functions for both large and small departments located in a designated geopolitical area. Trainees are hired by a police department and then assigned to the academy for the duration of the basic recruit training. Regional training academies also provide specialized and in-service courses besides basic police training. College-sponsored training academies operate on the premises of post-secondary institutions, particularly community colleges, and allow recruits to take police training and college credit courses (Thibault et al., 2010).

Academy curriculums and standards for certification vary state by state. Training and certification standards are established for each state under its **Peace Officer Standards and Training Act (POST)**. Each state's mandated training standards establish the length of entry-level training and the curriculum for certification as a police officer in its respective state. They also set in-service training requirements for officer certification and qualifications for state-certified instructors and training providers. In some states the POST conducts training for all sworn personnel in the state. All departments within the state must meet the minimum training and certification standards for their officers. However, there are departments that provide more training than required by state standards. The average length of basic recruit training programs includes 761 hours of classroom time, or about 19 weeks of training (Reaves, 2009).

In March 2003, the Kentucky Department of Criminal Justice Training (DOCJT) became the first public safety training academy in the United States and Canada to be accredited by the Commission on Accreditation for Law Enforcement Agencies (CALEA) under its newly created program, **Public Safety Training Academy Accreditation**. Accreditation requires compliance with a predetermined number of nationally recognized standards and benefits the Training Academy by strengthening its position in litigation involving officer training. The Kentucky Department of Criminal Justice Training (DOCJT) provides entry-level and in-service training for approximately 11,000 students each year, including city and county police officers, sheriffs, deputy sheriffs, university police, airport police, law enforcement telecommunicators, and coroners. Training is also provided for officers charged with water enforcement, motor vehicle enforcement, alcoholic beverage control, mining reclamation, and personnel from several other state and federal agencies (2014, DOCJT, https://docjt.ky.gov/).

Police entry-level training contains a variety of topics all based upon tasks that a job analysis has identified as the frequent and critical ones performed by an officer every day. The training provides the recruit officer with the necessary knowledge, skills, and ability to function as a police officer and improve the operations of the police department. The Bureau of Justice Statistics (Reaves, 2009) found that nearly all academies train their students in procedures related to patrol, investigations, and emergency vehicle operations. However, the academies spend the most time on firearm and self-defense skills. The next-highest median of training time is for health and fitness training. All academies include in their curriculums legal training, basic first aid, report writing, cultural diversity, Community Policing strategies, and mediation/conflict management skills. Recruits also receive training in computers and information systems, domestic violence, juveniles, domestic preparedness, and hate crimes. An indication of the changing nature of police work is the survey's finding that 90 percent of academies provided basic training on terrorism-related topics (Reaves, 2009).

For entry-level training to be effective, it must be relevant and presented in a manner conducive to learning. The basic training academy must ensure that important skills and abilities have been internalized by the trainees. Recruits must understand that their formal academy training does not provide all the answers and that they will need to continually build on and expand the knowledge base created during their academy training. It is a place where they are taught the fundamentals of policing, but it is also the beginning of a social-ization process in which they learn unofficial boundaries and rules of acceptable behavior in the police world (Bayley & Bittner, 1984; Niederhoffer, 1967).

After the completion of entry-level training, the majority of police academies in United States require that new officers undergo a post-academy period of **field training.** Field train-ing is a carefully structured training period in and evaluation of the application of basic police skills and knowledge. It serves as the new officer's introduction to the occupational setting and its requirements, the mission, vision, and values of the department, and how the employee contributes to these ends. It should also provide the employee with basic back-ground information on the department and the community it serves. This training con-ducted on the job is the responsibility of the officer's department.

Field training should be conducted by specially trained officers selected for this duty because they have proven themselves to be masters of their craft. These officers should be trained to coach and evaluate the new officer in the day-to-day performance of police tasks. This training should begin the process of synthesizing the department and the employee's goals. Field training introduces the officer to the department's strategic mission and vision and how his or her performance contributes to these ends. During field training, the process of actual-izing the book learning of the academy to the daily street work of the officer takes place. It is a reality orientation to the true nature of police patrol work and organizational life. It is also the period in which peer socialization and support network development takes place.

In 1999, the COPS Office funded a national model for field training that would incorporate Community Policing and problem-solving principles developed by the Reno (Nevada) Police Department and the Police Executive Research Forum (PERF). The **Police Training Officer (PTO) Program** incorporates contemporary methods of adult education and a version of the Problem-Based Learning (PBL) method of teaching adapted for police. It is designed to ensure that academy graduates' first experience as law enforcement officers is one that reflects policing in the 21st century.

The Office of Community Oriented Policing Services claims that this new approach to training sets a foundation for life-long learning that prepares new officers for the com-plexities of policing today and in the future. It allows a department to tailor the program to its unique needs. First tested in the Reno Police Department and subsequently tested by five other agencies, the PTO program has produced outstanding results. New officers enter the field with problem-solving skills that are rarely seen at that career level. The officers also display remarkable leadership and willingness to work as partners with the local community to fight crime and disorder problems. COPS concluded that the PTO program is producing officers who have the necessary knowledge, skills, and attitude for today's law enforcement environment (www.cops.usdoj.gov/default.asp?Item=461).

RAND's Public Safety and Justice Unit's (Glenn et al., 2003) evaluation of police train-ing in LAPD found that departments implementing the changes needed for community police training have found success through the following sequence:

1.   At the leadership and command levels of the department, there has to be total adherence to and understanding of community. This requires leadership by the chief executive

and his or her staff supplemented by well-crafted leadership training throughout the organization.

2. Entry-level and field training programs must be altered to reflect new training goals. The recruit and in-service training cadre must share the philosophy and goals of the department leadership and integrate them throughout training.

3. Promotion requirements should include training in and a demonstrated understanding of community policing.

4. Such philosophical shifts as Community Policing are best introduced at the division or station level to engage line supervisors and the informal leaders of the organization in the processes of training and field implementation.

RAND found that implementing the most effective training practices is not an overnight process. Significant investments are needed for training innovations. While certain innovations can be implemented without great cost in the short term, it appears that the most significant changes for LAPD training will require a long-term leadership commitment and significant investment in resources, most notably that of time (Glenn et al., 2003).

Several issues associated with the field training process include:
Organizational orientation.
Socialization to the organization's culture.
Selection of field training officers.
Training of field training officers.
Supervision of FTOs and the program.
Evaluation process of FTOs and recruits.
Validity issues.

Specialized/In-Service Training

Besides meeting mandatory training required by each state's POST system, police departments should identify their own training needs, establish training objectives, select or develop a training program to meet the department's strategic objectives, deliver the training, and evaluate its effectiveness. Police departments are responsible for keeping their personnel up-to-date with new laws, technology, and revision in the department's policy, procedures, rules and regulations. Mandatory training may also be required to provide specialized training to specific groups of officers and to maintain certain types of technical certification. Specialized training includes supervised on-the-job training by the department, training mandated by governmental authority such as training for certification as a breathalyzer operator, and enhancement of the skills, knowledge, and abilities particular to a specialization such as crime scene processing (CALEA, 2006, 33.6). This raises several critical questions such as:

• Which knowledge, skills, and abilities (KSAs) are required to address present or future department needs and strategy?
• To what extent do employees and managers have the mandatory KSAs?
• What is the most cost-effective way of ensuring adequate KSAs?

- What is the role of employees and managers in this effort?
- How can training and development outcomes be evaluated so as to improve these efforts?

All in-service training and development programs should be based upon a needs assessment. A training **needs assessment** is conducted to identify what training is required to meet the needs of the department and its employees. There are a variety of ways to conduct a needs assessment to identify the skills and knowledge required for effective performance. The first step involves a job analysis, which is a detailed study of a job to determine the specific skills that are required for effective performance. This analysis should generate a list of tasks and the knowledge, skills, and abilities associated with each task (Peak, Gaines, & Glensor, 2009). Another source of information is the department's existing information on job duties and responsibilities. These are usually found in the department's job descriptions, job specifications, and list of responsibilities found in policy and procedure manuals. A review of the department's performance evaluation reports, lawsuits, and citizen complaints are additional sources of information about officer performance effectiveness and deficiencies. Last, officers and operational supervisors should be surveyed and interviewed to obtain their input about their training needs. Dessler (2006, p. 154) suggests that the following informational sources can be used to identify employees' performance deficiencies and training needs:

- Supervisor, peer, self, and 360-degree performance reviews.
- Job-related performance data.
- Supervisor observations.
- Interviews with employees and supervisors.
- Assessment of employee knowledge, skills and abilities.
- Attitude surveys.
- Individual daily performance report.

Once training needs are identified objective and measurable training objectives can be established. Instructional objectives should specify what employees should be able to accomplish after completing the training program. The objectives provide the key focus for the development of the training program and a benchmark for evaluating its success.

Training can be delivered by a variety of methods such as lectures, demonstrations, discussions, case studies, online or computer-based instruction. Many training programs combine several of these methods. In-service training should be as meaningful as possible for the attendees. Training and development programs should be designed to meet the needs of adult employees. Adult learners bring experience to the learning process and will seek to have an active participation in that process. Thus it is important that both managers and trainers understand the following "**Principles of Learning**" for adults.

- **Motivation** is important for creating the participants' desire to learn. Trainees will be motivated to learn when they understand the relevance of the training to their work effort. Managers should explain the reasons for the training and how it relates to the employee's job performance.
- **Relevance and Transference** are enhanced when the training is directly related to work issues, problems, and employee needs. Issues and problems relating to the training

subject should be openly discussed and employees' suggestions to resolve them. Content can be made meaningful by summarizing the material, and ensuring that the program uses familiar job-related examples to illustrate key points (Wexley & Latham, 2002). The relevance of the training and its benefit for the department's employees should always be explained.

- **Repetition**. It is important to remember that people learn at different rates, ways they process information, and levels of retention. Repetition helps the learning process by allowing people to handle information at their own pace. Repetition can be accomplished through the use of lectures and practical exercises.
- **Feedback and Positive Reinforcement** helps reduce errors, enhance motivation, and increase attention to standards. Feedback that includes periodic performance assessments and more frequent verbal critiques should be used to reinforce behavior and negative feedback to stop it (Berman et al., 2006, pp. 224–225).

Evaluations are a critical part of the training process. All training programs upon completion should be evaluated to measure their effectiveness and if they have achieved their objectives. Evaluation should take two forms. A **process evaluation** should address issues of instructor quality and content delivery. An **outcome evaluation** should access the impact of the learning process on the student, that is, passing the final course exam, improved performance, enhanced abilities and skills. These can be difficult to assess. Evaluators should be aware that trainees may evaluate a program highly because of the charisma of the instructor. Also, performance improvements may take time to develop and the impact of the training may not be felt till sometime after the training program has been completed. Validity must be considered and addressed in all training evaluations.

Last, each department should develop an in-service training plan to maintain appropriate levels of performance and delivery of their training programs. This plan should identify the department's training needs in terms of officers and units that require training. It should establish a timetable for the training. The training schedule should consider training, training needs, and personnel availability. The goal of this plan is to ensure that all employees received proper training. The training plan helps to ensure that sufficient officers are available for each assignment within the department (Gaines & Kappler, 2011).

Roll Call Training

A well-managed appropriately planned roll call training program is a positive training supplement. Roll call training occurs 15 to 30 minutes prior to the beginning of a duty shift. The objective of this training is to keep officers up to date and present new ideas and techniques between formal training secessions. Roll call is the time unit commanders use to prepare officers for their patrol shift. Sergeants assign officers to their beats, disseminate information about major incidents occurring on previous shifts and wanted or dangerous persons and vehicles. Other matters may also be addressed, such as issuing court subpoenas, explaining new policies and procedures, and discussing shift and beat-related matters (Peak et al., 2009). Roll call training programs should be well structured and reflect the department's needs while being flexible enough to fit into a roll call setting.

Managerial Development

Management in a police department is a complex and challenging function. Managers face an array of responsibilities regarding personnel, unit effectiveness, ensuring obedience with policies and procedures. They must make sure that their department and its employees comply with federal, state, local law and regulations and community safety needs. All department sworn and non-sworn managers, no matter what their organization level, play an essential role in the effective and efficient operations of their department. Police departments should therefore make a considerable commitment to both the initial and ongoing preparation and development of their managers because of the significance of their role in creating and maintaining the effectiveness and efficiency of the department. Without it, a department operational effectiveness will quickly become stagnant and inert (O'Keefe, 2004). Traditionally, police supervisors and managers frequently are not provided with training after promotion and later are not provided with appropriate in-service-training (Gaines & Kappler, 2011).

Managerial training differs by states and organizations in law enforcement. Training and development programs for managers should be designed to improve current and/or future performance by imparting knowledge, changing attitudes, or increased skills. These programs vary by the size of the agency with large departments usually conducting internal programs and smaller agencies using external training. The Commission on Accreditation for Law Enforcement (2006, 33.8.2) holds that managerial training should be commensurate with the position's duties and should take place prior to promotion or within the first year following promotion.

Training of first-line supervisors is the initial step in the development of a department's present and future management. All police managers begin their managerial careers at this rank. First-line supervisors function at the technical/operational level of the department and as a result make decisions that affect their subordinates, departmental effectiveness, and financial liability. This initial managerial training should establish a foundation upon which the development of future organizational leaders are based. Supervisory classes for newly promoted sergeants must provide enough technical knowledge and managerial techniques for them to understand their role and manage the employees assigned to them. It should be focused on the skill set, knowledge, specific policies, procedures, personnel, and operational responsibilities of the rank (O'Keefe, 2004). In-service supervisory training should be focused on management techniques and leadership issues.

Middle managers who are either lieutenants, captains, or civilian managers in administrative staff positions function at the managerial and administrative level. Managers at this level create and interpret policies and procedures and translate the department's goals and objectives into the day-to-day tasks of their operational units. These managers organize, coordinate, and control department resources and personnel. They also evaluate supervisory accountability and unit performance (More, Vito, & Walsh, 2012). Promotional and in-service classes should be educationally based, reviewing new or specifically significant policies, procedures, and problems of the position but focusing heavily on the conceptual principles of change, critical thinking, problem solving, and organizational leadership. Many departments utilize the 12-week Administrative Officer's Course at the University of Louisville's Southern Police Institute, the 3-month police administration course offered by Northwestern University, or the 10-week FBI National Academy for middle-management developmental training. Besides these programs, managers can take part in a variety of seminars, workshops, and retraining conferences that provide instruction on developments and critical law enforcement issues. These programs are provided by a variety of organizations such as the International Association of Chiefs of Police; the Southern Police Institute; Institute for Law Enforcement Administration at the University of Texas, Dallas; Police Training Institute at the University of Illinois; the Justice and Safety Institute at Pennsylvania State University; the Federal Bureau of Investigation; and many in-state training programs such as the Department of Criminal Justice Training in Kentucky.

Discipline

Police departments are similar to other organizations in their need to control employee behavior through the maintenance of discipline. They develop policy, rules, regulations, standards of performance and conduct in order to prevent and control undesirable behavior. Employees are human, mistakes are made, and problems arise. However, the public's trust is quickly lost because of improper police employee behavior, misuse of authority, and the improper departmental handling of allegations of misconduct (Peak, 2014). The test of a properly administered human resource process is not the identification of how many problems are identified, but how effectively the department addresses and prevents them. Unfortunately, the administration of police discipline is often a source of frustration and dissatisfaction for everyone involved. The most effective disciplinary system combines the reinforcement of the right set of values in all employees with behavioral standards that are consistently and fairly applied (Swanson, Territo, & Taylor, 2005, p. 412). Policing requires a disciplinary process capable of serving the interest of community, the officers, and the department in a fair and equitable manner (Stephens, 2011).

The primary objective of discipline is to control behavior. It reflects the administrative goal to achieve maximum conformity with legal requirements, established policies, professional standards, and prevailing norms of conduct. Most organizations have implemented a formal policy or set of guidelines governing the application of discipline. A department's disciplinary process should include training, rewarding, counseling, and punitive actions in the interest of discipline. It is recommended that disciplinary procedures include:

1. A code of conduct and appearance that is made available to all department personnel.
2. Criteria for recognizing and rewarding employees, including letters of commendation, compensation, and awards for merit.
3. A written directive that prohibits sexual and other forms of unlawful harassment in the work place as well a means by which harassment can be reported.
4. Procedures and criteria for using counseling as a function of the interest of discipline.
5. Procedures and criteria for using training as a function of discipline.
6. Procedures and criteria for using punitive actions in the interest of discipline including oral reprimand, written reprimands, loss of leave, suspension, demotion and termination.
7. Specification of the role of supervisors and the authority attendant to each level of supervision and command relative to disciplinary action.
8. Appeal procedures that specifies initiation procedures, time frames, method of recording and scope of the appeal process.

9. An employee notification process in dismissal cases that states the reason for dismissal, effective date of the dismissal and the status of fringe and retirement benefits after dismissal.
10. Procedures for the maintenance of records of disciplinary actions that specifies under what circumstances they should be purged.

(CALEA, 2006, 26)

Discipline can be negative and positive as well as confusing and conflicting. This lack of clarity and confusion results from the negative connotation many have attached to the word since our early childhood conditioning. This has led to the belief that the only purpose of discipline is punishment. **Negative discipline** simply means punishment. Punishment is used to eliminate undesirable work-related behavior or undesirable individuals from the organization. It is used to accomplish an organizational purpose, not a personal one. It serves the specific purpose of punishing the offender and the general purpose of notifying other employees that the sanctioned behavior will not be tolerated by the organization. Examples of employee behavior that would be appropriate for this type of discipline include acts of corruption, sexual harassment, civil rights violations, substance abuse, insubordination, absenteeism, abuse of power, and poor work performance. This area is fully discussed in Chapter 11. Forms of punishment may involve an oral or written reprimand, voluntary surrender of regular days off, or annual leave, demotion, loss of salary, suspension, or dismissal. Some departments prefer to use loss of regular days off, annual leave, or accumulated compensatory time instead of outright suspension. In this manner the employee's family does not suffer from lost wages because of their infractions.

In cases of negative discipline a department must clearly identify what rule or procedure was violated, what performance standard was not met, or what duty was breached. Also, that the employee knew and understood the rule, procedure, performance standard and/or duty, in order to successfully establish incompetency or misconduct. The department must conducted a fair and complete investigation to establish the facts in each case before discipline is taken. A department's policy and procedures manual should clearly set forth its personnel policies, code of conduct, rules, directives, and standards of conduct. The clearer the "rules" are, the easier it is for employees to understand what is expected, and for the department to discipline the employee if he or she violates those "rules." It is also important for all employees to understand that a failure to abide by the "rules" or to meet minimum standards of competence may result in disciplinary action. Employees must have the understanding that everyone in the organization is held accountable for their behavior, and if sanctions are different for similar behaviors, that they are appropriate for the circumstances (Stephens, 2011). Last, the punishment must fit the offense and the employee. Arbitrators and courts have reversed disciplinary punishment that they found to be excessively harsh or inappropriate based upon the employment record of the offender.

Positive discipline is used to reinforce appropriate performance or correct performance deficiencies without using punishment. It involves training and the use of techniques of attitudinal conditioning designed to ensure the employee's commitment to organizational norms, values, and procedures without invoking punishment. Discipline is positive when employees share a common sense of purpose, practice self-discipline, and voluntarily follow the policies, procedures, rules, regulations, and standards of performance established to promote order and facilitation of the work of the organization. Through the application of positive discipline and the example set by organizational managers who demonstrate, guide, and counsel their employees, the need for negative discipline should be lessened.

Some commonsense guidelines for the use of discipline include:
Always base disciplinary decisions on facts, not hearsay or "subjective opinion."
Make sure the evidence supports the charge.
Base employee-related decisions on legitimate job-related/objective criteria.
Treat all employees in a fair and consistent manner.
Employees should be warned of the disciplinary consequences of their behavior.
Acts of misconduct should be fairly and adequately investigated.
Employee's due process rights must be protected.
Maintain the employee's right to counsel.
Apply policy, rules, orders, and penalties even handedly.
Provide timely and accurate feedback on your decisions to employees.
Make sure the penalty is reasonably related to the violation and to the employee's work history.
Be prepared to defend disciplinary decisions.
The burden of proof is always with the department.

First-line supervisors are the most important individuals in the disciplinary process because they directly manage more employees than any other position in the department. Their role requires that they work closely with their employees and monitor their performance and behavior. They are often the first managers to observe behavioral changes or signs of misconduct in the members of their unit. As a result in many police departments first-line supervisors are required to conduct the initial investigation into a citizen's complaint. While they are expected to follow the department's directives, discretion in their use of discipline enhances their ability to influence the future behavior of their subordinates.

When it comes to their use of positive and negative discipline, there are some essential concepts that relate to all managers and administrators. They should always use a positive approach to their use of discipline. However, they should take appropriate action to address mistakes and misconduct as soon as they occur. Additionally managers should never display their emotions and temper when disciplining employees. An unstable manager will quickly lose his or her authority and the employee's respect. Consistency in the manager's mode of supervision is important. The creditability, morale, disposition, and allegiance to the department displayed by managers will be imitated and repeated by their subordinates. Never oversupervise in petty situations. This is a common fault among newly appointed sergeants. Praise and acknowledgment of good work should vastly overpower criticism. Keep in mind, the department's employees are entitled to respect and consideration.

Employee Procedural Rights

The procedures that law enforcement administrators must follow to balance the rights of their employees and the department's disciplinary concerns have been clearly established in case law. In *Garrity v New Jersey (385 U.S. 493 1967)* officers were placed under investigation for fixing traffic tickets. When the officers were called in to be interrogated, they were properly informed that anything they said could be used against them in a criminal proceeding. They were also informed that they could refuse to answer any questions that they felt could incriminate them. However, they were warned that if they refused to answer any questions, they would be fired from their jobs. The officers answered the questions and were subsequently prosecuted and convicted for their crimes. They appealed to the United States Supreme Court, who held that "policemen, like teachers and lawyers, are not relegated to a watered-down version of constitutional rights." The court ruled that statements given by a police officer under threat of possible forfeiture of his or her job could not be used against the officer in a criminal prosecution.

Garrity establishes a set of protections that apply automatically whenever a police officer is questioned during a disciplinary investigation. Managers must:

1.   Advise the officer that the purpose of the interview is to obtain information that will assist in determining whether disciplinary action is appropriate, and that the answers furnished may be used in disciplinary proceedings against the employee.
2.   Advise the officer that the answers to the questions will not be used against the officer in criminal proceedings.
3.   Advise the officer that all questions relating to his or her performance of official duties must be answered fully and truthfully, and that disciplinary action, including dismissal, may be taken if the employee refuses to answer.

If the above warnings are given, the employee is required to answer questions that have a direct bearing on the individual's job performance. Refusal to answer can result in the department taking disciplinary action, including dismissal. If the department during a disciplinary investigation insists that the officer answer questions beyond those limited by *Garrity* and if they include areas of personal concerns, it is violating the employee's right to privacy.

Police departments have the right to question an employee about the discharge of his or her official duties during an internal investigation. The employee, however, may have a right to be represented during any such questioning, either by a lawyer or a representative of a union. This representation does not have to be an attorney unless specifically established by local statute or collective bargaining agreement. The right to such representation was established by the Supreme Court in *Weingarten v. United States (420 U.S. 251, 1975)*. The Court established the following rules for representation in disciplinary interviews:

1.   The employee's right to request representation as a condition of participation in an interview is limited to situations where the employee reasonably believes the investigation will result in disciplinary action.
2.   The right is only activated upon the employee's request for representation.
3.   The exercise of the right may not interfere with the legitimate needs of the employer.

Law enforcement employees are also entitled to the protection of the Due Process Clause of the Fifth Amendment to the United States Constitution. This clause states that: "No person shall be deprived of life, liberty, or property, without due process of law." Tenured, non-probationary employees are considered to have property rights in their job (*Wilson v. Robinson 668 F.2nd. 380, 1981*). Procedural due process must be followed in cases of discharge from employment, temporary suspensions without pay, demotions, and the removal of employees from premium pay, special assignments. These process rights for police officers during a police hearing were established by the U.S. Supreme Court in *Morrissey v. Brewer* (*408 U.S. 471 1972*).

In disciplinary action involving the possibility of these punishments, the following actions will ensure that the due process rights of the employee are protected.

1. The employee must be clearly put on notice that his/her job related conduct or performance is unacceptable.
2. The notice to the employee must clearly describe the specific instances of poor performance or unacceptable behavior that are the subject of the charge(s).
3. The employee must have been specifically informed of what s/he must do to conform to the employer's standards or policy.
4. The employee was offered assistance to overcome the deficiencies. Assistance should be in the form of formal training, counseling, or on-the-job instruction by the manager.
5. The employee was informed of the consequences that would occur if s/he failed to improve his/her performance or conduct.
6. The employee was given a fair opportunity to bring his/her conduct or job performance up to an acceptable level.

The actions recommended above are also found in various forms in the **Police Officer Bill of Rights**. The Police Officer Bill of Rights varies from state to state but as of of April 2015, 14 states have adopted versions of the Bill and more are considering similar legislation. These all include protections that are designed to make sure that investigations remain private and confidential until they are closed and discipline is administered. They also make sure that investigations are conducted in such a way as to afford officers due process rights and protection from overly biased supervisors and political influence.

Thus it is a matter of law and employee rights that managers who will take a disciplinary action against an employee ensure that they are not only correct in their decision but also that the disciplinary process is being followed properly and legally. Any disciplinary action taken by a police department should be fair, firm, and appropriate for the degree and type of behavior or performance problem to which it is being applied. The minimum due process requirements for discharging a police department employee include that employee be afforded:

1. A public hearing
2. Be present during the presentation of evidence against them and have an opportunity to cross-examine their superiors
3. Have an opportunity to present their own witnesses and other evidence concerning their side of the controversy
4. Be permitted to be represented by counsel
5. Have an impartial referee or hearing officer presiding
6. Have an eventual decision based on the weight of the evidence introduced during the hearing.

(Peak, 2014)

To ensure that the procedural rights of the employee are protected, many police departments have incorporated a system of progressive penalties in their discipline procedures. This system is commonly known as **progressive constructive discipline** (PCD).

Progressive Constructive Discipline

The progressive constructive discipline process employs a graduating sequence of penalties, with each penalty level having a greater degree of severity. The theory is that discipline should start at the lowest appropriate level and work up to more significant penalties. It is based on the belief that repetition of infractions, misconduct, and serious offenses will eventually lead to termination of the employee. Termination of employment should take place when an employee has demonstrated that he or she is unwilling to respond to less drastic disciplinary measures. Termination is a last resort that comes after the employee has been put on notice repeatedly and warned of the consequences of his or her failure to comply. The severity of each level of the process is based on the actions of the employee. This process does not imply a required sequence for all acts of employee misconduct. Serious offenses such as acts of brutality, accepting bribes, and drug use are subject to immediate suspension and possible discharge. The steps in the sequence of penalties are as follows.

The oral reprimand: This occurs during a discussion between the manager and the offending subordinate. The manager should clearly inform the subordinate that their misconduct or poor performance has occurred and explains the correct behavior to the employee. The focus of this discussion should be on the problem, not the punishment of the employee. The objective is to eliminate misunderstanding and to make sure the employee clearly understands what is required in this matter. It is a way for managers through communication and coaching to maintain desired standards of performance and conduct.

In many departments, the manager who delivers an oral reprimand must write a brief description of the incident and the conversation with the subordinate in his or her critical incident file. Some departments require the manager and the employee to both initial this critical incident report. Usually the report is kept out of the employee's official record, or if placed in it, removed when the manager feels that the condition is corrected.

Written reprimand: This is a written notice on an official department form. A copy should be placed in the individual's personnel file. This step should be taken after previous oral reprimands have failed to correct the condition or the offense is serious enough to require it. Department policy directives, rules, and labor contracts will provide guidelines for the use of written reprimands. A good manager does not write up everyone, only those who deserve it. Those who deserve it are employees who have engaged in:

1. Serious misconduct.
2. Major violations of departmental rules.
3. A pattern of poor performance after performance consultations and coaching by the manager.
4. A continual behavioral pattern (i.e., lateness) after previous oral reprimands.

A written reprimand should contain:

1. The name of the employee it is addressed to and the name of the manager who is filing the written reprimand.
2. Descriptive statement of the problem, incident, behavior, or performance. This should be a specific factual account. It should answer the following questions:
When did it happen (time of the incident)?
Where did it happen (exact location)?
What happened (specific descriptive account)?
What is wrong? This should be described in a descriptive statement that may include a history of events, description of specific rule, policy, or performance standard and employee's behavior.
3. A description of what the employee must do to improve or correct their performance. This statement should describe level of performance desired to correct the issue.
4. The consequences if the employee fails to improve or correct their performance. This should include any future action that will be taken by the manager if the employee continues to perform below standards.

Written reprimand meets the legal requirement of establishing notice for the employee. It should specifically inform the employee what is wrong in clear and concise terms. The written reprimand's purpose is not to punish but to inform the employee that there is a problem and what must be done to correct it. The reprimand also informs the employee of the consequences for failing to correct the problem. The ultimate objective of this step in the process is for the employee to correct the condition before more serious punishment is necessary. In effect, it makes the employee master of his or her own fate. If the employee takes corrective action, the manager has achieved what they desired but, if not, the next step in the disciplinary process is attained.

Suspension: This is an order releasing the employee from duty for a specific period of time. The exact number of days off should be designated in departmental policy and procedures. Suspension may either be with or without pay. The employee should receive a written notice of the cause for suspension that includes the facts in the case and information regarding the employee's right to reply in this matter. Employees, in some cases, may be offered the right to reply before the suspension takes place. However, in specific cases of serious misconduct or the commission of a crime, immediate suspension is appropriate. For example, the manager should have the authority to suspend an officer who reports to work late and unfit for duty because of intoxication or substance abuse.

A suspension is not always used as a form of punishment. In some departments suspension is used administratively to:

1. Provide a period of time for the organization to conduct an investigation of an incident, for example, use of deadly force.
2. Allow time for an investigation of a suspected but not fully substantiated complaint of a serious act of misconduct.

Dismissal: This is the most severe act of punishment a department will take against an employee. It is used when lesser disciplinary steps have failed, or when the employee's conduct constitutes a serious violation of public trust or department regulations. It is critical that the manager involved in a discharge recommendation have appropriate supporting documentation. Actually, managers should always have sufficient documentation to support their disciplinary decisions. Discipline decisions should never be made because of arbitrary or subjective reasons. The manager must be able to support their decision with objective job-related criteria. Documentation would include:

1. Critical incident reports.
2. Department records.
3. Civilian complaints (if any).
4. Performance evaluations.
5. Reports of interviews or conferences.
6. Witness statements.
7. Work examples.

Departments must be able to tie their disciplinary actions with job-related activities in a fair and equitable way. Employees who feel as though they are being arbitrarily punished because of vague, subjective interpretations of policy or rules are quick to file grievances. The subordinate who is seeking redress will rely on past appraisals of performance to make a case. If unsuccessful at the grievance level, the subordinate will take the next step, usually appealing to a civil service commission or a court. It is at this point that the basis for the departments charges against the employee come under close scrutiny.

The principle underlying the evaluation of the appropriateness of a disciplinary action is referred to as **just cause**. Just cause has become a common standard in labor arbitration, and is included in labor union contracts. A police department must prove just cause to sustain an employee's termination, suspension, or other discipline. Usually, the employer has the burden of proof in discharge cases or if the employee is in the wrong. To determine whether there is just cause for discipline they should ask themselves the following questions:

*   Was the employee aware or should have been aware of the rule or standards they are accused of violating?
*   Is the rule or standard reasonable?
*   Did the department conduct a reasonable investigation into the employee's wrong doing or misconduct?
*   Was the investigation conducted fairly and objectively?
*   Has it been established that the rule or standard was violated?
*   What mitigating or aggravating factors are present in the employee's work history?
*   Have comparable situations occurred in the past, and if so, how have the employees involved been treated.

(Freyss, 2004, p. 204)

The just cause test is important because the department must be sure that the its corrective actions and punishment fit the employee's behavioral violation. Using progressive discipline provides it with a documented history of actions designed to correct employee behavior that is an advantage in lawsuits and arbitration.

▦ Developing a Positive Work Environment

Police administrators need to establish a positive organization environment based upon positive instead of negative discipline. When it comes to human resource management the department's operational managers need to be trained to be problem preventers and problem solvers. Negative discipline should only be used when it is clear that other methods have failed or when the subordinate's intentional behavior requires it. The following suggestions will assist departments in creating a positive problem-prevention work environment.

1. Set Boundaries

Setting boundaries involves letting employees know what is expected regarding their work performance and on-the-job conduct. To hold employees responsible for their behavior and performance, they must know what is expected of them. Department managers must be trained to interpret and implement department directives, policy, rules, and regulations that relate to employee performance and conduct. When managers translate regulations into action, they are setting boundaries and standards of performance for their work groups. How this is accomplished will depend upon the development and training of the manager and their perception of their role.

The department's leadership must communicate its standards of performance and acceptable behavior to all employees along with an explanation of the probable consequences of non-compliance. Besides by directives, police rules and procedures, this communication is also accomplished through the spoken word and managerial action. Officers will test their organization to find out what the boundaries are. Most veteran administrators have experienced these tests on numerous occasions. Departments have an obligation to let their employees know what they will or will not tolerate on the job. This will not be accomplished overnight or at one roll call. It will be an evolving process of testing, monitoring, evaluating, and communicating. The integrity of the department is established by the decisions managers make.

Employees should have no doubt where their department draws the line on performance and conduct. If they do not, administrators may find they are constantly resorting to negative discipline. The results will be that the department's internal environment will be adversarial instead of positive. All of which will mean that administrators will work harder putting out disciplinary fires and accomplishing very little for the department.

2. Train Your Employees

Training is a positive form of discipline that should reinforce standards of performance. It assists administrators with maintaining standards and correcting performance problems. Training is a problem-prevention activity that is an important responsibility of all department managers. While most departments schedule formal training for employees, managers cannot rely on these alone to maintain employee proficiency. All managers should use on-the-job instruction to train their employees.

An excellent method of on-the-job instruction is to manage by asking questions. This technique involves encouraging operational managers to ask questions of employees after an incident in which the manager observed their work performance. First, the manager should not offer direction unless the officers are truly incompetent. Letting the officers finish their assignment without interference signals they are trusted. Second, after the incident, ask questions such as: "Why did you handle that situation in that manner?" or "Do you always handle situations like this in that manner?" The elicited response will provide the manager with an idea of the employee's skill level as well as their overall job knowledge. If policy has not been followed correctly or the performance was poor, instruction can be given immediately.

Questioning employees as to how and why they do what they do is a form of testing. It will reveal the employee's strengths and weaknesses, but it may also reveal weaknesses in policy and procedure. This is important problem-prevention information that will assist the department in developing reasonable procedures to govern behavior in the workplace and meet subordinate and departmental needs.

3. Give Feedback

Feedback has been called "the Breakfast of Champions" (Blanchard, 2007). Employees should be informed when their performance is or is not meeting standards. This is a form of positive discipline that supports compliance with standards and initiates employee improvement measures. Recognition should support employee accomplishments, large or small. If a subpar performer improves, let the officer know that the department is aware of their efforts. If an employee develops an innovative approach to solving a problem, the manager should be quick to recognize this type of risk taking. Recognition is one of the most powerful and underutilized tools for establishing and maintaining high levels of performance.

Discipline can be positive as in rewards and/or recognition, or it can be negative as in punishment. A positive work environment is characterized by employees sharing a common sense of purpose, practicing self-discipline, and voluntarily following the policies, procedures, rules, regulations, and standards of performance established to promote order and to facilitate the work of the department. Employees should have no doubt where their department draws the line on performance and conduct. Effective discipline requires consistency in the application of rules, regulations, and operational procedures by managers. Administrators should strive to create a positive work environment for their departments through the establishment of boundaries, training, and feedback.

Conclusion

This chapter discusses the human resource management function in police administration. Human resource management (HRM) refers to the functions, policies, and activities a police department uses to enhance the effective utilization of its human resources now and in the future. Strategic management of human resources is emerging as the prevailing approach to the development of effective police organizations. It is the art and science of linking a department's human resource management with its strategic goals and objectives to improve organizational performance and develop a culture that fosters commitment, learning, innovation, and flexibility. Recruitment, selection, training, discipline, and development of employees are critical human resource functions. However, these functions are influenced by the law, both federal and state, local charters and ordinances, political motives, jurisdictional size, community values, and the department's culture. The department administrative leadership creates human resource policy and practices that produce employee competencies and behaviors it needs to achieve its strategic objectives.

A department's administrative leadership structures the human resource function through its philosophy and practices. The department's strategic direction should provide the framework that guides the design of specific human resource activities such as recruitment, training development, and discipline. Administrators need to develop an integrated framework that systematically links human resource activities with the department's strategic need. This means that the management of human resources should be in perfect fit with the management of the organization and its strategic direction. In this way, employee behavior and skill sets form the bridge between the department's strategic direction and its effectiveness. The department should create a work environment in which employees are encouraged to develop and utilize their skills and abilities to the maximum extent. Thus, how an organization goes about organizing its human resource functions has significant consequences on what it can actually accomplish.

KEY TERMS

Deliberate indifference
Development
Discipline
Employee procedural rights
Entry-level training
Equal employment legislation
Field training
Hawthorne Studies
Human Relations School
Human Resource
Management
Job task analysis
Just cause
Labor market
Multiple hurdle process
Needs assessment
Negative discipline

Organizational image
Outcome evaluation
Peace Officer Standards and
Training Act (POST)
Personnel
Police Officer Bill of Rights
Police Training Officer
Program
Positive discipline
Positive work environment
Pre-employment academies
Principles of Learning
Procedural rights
Process evaluation
Progressive constructive
discipline

Public Safety Training
Academy Accreditation
Recruiter
Recruitment
Recruitment Plan
Roll call training
Scientific Management
Selection
Special Population
Recruitment Plan
Specialized/In-service training
Strategic Human Resource
Management
Training
Validity

References

Alpert, G., & Smith, W. (1991). Beyond city limits and into the wood(s): A brief look at the policy impact of city of *Canton v. Harris* and *Wood v Ostrander*. *The American Journal of Police, 10,* 19–40.

Bayley, D., & Bittner, E. (1984, Fall). Learning the skills of policing. *Law and Contemporary Problems,* 35–59.

Beres, J. (Ed.) (2009). *Law enforcement recruitment toolkit*. Washington, DC: COPS/IACP Leadership Project Office of Community Oriented Policing Services, U.S. Department of Justice.

Berman, E.M., Bowman, J.S., West, J.P., & Van Wart, M. (2006). *Human Resource Management in Public Service*. Thousand Oaks, CA: Sage.

Berman, E.M., Bowman, J.S., West, J.P., & Van Wart, M. (2013). *Human resource management in public service*. Thousand Oaks, CA: Sage.

Blanchard, K. (2007). *Leading at a higher level*. Upper Saddle River, NJ: FT Press.

The Commission on Accreditation for Law Enforcement Agencies (2006). *Standards for law enforcement agencies*. Fairfax, VA: CALEA.

Community Oriented Policing Services, www.cops.usdoj.gov/default.asp?Item=461.

Decicco, D.A. (2000). Police officer candidate assessment and selection. *FBI Law Enforcement Bulletin, 69*(12), 1–6.

Dessler, G. (2006). *A framework for human resource management*. Upper Saddle River, NJ: Pearson Prentice Hall.

Dessler, G. (2013). *Human resource management*. Upper Saddle River, NJ: Pearson-Prentice Hall.

Dickerson, N. (2003). *Navigating the U.S. labor market: Trends and prospects for workers*. Washington, DC: U.S. Department of Labor.

Drucker, P. *On the profession of management*. Boston: Harvard Business School Press, p. 24.

Equal Employment Opportunity Commission. (1978). *Uniform guidelines on employee selection procedures*. In Code of federal regulation (41 CFR Ch.60) Washington, DC: Department of Labor.

Freyss, S.F. (Ed.) (2004). *Human resource management in local government: An essential guide*. Washington, DC: International City/County Management Association.

Fyfe, J.J., Greene, J.R., Walsh, W., Wilson, O., & McLaren, R. (1997). *Police administration*. New York: McGraw-Hill.

Gaines, L.K., & Kappler, V.E. (2011). *Policing in America*. Walthham, MA: Anderson.

Glenn, R.W., Panitch, B.R., Barnes-Proby, D., Williams, E., Christian, J., Lewis, M.W., Gerwehr, S., & Brannan, D.W. (2003). *Training the 21st century police officer: Redefining police professionalism for the Los Angeles police department*. Santa Monica, CA: RAND Public Safety and Justice.

Gomez-Mejia, L.R., Balkin, D.B., & Cardy, R.L. (2012). *Managing human resources*. New York: Pearson.

Koper, C. (2004). *Hiring and keeping police officers*. Washington, DC: U.S. Department of Justice, National Institute of Justice.

Langworthy, R. Hughes, T.W., & Sanders, B. (1995). *Law enforcement, Recruitment, selection, and training: A survey of major police departments in the U.S.* Highland Heights, KY: ACJS, 1995.

Macan, T. (2009). The employment interview: A review of current studies and directions for future research. *Human Resource Management Review, 19*, 203–218.

Marenin, O. (2004). Police training for democracy. *Police Practice and Research, 5*(2), 107–123.

Niederhoffer, A. (1967). *Behind the shield: The police in urban society*. New York: Doubleday.

Nowicki, D.E. (2003). Human resource management and development. In W.G. Geller, & D.W. Stephens (Eds.), *Local government police management* (pp. 353–390). Washington, DC: ICMA.

O'Keefe, J. (2004). *Protecting the republic: The education and training of American police officers*. Upper Saddle River, NJ: Prentice Hall.

Peak, K (2014). *Policing America: Challenges and best practices*. Upper Saddle River, NJ: Prentice Hall.

Peak, K.J., Gaines, L.K., & Glensor, R.W. (2009). *Police supervision and management: In an era of community policing*. Upper Saddle River, NJ: Prentice Hall.

Posthuma, R.A., Morgeson, F.P., & Campion, M.A. (2002). Beyond employment interview validity: A comprehensive narrative review of recent research and trends over time. *Personnel Psychology*, 55, 1–81.

Raymond, B., Hickman, L., Miller, L., & Wong, J. (2005). *Police personnel challenges after September 11: Anticipating expanded duties and a changing labor pool*. San Monica, CA: Rand, www.rand.org/pubs/occasional_papers/2005/RAND_ OP154.pdf.

Reaves, B.A. (2009). *State and local law enforcement training academies, 2006*. Washington, DC: The Bureau of Justice Statistics, U.S. Department of Justice.

Reaves, B.A. (2012). *Hiring and retention of state and local law enforcement officers, 2008 statistical tables*. Washington, DC: The Bureau of Justice Statistics, U.S. Department of Justice, www.bjs.gov/index.cfm?ty=pbdetail&iid=4514.

Rice, G.E., & Rizzo, T (2014, August 23). Like Ferguson, area police departments lack racial diversity. *The Kansas City Star*, www.kansascity.com/news/local/crime1282013.html.

Robbins, S.P., & Judge, T.A. (2013). *Organizational behavior*. Upper Saddle River, NJ: Prentice Hall.

Roberg, R., Kuykendall, J., & Novak, K (2002). *Police management*. Los Angeles, CA: Roxbury.

Roberg, R., Novak, K., Cordner, G., & Smith, B. (2012). *Police & society*. New York: Oxford University Press.

Ross, D.L. (2000). Emerging trends in police failure to train properly. *Journal of Police Strategies and Management*, 23(2), 169–193.

Rydberg, J., & Terrill, W. (2010). The effect of higher education on police behavior. *Police Quarterly*, 13(1), 92–120.

Schuler, R.S. (1992). Strategic human resources management: Linking the people with the strategic needs of the business. *Organizational Dynamics*, Summer, 18–32.

Stephens, D.W. (2011). *Police discipline: A case for change*. Washington, DC: U.S. Department of Justice, National Institute of Justice.

Swanson, R., Territo, L., & Taylor, R.W. (2005). *Police administration: Structure, processes, and behavior*. Upper Saddle River, NJ: Prentice Hall.

Taylor, B., Kubu, B., Fridell, L., Rees, C., Jordan, T., & Cheney, J. (2006). *Cop crunch: Identifying strategies for dealing with the recruiting and hiring crisis in law enforcement*. Washington, DC: National Institute of Justice.

Taylor, F.W. (1911). *Principles of scientific management*. New York: Harper & Row.

Thibault, E.A., Lynch, L.M., & McBride, B.R. (2010). *Proactive police management*. Upper Saddle River NJ: Prentice Hall.

Vosburgh, R. (2006). The evolution of HR: Developing HR as an internal consulting organization. *Human Resource Planning*, 30(3), 11–23.

Wexley, K., & Latham, G. (2002). *Development and training human resources in organizations*. Upper Saddle River, NJ: Prentice Hall.

Cases

Albemarle Paper Co v. Moody 95 S.Ct. 2362, 1975.
City of Canton v. Harris 109 S.Ct. 1197, 1989.
Garrity v New Jersey 385 U.S. 493, 1967.
Griggs v. Duke Power Co. 401 U.S. 424, 1971.
Meritor Savings Bank, FSB v. Vinson 109 S.Ct.2399, 1986.
Morrissey v. Brewer 408 U.S. 471 1972.
Oncale v. Sundowner Offshore Services, 523 S.Ct. 75, 1998.
Segar v. Civilliti 25 FEP 1425, 1981.
Weingarten v. United States, 420 U.S. 251 1975.
Wilson v. Robinson 668 F.2nd. 380, 1981.

10 Measuring Police Performance

Crime is one element of the bottom line of policing; it is not the bottom line. Police practitioners, scholars and city officials will have to be extraordinarily careful to develop measures of accountability that fully reflect the values that police departments serve— indicators of justice, integrity, wise use of force, citizen satisfaction, efficiency, and so on.
George L. Kelling, *Defining the Bottom Line in Policing* (1996)

Learning Objectives

1. To understand the methods of police performance measurement at both the departmental and individual levels.

2. To discuss the differences between input, output, and efficiency measurement.

3. To distinguish the differences between general, macro, and specific measures of agency performance.

4. To understand the differences between success and performance indicators.

5. To learn the differences between baseline and target measures.

6. To understand the basic principles of police performance appraisals

Introduction

Performance measurement is a critical strategic management tool. Creating appropriate quantitative and qualitative performance measures enables law enforcement managers to determine the effectiveness and efficiency of their activities. Performance measurement is used to not only evaluate organizational accomplishments but also to identify areas where improvement may be needed or where organizational assets should be directed. It can also provide a link between public priorities and budgetary decisions, and a means for communicating with elected officials and the public about police performance. Above all, it is a primary tool for establishing the police department's credibility.

Monitoring, gathering data, measuring, and evaluating organizational activities are critical factors for determining managerial success. A department's managers must develop a performance measurement system that is valid, reliable, and capable of letting them know how effective their operations are. Establishing appropriate quantitative and qualitative performance measures can assist law enforcement managers in meeting the demands of their external environment by linking the use of resources to specific outcomes. If there isn't any hard data to support their managerial decisions and strategies, police managers are placed in the position of being "just another individual with an unfounded opinion." Monitoring, measuring, and evaluating organizational activities are keys for preventing this from happening.

Kouzes and Posner identify performance measurement as a crucial aspect of organizational leadership. It also recognizes that "What Gets Measured Gets Done" and gives leaders the ability to influence outcome by providing the tools for measuring progress. They stress that organizational goals must reflect the values of the organization—doing the things that mean something, not just those that "count" (Kouzes & Posner, 2012).

Performance measurement is defined as the process of collecting, analyzing, and/or reporting information regarding performance to determine the extent to which a police organization accomplishes what is expected of it. The reasons behind its use include: (1) to establish the police capacity to accomplish an objective, and (2) to monitor the extent to which a department or program is accomplishing an objective (Mastrofski, 2003, p. 464). In this chapter, we review the measures and issues surrounding police performance at both the departmental and individual levels.

What Should Be Measured?

Establishing appropriate quantitative and qualitative performance measures can assist law enforcement managers in determining the effectiveness of their operational activities. If they are not gathering and measuring data to support their managerial initiatives and strategies, they are placing themselves in the position of not knowing what they have actually accomplished.

Traditionally police performance measures have been based upon such categories as (a) numbers and types of arrests, (b) clearance rates, (c) ratios of police to civilian resident population, (d) citations/parking tickets issued, (e) reports taken, (f) property recovered, (g) bars checked. These areas are considered objective, concrete, and provide for easy measurement. They are collected in the normal course of business by police departments and are recorded not so much for measurement as for documentation for later use (Klockars, 1999, Sparrow, 2015). They are typically used to determine what is accomplished, how efficiently resources are allocated, or the quality or effectiveness of the resources used.

Several police scholars and expert practitioners offered their thoughts on this subject in an influential monograph from the National Institute of Justice, *Measuring What Matters* (1999). Most often, these policing experts stressed the need to collect data on measures other than Index Crimes to better reflect the total functions of policing. For example, Kelling (1999, p. 29) recommended that the police collect data on disorder: "Fighting disorder, by solving the problems that cause it, is one of the best ways to fight serious crime, reduce fear, and give citizens what they actually want from the police force." He believes that the police should move away from an emphasis on the UCR Index Crimes toward arrest and police response reports on the crimes that most concern the daily lives of citizens—drugs, parking and traffic, disorderly groups, auto larceny, prostitution or gambling, burglary and robbery.

Skogan (1999, p. 51) offers suggestions on assessments of the quality of police service and of citizen encounters with police: "People who were stopped by the police are asked if they were given reasons for being stopped; if they were questioned, searched or breath-tested; and if they were arrested, prosecuted, or otherwise sanctioned." Moore and Poethig (1999, p. 153) concluded that "the police are a more valuable asset when viewed from the vantage point of trying to strengthen urban life than they are when viewed from the narrower perspective of reducing crime through making arrests." Measures of police performance should consider the totality of police performance activity and its impact on community safety in order to judge their effectiveness. The police on a daily basis deal with things other than crime: managing disorder in public places, reducing fear, controlling traffic and crowds, and providing various emergency services are but a few of the activities they engage in to keep communities safe.

A related problem is the difficulty in measuring when the police prevent crime—when they act as "sentinels" rather than apprehenders. Nagin, Solow, and Lum (2015) constructed a mathematical model to estimate the distribution of offender opportunities and decsion making on both their opportunities to victimize and their risk of apprehension. When police are effective in the sentinel role, they deter crime from occuring in the first place, negating the need for arrest. This outcome was stressed by Sir Robert Peel; it's impossible to ascertain and remains as a challenge to performance measurement (Nagin et al., 2015, p. 93).

Why Measure Performance?

Generally law enforcement managers are responsible for the evaluation of either some or all of the following functions (Oettmeier & Wycoff, 1996; Behn, 2003):

1. **Administration**: to help managers make decisions about promotion, demotion, reward, discipline, training needs, salary, job assignment, retention, and termination. These measurements provide a **control function** and answer the question: *How can I ensure that my subordinates are doing the right thing?*
2. **Guidance and Counseling**: to help supervisors provide feedback to subordinates and assist them in career planning and preparation, and to **improve employee motivation**: *How can I motivate line staff, middle managers, non-profit and for-profit collaborators, stakeholders, and citizens to do the things necessary to improve performance?*
3. **Research**: to validate selection and screening tests and training evaluations and to assess the effectiveness of interventions designed to improve individual performances. The purpose here is **evaluation**: *How well is my agency performing?*
4. **Socialization**: to convey expectations to personnel about both the content and the style of their performance and also to reinforce other means of organizational communication about the mission and values of the department. **Celebration** is the desire: *What accomplishments are worthy of the important organizational ritual of celebrating success?*
5. **System improvement**: to identify organizational conditions that may impede improved performance and to solicit ideas for changing the conditions. Success at this point can lead to **promotion**: *Convincing political superiors, legislators, stakeholders, journalists, and citizens that the agency is doing a good job.*
6. **Documentation**: to record the types of problems and situations officers are addressing in their neighborhoods and the approaches they take to them. Such documentation provides for data-based analysis of the types of resources and other managerial support

needed to address problems. It also allows officers the opportunity to have their efforts recognized. **Improvement** is the aim: *What exactly should we do differently to improve agency performance?*

7. **Strategy**: examining the effectiveness of a project or program. **Learning** is the goal: *To know why something is working or not.*

However, judging performance of law enforcement operations is more than a technical matter of choosing appropriate measurement criteria and methodologies. It involves controversial decisions about what we should do (*Function*) and how we should do it (*Process*). For example, if we have a location, a "hot spot," that generates numerous incidents of drug sales, assaults, robberies, disorderly conduct, and quality-of-life violations, the initial question faced by the command staff is: How should we address this problem? A quick immediate way is to use a concentrated strike, involving many officers to sweep the area and make several arrests. This tactic could cause a temporary displacement of the offenders and several traditional performance statistics (arrests) for the department. However, in time if the customers remain, the dealers will return and the problems in the area will resurface. An alternative strategy would be to form a problem-solving team of officers under the direction of a team manager. The team should be charged with identifying the factors that contribute to the problem and suggesting several responses to address these factors that will result in a long-term solution for this problem.

Whatever strategy is selected, it should not be based on a knee-jerk response to pressure from the community. Instead, it should be based upon clear assessment of the intelligence about the location, agreement among the command staff as to the desired methods and outcomes, and the identification of appropriate tactics to accomplish them.

Accurate performance measurement requires the use of indicators that are both valid and reliable. *Valid measures* correctly capture the concept under consideration. For example, does a drop in the number of reported burglaries indicate that a Citizen's Crime Watch program is effective or have citizens stopped reporting burglaries because they have lost faith in their police and feel that nothing will be done? *Reliable measures* yield the same result upon repeated applications. For example, do police officers using a form to record traffic stop information classify the same events in the same manner?

Valid and reliable evaluation of police organizational performance requires:

1. Clearly defined outcomes (goals and objectives).
2. Fixed command accountability for the achievement of these outcomes.
3. Identification of appropriate measurement data that will tell us how successful we are in achieving the outcomes.
4. Creation of a reporting system that will monitor strategy implementation and impact.
5. Managerial oversight through implementation, follow-up, and assessment.

However, there are also several problems that must be overcome to implement such an information system. First, the criteria to determine agency effectiveness are seldom established. Traditional standards of response time, crime rates, and arrest rates continue to be offered as benchmarks with which the public should assess agency accomplishments. These are not "one-size-fits-all" performance measures and are only appropriate with certain, clearly specified tactical responses. Second, the quality of data is often sorely lacking. For example, police in many jurisdictions were given the task of recording and collecting data about traffic stops to address racial profiling. Here are two examples of how this process can go wrong. State troopers in New Jersey were accused of "ghosting"—stopping a Black motorist, recording the facts of the stop, and then recording the plate number of a passing car driven by a White person (Skolnick & Caplovitz, 2001, p. 418). Another racial profiling study observed that the police did not record about 25 percent of the stops they made even though they used mobile data terminals in their cars to record traffic stop data (Meehan & Ponder, 2002, p. 420). Even when the data is accurate, the third and most damaging problem is failing to use the data to guide operations.

Performance measurement involves the selection of indicators, their measurement, transparency, and the auditing of efficiency and effectiveness (Fleming & Scott, 2008, p. 322). It can also provide a means for communicating with elected officials and the public about police performance. Above all, it is the primary tool for establishing organizational credibility and professionalism. In Australia, it is linked to "managing for outcomes" and showing "value for money" in the measurement and evaluation of government outcomes (Fleming & Scott, 2008, p. 323). As organizational managers, police administrators are confronted with several basic questions.

- What works?
- What criteria do we use to measure the performance and impact of ourselves, or people and the programs we create?
- How can we demonstrate to elected officials and citizens that our people and programs and services are effective and efficient?

Although new policing strategies are being tested in many departments, the success of these efforts needs to be measured to prove their effectiveness. One reason for this perception is the difficulties administrators have in determining what measures should be used to determine the success of their programs. If a program increases the quality of life in a neighborhood, then measuring response time and arrest rates will not provide a true measure of program effectiveness. For example, measuring the impact of police tactics designed to reduce residents' fear levels in a community defy the simple quantitative measurement systems now used by many departments.

Police managers are responsible for the evaluation of either some or all of the following actions:

1. Individual performance.
2. Unit performance.
3. Project or program performance.
4. Divisional performance.
5. Organizational performance.

However, accomplishment of these tasks is often difficult to achieve. Their achievement requires more than a technical matter of choosing appropriate measurement criteria and methodologies; it involves controversial decisions about what should the department and its personnel be doing and how it should do it. Fleming and Scott (2008) recommend measuring the "complexity of police work" through a combination of product and process measurement (using both quantitative and qualitative data) to obtain a strong and accurate picture of a police organizations' achievements (Fleming & Scott, 2008, p. 323).

One common and readily available measure typically used to assess police performance is the crime rate—statistics reported to the FBI and published yearly in the *Uniform Crime Reports*. However, the reporting and recording of a crime is subject to the following chain of events:

1. A crime event occurs.
2. It is observed by the victim or someone else (the police directly or a neighbor).
3. The police are notified of the offense.
4. The police decide if the event is a crime and how (and whether) it is recorded.
5. Often, this decision is reviewed (and can be dismissed) at another point in the police hierarchy.
6. The police decide which of the FBI Uniform Crime Reporting categories is appropriate.
7. The statistics are made public.

(Seidman & Couzens, 1974, p. 458)

In this fashion, the validity of crime rates is attributable to three basic sources: factors influencing the reporting of the crime to the police, recording practices of the police themselves, and subsequent problems in the official presentation and interpretation of the UCR statistics.

Crime rate figures are also subject to the reporting practices of victims. For example, victims are unlikely to report a crime to the police when:

1. The victim consents or agrees to the act (drug use, gambling, and prostitution).
2. The victim believes that the crime is trivial.
3. The victim does not wish to embarrass the offender (relative, friend, acquaintance, fellow employee).
4. The victim is in an embarrassing situation (the married man on a business trip who is robbed by a prostitute).
5. The victim believes that nothing will be done.
6. The victim is unaware of the crime due to the skill of the offender.

(McClintock, 1977)

Thus, selective reporting by victims can influence the accuracy of crime rates.

Measurement Criteria

Three levels of measurement are available to managers (Bayley, 1996):

1. **Macro measures** are direct outcome measures that focus on overall agency indicators. Examples of these include agency-wide *crime rates, cases cleared, victimization rates, cost of services, and sustained complaints about employee behavior*. Most of these are valid, traditional measures of police performance. However, Bayley suggests the following indicators can also tell us how successful a police department is in providing public safety:

    *   Real estate values.
    *   Public utilization of common space.
    *   Community commercial activity.

2. **General measures** are broad indicators of effectiveness based on the subjective reflection of people's impressions of quality, accomplishments, service levels, and participation in police activities. Examples of these measures include:

    •   Citizen perception of community safety.
    •   Citizen fear levels.
    •   Percent of citizens assisting in problem-solving activities.
    •   Satisfaction with police activities.
    •   Perception of police integrity.

3. **Specific measures** are designed to evaluate individual and unit performance and efficiency. These measures should be developed at all levels of the organization; however, they are extremely important for operational units. These include performance goals and measurement indicators that should be established by supervisors to evaluate the success of operational personnel. Examples of these measures include:

    •   Targeted crime rates in a specific geographical area.
    •   Numbers of identified and resolved incidents of social or physical disorder.
    •   Percentage of problems identified and resolved in an area.
    •   Number of community meetings attended.
    •   Numbers of specific performance outcomes achieved by the officer or unit (arrests, citations, incidents, and/or calls for service reduced, etc.).

In addition, performance measures must reflect the mission of both the department and the operational unit. The design and implementation of the evaluation of a strategy will depend upon the specific purpose it serves and the outcomes it is expected to achieve. These will differ according to the specific strategy and the type of measurement information needed by the manager (Stephens, 1996). Measures should focus on service delivery as opposed to internal operations. They can be developed only after mission, strategy, and tactics have been identified. Measures must reinforce department priorities and quality of service delivery. They should include the quality of work accomplished and the amount of resources devoted to complete certain activities.

Police performance measures should include the following elements:

1. **Success indicator**: It defines the attribute to be measured—a characteristic used to measure an output or outcome.
2. **Performance indicator**: It describes what is to be measured (i.e. number of arrests or percentage of crimes solved by arrest).
3. **Baseline**: determines the initial level of a measurement against which targeted progress and success is compared. A baseline includes both a starting date and/or starting level or value and a
4. **Target**: the part of a performance measure that establishes the desired level to be reached in a defined time period, usually desired to be an improvement over the baseline.

(Shane, 2007, p. 32)

The establishment of such elements are crucial but can be difficult. For example, West (2003) notes that one of the most controversial components of research on racial profiling by police during traffic stops relates to the "baseline" or comparison group. Researchers have struggled with determining whether agencies are engaging in racial profiling when making traffic stops without some measure of what the world would look like in the absence of it. Baselines used in these studies have included: (1) the racial distribution of the area as defined by census tract data, (2) the racial distribution of persons of driving age in the area, (3) the racial distribution of licensed drivers in the area, (4) the racial distribution of drivers driving on the roadways, as determined by stationary observation; (5) the racial distribution of speeders driving on the roadways, and (6) the racial distribution of drivers involved in accidents (West, 2003, pp. 64–65). All of these measures served as proxies for the population of drivers who could have been stopped but they are all imperfect. Consider measures 1 through 3 above. Do they consider the possibility that drivers who do not reside in the area will use roadways not in their particular neighborhood? Or that drivers outside of the city under observation will not use these roadways? For such reasons, criminologists have focused upon what happens after the stop (search, citation, arrest) and compared the percentage rates between African American and White drivers (Higgins, Vito, & Grossi, 2012). These are examples of the problems that must be faced when developing performance measures.

Some proposed measures of police organizational performance measures are summarized in Table 10.1.

There are several factors that can increase the likelihood of success of performance measures. The first is buy-in by middle management and first-line supervisors. They will do much of the assessment of the measures and the data collection procedures necessary to conduct the analysis. Second, a consensus on the meaningfulness of measures and their measurability must be established. This factor depends upon the reliability and validity of the measures and requires input from all levels of the organization to ensure such a result. The benchmarks for performance must be appropriate and measure success rather than failure. The evaluation process should include the adoption of a problem-solving approach for resolving identified deficiencies that indicate the need for improvement rather than levying punishment. Last, performance information systems require the availability of technical support to provide timely reports and follow-up analyses.

Evaluating Strategy

Strategy evaluation is defined as the systematic attempt to examine strategy process, implementation, and impact. Managers need this information to judge the operational performance of their strategic initiatives and to change the ways day-to-day activities are conducted. Ideally, strategic evaluation should focus on the effectiveness and efficiency of the strategy. It seeks to determine the answer to the following questions:

1.   Did the strategy impact the problems or conditions it addressed?
2.   To what extent was that impact (% decrease, increase)?
3.   Was the process and service delivery consistent with strategy design specifications?
4.   What is the cost-benefit analysis of expanded resources to strategy outcomes?
5.   Were organizational resources used properly?

TABLE 10.1 Measures of Police Performance

Issue	Elements	Measures

Community Security	Measures of disorder: 1. The vulnerability of its citizens to various crimes of violence. 2. The risk of property loss through theft or vandalism existing in the community. 3. The probability of being a victim from an accident on the highways of the community. 4. The extent of activities defined to be illegal existing in the community.	• UCR crimes reported to police.
		• Calls for service to police.
		• Location of the crime (addresses, parks, schools, public transit).
		  — Facilitates GIS analysis for "hot spots" of crime.
		• Victimization surveys.
		• Accident investigation reports.
		• Fear of crime via community surveys:
		  — How do people assess their victimization risk?
		  — What is their perceived threat of crime in their neighborhood?
		  — What actions do citizens take in response to their fear of crime?
		• Data from hospital emergency rooms (trauma, stabbings, gunshot wounds).
		• Focusing on observable behavior:
		  — graffiti
		  — junk, trash, and litter
		  — vacant and boarded-up buildings
		  — abandoned vehicles
		  — public drug use, drinking, and gambling
		  — street-level prostitution
		  — verbal harassment on the street

Efficiency and the quality of police service delivery	Police response time. Workload (self-initiated activity). Handling of major events. Response to civil disturbances.	• When the call is received.
		• When the police unit is dispatched.
		• When the police unit reports arrival at the scene.
		• Number of calls for service per sworn officer.
		• Number of police-initiated actions in the field (pedestrian and traffic) per sworn officer.
		  — number of cars stopped.
		  — parking and traffic tickets issued.
		  — suspicious subjects checked.
		  — buildings checked.
		  — field interview reports completed.
		  — warrants (both checked and issued).
		• Traffic control (disbursement traffic).
		• How much crime occurred?
		• Complaints on how the police handled the event.

	Arrests: Demonstration that something has been done about crime; exercising control over a certain problem.	• Arrest reports. • Clearance rate: number of crimes cleared by arrest. • Should also address the "quality" of the arrest (that it was conducted in a manner consistent with legal due process requirements and held up in court). — conviction rate. • Use of weapons. • Authorized wiretaps.

(Continued)

TABLE 10.1 (Continued)

Issue	Elements	Measures
Citizen Contacts	Traffic and street-level stops: Establishing accountability—requiring the police to act within the limitations of the law and rules established by governmental authority. Public satisfaction with police service.	• Citizen observation of police operations: Reported, sustained, not sustained, exonerated, or unfounded. • Number and disposition of citizen complaints against police officers. • Observation of video recordings. • Community surveys and call-in reports. • Adequacy of coverage of calls for service. • Crime victim satisfaction with police handling of cases. • Results of use of force complaints.
Legitimacy	Customer satisfaction. Business community satisfaction.	• Citizen/police contact survey. • Retail business survey.
Organizational Environment Officer Misconduct	Employee job satisfaction and morale (including perception of agency leadership). Absenteeism. Number of disciplinary actions/sworn officer. Community perceptions of police abuse.	• Officer survey. • Mean number of sick and family leave time taken by sworn staff. • Self-assessment form. • Community survey.
Cost of Police Services	Dollar cost/custodial arrest. Dollar cost/call for service answered. Dollar cost of police department/resident.	• Self-assessment form.

Sources: Alpert, G.P. & Moore, M.H. (1993). Measuring police performance in the new paradigm of policing. *Performance measures for the criminal justice system* (p. 109). Washington, DC: U.S. Department of Justice; p. 111. Bayley, D.H. (1996). Measuring overall effectiveness or, "Police-force show and tell." In L.T. Hoover, *Quantifying quality in policing* (p. 46). Washington, DC: Police Executive Research Forum; Davis, R.C., Ortiz, C.W., Euler, S. & Kuykendall, L. (2015). Revisiting "Measuring What Matters": Developing a suite of standardized performance measures for policing. *Police Quarterly*, 18(4) (pp. 489–492). Mastrofski, S.D. (1996). Measuring police performance in public encounters. In L.T. Hoover, *Quantifying quality in policing* (pp. 223–224). Washington, DC: Police Executive Research Forum; Moore, M.H. & Braga, A. (2004). *The "bottom line" of policing: What citizens should value (and measure!)* In *Police performance* (pp. 79–86). Washington, DC: Police Executive Research Forum; Ostrom, E. (1973). On the meaning and measuring of output and efficiency in the provision of urban police services. *Journal of Criminal Justice*, 1 (p. 98); Skogan, W.G. (1999). Measuring what matters: Crime, disorder, and fear. In Langworthy, R.H. *Measuring what matters: Proceedings from the policing research institute meetings* (pp. 42–43) Washington, DC: National Institute of Justice and the Office of Community Oriented Policing Services, 1999); Stephens, D.W. (1996). Community problem-oriented policing: Measuring impacts. In L.T. Hoover, *Quantifying quality in policing* (pp. 103–108).Washington, DC: Police Executive Research Forum.

6. Were targeted populations or neighborhood groups reached?
7. How did the officers perform?

Operational planning should always be conducted with evaluation in mind. It should be clear that evaluation is centered on the identification and measurement of what has in fact occurred as opposed to what should have occurred. Measurable objectives must be incorporated into the feedback system that tests strategy. An action plan that incorporates the following system elements will allow managers to avoid setting unrealistic or unattainable expectations. Outcomes and objectives should be realistically set to provide the organization with a way to assess progress. Baseline measures (what conditions existed before operations began) should be identified so that a before-and-after comparison of performance indicators is possible. Individual measures should always be linked to unit and strategy outcomes.

Typically, the evaluation of an anti-crime strategy considers the level of crime that is prevented or controlled following its implementation. The baseline measures compare the crime level after a specific time period during which the strategy was applied with what existed before the strategy was adopted. Also, tactics often have several aims. Multiple measures are usually appropriate because crime problems are not isolated incidents. For example, an attempt to move against an open-air drug market may attempt to reduce citizen fear of crime, community disorder, or even traffic-related problems. Different outcome measures are required to capture these elements.

As a result, the strategy selected to eliminate the drug market may have several measurable outcomes that could include elimination of the distribution center, reduction of ancillary criminal incidents, stabilization of the neighborhood, reduction of citizens' fear, and increased use of neighborhood space by ordinary citizens. Operational strategies are expected to have an impact. The amount of the impact should be projected, planned for, and measured. Managers have to identify measurement criteria that will accurately inform them, both positively and negatively, of what they have accomplished. Efficiency and legality are also important evaluation strategy issues. The cost-benefit (efficiency) analysis of operational strategies is a necessary consideration when deciding how to best evaluate the use of resources. An operational strategy may be an efficient use of resources or a terrible waste of them. A planned strategy evaluation that provides data on implementation, resource use, and associated costs (direct and indirect) should provide the information needed to determine cost-benefit in a timely manner. Operational managers also must make sure that their strategy meets appropriate legal and ethical standards. The ends do not justify the means.

The monitoring of operational systems either involves identifying deficiencies in strategy implementation and unidentified consequences that prevent strategies from delivering what they were originally designed to do or what in fact makes them work. The analysis of monitoring data addresses the actual strategy process to its design and outcomes. Key factors in evaluating an operational program's performance involve describing the activities undertaken in implementing the strategy (process outputs) and the specification of objectives in measurable terms (impacts/outcomes). Data for monitoring purpose can be collected from four sources:

•   Direct observation.
•   Official records.
•   Operational statistics.
•   Interviews of officers involved, and program participants (community surveys).

Efficiency analysis provides a framework for relating program cost to results. Cost-benefit analysis directly compares program outcomes to process output costs in monetary terms. This analysis requires that program costs and benefits be known, quantified, and transformed to a common measurement unit. It should be remembered that the true outcomes of programs include spillover effects, and these should be in any cost-benefit analysis. Spillover effects are unanticipated outcomes or issues created by implementing the strategy; for example, the cost of the unanticipated need for additional community outreach meetings during the initial stage of the strategy's implementation. A well-defined impact model is essential to both program design and evaluation. However, every evaluation must be tailored to the specific strategy being designed and implemented.

Naturally, when measuring police operational performance, outcomes generate the most concern. Political and community representatives and policy makers want to know: Is the department accomplishing what it said it would? Did crime go down, was disorder reduced, and are citizens satisfied? It should also be understood that the strategy used to accomplish the outcome would influence the outcomes we obtain. Thus, the strategy implementation process is also important. Did we select the right people for the task? Were they trained properly? Did first-line supervisors do their assigned tasks? Was it efficient, effective, legal, and ethical? We need to know what parts of the strategy worked and which did not. So we can avoid mistakes. To answer these questions, law enforcement departments should:

1. Take maximum advantage of the data they routinely collect by analyzing the patterns and trends (intelligence) they contain.
2. Analyze and disseminate this intelligence to operational commanders who need it in a timely and understandable fashion.
3. Look for cost-effective ways to enhance their routine data collection and intelligence analysis.
4. Undertake special measurements when the cost is not prohibitive and the need is substantial enough to warrant the extra effort.
5. Use intelligence data to support operational decision making.
6. Employ GIS systems.
7. Use volunteers, senior citizens, or college students enrolled in research methods classes in nearby colleges to conduct telephone surveys focused on citizen fear of crime, satisfaction with the department, and other topics.
8. Set realistic outcomes and objectives to provide the organization with a way to assess progress accurately; cite success, identify effective strategies, and refocus resources accordingly.
9. Remember to establish appropriate baseline measures so that a before-and-after comparison of relevant factors is possible.

Performance measurement is a management tool. It is only as good as its design and the individual(s) who use it. The measurement of effectiveness is concerned with outcomes rather than outputs. **Input measures** address the amount of resources used to provide a particular service, such as the number of hours spent patrolling a particular area—human, financial, and in-kind assets. **Output measures** consider the quantity of the service delivered—number of arrests, total dollars collected in seized assets, number of cases resulting in conviction (Shane, 2007, p. 27). **Outcome measures** describe results achieved. They compare the actual results achieved to those desired. Thus, they are concerned with measuring the effectiveness of the process used to achieve the desired outcome. It is not sufficient to know that a change occurred; managers need to determine whether the strategy and tactics in question caused the observed change. Have crime incidents been reduced? Do community residents feel safer? Is there an improvement in officer performance after their attendance at a training program?

Measures of efficiency consider the amount of resources used to achieve an output, like hours spent per arrest and the cost thereof. Efficiency is tied to doing more work in less time and at less cost. The measure of *committed time* is concerned with the time that an officer spends on a particular call for service (the combination of response and handling time). The ratio of these times to the available time for patrol (i.e., duty hours minus lunch breaks, report writing, and other non-patrol time) represents the proportion of the officer's day that is devoted solely to dispatched calls for service (Vega & Gilbert, 1997).

The above categories are crucial elements of performance measurement. It is not just the number of arrests made but the condition of the community after the arrests were made that should concern us. Has the safety and security of the citizens in that community increased in a measurable way because of the arrests? Have we displaced the problem to another place that will require a new strategy and resources? Last, performance measurement should not be an end but the pathway to a more effective law enforcement department. It is used best when it is a feedback mechanism to help decision makers focus on goals, strategies, and resource allocation to accomplish the department mission and improve service to the community.

One key question is: Can the police have an impact upon crime? The research presented in Chapter 13 (Strategic Policing) reveals that the answer is a resounding "Yes!" Many experts consider crime control to be the "Bottom Line" of policing but they also note it should not be the sole indicator of output (Stephens, 1996; Moore & Braga, 2004). Another reason to develop different performance measures is to monitor and evaluate how police officers use their discretionary authority. The aim is to provide data to judge the quality of service provided by police officers. For example, citizens stopped by the police can be asked if they were given the reasons for the stop; if they were questioned, searched, or breath-tested; and if they were arrested, prosecuted, or otherwise sanctioned. Judging citizen satisfaction with the quality of the service received from their police department is an important element of police perforamce measurement (Skogan, 1999, p. 51).

Some innovative methods have been developed to measure the effectiveness of new policing initiatives. For example, Ridgeway and MacDonald (2014) have established a method to compare police performance between neighborhoods through internal benchmarking. Rather than compare police performance in one city to another outside entity, internal benchmarking makes comparisons within the city in question. In this example, comparisons regarding the average level of satisfaction with the police, perceptions of racial profiling behavior by the police, and personal experience with racial profiling were made in each Cincinnati neighborhood to a weighted comparison group of similarly situated residents within the city through the use of propensity score matching. The results showed that some neighborhoods stood out in contrast to the comparison neighborhoods in terms of their dissatisfaction with police performance. These differences can guide and focus policy interventions where they are needed. The internal benchmark provides a method to scrutinize police performance in problem neighborhoods with a more accurate gauge that matches the unique characteristics of a department's community. The results could improve the professionalism of the police, produce more effective and humane practices, and improve citizen's perceptions of the police (Ridgeway & MacDonald, 2014, p. 160).

Similarly, Coleman (2008) surveyed Canadian police agencies to determine if they had strategic performance measurement systems in place congruent with the goals of Community Policing. The survey results showed that departments were still focused upon outputs instead of outcomes as performance measures. Measures like the time taken to respond to non-emergency calls for service, the crime rate, and caseload per officer based on reported crime (and failing to take unreported crime into account) remained as key features of police performance. A strategic performance measurement system should develop measurable outcome goals based upon their mission while establishing internal measurement systems to hold employees accountable and ensure that they are working toward the achievement of organizational goals (Coleman, 2008, p. 310).

The International Association of Chiefs of Police developed a new method to consider benchmarks—the Law Enforcement Benchmarking and Performance Analytics Portal (www.theIACP.org/benchmarking). The Portal provides information on comparative reports on such issues as budgeting, calls for service, sworn strength, complaints, use of force statistics, and median salaries (Phillips, 2017, p. 80).

Shane (2007, p. 44) reminds us that the purpose of developing police performance measures is to establish accountability for improving service delivery. The performance of public agencies is typically focused on "the three Es" of: (1) Economy, (2) Efficiency, and (3) Effectiveness (Boland & Fowler, 2000, pp. 419–420). Measures of economy typically focus upon the fiscal cost per output measured—cost per case, cost per service type, and numbers and categories of staff involved. Efficiency measures are concerned with the ratio of inputs to outputs such as the percentage of crimes solved by arrest. Indicators of effectiveness attempt to measure the extent to which outputs meet a perceived societal need. Such measures are difficult to develop and measure and are tallied in qualitative terms. The typical result of the attempt to measure police performance is the use of quantitative indicators that recognize the intangibility of outcomes while still providing useful data on how agencies are handling the obligation to meet their goals while making the best use of public resources—an exercise in accountability that impacts resource allocation (Boland & Fowler, 2000, pp. 420–421).

Individual Performance Appraisal

The evaluation of police performance is also conducted at the individual level. The typical goal of an employee performance appraisal is to hold individual employees accountable and ensure that their actions are in concert with their organizational position and the achievement of department goals. To do this properly, police managers must: (1) clarify what is expected to their employee, (2) examine officer activities and performance accomplishments and compare actual performance with what is expected, (3) act on findings to improve officer performance, and (4) communicate findings under agency and regulatory policy (Shane, 2007, p. 20).

There are three primary uses for the information provided by individual police performance appraisals: (1) to provide data for administrative decisions, (2) for research, and (3) for counseling of personnel (Landy, 1977, p. 4). The law requires that measurement indicators used in personnel evaluations be based upon job-related criteria. This legal standard requires that a manager's performance evaluation decisions must be relate to the responsibilities of the employee's position (*Griggs v. Duke Power Co., 401 U.S. 424, 1971*). The creation of measurement indicators that serve as the basis for performance appraisals must be based upon a job analysis. In *Segar v. Civiletti (25 FEP 142, 1981)* the federal courts define a job analysis as:

> systematic detailed study of the content of a job so that one can develop an accurate description of what the job entails, the conditions under which the job is performed and the knowledge, skills and abilities needed to perform that job.

Conducting a job analysis includes five basic steps: (1) a review of the department's sources of information (policy, rules, procedures) on job duties and responsibilities, (2) analyze department records that will provide information on work demand and output, (3) obtain information from persons familiar with the job—both employees and their supervisors, (4) observe on-the-job performance, and (5) identify a comprehensive list of job-related tasks (Walsh & Donovan, 1990). A properly conducted job analysis will provide the answers to four basic questions:

1. What should be done?
2. What is actually being done?
3. Who is doing it?
4. How is it being done?

One of the leading experts in police administration, O.W. Wilson (1963), noted that police performance appraisal is a difficult task but one that should be conducted every six months.

Mangers should be aware that individual attributes can affect their employee's performance appraisal process. Barrick and Mount (1991) conducted a meta-analysis of 117 studies that examined the relationship between the "Big Five" personality dimensions (extraversion, emotional stability, agreeableness, conscientiousness, and openness to experience) and job performance. Police departments were one group included in this study. The conscientiousness dimension was determined to be a predictor of job performance across all occupational categories. Traits associated with conscientiousness (a strong sense of purpose, obligation, plan-oriented, organized, hardworking, achievement-oriented, and persistence) were found important to performance in all jobs. These authors concluded that "it is difficult to conceive of a job in which the traits associated with conscientiousness would not contribute to job success" (Barrick & Mount, 1991, pp. 21–22).

Criticisms of the performance appraisal process center on complaints it is based on inaccurate measures of performance, sponsors dysfunctional employee conflict and competition, overemphasizes holding individual employees responsible for poor performance and undervalues the overall work process in the organization, fails to recognize group contributions, and is a "Theory X" control device by management (Roberts, 2003, p. 89). Unfortunately, dissatisfaction with police performance appraisal appears to be the norm. An investigation of the constructs underlying performance appraisals in a medium-sized police departments found no consistent pattern to this method of evaluation (Falkenberg, Gaines, & Cordner, 1991). Walsh (1990) conducted research on how performance evaluation was used in small and medium departments through a survey of 150 sergeants attending continuing education courses in police supervision. He found that the majority of these departments borrowed their forms and processes from other departments—a threat to their validity. Personnel appraisal systems were typically imposed by higher-level administrators without supervisors' input. The administrators stressed the use of performance evaluation in their departments' personnel process but provided no training regarding their use to supervisors. Last, the evaluation criteria used by these departments were not the result of a formal job analysis as required by court decisions.

In the United Kingdom, sergeants were surveyed about their experiences and attitudes toward introducing the New Public Management (NPM) system implemented nation-wide in the 1990s (Butterfield, Edwards, & Woodall, 2004). These sergeants were operational officers who had supervisory responsibilities for the performance appraisal of constables under their charge. Under the NPM, their roles became more managerial and less operational. Their duties were expanded to include responsibility to supervise crime investigation, budgets, work planning, deployment of teams, and handling complaints from the public. They were subject to more scrutiny and experienced an increase in paperwork that included performance appraisals of the constables. These sergeants complained that this role transformation increased their workload, with little training on how to perform their new duties. Performance appraisals were viewed as necessary exercises that relied upon invalid data and measures. In particular, there was an emphasis on the selective use of outputs (as recorded on computer systems) to the expense of demonstrated outcomes of the service delivered (Butterfield et al., 2004, p. 407). The sergeants believed that performance indicators were selected because they were easily measured but not strategically useful—with no particular relevance to the detection and prevention of crime (Butterfield et al., 2004, pp. 408–409). "The impact of the performance measures was that sergeants undertook those aspects of their work that were measured, relegating other work to secondary importance" (Butterfield et al., 2004, p. 411). The sheer volume of work, the nature of the performance measures, and the computer system under the NPM constrained the operational autonomy of the sergeants. Pressures for accountability backfired and led to frustration and inflexibility caused by centralized control over the sergeants. This "Neo-Taylorism" contributed to a division between line supervisors and their superiors.

Negative attitudes toward police performance evaluation have also been documented in a Canadian study of constables and sergeants ($n = 393$) in 15 municipal agencies. The majority of the officers reported that they were appraised on the basis of their personal traits and that they had little or no input on their perfomance evaluation. Few officers stated that they received informal performance feedback from their supervisors regularly. One third of the respondents showed that they did not receive formal face-to-face feedback following their perfomance appraisal. The study found that little training was provided to police supervisors to conduct performance appraisals (Coutts & Schneider, 2004, pp. 76–78).

Several recommendations have been made to improve individual police performance appraisals (Walsh, 1990, p. 103; Coutts & Schneider, 2004, pp. 68–69):

1. A job analysis of each position should be conducted and job data should be matched to the position under evaluation. To be legally sound, performance appraisals should be job-related and based upon performance behaviors rather than traits.
2. These matched criteria should then be retained as rating factors and the others should be discarded and replaced after a review by a committee of representatives from all ranks in the department.

3. To enhance perceptions of fairness and legitimacy, employees should have meaningful input to the evaluation process. Direct participation by employees in the performance appraisal process has been determined to be a crucial attribute in its acceptance and effective implementation.

4. When employees are confident that the appraisal process is fair and impartial, they are more likely to accept the results of the evaluation, even when it is negative or adverse. In addition, the validity of the assessment increases when employees contribute to the construction of performance measures. They provide information that may not be readily perceived or available to the rater (Roberts, 2003, p. 90).

5. This committee should then develop a set of behavioral descriptions of unacceptable and outstanding performance based upon their matched criteria ratings.

6. Reviews should be conducted annually, documented, filed, and reviewed with every employee. "Comprehensive and effective participation within the performance appraisal process consists of joint rater-ratee development of: a) performance standards, b) the rating form, c) employee self-appraisal, and d) rater participation in the interview" (Roberts, 2003, p. 91).

7. To foster growth and development, a continuous feedback process based upon two-way communication must take place between superiors and subordinate employees. Employees should be able to expect accurate, meaningful, and timely feedback about their performance.

8. Supervisors should assess important, job-related aspects of performance and inform employees about their shortcomings and offer suggestions for improvement. The officer in question should be permitted to protest the results (if appropriate) and sign the final report. Performance appraisal should sponsor the achievement of individual and organizational goals. If the employees have confidence in the appraisal process, they will use the information to systematically assess their own performance (Roberts, 2003, p. 91). With feedback on performance, employees can make adjustments, receive positive reinforcement when they prove effective, and thus lead to greater job satisfaction and the improved performance that the organization desires.

Employee performance evaluation has an importance beyond that of an administration system. It should be a major factor in the manager's approach to his or her role. It is an integral part of the manager's efforts to motivate, change, and monitor employee performance. It also benefits the employee by letting them know what they will be held accountable for and what their manager thinks of their work.

The chief (or highest-ranking officer in the department) should conduct an annual inspection of the system to identify instances of supervisory rating error, determine the reasons for error, and take appropriate actions to correct them. Senior mentors should be provided to raters to continually evaluate the appraisal process and employees should also be a part of this review (Roberts, 2003, p. 95). Administrators should continuously evaluate the purpose and content of the appraisal, provide rater training regarding its proper and valid use, and ensure that these elements are consistent with organizational objectives to accurately evaluate meaningful officer performance (Lilley & Hinduja, 2006, p. 35). The key is to develop measures that capture essential job duties and responsibilities by balancing process, outcome, and group and individual performance standards (Roberts, 2003, p. 91).

Employee participation in the performance appraisal process is crucial to its acceptance and ultimately its effectiveness. They are more likely to accept the system when they understand the process, agree upon its value orientations, share a consensus with management on the measures developed and used, are confident in their validity, and perceive that the raters are unbiased (Roberts, 2003, p. 93). If employees believe that the process is tainted by favoritism toward an "in-group," trust will be completely extinguished. A meta-analysis of 27 studies that analyzed the appraisal process determined that there was a strong and stable relationship between employee participation and satisfaction with the results of the evaluation (Cawley, Keeping, & Levy, 1998, p. 626). The authors listed five ways to involve employees in the appraisal process: (1) offer them the opportunity to voice their opinions, (2) allow them to thus influence the process, (3) allow them to perform self-appraisals, (4) allow them to take part in its development, and (5) allow them to participate in goal setting as a part of the process (Cawley et al., 1998, p. 628).

The manner in which a negative appraisal is delivered is a vitally important part of the appraisal process. Roberts (2003, p. 94) counsels managers to take a "courtroom perspective" and question their beliefs about worker motivation, ability, and poor performance assuming that the employee is "innocent until proven guilty" through a thorough analysis of all available information that may provide explanatory, mitigating, or extenuating factors that influenced the employee's performance.

Cederblom and Pemerl (2002, p. 132) suggest that agencies move from performance appraisal to performance management.

> Performance management refers to an umbrella of all organizational components and activities affecting individual, work group, and agency performance. A performance management system would include performance appraisal, and other components such as strategic plans, manager accountability, pay, promotion, training/development, and discipline.

Rather than pursuing numbers, departments should also evaluate how officers identify and resolve community safety issues by soliciting input from citizens. Such a system would promote problem solving, Community Policing and Compstat approaches to increase the relevance of police performance appraisals. In fact, a survey of 600 U.S. police organizations revealed that job satisfaction in agencies engaged in Community Policing increased. Job satisfaction was heightened because engagement in Community Policing led to improved methods of performance appraisal by providing more training for raters, greater evaluative emphasis upon officer development, and the use of a broad range of performance criteria (Lilley & Hinduja, 2007, p. 147). Police administrators should think of new ways to drive police performance through improved recording, reporting, and communication with an eye toward "big picture" organizational objectives (Cederblom & Pemerl, 2002, p. 138). This is a strategic approach to performance management that evaluates all that an officer does and links it to the achievement of departmental goals and objectives.

However, the promise that Community Policing will lead to changes in police performance evaluation appears limited (Lilley & Hinduja, 2006). Lilley and Hinduja (2007) conducted a content analysis of 1,474 individual rating items on 150 officer evaluation instruments from police departments across the United States. They examined these evaluation instruments for five appraisal ratings: (1) stakeholder focus, (2) officer role emphasis, (3) level of service expectation, (4) employee traits encouraged, and (5) type of motivation used. In addition, they surveyed 197 agencies engaged in Community Policing from LEMAS data for 1997 and also randomly selected more traditional departments. The results revealed that, although supervisors from the Community Policing departments placed greater emphasis upon problem solving and neighborhood crime and disorder in their assessment of officer performance, the content analysis of the evaluation instruments demonstrated no substantial difference from more traditional agencies in terms of focus, role emphasis, service effort, or any other variable (Lilley & Hinduja, 2007, pp. 147–148). Although the Community Policing departments emphasized a different level of service delivery and performance evaluation, these changes were yet to be reflected in their performance appraisal instruments. In fact, rating items overall appeared to be directed toward a desire to avoid citizen complaints and maintain conformity (i.e., personal appearance assessment) as an important officer trait. Innovation was not valued over the prevention of unwanted officer behaviors. Lilley and Hinduja (2007, p. 148) conclude from their analysis that the primary objective of performance appraisals was the desire to reduce the workload of management in the police bureaucracy.

In addition, NYPD's Compstat process has also revealed issues with performance measurement. A survey of 1,770 NYPD retirees in three separate waves determined that performance pressures under the Compstat system led many to manipulate crime statistics for their benefit (Eterno, Verma, & Silverman, 2014). Statistical analysis of crime reporting data found that the pressure to downgrade crime statistics was highest during the Bloomberg–Kelly era of Compstat in the NYPD and that there was similar pressure to obey legal/Constitutional rules (Eterno et al., 2014, p. 16). The data show that, over time, the initially productive Compstat system morphed into a culture of "gaming numbers" to keep the crime decreases going (Eterno et al., 2014, pp. 18–19). The authors suggest that transparency in police agencies can remedy the pressure to manipulate performance measures.

Conclusion

Police performance should be gauged at both the organizational and individual level. Agencies must do a credible job of both by establishing valid and reliable measures for each type of appraisal. The thoughts and feelings of employees at all levels should be a significant part of both processes to ensure accuracy and legitimacy of the measures. Police organizations do not have a readily definable bottom line and the intensive focus on numbers of crimes and arrests may lead police agencies to lose sight of other important goals like equity, fairness, and justice (Maguire & Uchida, 2000, p. 506). Qualitative and quantitative measures should be included in these appraisals.

Benefits of performance evaluation outweigh the drawbacks of the process. Employees wish to know where they stand and evaluations offer transparency, allowing employees to understand how their performance is viewed in the organization. They provide a regular method to recognize and reward top performance. The information helps to develop employees by assessing their strengths and weaknesses—building an organizational culture promoting improvement and growth (Goler, Gale, & Grant, 2016).

Measurement is the first step that leads to control and eventually to improvement. Studies have found: "When performance is measured, it improves. When performance is measured and compared, it improves further. When performance is measured, compared, and appropriately recognized and rewarded, it improves even more, dramatically more" (Creech, 1995, p. 473). Performance measurement is not just about numbers When assessing feelings about public safety, counting incidents of crime, numbers of arrests, victims of violent crime, or drug sales in a public park, numbers are not the end of the process. The bottom line is actually the beginning of a continuing process of problem solving, evaluation, managerial oversight, and constant improvement. It is important to remember that performance measurement is not a one-time event; it is a continual process of improvement.

KEY TERMS

Baseline	Measures of efficiency	Specific measures
General measures	Outcome measures	Success indicator
Input measures	Output measures	Target
Macro measures	Performance indicator	

References

Alpert, G.P. & Moore, M.H. (1993). *Measuring police performance in the new paradigm of policing. Performance measures for the criminal justice system* (p. 109). Washington, DC: U.S. Department of Justice.

Barrick, M.R., & Mount, M.K. (1991). The big five personality dimensions and job performance: A meta-analysis. *Personnel Psychology, 44*(1), 1–26.

Bayley, D.H. (1996). Measuring overall effectiveness or police force "show and tell". In L.T. Hoover (Ed.), *Quantifying quality in policing* (pp. 37–54). Washington, DC: Police Executive Research Forum.

Behn, R.D. (2003, September/October). Why measure performance? Different purposes require different measures. *Public Administration Review, 63*(5), 586–606.

Boland, T., & Fowler, A. (2000). A systems perspective on performance in public sector organizations. *The International Journal of Public Sector Management, 13*(5), 417–446.

Butterfield, R., Edwards, C., & Woodall, J. (2004). The new public management and the UK police service. *Public Management Review, 6*(3), 395–415.

Cawley, B.D., Keeping, L.M., & Levy, P.E. (1998). Participation in the performance appraisal process and employee reactions: A Meta-analytic review of field investigations. *Journal of Applied Psychology, 83*(4), 615–633.

Cederblom, D., & Pemerl, D.E. (2002). From performance appraisal to performance management: One agency's experience. *Public Personnel Management, 31*(2), 131–140.

Coleman, T.G. (2008). Managing strategic knowledge in policing: Do police leaders have sufficient knowledge about organisational performance to make informed strategic decisions? *Police Practice & Research, 9*(4), 307–322.

Coutts, L.M., & Schneider, F.W. (2004). Police officer performance appraisals: How good are they? *Policing, 27*(1), 67–81.

Creech, R. (1995). Employee motivation. *Management Quarterly, 36*(2), 33–40.

Davis, R.C., Ortiz, C.W., Euler, S. & Kuykendall, L. (2015). Revisiting "Measuring What Matters": Developing a suite of standardized performance measures for policing. *Police Quarterly*, 18(4), 489–492.

Eterno, J.A., Verma, A., & Silverman, E.B. (2014). Police manipulations of crime reporting: Insiders' revelations. *Justice Quarterly*, 33(5), 1–25.

Falkenberg, S., Gaines, L., & Cordner, G. (1991). An examination of the constructs underlying police performance appraisals. *Journal of Criminal Justice*, 19(4), 351–360.

Fleming, J., & Scott, A. (2008). Performance measurement in Australian police organizations. *Policing: A Journal of Policy and Practice*, 2(3), 322–330.

Goler, L., Gale, J., & Grant, A. (2016, November). Let's not kill performance evaluations yet. *Harvard Business Review*, 90–94.

Higgins, G.E., Vito, G.F., & Grossi, E.L. (2012). The impact of race on the police decision to search after a traffic stop: A focal concerns theory perspective. *Journal of Contemporary Criminal Justice*, 28(2), 166–183.

Kelling, G. (1999). Measuring what matters: A new way of thinking about crime and public order. In R.H. Langworthy (Ed.), *Measuring what matters: Proceedings from the policing research institute meetings* (pp. 27–36). Washington, DC: National Institute of Justice & the Office of Community Policing Services.

Kelling, G.L. (1996). Defining the bottom line in policing: Organizational philosophy and accountability. In L.T. Hoover (Ed.), *Quantifying quality in policing* (pp. 23–39). Washington, DC: Police Executive Research Forum.

Klockars, C.B. (1999). Some really cheap ways of measuring what really matters. In R. Langworthy (Ed.), *Measuring what matters: Proceedings from the policing research institute meetings* (pp. 195–214). Washington, DC: U.S. Department of Justice.

Kouzes, J., & Posner, B. (2012). *The leadership challenge*. San Francisco, CA: Jossey-Bass.

Landy, F.J. (1977). *Performance appraisal in police departments*. Washington, DC: The Police Foundation.

Lilley, D., & Hinduja, S. (2006). Officer evaluation in the community policing context. *Policing*, 29(1), 19–37.

Lilley, D., & Hinduja, S. (2007). Police officer performance appraisal and overall satisfaction. *Journal of Criminal Justice*, 35, 137–150.

Maguire, E.R., & Uchida, C.D. (2000). Measurement and explanation in the comparative of American police organizations. *Criminal Justice*, 4, 491–557.

Mastrofski, S.D. (1996). Measuring police performance in public encounters. In L.T. Hoover (Ed.), *Quantifying quality in policing* (pp. 223–224). Washington, DC: Police Executive Research Forum.

Mastrofski, S. (2003). Personnel and agency performance appraisal. In W. Geller (Ed.), *Local government police management* (pp. 447–486). Washington, DC: International City Management Association.

McClintock, F.H. (1977). The dark figure of crime. In L. Radzinowicz, & M.E. Wolfgang (Eds.), *Crime and justice: Volume I—The criminal in society* (pp. 126–139). New York: Basic Books.

Meehan, A.J., & Ponder, M.C. (2002). Race and place: The ecology of racial profiling African American motorists. *Justice Quarterly*, 19(3), 399–430.

Moore, M.H., & Braga, A.A. (2004, Winter/Spring). Police performance measurement: A normative framework. *Criminal Justice Ethics*, 3–19.

Moore, M.H., & Poethig, M. (1999). The Police as an agency of municipal government: Implications for measuring police effectiveness. In R.H. Langworthy (Ed.), *Measuring what matters: Proceedings from the policing research institute meetings* (pp. 151–168). Washington, DC: National Institute of Justice & Office of Community Policing Services.

Nagin, D.S., Solow, R.M., & Lum, C. (2015). Deterrence, criminal opportunities, and police. *Criminology, 53*(1), 74–100.

Oettmeier, T.N., & Wycoff, M.A. (1996). Police performance in the nineties: Practioner perspectives. In G.W. Cordner, & D.J. Kenney (Eds.), *Managing police organizations* (pp. 131–156). Cincinnati: Anderson.

Ostrom, E. (1973). On the meaning and measuring of output and efficiency in the provision of urban police services. *Journal of Criminal Justice, 1*(2), 93–111.

Phillips, T. (2017, July). IACP working for you: Benchmarking and performance analytics: Your new tool for data-driven decision making. *The Police Chief,* 78–80.

Ridgeway, G., & MacDonald, J.M. (2014). A method for internal benchmarking of criminal justice performance. *Crime & Delinquency, 60*(1), 145–162.

Roberts, G.E. (2003). Employee performance appraisal system participation: A techinque that works. *Public Personnel Management, 32*(1), 89–98.

Seidman, D., & Couzens, M. (1974). Getting the crime rate down: Political pressure and crime reporting. *Law and Society Review, 8,* 456–493.

Shane, J.M. (2007). *What every police executive should know: Using data to measure police performance.* Flushing, NY: Looseleaf Law Publications, Inc.

Skogan, W. (1999). Measuring what matters: Crime, disorder and fear. In R.H. Langworthy (Ed.), *Measuring what matters: Proceedings from the policing research institute meetings* (pp. 37–54). Washington, DC: National Institute of Justice & Office of Community Policing Services.

Skolnick, J.H., & Caplovitz, A. (2001). Guns, drugs, and policing: Ways to target guns and minimize racial profiling. *Arizona Law Review, 43,* 413–438.

Sparrow, M.K. (2015). Measuring performance in a modern police organization. *New Perspectives in Policing Bulletin.* Washington, DC: US Department of Justice, National Institute of Justice.

Stephens, D.W. (1996). Community problem-oriented policing: Measuring impacts. In L.T. Hoover (Ed.), *Quantifying quality in policing* (pp. 95–129). Washington, DC: Police Executive Research Forum.

Vega, A., & Gilbert, M.J. (1997). Longer days, shorter weeks: Compressed work weeks in policing. *Public Personnel Management, 26*(3), 391–402.

Walsh, W.F. (1990). Performance appraisal in small and medium police departments. *American Journal of Police, 9,* 93–109.

Walsh, W.F., & Donovan, E. (1990). *Supervision of police personnel: A performance-based approach.* Dubuque, IA: Kendall Hunt.

West, A.D. (2003). Chicken little, three blind Men and an elephant, and "racial profiling": A commentary on the collection, analysis, and interpretation of traffic stop data. *The Journal of Forensic Psychology Practice, 3*(2), 63–77.

Wilson, O.W. (1963). *Police administration.* New York: McGraw-Hill.

Cases

Griggs v. Duke Power Co., 401 U.S. 424, 1971.

Segar v. Civiletti, 25 FEP 142, 1981.

11 Maintaining Integrity and Professional Standards

Most police departments have members who commit corrupt acts from time to time.
Only some police departments, however, become corrupt police departments.
L.W. Sherman, *Controlling Police Corruption* (Sherman, 1978, p. 32)

Learning Objectives

1. Describe police deviance, misconduct, and corruption.

2. Identify the dimensions of police corruption.

3. Describe the ways police departments can control officer deviance.

4. Identify the characteristics of the internal affairs process.

5. Describe the police inspectional process.

6. Describe police early warning systems.

7. Describe the use of disciple to control deviance.

Introduction

This chapter discusses the maintenance of organizational integrity and **professional standards** in policing. Its objective is to provide an understanding of police **misconduct** and corruption, its causes, and organizational strategies for its prevention. Policing in a democracy requires high levels of integrity. Police officers are entrusted with powers and responsibilities that set them apart from their fellow citizens. When the police are corrupt and operate without integrity, their actions result in an erosion of public confidence in the very democratic principles they are sworn to protect.

Police **deviancy** is a recurring occupational hazard. Police officers and their organizations throughout history have engaged in illegal and unethical activity (Reppetto, 1978; Monkkonen, 1981; Whalen & Whalen, 2014). There have been persistent incidences of corruption, misconduct, and violation of professional standards of conduct and the law by all ranks in policing. Instances of organized police corruption have been found in Boston, Chicago, New York, Detroit, Los Angeles, Miami, and Philadelphia (Norwicki & Punch, 2003). Traditionally, police deviancy has been viewed as a big city problem but misconduct and corruption are potential problems for all departments no matter what their size.

Throughout the history of policing, officers have been found to have engaged in a variety of corrupt activities that include bribe taking, extortion, protection of gambling, and suppression of evidence, excessive use of force, tampering with evidence, perjury, and accepting graft. Receiving free meals, tickets, tips, and discounts are accepted behaviors in many departments but considered acts of misconduct in others. Deviant activities will thrive in departments where administrators and managers are negligent in their responsibility to prevent and detect wrongdoing by subordinates. For example, the Los Angeles Police Department's investigation into corruption in its Rampart Area Division found that inadequate discipline, lax supervision, and a general culture of acceptance of mediocre performance created a climate in which corruption flourished. This climate resulted from a lack of commitment, laziness, excessive tolerance, and the failure by the division's managers to hold officers responsible and accountable (Parks, 2000). When misconduct and corruption exist in a department, they represent a failure of leadership, command accountability, policy, and discipline.

Klockars (1999), after extensive research into police corruption, concluded that policing is an occupation ripe with opportunities for misconduct of many types. Inappropriate and illegal behaviors exist in policing because it is a highly discretionary, coercive activity that routinely takes place in private settings, out of the sight of supervisors and witnesses. Policing involves the exercise of authority over citizens and thus requires a high level of ethics and integrity to be perceived as legitimate in the eyes of the public. Close contact with citizens, the monitoring and control of vice activities, and the discretionary power exercised by officers make policing a "morally dangerous occupation" (Barker, 2006). It is because police officers are charged with such important responsibilities and power that it is necessary that their behavior be monitored and controlled. A police agency noted for its integrity and transparency will have an occupational culture that supports the discipline of officers who violate the law and not tolerate those who abuse the rights and privileges of their office (Klockars, Ivkovic, & Haberfeld, 2006).

The proper utilization of police power and discretion requires a strong sense of ethical awareness and adherence to norms of professional conduct. Integrity is more than just officers following the department's rules. It involves reflective, self-prescribed, and self-governing discretionary decisions made in situations involving ethical standards of conduct and individual rights (O'Keefe, 2004). *Integrity* is the normative inclination among police to resist temptations to abuse the rights and privileges of their occupation (Klockars et al., 2006). To a large degree, the public's image of the police is determined by the department's maintenance of standards of integrity and its actions in responding to allegations of corruption, violations of professional standards, and serious misconduct by the agency or its employees (CALEA, 2006). When the police perform their duties with fairness, equity, and integrity, public trust is maintained.

Democratic policing is citizen-focused policing that combines crime control and crime prevention with a welfare and service role. It fulfills the institutional responsibilities of enforcing law and ensuring public social order while following four key principles (Bayley, 2001):

Police must be accountable to the law rather than to the government. Police actions in a democracy must be governed by the rule of law.

Police must give top operational priority to servicing the needs of individual citizens and private groups. The most dramatic contribution police can make in a democracy is to become responsive to the needs of individual citizens, instead of primarily serving the interest of government.

Police must protect human rights, especially those that are required for the sort of unfettered political activity that is the hallmark of democracy. Democracy requires not only that the police be constrained by law but also that they make a special effort to safeguard activities that are essential to the exercise of democracy.

Police should be transparent in their activities. Police activity must be open to observation and regularly reported to outsiders.

These principles hold that the police should be accountable to the communities being policed, to the taxpayers who pay the bills, and to the legal order governing their authority. Police organizations should not be closed, insular, or cut off from citizens and the communities from which their power derives. Sir Robert Peel noted that the ability of the police to perform their task is dependent on public approval of their existence, actions, behavior, and on the ability of the police to secure and maintain public respect (Lee, 1901).

Public confidence in the police depends on police officers demonstrating the highest levels of personal and professional standards of behavior. Each department employee's performance and behavior should reflect the goal of honorably and lawfully serving and protecting the public. Strategically, police administrators and managers must see themselves as part of an organizational system whose ultimate goal is to create an environment in which each officer is challenged to do their best in a legal and ethical manner (Murphy & Caplan, 1991). The integrity of a police department depends on the personal integrity and discipline of each of its employees. Police administrators and managers have a responsibility to ensure that they and their employees adhere to the law as well as a code of professional values, standards, and behavior. **Integrity** is the most important characteristic and strength of a police department and its employees. It is the foundation of police legitimacy in the eyes of the public.

Defining Police Deviance, Misconduct, and Corruption

In order to understand and manage police, deviance it is important to establish what it entails and who it involves. *Police deviance* includes activities inconsistent with expected norms, values, or ethics from both a societal and police perspective. *Police misconduct* violates accepted standards, departmental policies and procedures (e.g., drinking alcohol on duty, not responding to calls for service, sleeping on duty, filing false reports). It is classified as follows:

Malfeasance—performance of a prohibited unjustified, harmful act or activity that is in violation of the public trust (e.g., seeking a gratuity, use of police resources for personal use).

Misfeasance—the wrongful performance of a normally lawful duty or authority (e.g., conducting improper searches, selective enforcement, verbally abusing a citizen).

Nonfeasance—failure to perform a required duty when it is required (e.g., failure to file reports, improper stop and frisk, security breach).

Corruption involves an officer's misuse of police authority to do or not do something for the purpose of deriving some form of personal gain for the officer or others (Bayley & Perito, 2011). Roebuck and Barker (1974) offered a broad definition by identifying police corruption as any form of deviant, dishonest, improper, unethical, or criminal behavior by a police officer. It typically involves an officer taking bribes (Norwicki & Punch, 2003). Kleinig (1996, p. 166) suggests that "Police officers act corruptly when, in exercising or failing to exercise their authority, they act with the primary intention of furthering private or departmental/divisional advantage." Skogan and Meares (2004) propose that **types of corruption** can be understood according to their intention. Examples include abuse of authority, physical abuse (e.g., police brutality and/or excessive force), psychological abuse (most often in the context of police interrogations), and legal abuse (generally in the form of perjury to achieve an organizational goal or to protect corrupt practices). Kappeler, Sluder, and Alpert (1998) identify **police crime** as a separate category of corruption that occurs when the officer's behavior involves violation of existing criminal statutes. Courtemanche (2011) warns that misconduct gets police officers fired; however, corruption results in police chiefs being fired.

Corruption may be carried out for "personal gain" as well as organizational gain. The latter is known as ***"noble cause"*** corruption because it involves the use of inappropriate or illegal means to obtain legitimate ends, such as committing illegal searches to achieve an arrest and/or lying on the witness stand to establish probable cause for an arrest. Klockars (1980) labeled these noble cause activities as the "Dirty Harry Problem." The key element in this form of corruption involves the misuse of official authority. The officer or officers involved believe that the good consequences (i.e., criminal convictions, removal of bad people from the community, suppression of drug sales) they seek justify their inappropriate or illegal behavior.

Corruption can be an activity engaged in by both an individual and organization. For example, some police administrators foster a culture in their organizations that tolerates the use of excessive force commonly known as "street justice" by their officers to maintain public order and respect for authority (Skolnick & Fyfe, 1993). In these instances the desire to solve and control crime and teach bad guys a lesson may sometimes result in the officer violating a citizen's constitutional rights by making an illegal arrest or conducting overly broad searches, coercing confessions, or using excessive force as a form of retribution. Some police managers tend to avoid disciplining officers in these situations especially when felony arrests and cases are solved as a result of these practices. However, practices of this type resulted in the city of Chicago spending nearly $100 million on settlements and legal fees relating to a police commander's use of a torture ring during the 1970s to the 1990s that used electrical shock, burning, and mock executions to elicit confessions from suspects (USA Today, 2015).

Dimensions of Police Corruption

Corruption has been the target of numerous efforts at creating topologies. Newburn (1999) synthesized a typology of nine types of police corruption based on the work of Roebuck and Barker (1974) and Punch (1985).

Corruption of authority: When an officer receives some form of material gain due to his or her position without violating the law p*er se* (e.g., free drinks, meals, services).

"Kickbacks": Receipt of goods, services, or money for referring business (e.g., recommendation of a lawyer to arrestees).

Opportunistic theft: Stealing from arrestees, traffic accident victims, crime victims, and the bodies or property of dead citizens.

Shakedowns: Acceptance of a bribe for not following through on a criminal violation, that is, not making an arrest, filing a complaint, or impounding property.

Protection of illegal acts: Police protection of those engaged in illegal activities (e.g., prostitution, drugs, pornography) enabling the activity to continue operating.

The fix: Undermining criminal investigations or proceedings. (e.g., giving inaccurate or false testimony).

Direct criminal activities: A police officer commits an actual crime in clear violation of both departmental and criminal norms. (e.g., committing a burglary on duty).

Internal payoffs: Entitlements available to police officers (holidays, shift, allocations, days off, promotion) are bought, bartered and sold.

"Flaking" or "padding": Planting of or adding to evidence (increasing the weight of a narcotics seizure from a misdemeanor to felony level).

The Knapp Commission (1972) investigation of the New York City Police Department identified two types of corrupt officers, "grass eaters" and "meat eaters." **Grass eaters** engaged in opportunistic corruption. They accepted bribes and gratuities that were offered to them but did not actively seek these out. **Meat eaters** proactively seek gratuities and bribes. They would attempt to obtain assignments in enforcement units that offered many opportunities for illegal payoffs such as those that enforced gambling, prostitution, and narcotics laws.

Kane and White (2009, p. 745) developed a classification scheme of police misconduct based on a study of 1,543 New York City police officers who were involuntarily separated from the NYPD for career-ending activity during 1975–1996. They classified police misconduct into eight categories:

1. *Profit-motivated crimes*: All offenses, other than drug trafficking and whether on duty or off duty, in which the end or apparent goal of officers' wrongdoing was a profit.
2. *Off-duty crimes against persons*: All assaultive behavior, except for profit-motivated robberies, by off-duty officers.
3. *Off-duty public order crimes*: All offenses, other than drug trafficking or possession, against public order, including driving while intoxicated and disorderly conduct.
4. *Drugs*: Possession and sale of drugs, and related conspiracies, as well as failing or refusing to submit to departmental drug tests.
5. *On-duty abuse*: All offenses by officers that involved the use of excessive force, psychological abuse, or discrimination based on citizens' membership in a class (i.e., gender, race, ethnicity, or sexual preference).
6. *Obstruction of justice*: Conspiracy, perjury, official misconduct, and all offenses in which the apparent goal is obstruction or subversion of judicial proceedings.

7. *Administrative/failure to perform*: Failure to abide by departmental regulations concerning attendance, performance, obedience, reporting, and other conduct not included in other offense types.
8. *Conduct-related probationary failures*: All misconduct-related terminations of probationary officers in which misconduct in types 1–7 is not specified, and excluding simple failure.

Sherman (1974) took an organizational approach and classified police departments according to the level of pervasiveness of their corruption. *Type I* departments are characterized by small numbers of individual officers and groups of officers who engage in unorganized corruption. He identified these officers as rotten apples and rotten pockets. *Type II* departments contain pervasive unorganized corruption in which a majority of police officers are corrupt, but they have little relationship to each other in that there is no informal organization of engaging in corruption. *Type III* departments have pervasive organized corruption in which a hierarchical and authoritarian system exists to control corrupt activity involving individuals from not only within the department but also political figures.

Fyfe, Greene, Walsh, Wilson, and McLaren (1997, p. 461) suggest a series of questions that will identify whether a department's corruption is an indication of individual employees (grass eaters) or a deeper systematic Type III organizational problem.

1. How many officers are involved in the corrupt activity?
2. How high up the chain of command does the corruption extend?
3. How many nonparticipating officers, members of the community or other officials knew about the corrupt activity?
4. Did any nonparticipating persons who knew of this activity report it? If so, how long did it take, and under what circumstances did it occur?
5. Have previous attempts to report the misconduct gone unheeded?
6. Is the corruption associated with the activity that very visibly provides illegal goods or services for a large clientele?
7. Is the corruption associated with the enforcement of laws or administrative ordinances that are routinely ignored and that have no support in the community?
8. Is the corruption associated with a law enforcement activity about which the agency has not formulated a clear policy?
9. Is the corruption consistent with some partisan end?

Controlling Deviance

The police chief executive and his or her management team are responsible for their organization's integrity and controlling deviant employee behavior. Deviance, corruption, and misconduct undermine the integrity of the police officer as well as the department in the minds of the citizens they have sworn to protect. All too frequently, citizens' confidence in the police has been damaged by repeated acts of deviant police behavior reported in the media. Incidents of excessive use of deadly force, brutality, and corruption around the country have become daily news items—all of which contribute to the erosion of public confidence in their police. The broad range of behaviors identified as being deviant or corrupt suggests that, when investigating and attempting to prevent these activities, it is important to employ a targeted, yet complex, approach to their prevention. This approach must focus not only on the most frequently occurring incidents of deviance but, more important, seek to control the multiple factors that combine to produce corrupt behavior and a culture of deviance in the department (Porter & Warrender, 2009).

The control of employee deviance requires constant attention, collection and analysis of data, confronting the reality of practice, and holding all employees accountable. It also necessitates the development of a long-term, multifaceted strategy that includes speaking out, setting clear standards and policy, holding those in authority accountable, improving the use of discretion, promoting integrity through training, enlisting outside help, and robustly and proactively tackling corruption and deviance (Norwicki & Punch, 2003, p. 333).

There are three major categories of standards defining police behavior: ethical, organizational, and legal. **Ethical standards** are principles of appropriate conduct. Ethical behavior is an expression of these principles. For example, the Northumbria Police Service (2015) in the United Kingdom states on its website that the department takes pride in all we do, putting the citizen first and applying the principles of integrity and high-quality service in our six Ethical Principles. These principles are defined as:

Attentive—by listing to communities
Responsive—by responding to the needs of the communities
Reliable—by not letting people down
Skilled—by having staff with the right tools to do the job
Polite—to the public
Fair—at all times in carrying out our duties.

Organizational standards can be both formal and informal; they are derived from policy, procedures, rules, and regulations of the department (formal) and from the expectations of one's peers (informal). **Legal standards** are represented by the laws officers are sworn to uphold and by due process, which establishes the means officers may use to achieve good ends (Roberg, Novak, Cordner, & Smith, 2012, p. 291).

In 1979 the Commission on Accreditation for Law Enforcement Agencies (CALEA) was created through the joint efforts of the International Association of Chiefs of Police, the National Organization of Black Law Enforcement Executives, the National Sheriffs Association, and the Police Executive Research Forum for the purpose of establishing a body of professional standards for police agencies. CALEA developed an accreditation process based upon these standards to provide law enforcement agencies with the opportunity to voluntarily demonstrate that they meet an established set of professional standards. CALEA's *Standards for Law Enforcement Agencies* and its Accreditation Programs have evolved as the accepted set of standards by which a police department can demonstrate commitment to professional excellence in law enforcement. The standards upon which the Law Enforcement Accreditation Program is based are acknowledged nationally as benchmarks for evaluating the professionalism of law enforcement agencies. Since the creation of CALEA, many individual states have established their own accreditation programs for their police departments.

CALEA's accreditation program expects accredited police departments to be in compliance with the established set of professional standards and demonstrate that they:

Have a comprehensive, well thought out uniform set of written directives.

Provide the necessary reports and analysis a Chief Executive Officer needs to make fact based, informed management decisions.

Have a preparedness program so the agency is ready to address natural or man-made critical incidents.

Develop or improve the agency's relationship with the community.

Have a continuum of standards that clearly define authority, performance and responsibility that strengthens the department's accountability.

(CALEA, 2006)

Recent research on police integrity and corruption over the last 5 to 10 years has concluded that acts of police misconduct and corruption are not isolated activities engaged in by a few individual "grass eaters" or "bad apple" officers (Klockars et al., 2006). They are aspects of the influential organizational culture that exists within police departments (Leuci, 2004; Courtemanche, 2011). The United States Department of Justice recommends that departments place a greater emphasis on building internal systems that continually reinforce a culture of integrity by reflecting core values in its daily processes (USDOJ, 2010).

An organization's culture is a shared system of beliefs, values, traditions, and behaviors that employees share (Schein, 1990). It manifests itself in the continuous patterns of employee behavior as well as official and unofficial ways of doing things. It is also reflected in the manner in which employees treat each other as well as those outside the department and the types of behavior in which they consistently engage. Instead of focusing on personal ethics and morality of individual officers, departments should focus on the creation of an organizational value system that perceives integrity as the responsibility of every organizational member.

When individuals enter policing they undergo a socialization process that begins in the training academy and continues in the department's field training program that is intended to prepare them for police work. During this experience they acquire new ideas, beliefs, values, attitudes, motives, and norms and internalize these into their frame of reference by which they judge the world they are in. This process helps recruits adapt to the police organization's definition of the world and how it operates within it. When they undergo field training, they are immersed in the day-to-day experiences of police patrol work. During this process they are mentored by their fellow officers and supervisors who school them in the organization's cultural system as well as the techniques of police work. These experiences provide the new officers with an understanding of their job, commonsense methodologies for handling police incidences, justifications and rationalizations for dealing with the demands of their job.

These methodologies and rationalizations form the critical elements of the police culture that guides officers' behavior in the performance of their duties. Consequently, a police officer is a dynamic composite of past learning, socialization, and knowledge modified by current experiences. Research has consistently found that how officers adjust to their day-to-day operational experiences and rationalize their behavior are the most important factors in the development of good or bad individual police officer behavior (Brooks, 2010).

Training should prepare officers to realistically handle the challenges of their jobs. It should support the department's value system, its policies and procedures for controlling corruption and misconduct. The department's entry-level and in-service training should instruct officers in how to identify and reject the corrupting influences they are exposed to as part of their work. This training should contain instruction and analysis of past department cases involving corruption and misconduct as well as how to address potential violations of professional conduct. Additionally, all department employees should have a clear understanding of the consequences of inappropriate behavior and performance.

A department can establish a culture of integrity through the development of a clear set of standards and values that define to its employees and citizens its expectations of professional conduct. These then should act as a guide for employee performance on a daily basis. For example, the 44-person Green Cove Springs Police Department in Florida defines its mission, purpose, and core values as follows:

MISSION:

The Green Cove Springs Police Department is unwavering in our duties of protecting life, property and rights of all people, by resolving issues and promoting peace in our community through partnerships and the continuous development of our organization and its members.

PURPOSE:

The Green Cove Springs Police Department, in partnership with our community is committed to the protection of life and property, safeguarding of order and enforcement of criminal laws, through the continuous application of proactive policing practices. The members of your Police Department proudly carry out their duties by exhibiting a professional demeanor, exemplifying their commitment to public service and professional integrity.

CORE VALUES:

S Safety: We are committed to providing safety within our community, through continuous partnerships and problem solving methods.
P Professionalism: We are committed to providing service excellence to our community in all aspects of our duties.
I Integrity: We are committed to unwavering legal, ethical, and moral standards in the lives we lead.
R Respect: We are committed to valuing and promoting human dignity in all of our duties.
I Innovation: We are committed to the continuous improvement of the services we provide to our community.
T Training: We are committed to being a leader through continuous education and development of our personnel and the agency.

The department's mission, purpose, and core values are displayed on its website, reflected in its policy and procedures and used as a means to evaluate the performance of its officers. Once a department establishes these defining characteristics of the organization's culture, its policies and reward system should be structured to support these standards and values. In this manner they become guiding tools of accountability that inform all department employees of what is expected of them.

All organizational managers should be held responsible for maintaining integrity and accountability throughout the department. Developing and preserving a strong ethical organizational culture must become a primary responsibility of every department manager. In this manner accountability will become the foundation upon which the department's culture and its integrity rests. Holding all managers and supervisors accountable as well as their employees represents the extension of accountability throughout the department. In addition to making clear the existence of positive core values, managers must continue to communicate and reinforce them daily through their personal example. To succeed in enhancing its integrity, the department's redirection and culture of accountability must be institutionalized and sustained. This can be accomplished through maintaining a climate of transparency supported by an internal affairs process, inspections, and discipline.

As part of the process of institutionalizing an ethical culture, the executive command team and managers should control and eliminate arrangements, discriminatory practices, and traditions that are a breeding ground for corruption and misconduct within the department. Fundamental changes will only occur after the culture of integrity is operationalized and sustained throughout the department. This can be accomplished by confronting managers with current conditions and creating dissatisfaction with the status quo. The chief executive must put the department employees face-to-face with the true state of the organization's integrity. This can be accomplished by conducting a real discussion and open communication about what is actually happening as opposed to what should be happening. Key managers need to come to consensus about the cause of these problems and what needs to change in the department. Once the beliefs and energies of this critical mass of the organization are engaged, conversion to a new culture of integrity will spread, bringing about fundamental change very quickly (Gladwell, 2000).

This discussion should focus on three important relationships: police to the community, management to officers, and officers to officers (Gaffigan & McDonald, 1997, p. 66). The objective is to create an understanding within the department as to why change is necessary and to develop a sense of urgency to bring about the change. Employee motivation should then be directed into a focused organizational improvement effort. Chief executives can create a culture of integrity dissatisfaction in their organizations by:

1. Communicating information about potential crises or threats to the organization's integrity to its members.
2. Provide employees with objective data about organizational integrity. Inform them what is actually happening as opposed to what should be happening.
3. Engaging in frank discussion and dialogue about the organization's integrity and standards.
4. Setting realistic standards and expectations that will create the desire to change.
5. Hold all employees accountable for maintaining the department's integrity and standards of professional conduct.

The end result is for the department to establish and sustain a culture of integrity, transparency, and adherence to professional standards. This transition will only be sustained if all department employees are aware of and held accountable for the highest standards of the police profession.

Internal Affairs

The function of internal affairs is to assist in maintaining the professional integrity of the department and preserve public trust by inspecting and controlling, preventing and detecting and investigating allegations of employee misbehavior and violations of professional standards. Differences in state and local law, collective bargaining, and organizational and political cultures make it impossible to create a one-size-fits-all approach to internal affairs (Courtemanche, 2011). Despite this each police department should develop a system of inspection and internal control as well as the capacity to deter, detect, and punish employee wrongdoing. The internal affairs section is responsible for conducting investigations and carrying out all assignments related to resolving issues of integrity, misfeasance, malfeasance, and nonfeasance by employees, and professional standards (CALEA, 2006, p. 52). Minor violations of a lesser importance are usually assigned to be investigated by supervisory personnel. However, all members of the department from the chief down to the officers on patrol have a responsibility to uphold the integrity of the department (Fyfe et al., 1997). This function should be conducted in a fair, accessible, and transparent manner.

When a department employee is accused of misconduct or criminal activity, he or she should be subject to an honest and fair fact-finding process that uncovers the truth in this matter. In large police departments this is the responsibility of a special unit staffed by investigators with the rank of sergeant and above whose commander reports directly to the chief of police (CALEA, 2006). In smaller police departments this function is usually carried out by a ranking officer or the chief executive (Thurnauer, 2004). Personnel assigned to internal affairs are either volunteers or individuals serving by the direction of the chief executive. Some departments require that individuals be assigned to internal affairs as part of their development for promotion to command rank.

Fyfe et al. (1997, pp. 472–473) identifies three desirable outcomes from this assignment practice. First, internal affairs would be destigmatized and humanized, less isolated from the field, and no longer vulnerable to criticism. Second, it will become more objective because of the regular entry into it of new blood. Third, over the long term this assignment would fill the agency's top rank with personnel who have an understanding of and sympathy for the work of internal affairs and would therefore share its goals. The sensitive nature of this assignment requires that personnel selection must be based on established criteria. Internal affairs investigators should possess a reputation for integrity, knowledge of the law and employee rights, and have proficiency in investigation, interviewing, and interrogation techniques (Norwicki & Punch, 2003).

Complaints

A primary feature of the internal affairs process is a procedure for dealing with complaints against police officers. This procedure must ensure that citizens can file a complaint directly with the police and that all allegations of misconduct, regardless of their source, are reviewed, validated, and an investigation is conducted if required. Procedures for registering complaints should be made available to the community through the media or the department's community relations programs and disseminated to all department employees (CALEA, 2006). The complaint process from intake to final disposition should be clear to all involved, and should include a general description of the categories the agency uses to group complaints and the procedures for handling each category (DOJ, 2009). These descriptions and procedures should be in writing and easily accessible to the public. The procedures should provide guidelines regarding the types of complaints to be handled by internal affairs and which by the department's disciple process. It should also specify the nature of those complaints that should be brought immediately to the department's chief executive.

A *complaint* is one or more allegations by any person that an employee of the department, or the department itself, has behaved inappropriately as defined by the person making the allegation. Each event of alleged inappropriate behavior is an allegation, whether reported verbally or by other depiction (DOJ, 2009). Not all complaints are about police misconduct but may relate to how people feel about the police service they received, policing standards, operational guidelines or policies. Such so-called service complaints will not always require an investigation but nevertheless warrant an effective and timely response, just like any other complaint. However, the information they contain may provide the police department with a learning opportunity or an awareness of where change is needed (U.N., 2011).

Complaints that are best resolvable beyond the realm of the internal affairs function should be redirected to other areas of the department as the nature of the complaint dictates (e.g., supervisory issues, personal grievances, employee disputes, etc.). Complaints are a source of information for the department to evaluate employees' performance, identify areas of police misconduct, monitor police relations with the public, and identify the need for new or revised policies or improved training (Norwicki and Punch, 2003, p. 342). Thus, they are a critical source of data for the management of the department's external and internal environments.

Handling of Complaints

A responsive police department that desires to maintain its integrity will accept complaints in any form, by phone, mail, in person, email or web form. Anonymous complaints should be accepted. Departments run the risk of losing valuable community input if the complaint process is not clear and simple. The practice of discouraging people from making complaints or refusing to accept or record complaints should be avoided at all times. A failure to register a complaint should be considered neglect of duty representing a disciplinary offense. The department should keep records of all complaints received. Each complaint should be tracked through to its final disposition. The person making the complaint should receive verification that it has been received by the department. The status of the complaint and its investigation should be communicated in a timely manner to the complainant throughout the process. Departments should conduct regular inspections of this process to verify that complaints are being taken properly, procedures are being followed, and that all employees are adhering to the department's complaint policy and procedures.

During intake, the complaint should be classified for purposes of determining where, when, and how the complaint will be investigated and resolved. It is helpful to classify complaints into either of two categories: criminal or administrative. **Criminal complaints** are investigated quite differently from administrative complainants. Criminal misconduct involving violations of law may lead to prosecution. An administrative complaint may lead only to internal discipline or other corrective action. Administrative complaints can be further classified as personnel or service complaints. Personnel complaints address alleged misconduct by an employee. Service complaints address problems in the provision of service not linked in any way to an employee's possible misconduct, such as a complaint that the agency's response times to public housing areas are routinely too long. A department will demonstrate transparency by disclosing its complaint statistics. This report should be published on an annual basis and contain the number and nature of the complaints received, number of officers involved and their disposition.

Credibility and transparency are important factors in maintaining a department's integrity with the public as well as with the department's employees. The employee(s) who is the subject of the complaint should be notified of the circumstances of the complaint. The department's policy and procedures should indicate when employee notification of a complaint should take place. Normally, the employee is notified the day the complaint is received. This can be done in several different ways. It is preferable to provide the employee with a copy of any written complaint. Administrators may also have guidelines in collective bargaining agreements that have to be met concerning complaint procedures (Thurnauer, 2004).

Complaint Investigation

Once a complaint has been received the next step is to determine whether the case requires investigation. The guiding principle should be that all complaints made by members of the public and all internal complaints of a serious nature, as determined by the agency, must be investigated. Internal Affairs should be responsible for conducting all serious investigations, including but not limited to officer-involved shootings, suspected criminal activity, in-custody deaths, alleged constitutional violations, allegations of racial profiling or discriminatory policing or racial prejudice, dishonesty, drug use, sexual misconduct, cases handled for other jurisdictions, interagency cases, and cases referred directly by the agency head or command staff. Internal Affairs should also conduct all administrative investigations of allegations of misconduct that are likely to result in litigation against the agency or its members. Unless there is a specialized unit to handle internal complaints by employees of discrimination, sexual harassment, and other unlawful employment practices, Internal Affairs should conduct such investigations (DOJ, 2009).

Internal affairs investigations should be factually focused, timely, and free from conflict of interest, bias, prejudice, or self-interest. The extensiveness of the investigation will vary from complaint to complaint commensurate with the seriousness and complexity of the case. The policy and procedures of the department should describe what the investigation should include and identify each step of the internal investigation. This serves as a guide to the process and lets the subject of the complaint know what to expect (Thurnauer, 2004).

All complaints brought to Internal Affairs should require at least a preliminary investigation. **Preliminary investigations** are conducted to verify whether there is a need for a disciplinary or criminal investigation. This investigation should involve an effort to gather key statements or evidence if reasonably attainable. Its objective is to determine if the complaint should be further investigated and, if so, by whom. The advantage of conducting a preliminary investigation is that it can guide decision making and prevent damage to the reputation of a police officer found to be innocent (UN, 2011). Enforceable time lines for investigations are critical. The complainant and witnesses should be interviewed by the investigator within

24 hours of filing the complaint, and preferably, within 24 hours of the complaint being reported. This allows the investigator to get information from the complainant and witnesses while it is still fresh in their minds and before they have an opportunity to taint their memory by second-guessing, talking with other witnesses, speaking with an attorney, or even being contacted by the subject of the complaint. A thorough and complete interview also locks the complainant and witnesses into their statements and helps identify any discrepancies or embellishments that may occur.

An investigation is completed when all relevant information is acquired and a finding in the case can be made. A **complete investigation** should take place where the allegations, if true, would likely result in formal discipline. If the investigation concludes that charges against an officer are not sustained, he or she should be notified in writing and the case closed. Regardless of whether charges are sustained, the allegation and disposition should be retained in the officer's personnel file, while the record of the investigation should remain with Internal Affairs (Fyfe et al., 1997, p. 472).

Likewise, a complete investigation should be considered if it appears from a preliminary review that an agency's policy, standard, or training may be a factor in unintended consequences apparent in the complaint. Any decision made to proceed or not after the completed investigation should be made by the commander of Internal Affairs with a written explanation included in the file and notification to the complainant (DOJ, 2009). Many investigations do not require the expertise of Internal Affairs investigators. These cases can be investigated at the unit level.

There are four possible **dispositions** of complaints received:

Unfounded: The allegation is found to be false or there is a lack of credible evidence to support it.
Exonerated: The allegation is true but the action of the department member is consistent with department policy, justified and legal.
Not Sustained: The investigation failed to disclose sufficient evidence to either prove or disprove the allegation.
Sustained: The allegation is supported by sufficient evidence and the action(s) of the department member is not consistent with the department's procedures, policy, or the law.

Once a disposition is rendered, the employee(s) involved and the complainant should be notified (CALEA, 2006, 52.2.8). The employee should be notified of the findings and, if sustained, told that he or she will be disciplined. In all cases, the subject officer should receive a complete copy of the investigative report (DOJ, 2009). Similarly, the complainant should receive written notification of the final disposition of the complaint and, at a minimum, the name and contact information of the commanding officer who can answer any questions (Noble & Alpert, 2009).

Internal Affairs Files and Confidentiality

Once the internal affairs process is complete, all documents and files must be remain under control of the Internal Affairs unit, if applicable, or to the law enforcement executive who oversees Internal Affairs. These files should be kept separate from all other personnel files, and should always remain locked, accessible only to appropriately credentialed personnel. All files must remain confidential and should be retained for a period of time required by law or, if no law exists, for an appropriate length of time determined by the chief of police (CALEA, 2006).

Finally, executives and investigators should operate on the assumption that all written interviews, statements, and reports may be reviewed by the public. All 50 states and the District of Columbia have public records laws. Some states have enacted multiple statutes, but generally, these laws enable members of the public to obtain documents and other public records from state and local governments. Although these laws are similar to the federal Freedom of Information Act (FOIA), there are important differences between and among the laws. At the very least, every police chief and Internal Affairs unit commander must familiarize him or herself with the FOIAs within his or her state, thereby knowing what information is vulnerable to public inspection (USDOJ, 2009).

Inspections

Police departments should conduct two types of inspections:

1. **Staff inspections** are conducted by those who do not have direct control but who have the responsibility to determine how well employees do their jobs.
2. **Line inspections** are conducted to see that tasks are performed satisfactorily by those in direct control of the employees and things being inspected.

The *staff inspection* is a system of reviews and audits conducted by administrators to analyze and monitor the alignment of the department's policy and procedures with unit and individual performance. It is a way to ensure that the department's units and personnel are complying with policies and procedures and to discover potential problems before they negatively affect the department and its integrity. However, all department managers and supervisors are responsible for monitoring and inspecting the performance of their employees on a continual basis in order to ensure that their employees are acting in accordance with the rules, regulations, and policies of the organization as they relate to their assignments. These managerial monitoring audits, known as *line inspections*, are designed to identify and correct minor infractions by supervisors through coaching and on-the-job training. The complexity of line inspections vary according to the length of the chain of command and number of employees the manager supervises. They are a primary means of ascertaining employee fitness for duty that include, but are not limited to, the following, if applicable:

1. Uniforms.
2. Appearance.
3. Equipment.
4. Vehicles.
5. Firearms.
6. Personnel.
7. Facilities.
8. Performance.

Staff inspections complement and augment the line inspection function. It is designed to access the effectiveness of operational procedures and report on their shortcomings. It can be used to audit financial records, inventory agency property, inspect equipment, and conduct surveys. It is an excellent administrative practice for the chief of police to schedule unit inspections on a periodic basis. Many departments have developed standardized check lists to be used in the inspection process in order to ensure uniformity. The unit to be inspected should receive an advance notice of the inspection. These inspections address items that are for the most part a matter of record.

There are six objectives of a staff inspection:

- To determine whether the department's procedures and policies are being properly implemented;
- To determine whether the department's procedures and policies are adequate to attain the department's goals and maintain its integrity;
- To determine whether the department's resources (such as personnel) are being used fully and sensibly;
- To determine whether the department's resources are adequate to attain the department's goals;
- To discover any deficiencies in integrity, training, morale, or supervision; and
- To help operating line units plan their line inspections.

(Fuller, 2004, p. 68)

In large departments, staff inspections are generally the responsibility of a special unit of supervisors while in smaller departments they are conducted by individual managers. Unit commanders and individuals responsible for inspections should always report directly to the police chief executive or agency head. In small agencies staff inspection should be conducted by the chief executive. This oversight responsibility of the chief is particularly critical, as it validates the independence and objectivity of the inspection process (Thurnauer, 2004).

The effectiveness and integrity of the staff inspection process depends on the quality of personnel selected for this assignment. These individuals should be at minimum first-line supervisors with extensive operational experience. Ideally, they should possess a strong sense of personal integrity, excellent analytical, communicative, investigative, and problem-solving skills as well as the ability to operate with little or no supervision.

The culmination of a staff inspection is a written report to the chief executive that defines the results of the inquiry. It is not sufficient to just to provide data or announce performance failures. This report should contain a clear and comprehensive communication about what is really happening as opposed to what should or could be happening. It should also provide the chief executive with a list of recommendations to consider in order to correct the issue.

Early Warning Systems

During the late 1990s police departments began to use early warning systems to proactively address issues of officer integrity. Early warning systems are data-based management information systems designed to identify those officers who are becoming problematic and subject them to an intervention to correct their future performance. It is a commonly held managerial belief that the majority of a department's behavioral problems are caused by a small number of officers. These officers are known to their supervisors, to their peers, administrators, and to the residents of the areas in which they work (Goldstein, 1977, p. 171; Walker, Alpert, & Kenney, 2001). The purpose of these systems is to acquire performance information, document it, analyze it, and transfer the result of this analysis to operational managers in order to correct future behavior. This process is a strategic learning organization technique. Walker (2003, p. 30) identified the following goals and impacts of early warning systems:

GOALS AND IMPACTS OF EARLY WARNING SYSTEM

The Individual Officer

- Improved Performance.
- Higher Standards of Accountability.

Supervisors

- Improved Supervisory Practices.
- Higher Standards of Accountability as Supervisors.

The Department

- Higher Standards of Accountability.
- Reduction in Litigation.
- Improved Community Relations.

It is hoped that early identification and intervention response will correct the problem and prevent the behavior from becoming a greater issue for the department. Early intervention usually involves some combination of deterrence, counseling, or training. At the end of the 20th century, approximately 40 percent of all municipal and county police departments serving populations greater than 50,000 people either had an early warning system or were planning to implement one (Alpert & Walker, 2000).

Early warning systems involve three distinct stages: selection, intervention, and a follow-up process of post-intervention monitoring. A list of recommended standards has not been established for selection of officers for inclusion in the program. However, most selection programs are designed to identify problematic officers based upon a combination of factors that include a variety of behavioral criteria such as:

1. Citizen complaints and commendations.
2. Discharges of firearms.
3. Use of force incidents.
4. Misconduct allegations.
5. Involvement in civil litigation.
6. A disproportionate number of resisting-arrest incidents.
7. Involvement in high-speed pursuits.

8. Use and abuse of sick leave.
9. Occurrence of incidents causing vehicular damage.
10. Preventable motor vehicle accidents.
11. Habitual lateness.
12. Ongoing poor performance or sudden poor performance.
13. Unusual behavior.
14. Garnishment of wages.
15. Being the subject of a restraining order.
16. Reports of prisoner problems and complaints.
17. Unfavorable traffic and pedestrian stop data.

The department should track all complaints, justified or not, to identify officer behavior patterns. Analysis of complaint patterns provides objective data on types of officer discretionary behavior (Gaines & Kappeler, 2011). Those police departments using citizen complaints as an identifying criteria usually require three complaints within a given time frame such as a 12-month period (Walker, Alpert, & Kenney, 2001). Research into the characteristics of officers who most frequently receive complaints disclosed that number of arrests, officer age, and officer gender differentiated officers with high numbers of complaints. Female officers received fewer complaints while younger officers were more likely to use force and received more complaints (Brandl, Stroshine, & Frank, 2001).

Selection and intervention consist of both specific and general deterrence. Specific deterrence occurs when an officer is selected for inclusion in the program and his or her performance behavior is changed for the better. General deterrence assumes that the officers not selected will also adjust their behaviors to not be identified by the system. In addition, any counseling and training that is part of the intervention has the potential to correct officers' mistakes and help them improve their performance. The initial response in most systems involves a review by the selected officer's immediate supervisor. Some departments have command officers participating in counseling the officer as well as assigning identified officers to training classes (Walker, Alpert, & Kenney, 2001). However, supervisors involved in the process should be trained in the techniques of counseling and their efforts to change officer behavior should be documented. Once intervention is completed, the selected officers are monitored to determine if the effort has had an impact on their performance. Departmental monitoring programs vary as to time frame and formality and can be developed on a case-by-case basis. A properly managed early warning system requires a commitment to accountability and a significant administrative and supervisory effort from the department. However, they can be effective in raising standards of performance and improving the quality of the department (Swanson, Territo, & Taylor, 2011).

The impact of early warning systems in Minneapolis, New Orleans, and Miami-Dade County discloses that, overall, the systems in these cities appear to have been successful at reducing citizen complaints against officers as well as other indicators of problematic police performance. In Minneapolis, for example, complaints against selected officers dropped by 67 percent within one year of the initial intervention. In New Orleans, the reduction was 64 percent, while in Miami-Dade the numbers of selected officers having no use of force went from only 4 percent to at least 50 percent following the early warning intervention (Walker, Alpert, & Kenney, 2001).

Sustained Complaint

A complaint against an employee will be sustained when it is supported by sufficient evidence that the action(s) of the individual is not consistent with the department's procedures, policy, or the law. Disciplinary action must then be taken by the department. The chief of police should have unrestricted disciplinary power subject only to the general direction and approval of the jurisdiction chief executive officer to address employee misconduct (Fyfe et al., 1997). Discipline is imposed to:

- To modify the employee's behavior.
- To set expectations for other employees.
- To maintain public trust by holding employees accountable.

The goal of discipline is to bring employees into compliance with established standards, guiding principle, and core values of the department. However, before discipline is enacted, the department must be certain to adhere to state and local laws and collective bargaining agreements to ensure compliance with the employee's legal and contractual rights. All disciplinary action should be fair, consistent, and flexible. The application of discipline should not be to select a penalty to fit the offense, but to maintain the integrity of the department (Noble & Alpert, 2009).

Police departments use a variety of ways to handle disciplinary proceedings, such as review and disposition by the department's chief executive, administrative hearings, individual hearing officers, police or civilian review boards. This process should include a procedure that allows for disposal of minor infractions which require some sort of formal action but are not serious enough to be heard before a formal board of discipline. In the disciplinary process the corrective action is calculated according to the degree of misconduct, modified by the offender's prior record and the extent to which systemic defects in the department may have contributed to the offense. Each case should be judged on its own merits with penalties depending on the circumstances (Norwicki & Punch, 2003).

Administrative hearings are quasi-judicial fact-finding proceedings. Conclusions are reached based upon preponderance of the evidence, not a guilty-beyond-reasonable doubt standard. All parties involved should be aware of the rules for the hearing. The procedures include opening statements for both the accused and the department, as well as provisions for cross-examination, and questioning of board members. The following rules should apply:

- The accused employee should be notified in advance of the charges.
- The accused employee should receive reasonable notice of the time and place of the hearing.
- The accused employee must have the opportunity to call witnesses, to cross-examine opposing witnesses, and to testify in his or her behalf.
- The hearing should be held before those who will decide the issues.
- The disciplinary hearing should close with a decision, accompanied by a statement summarizing the essentials of the proceedings and findings. If there are multiple charges, each one should receive a separate finding. If the hearing finds that the employee should be charged, one of the following can be recommended:

- Oral reprimand.
- Written reprimand in the officer's personnel file.
- Disciplinary transfer from a special assignment.
- Loss of time or annual leave in lieu of suspension.
- Suspension with or without pay.
- Monetary fine, to be deducted from salary or pension payments.
- Demotion in rank.
- Pass over for promotion.
- Removal from service.

Before the recommended disciplinary action is imposed, the employee should receive written notification of the hearing's outcome and his or her right to formally respond to the finding. CALEA Accreditation Standard No. 52.2.7 requires an agency to have a written directive specifying the circumstances in which an employee may be relieved from duty. The employee should be allowed to address the charges against him or her and request a reduction in any proposed disciplinary action (IACP, 2007). Once the chief of police reviews the employee's response and makes a final ruling on the proposed discipline, the chief may order the disciplinary action implemented. It is important to note that some union contracts require that, before any corrective action or termination takes place, the agency must demonstrate just cause in determining whether management acted reasonably in its decision to implement discipline or termination (Noble & Alpert, 2009).

When an employee willingly follows agency policy, meets or exceeds expectations, and practices good judgment, it is indicative of effective discipline and self-monitoring. There may be many ways to accomplish this goal and maintain positive relationships between the employee and supervisors through coaching, mentoring, and discipline.

Conclusion

Since the development of professional policing in the 19th century, police deviance, misconduct, and corruption have been persistent problems. Democratic policing requires high levels of integrity and transparency if the police are to earn the trust of those whom they are sworn to protect and serve. All too often throughout the history of policing, citizen confidence in their police has been shaken by the disclosure of incidents of major corruption, excessive use of deadly force, brutality, and sexual misconduct. This has contributed to the erosion of the public's confidence in the integrity of policing. The police chief executive and his or her management team are responsible for controlling deviant employee behavior and maintaining department integrity.

Police behavior is governed by ethical, organizational, and legal standards. However, as this chapter has identified, there are numerous ways by which these standards have been violated. Control of deviance requires constant attention, collection and analysis of data, as well as confronting the reality of practice and holding all employees accountable. Identifying a few "rotten apples" and individual punishments have proven to be an inadequate response to this problem. Departments need to develop a long-term multifaceted strategy to proactively tackle corruption and deviance. All organizational managers should be held responsible for maintaining a culture of integrity and accountability throughout the department. Accountability is the foundation upon which the department's integrity rests. The department's culture of accountability must be institutionalized and sustained. This can be accomplished through maintaining a climate of transparency supported by an internal affairs process, inspections, and discipline.

KEY TERMS

Administrative hearing	Grass eaters	Organizational standards
CALEA's *Standards for Law Enforcement Agencies*	Integrity	Police crime
	Internal affairs	Preliminary investigation
Complaint	Legal standards	Professional standards
Complaint disposition	Line inspection	Staff inspection
Complaint investigation	Malfeasance	Sustained complaint
Corruption	Meat eaters	Type of corruption
Democratic policing	Misconduct	Type I Department
Deviancy	Misfeasance	Type II Department
Early warning system	Noble cause corruption	Type III Department
Ethical standards	Nonfeasance	

References

Alpert, G., & Walker, S. (2000). Police accountability and early warning systems: Developing policies and programs. *Justice Research and Policy, 2*(2), 59–72.

Barker, T. (2006). *Police ethics: Crisis in law enforcement.* Springfield, IL: Charles C Thomas.

Bayley, D.H. (2001). Democratizing the police abroad: What to do and how to do it. In *Issues in international crime.* Washington, DC: National Institute of Justice.

Bayley, D., & Perito, R. (2011). *Police corruption: What past scandals teach about current challenges—Special report.* Washington. DC: United States Institute of Peace.

Brandl, S., Stroshine, M., & Frank, J. (2001). Who are the complainant-prone officers? An examination of the relationship between police officers' attributes, arrest activity, and assignment. *Journal of Criminal Justice, 29*(6), 521–529.

Brooks, L.W. (2010). Police discretionary behavior: A study in style. In R.G. Dunham, & G.P. Alpert (Eds.), *Critical issues in policing: Contemporary readings* (pp. 122–142). Long Grove, IL: Waveland Press.

Commission on Accreditation for Law Enforcement Agencies (2006). *Standards for law enforcement agencies.* Fairfax, VA: CALEA.

Courtemanche Jr., R.D. (2011, November). Internal affairs: An evolution in organizational culture? *The Police Chief, 78,* 14–15.

Fuller, J. (2004). Staff inspection: A strong administrative tool. *The Police Chief, 71*(12), 66–72.

Fyfe, J.J., Greene, J.R., Walsh, W., Wilson, O., & McLaren, R. (1997). *Police administration.* New York: McGraw-Hill.

Gaffigan, S.J., & McDonald, P.P. (1997). *Police integrity, public service with honor.* Washington, DC: U.S. Department of Justice.

Gaines, L.K., & Kappeler, V.E. (2011). *Policing in America.* Waltham, MA: Elsevier.

Gladwell, M. (2000). *The Tipping point: How little things can make a big difference*. New York, NY: Little, Brown and Company.

Goldstein, H. (1977). *Policing a free society*. Cambridge, MA: Ballinger.

Kane, R.J., & White, M.D. (2009). Bad cops: A study of career-ending misconduct among New York City Police Officers. *Criminology & Public Policy, 8*, 37–769.

Kappeler, V., Sluder, R.D., & Alpert, G.P. (1998). *Forces of deviance: Understanding the dark side of policing*. Prospect Heights, IL: Waveland Press.

Kleinig, J. (1996). *The ethics of policing*. Cambridge: Cambridge University Press.

Klockars, C.B. (1980). The dirty harry problem. *The Annals of the American Academy of Political and Social Science, 452*(1), 33–47.

Klockars, C.B. (1999). Some really cheap ways of measuring what really matters. In R.H. Langworthy (Ed.), *Measuring what matters: Proceedings from the policing research institute meetings* (pp. 195–214). Washington, DC: National Institute of Justice.

Klockars, C.B., Ivkovic, S.K., & Haberfeld, M. (2006). *Enhancing police integrity*. Dordrecht, NL: Springer.

Knapp Commission. (1972). *Report of the New York City commission to investigate allegations of police corruption and the city's anti-corruption procedures*. New York: Bar Press.

Lee, W.L.M. (1901). *A history of police in England*. London: Methuen.

Leuci, R. (2004). *All the centurions: A New York City cop remembers his years on the street, 1961–1982*. New York, NY: Harper Collins.

Monkkonen, E.M. (1981). *Police in America—1860—1920*. Cambridge: Cambridge University Press.

Murphy, P.V., & Caplan, G. (1991). Fostering integrity. In W.G. Geller (Ed.), *Local government police management* (pp. 239–270). Washington, DC: International City Management Association.

National Law Enforcement Policy Center. (2007). *Investigation of employee misconduct: Concepts and issues paper*. Alexandria, VA: International Association of Chiefs of Police.

Newburn, T. (1999). *Understanding and preventing police corruption: Lessons from the literature: Home Office Research Series Paper 110*. London: Home Office.

Noble, J.J., & Alpert, G.P. (2009). *Managing accountability systems for police conduct: Internal affairs and external oversight*. Prospect Heights, IL: Waveland Press.

Norwicki, D.E., & Punch, M.E. (2003). Fostering integrity and professional standards. In W. Geller (Ed.), *Local government police management* (pp. 315–352). Washington, DC: International City Management Association.

Northumbria Police U.K. (2015). *Our values at Northumbria police*, www.northumbria. police.uk/about_us/organisation/values/

O'Keefe, J. (2004). *Protecting the republic: The education and training of American police officers*. Upper Saddle River, NJ: Prentice Hall.

Parks, B.C. (2000). *Board of inquiry into the Rampart area corruption incident*. Los Angeles: Los Angeles Police Department.

Porter, L.E., & Warrender, C. (2009). A multivariate model of police deviance: Examining the nature of corruption, crime and misconduct. *Policing and Society, 19*(1), 79–99.

Punch, M. (1985). *Conduct unbecoming: The social construction of police deviance and control*. London: Tavistock.

Reppetto, T.A. (1978). *The blue parade*. New York: The Free Press.

Roebuck, J.B., & Barker, T. (1974). A typology of police corruption. *Social Problems, 21*, 423–437.

Roberg, R., Novak, K., Cordner, G., & Smith, B. (2012). *Police & society*. New York: Oxford.

Schein, E.H. (1990). Organizational culture. *American Psychologist, 45*, 109–119.

Sherman, L.W. (1974). *Police corruption: A sociological perspective*. Garden City, NY: Anchor Press.

Sherman, L.W. (1978). *Controlling police corruption: The effects of reform policies*. Washington, DC: U.S. Department of Justice.Skogan, W.G., & Meares, T.L. (2004). Lawful policing. *The Annals of the American Academy of Political and Social Science, 593*(1), 66–83.

Skolnick, J.H., & Fyfe, J.J. (1993). *Above the law: Police and the excessive use of force*. New York: Free Press.

Standards for Law Enforcement Agencies. (2006). Fairfax, VA: CALEA.

Swanson, C.R., Territo, L., & Taylor, R.W. (2011). *Police administration: Structures, processes, and behavior*. Upper Saddle River, NJ: Prentice Hall.

Thurnauer, B. (2004). *Internal affairs: A strategy for smaller departments*. Washington, DC: International Association of Chiefs of Police.

United Nations Office on Drugs and Crime. (2011). *Handbook on police accountability, oversight and integrity*. New York: United Nations.

USA Today. (2015, April 15). Deal set for Chicago police torture victims. *USA Today*, 3B.

U.S. Department of Justice, Office of Community Oriented Policing Services. (2009). *Standards and guidelines for internal affairs: Recommendations from a community of practice*. Washington, DC: Office of Community Oriented Policing Services, U.S. Department of Justice.

U.S. Department of Justice, Office of Community Oriented Policing Services and the Boston Police Department. (2010). *Enhancing cultures of integrity: Technical assistance guide*. Washington, DC: Office of Community Oriented Policing Services, U.S. Department of Justice.

Walker, S. (2003). *Early intervention systems for law enforcement agencies: A planning and management guide*. Washington, DC: Office of Community Oriented Policing Services.

Walker, S., Alpert, G., & Kenney, D.J. (2001). *Early warning systems: Responding to the problem police officer*. Research in Brief. Washington, DC: National Institute of Justice.

Whalen, B., & Whalen, J. (2014). *The NYPD's first fifty years: Politicians, police commissioners & patrolmen*. Lincoln, NE: University of Nebraska Press.

12 Creating Safe Communities

Trust between law enforcement agencies and the people they protect and serve is essential in a democracy. It is key to the stability of our communities, the integrity of our criminal justice system, and the safe and effective delivery of policing services.

President's Task Force on 21st Century Policing (2015)

Learning Objectives

1. Describe the police–community relationship.
2. Identify Kennedy's position on police and minority relations.
3. Describe the difference between effective and ineffective communities.
4. Define collective efficacy and police legitimacy.
5. Describe Broken Windows theory and its relationship to quality-of-life policing.
6. Identify the characteristics that contribute to the defense of neighborhoods.
7. Describe what community partnerships can accomplish.
8. Identify what police must do to implement community partnerships.
9. Identify how police can create community safety through community partnerships.
10. Identify the characteristics of successful community partnerships.

Introduction

All people wish to live in safety, free from the threat of personal violence and loss of their property. Unsafe communities collapse into themselves because residents live in fear, remain behind locked doors without a sense of wellbeing or connection to their neighbors. Creating safe communities is the responsibility of a community's residents and its civil authority represented by the police. The creation of safe communities represents a never-ending challenge to police because they can only provide public safety and crime control with the approval and cooperation of community residents. Sir Robert Peel recognized this in his famous 1829 *Principles of Law Enforcement* when he stated that "The ability of the police to perform their task depends on public approval of their existence, actions, behavior, and on the ability of the police to secure and maintain public respect" (Reith, 1956,p. 156). This principle received greater recognition with the establishment of Community Policing as a dominant philosophy and strategy of modern policing.

The ultimate goal of Community Policing is to engage community residents as equal partners with the police in addressing local crime and disorder problems. The basic aim of this partnership is to involve residents as active participants in the identification and prevention of crime and other street-level revitalization efforts. It is hoped that neighborhood residents and community institutions would share responsibility with the police for dealing with issues of community safety. This strategy requires police departments to actively seek to collaborate with the community in a planned manner and build partnerships of mutual trust. As the citation at the beginning of this chapter from the *President's Task Force on 21st Century Policing* notes, this mutual trust between police and citizens is essential in a democracy. It is key to the stability of our communities, the integrity of our criminal justice system, and the safe and effective delivery of policing services.

The police cannot achieve community safety if they lack the respect and trust of the people who live in the community in which they serve. Civil disturbances in Ferguson, Missouri; New York City; Baltimore, Maryland; Cleveland, Ohio; Oakland, California, and demonstrations in many other areas of the country because of controversial police encounters involving the killing of unarmed individuals have challenged the legitimacy of the police use of deadly force. These disturbances have also questioned the tactics used by police departments to provide community safety, especially in minority neighborhoods. They have contested the authority of the police and challenged their ability to provide public safety in inner-city African American communities.

David Kennedy (2011), drawing upon his many years of street-level experience attempting to reduce gun violence in inner-city America, provides an insightful perspective to understanding police–minority relations. He theorizes that at the heart of the problem is a general distrust and misunderstanding that minority residents and police have of each other. These opinions derive from the racial history of our country and the unintended consequences of recent criminal justice policy, in particular the "War on Drugs." Minorities often believe that the police are uninterested in protecting them; fail to keep their communities safe; are rude, corrupt, abusive; lock up their young men; use excessive force; and have no regard for their lives (Carter, 2002; Kennedy, 2011). Police believe that the inner-city community tolerates violent crime and drug dealing because it is corrupt or too broken to stand up against it. They believe that Black-on-Black homicide is a symptom of persistent lawless behavior by Black people and is a product of their tolerance for criminal behavior (Braga & Brunson, 2015).

However, research in Chicago found that residents were intolerant of teenage deviant behavior but racial, ethnic, and socio-economic groups differed substantially in their beliefs about the legitimacy of law and the police. The study found that a higher proportion of Blacks (29%) and Latinos (31%) than Whites (19%) view legal norms as not binding. These findings found that Blacks appear to be more cynical toward or dissatisfied with the police because they are more likely to live where disadvantage is concentrated (Sampson & Bartusch, 1998).

Kennedy concludes that each side's perceptions, and the resulting narratives, are entirely plausible and make sense when viewed from either side, but both are wrong. Both positions undermine community norms against crime and for the law, and prevent any possibility of meaningful partnership or community safety. What is true is that both sides deeply desire public safety but these core misunderstandings block each from shifting toward this common goal. Sampson, Raudenbush, and Earls (1997) suggest that the capacity of neighborhood residents to protect themselves against serious violence necessitates that they achieve a common set of goals and exert control over youth and public spaces. They labeled this effort "**collective efficacy**." Creating and supporting the development of neighborhood collective efficacy is a worthwhile objective for police–community partnerships. Weisburd, Davis, and Gill (2015) argue for the relevance of informal social controls in place-based policing in their analysis of an innovative Smart Policing collaboration between the Brooklyn Park (Minnesota) Police Department and the Center for Evidence-Based Crime Policy at George Mason University that implemented a department-wide program in which police lead interventions to increase collective efficacy in hot spots. Their study highlights the importance of police–community collaboration to improve public safety and reinforce informal social controls, and the emerging empirical evidence that social disorganization and collective efficacy may influence crime patterns at the micro-geographic level. This chapter examines the issues relating to the role of the police in collaborating with communities to develop safe neighborhoods through community partnerships. To understand the interrelationship between the police and the community, it is important to identify those terms and concepts commonly used to define it.

Community Concepts

Understanding the dynamics of "community" is important to the prevention and control of crime and disorder and fear of crime (Trojanowicz & Bucqueroux, 1994). The term "community" is a key analytical concept that is often left undefined in policing literature. Many Community Policing advocates use the term "community" as an objective phenomenon that collectively speaks with one unified voice and set of values. Nothing could be further from the truth.

Community is a social construct that refers to a fixed place (geographically defined area) where people live in a relationship of mutual interdependence, interact, have a sense of belonging and a psychological identification with a common locality. The interactions and behaviors that occur in a community are based on shared expectations, values, beliefs, and meanings held by the people who live and interact there. Communities will vary on the basis of their size, location, and degree of urbanization, social composition, and economic base. For the people who live there, it is their place, their home ground, and they feel a connection with it. The concept also denotes all individuals, groups, and institutions within a specific geographic area. These include civil and governmental organizations such as the police who are responsible for delivering security and other services in that area. However, when residents' shared sense of belonging and values breaks down, any sense of community will cease to exist.

Community analysis is concerned with the type, quality, and basis for the interaction of people in the community. This is because a community is a social place where families, friends, workers, neighbors, community associations, clubs, civic groups, churches, temples, ethnic associations, and governmental agencies interact. A community can comprise a politically defined municipal area, economic zone, residential subdivision, urban public housing area, a city block, as well as a psychologically defined area.

It is important to note that today's perception of community differs from the traditional view that described community as a homogeneous place of little change that demanded a high degree of conformity and is wary of strangers (Peak & Glensor, 2012). Today we live in heterogenetic communities that are influenced by and are subjected to consistent change because of their connectivity to the macro-society and world in which they exist. In these communities residents have little sense of relationship to one another, a minimal sense of belonging or opinion that the community is a significant social group. Residents occupy a space in the community but are more closely related to larger macro-system attachments such as work groups, professional societies, or other institutional associations than to components of the local community. As a result, the creation of community partnerships with active participation of residents is difficult unless there is a serious issue or problem that concerns their safety.

The term "neighborhood" is often used interchangeably with community. A **neighborhood** is a geographically smaller sublocation within a larger community where people live or work near each other, recognize their recurring closeness, and have a personal sense of identity to this place and one another. It is a place of intense interrelationships that includes a sense of personal belonging because of geographical and physical characteristics; racial, ethnic, and kinship networks; and emotional attachment of residents. Neighborhoods often are distinguished by their common ties of family, ethnicity, social class, religion, and occupation. The structure of a neighborhood is people acting together because they want to and need to.

In the City of Louisville, Kentucky, places like Newburg, Portland, the Highlands, and St. Matthews are considered neighborhoods. In the City of New York, neighborhoods include areas such as Yorkville, East Village, Chelsea, Harlem, the Hasidic community of Crown Heights, and Greenwich Village. Urban residents construct "cognitive maps" in which they allocate distinctive places as "their own" it is their neighborhood. For example, when one of the authors was an NYPD detective in the Bedford-Stuyvesant section of Brooklyn, New York, he often found that one city block was populated with individuals who came from or had roots in the same area in the South. People from this area migrating to New York City sought family, friends, and support from individuals they knew or had a connection with. They settled next to this support system and formed a neighborhood within the larger community.

The intensity of neighborhood relationships depends on many factors including geographical and physical characteristics of community, ethnic and kinship networks, affective attachment of residents, building construction features, local facility usage, pedestrian and automotive traffic patterns, the amount of time residents spend in the area, and demographic patterns.

A community or neighborhood can also be thought of as inter-actionable field where community-based organizational systems are linked. These systems are linked **vertically** through structural and functional patterns with the macro-system (government, economic, educational, public services). Macro-system attachments sustain the community's economic and socio-political base. They provide job preparation, access to employment, and governmental support services. They are also linked **horizontally** through structural and functional patterns with the various social units and subsystems in the local community. In a well-functioning **horizontal system**, community associations develop and provide a support place for residents. Horizontal community associations provide a special tool where belonging is the primary motivation, where people of all capacities are members, and creativity to address issues can be developed. Horizontal community associations are interdependent. For example, if an American Legion Post disbands, several community fundraising events they performed annually may also cease to exist. As a result programs supported by the legion post that serve the community such as the maintenance of the local ballpark and school scholarships will end. The interdependence of the local associations and the dependence of the community upon their work is a critical factor in the development of an effective community.

Communities that are crime-ridden, disorderly, and disorganized with an undeveloped sense of belonging often lack horizontal community associations and have limited ties to the macro-system. These are the communities characterized by housing dilapidation, high resident victimization, and fear, violent crime, drug markets, street gangs, unemployment, visible disorder, public drinking, and high unemployment. Time also changes neighborhood use and the way people feel about their area. At night people lock themselves in their homes, fear for their children, and stay off the streets, and do not use public places. The police by default are the primary social service in these communities. Unfortunately, residents rarely engage helpfully with the police due to strained relationships, skepticism of the sincerity of the police, and fear of reprisals from local criminals when cooperating with the police (Skogan & Frydl, 2004).

The literature that describes disorganized crime-ridden communities tends to link exclusively these conditions to urban areas. However, suburban and rural communities are not immune. Rural areas with limited policing resources have been plagued with the ravages of crime accompanying addiction to oxycodone, heroin, methamphetamine use and production, marijuana grow operations, and other controlled substances (Vito, Higgins, Walsh, & Vito, 2012).

Effective communities defend against crime and disorder through the interaction of private social control maintained by family, neighbors, religious and local organizations. In these communities, residents have a concern for the overall condition of their area beyond that of their own individual homes. They accept a certain amount of responsibility for what takes place in their community. Residents exercise some control over disorderly behavior of youth and others and ensure that common areas are free of litter and debris. This collective efficacy allows residents to create a safe and orderly environment (Sampson et al., 1997; Sampson, 2012).

Collective efficacy is the capacity of neighborhood residents to protect themselves against serious violence through the achievement of a common set of goals and the exertion of control over youth and public spaces. They care for and are concerned about the survival of the area in which they live. Collective efficacy involves residents monitoring children and other persons in public areas, acting to prevent disorderly conduct, and confronting individuals who exploit or disturb public spaces. Thus, creating safe communities depends upon residents trusting each other and cooperating with themselves and the police.

Kelling and Stewart (1989, p. 3) identified six characteristic that contribute to the defense of neighborhoods.

1.   Individual citizens act on their own or in association with police and criminal justice agencies.
2.   Individual citizens acting alone by engaging in activities to protect themselves, their property and their neighborhood.
3.   Private groups of citizens may act on their own behalf to protect the neighborhood, its residents and users by forming self-help groups to enhance community safety.

4.   Formal private associations such as funded community activist and community development organizations implement and maintain neighborhood programs.
5.   Commercial firms such as small shopkeepers and large corporations provide their own proprietary protective services. These security operatives often work closely with neighborhood police.
6.   Public criminal justice agencies such as the police operate on their own to provide safety to the community.

This discussion highlights the importance of residential participation and involvement in creating safe communities. This is what Community Policing hopes to restore and maintain through the development of community partnerships. It also negates the image that the police are the only source of community safety that is always ready to respond to citizen activation. It holds that the community and its members must be ready to take responsibility for their security problems in partnership with their police. The development of police–community partnerships is a key factor in the creation of a community's collective efficacy. This form of collaboration ensures residents have a voice in the identification of problems, and take part in the development and implementation of solutions that will affect them. Collaboration occurs when the police, residents, individual stakeholders, community organizations, and special interest groups work together to obtain the resolution of a problem or issue.

A **community partnership** is a working relationship between the police, residents, residential groups, and social organizations in a neighborhood. Community partnerships are an organizational strategy designed to prevent and eliminate crime while assisting in creating secure communities. They are a planned, more intense form of a collaborative relationship created to address serious issues of crime and disorder in a community. These partnerships are designed to achieve trust and legitimacy by establishing a positive presence at community activities and events, participating in proactive problem solving, and ensuring that communities have a voice and seat at the table working with officers (COPS Office, 2015). Effective community partnerships can achieve the following six results:

1.   Accomplish what individuals alone cannot.
2.   Prevent duplication of individual or organizational efforts.
3.   Enhance the power of advocacy and resource development for the initiative.
4.   Create more public recognition and visibility for the community policing initiative.
5.   Provide a more systematic comprehensive approach to addressing community crime and disorder problems.
6.   Provide more opportunities for new projects.

(Rinehart, Laszio, & Brisco, 2001, p. 175)

When the concept of community engagement through partnership is discussed, it should be remembered that the police are referring to a planned coordinated strategy in which the role, knowledge, and effectiveness of each partner is critical to its success. Individuals involved should be knowledgeable partners to assist in identifying community problems and developing solutions. Community partnerships are essential to the creation of safe neighborhoods.

Community safety is a generic term widely used by the police, academics, protestors, politicians, community workers, and others regarding reducing localized levels of violent crime and disorder. It also involves addressing resident's fear of crime and perceptions of safety. Community safety means varying things to different people at different times. Its focus alters as the nature of crime and anti-social behavior shifts. Crime and disorder coupled with one's feeling of personal safety and potential victimization (fear) are the greatest threats to our sense of community. Residents' fear is shaped less by their knowledge of specific criminals or crimes than by knowledge of dangerous and safe places in their community. Community safety is a byproduct of society's private control system that comprises the family, neighbors, religion, education, and social relationships. However, the strains and pressures of today's world have weakened the impact of this system. This strain places more emphasis on the public control systems which constitute the criminal justice system and governmental organizations. The police are members of this system and have primary responsibility for personal and community safety. However, in order for the community residents to collaborate and form partnerships with the police as Sir Robert Peel noted, they must believe and trust in the legitimacy of their police department and approve of its efforts.

Legitimacy/Procedural Justice

The effectiveness of police operations depends upon the public's willingness to provide information and otherwise help the police (Henry, 2002; Maple & Mitchell, 1999; Walsh, 2001). Police leaders increasingly are realizing that citizens' perception of their legitimacy and use of procedural justice are necessary conditions of gaining community residents' support and are worthy goals in themselves (Fischer, 2014). Police legitimacy and procedural justice are based on the belief that the police are entitled to call upon the public to comply with the law and their right to exercise power. This enables the police to control the behavior of citizens. The police need people to both accept their decisions and follow the law voluntarily through obligation and voluntary deference to police directives (Neyroud, 2009). **Legitimacy** is present when citizens believe that the police have moral authority to enforce the law and deserve respect and compliance with their initiatives (Fischer, 2014; Gau, 2013, p. 760). Police need to think about and understand how the public's perceptions of legitimacy and procedural justice can affect a department's efforts to achieve its goals and citizen compliance.

People voluntarily obey the law when:

1. It is instrumental. It creates a credible risk that people will be caught and punished for crime.
2. They believe in the moral rightness of the law.
3. They believe in the legitimacy of the authority enforcing the law.

Community residents will accept police decisions when they believe that they are legitimate and to the degree they consider the decisions as favorable and fair. Citizens are more willing to cooperate with the police by engaging in community activities, reporting crimes, or identifying suspects when they view police actions as fair and unbiased (Sunshine & Tyler, 2003). If they view the police as unfair and biased, it can lead to alienation, dissatisfaction, defiance, and a lack of public cooperation. Thus, the legitimacy of the police is linked to public judgments about the fairness of the processes through which the police make decisions and exercise authority. If citizens believe that police actions are morally justified and appropriate to the circumstances, they are legitimate.

The police can build trust in the community and increase residents' respect for police authority by listening to community residents about the issues that concern them and responding to those concerns. Citizens will cooperate with the police when they believe that police performance in fighting crime is effective and that there is a credible threat of punishment for crime (Tyler & Fagan, 2008, p. 263). Satisfaction with police control of disorder has been found to be significantly related to citizens' overall satisfaction with crime prevention (Zhao, Tsai, Ren, & Lai, 2012, p. 414). Visability is another factor in this process. When citizens see the police doing their job and quality service is provided, legitimacy is enhanced (Hawdon, Ryan, & Griffin, 2003, p. 485; Maguire & Johnson, 2010). A police chief familiar with the concepts of legitimacy and procedural justice and the research behind these ideas, and who works to incorporate these concepts in the practices in his or her department, will generate feelings of goodwill and support for the police among the public. This result is not a mere public relations success, but rather an important component of ensuring the overall success of the police (Fischer, 2014, p. 4).

Legitimacy may also facilitate community order maintenance. A survey conducted by Wolfe (2011) found that persons exhibiting low self-control were more likely to hold negative perceptions of police procedural justice. Such persons may also be more likely to be treated unkindly by the police because they challenge police actions and decisions. However, the results also showed that, if the police follow the tenets of procedural justice, they will gain voluntary compliance and lower levels of offending from people who have low self-control (Wolfe, 2011, p. 72). For example, when the police arrested James Eagan Holmes, the person responsible for the mass shooting in Aurora, Colorado, on July 20, 2012, he told the police that he had also rigged his apartment with homemade explosives. He later stated that he told this to them because they had treated him properly when he was arrested (Oates, 2016).

To summarize, there are three interrelated points concerning police legitimacy. First, to be effective in their public safety maintenance role, the police need voluntary public support and cooperation. Second, such collaboration is intimately linked to public perceptions of police legitimacy. Finally, police legitimacy is determined by public assessments of how the police exercise their authority (Tyler, 2004). Tyler and Huo (2002) advocate the development of a "process-based model of regulation" to promote procedurally fair treatment of citizens by the police. The aim is to obtain voluntary compliance with police decisions due to the fair treatment that citizens receive. Legitimacy is crucial to respectful and effective relations between the police and the communities they serve.

Order Maintenance: Broken Windows Policing

As noted earlier in this chapter order-maintenance policing has become a source of tension between minorities and many urban police departments. This form of policing is an outcome of a theoretical position expressed in a 1982 *Atlantic Monthly* article by James Q. Wilson and George Kelling that suggested that targeting minor disorder could help reduce more serious crime and resident fear and prevent neighborhoods from becoming crime-ridden. Police departments in the three most populous cities, New York City, Chicago, and Los Angeles, and many smaller cities throughout the United States have all adopted at least some aspect of Wilson and Kelling's theory, primarily through more enforcement of minor misdemeanor laws. As first proposed by Wilson and Kelling, the basic idea behind what today is known as the Broken Windows theory is that if the police engage in quality-of-life or order-maintenance policing, they could simultaneously impact serious crime, citizen fear, and prevent communities from becoming unsafe. They stressed the importance of addressing and solving neighborhood problems to reduce the opportunity for crime and the fear of it among residents. The theory suggests that citizen fear, created by disorder, leads to weakened social controls, thus creating the conditions in which crime and disorder can flourish. The justification for this emphasis on public order crime is drawn from history that in the past the police had carried out such activities and that the community from which the police gained legitimacy saw these as important police functions (Weisburd & Braga, 2006). The central theme of the article was that the link between minor incidents and serious crimes is exemplified by the metaphor of what happens to an abandoned building. If this building has all its windows intact, it can sit vacant and undisturbed for an indefinite period. But if one window is broken and not quickly repaired, more windows will be broken and the building will eventually be destroyed (Wilson & Kelling, 1982; Maple & Mitchell, 1999). Community disorder creates quality-of-life issues that, like the breaking of an abandoned building's windows left unchecked, eventually lead to the breakdown of community controls. Sousa and Kelling (2006) note that the policy implication is that if the police working with community residents manage minor disorders and maintain public order, the result will be a reduction in more serious criminal activity. This implication also implies that the police and the community should support each other and work together to achieve community safety.

William J. Bratton operationalized the Broken Windows theory when he was chief executive of the New York City Transit Police, the New York City Police Department, and the Los Angeles Police Department. He believes that taking care of small quality-of-life offenses in a neighborhood, like fixing the abandoned building's windows, will eventually head off more serious crime. Take a fare-beater, a low-level drug dealer, or disorderly drunk off the street and whatever criminal behavior he intended to engage in goes away with him. Bratton's strategist Deputy Police Commissioner Jack Maple (1999), however, warned that while one arrest can interrupt an active criminal career, quality-of-life enforcement is only fully effective if the department actively has its officers seek to obtain information about other crimes from their arrestees. Police officers should also be empowered to collaborate with residents to deal with small stuff that matters to communities and the serious stuff will be taken care of (Bratton & Tumin, 2012). Maple's strategic view was that all members of the department should become information gathers. This information and the data normally gathered by a department should serve as the basis for strategy development.

However, accomplishing this redirection requires changes in departmental administration. Broken Windows operations should give local commanders the discretion to target areas and focus on minor offenses based on residents' complaints and practices of their communities. Thus, policing an area should not follow a department's traditional mode of imposed operations but should reflect the needs of the community. This will require decentralizing control over personnel to allow them to concentrate on problem areas and engage in community-based problem solving, responding to problems rather than incidents, and making it possible for them to work directly with their counterparts in the community and other government service agencies, freeing them from the control of the chain of command

(Wilson & Kelling, 1989). Kelling has reiterated these ideas, emphasizing that the concept of Broken Windows has always been "a tactic of community policing, highly discretionary, easy to abuse, but when conducted properly contributes enormously to the quality of urban life" and the sense of security that grows out of close interaction between community residents and the police to maintain order and reduce crime (Kelling, 2015, p. 628).

This increased interaction between officers and residents requires that officers receive training in discretion and tactics for de-escalating confrontations. The manner in which officers engage citizens is a key component in the proper application of this form of policing and the source of minority displeasure with the tactic. For example, a study of the New York City Police Department's order-maintenance strategy "Stop and Frisk" conducted on behalf of the Center for Constitutional Rights claimed that the department engaged in a widespread pattern of unprovoked and unnecessary stops and racial profiling in carrying out the policy. The study examined police data cataloging the 2.8 million times from 2004 through 2009 that officers stopped people on the streets to question and sometimes frisk them (Baker & Rivera, 2010). It noted that many of these stops violated the United States Supreme Court position that held that in order for police officers to stop someone, they must be able to articulate a reasonable suspicion of a crime.

Stop, question, and frisk (SQF) is not Broken Windows Policing, although many police departments and the general public think it is. In New York City this tactic reached a peak of nearly 700,000 per year in 2011. A large percentage of those stopped were minorities, and critics and plaintiffs in federal court proceedings questioned whether all these stops could have been based on reasonable suspicion, especially when only 6 percent resulted in arrests. Largely because of the Stop, Question, and Frisk controversy, both a federal monitor and an inspector general have been appointed for the NYPD, and the department is now subject to the greatest level of continuous outside scrutiny in its history (Bratton & Kelling, 2015).

In the 1990s, the New York City Police Department targeted quality-of-life offenses (QOL such as subway fare-beating, aggressive panhandling, sleeping on public benches, smoking marijuana in public, and graffiti painting) in a program that began with Commissioner William J. Bratton and Mayor Rudy Giuliani and continued through the next 25 years. This tactic has been identified with Broken Windows and order-maintenance policing. It is designed for use in neighborhoods and places plagued by serious crime problems and have also displayed an inability to control these problems. Another example of this strategy is the **Hot Spots Policing Strategy** implemented in 2005 by the Lowell (MA) Police Department. It sought to improve social order in targeted high-crime areas (Hot Spots) and was intended to create broad crime-reduction results across the greater area (Braga & Bond, 2008). To be effective, this style of policing should not only involve reducing crime and disorder but also ways to facilitate community collective efficacy. Therefore, matching the policing style to conditions in a neighborhood represents only the first step. The second step should have the officers find ways for moving the community toward the development of a stronger self-reliant community (Noland, Conti, & McDevitt, 2005).

Early research on the effectiveness of **QOL** policing recorded mixed results. Sherman (1990) examined the effect of QOL policing on public drinking and parking violations to see if it also impacted robbery in Washington, DC. Although the operation failed to reduce street-level robberies, it enhanced citizen perceptions of safety in the area. A similar study reported the same results, cracking down on liquor law violations (public drunkenness, possession of alcohol by minors) failed to impact burglary and robbery offenses (Novak,

Hartman, Holsinger, & Turner, 1999). Both studies focused upon the enforcement of alcohol offenses but QOL policing often focuses on broader acts of public disorder.

Katz, Webb, and Schaefer (2001) conducted research on the effectiveness of Operation Restoration, a QOL operation in a Chandler, AZ, redevelopment district. Here, a specialized police unit focused upon disorder crimes (prostitution, street-level drug dealing, loitering) and physical conditons (graffiti abatement, property inspections, removal of trash and litter). The research determined that the operation impacted social and physical disorder. Public morals crimes (prostitution and public drinking) were reduced and physical disorder calls for service decreased. Evidence of crime displacement was also present—traffic violations and drug calls for service increased in surrounding areas (Katz et al., 2001, pp. 857–858). Clearly, the benefits of the operation were limited to the offenses it targeted.

One of the major policy issues is whether QOL policing has a deterrent effect, reducing disorder and enhancing public safety. A survey of 539 New York arrestees in 1999 revealed that they knew of the quality-of-life policing activities by the NYPD and that they had changed their behavior (about two thirds) in the last six months. The deterrent effect was especially pronounced among those who had engaged in disorderly behavior (Golub, Johnson, Taylor, & Eterno, 2003).

Another serious criticism of QOL policing is that it "widens the net" for arrests, especially among minority groups. Further analysis of the 1999 NYC QOL arrestee sample addressed this question by comparing them to arrestees for index and drug felonies. The research found that widening the net did not occur. While most (90%) of the QOL arrestees were Black or Hispanic, so were most of the serious felony arrestees during this time period. QOL policing did not increase the targeting of minorities but it also did not reduce it (Golub, Johnson, Taylor, & Eterno, 2004, p. 41). One of the major complaints raised by activists about this form of policing is that it primarily targets people of color.

A meta-analysis of Broken Windows Policing studies confirms the effectiveness of the approach, particularly those designed to change social and physical disorder at particular places, rather than an aggressive order-maintenance strategy (Braga, Welsh, & Schell, 2015). The studies report the ability of the order-maintenance policing to reduce violent, property, drug, and disorder crimes. They concluded that these types of strategies used by police departments to control disorder seem to matter, and this holds important implications for police–community relations, justice, and crime prevention. This analysis underscores the conclusion that police "should continue to engage in policing disorder tactics as a part of their portfolio of strategies to reduce crime" (Braga et al., 2015, p. 581).

The question of effectiveness of Broken Windows Policing is tied to its implementation. Are operations carried out with an eye toward collective efficacy and procedural justice? Mears (2015, p. 620) notes there are two "curricula" surrounding such operations. First is the overt curriculum that emphasizes constitutional rights. Here, the message to citizens from police is: We are working for your good and especially for the good of those who live in high-crime communities. We are fighting crime while respecting your freedom and autonomy. Our goal is to maximize freedom, your freedom from crime and predation, and your freedom from the arbitrary power of the state. The second is the "hidden curriculum" of Broken Windows Policing that gives certain citizens the impression they are a "special, dangerous, and undesirable class." The benefits of Broken Windows Policing are counterbalanced by a potential threat to civil liberties. The desirable fruits of order maintenance must be framed by a constitutionally respectful implementation of operations if they are to be fully enjoyed. Unfortunately in the beginning of the 21st century the NYPD began to focus more on increasing misdemeanor arrests than situational crime prevention and enhancing social order.

In July 2014, the death in New York City of Eric Garner created a growning campaign against Broken Windows Policing. Garner, a 350-pound asthmatic, was committing a misdemeanor offense by selling untaxed cigarettes in a commerical area of Staten Island. A group of New York City police officers tried to arrest him. He resisted, and the officers brought the 350-pound asthmatic to the ground by pulling him down by his neck. Garner went into cardiac arrest and eventually died. Critics of Broken Windows Policing contend that this case illustrates the dangers of this form of policing, especially for minorities and that public order policing is a racist assault on poor minority neighborhoods that criminalizes inoffensive behavior. They claim it leads to harassment of Blacks and Hispanics and antagonizes residents of high-crime neighborhoods while doing nothing to fight serious crime (MacDonald, 2014). Critics claim that the police tactics fail to distinguish minorities who are ordinary working individuals from those who engage in criminal behavior. It is claimed that the application of Broken Windows encourages officers to indiscriminately stop and harass minorities. As a result, in many areas of the country, Broken Windows enforcement has lost the minority community's support because it is seen as an externally imposed measure targeting residents of their communities. Critics say applications of Broken Windows such as the stop-and-frisk policy of New York City stretched from Kelling's original design into a convenient rubric for intrusive policing measures. Many in the most affected communities complained that protection had felt like occupation. This debate, while critiquing police practice, is also creating a dialogue between the police and community members regarding what is an acceptable policing crime control strategy.

Creating Community Safety

The prior discussion of police tactics highlights the fact that community safety is a product of how well two very important stakeholders, the residents and the police, work together and respect each other. In a free society there must be a balance in the relationship between civil authority and citizens. Communities will never develop as safe and secure environments if the residents do not take ownership for their own security. Police departments, depending upon the size of the area they serve, can help to build community self-defense through legitimacy, procedural justice, consultation, collaboration, and partnership. The purpose of these efforts is for the police to support and increase the inherent strengths and self-governing capacities of neighborhoods that enable them to defend themselves against crime and disorder. Kelling and Stewart (1989, pp. 8, 9) maintain that the following principles shape that relationship.

1. Community self-defense against crime and disorder is primarily a matter of private social control supported, but never supplanted, by public police.
2. Because neighborhoods vary in their problems and in their capacity for self-help (their ecology of self-defense, collective efficacy), police tactics must be tailored to specific neighborhoods.

3. Tailoring tactics to neighborhoods will require decentralization of police authority and tactical decision-making to lower levels of the organization and the empowerment of sergeants and patrol officers to decide about the problems with which they will deal and the tactics they will use to deal with them.

4. Precinct (police subdivisions) and beat (officer assigned area) configuration must be changed to reflect community and neighborhood form.

5. In the most troubled neighborhoods, especially those now being ravaged by the problems associated with drugs and violent crime, police must at least seek authority from residents to act on their behalf. In neighborhoods that are most bereft of self-help capacities, in inner-city underclass areas, and in neighborhoods most plagued by lawlessness, it is tempting for police to operate independently and without community consultations. The problems are so acute and the resources so meager that consultations may appear inefficient and needlessly time-consuming. This serves neither police nor residents well. Deprived of community authorization, police are vulnerable to charges of both neglect and abuse. The willingness of police to fill in the gap and "do it themselves" deprives citizens of the kinds of experiences that American political philosophy suggests will lead them to "acquire a taste for order" and develop their capacities as citizens.

6. If it is believed that the function of police is to support and increase the inherent strengths and self-governing capacities of neighborhoods that enable them to defend themselves against crime and disorder, a priority of police in deprived neighborhoods is not only to gain authorization for police action but also to help develop capacities for community self-defense. Given the desperate circumstances of some inner-city neighborhoods, this will be a difficult task. It will be extraordinarily risky for citizens to defend their neighborhoods. The risk can be justified only if police commit themselves to pervasive presence for long durations of time. Such presence must always support and encourage self-help.

7. In neighborhoods capable of self-help and governance, police activities should be designed and implemented to strengthen neighborhoods. Police, like other agencies of government, should not do for citizens what citizens can do for themselves. There are reasons to believe that when government supplants self-help, the capacity of citizens for self-help diminishes.

8. Because different neighborhoods have different interests, interests that conflict with each other, police will have to manage inter-neighborhood, and intra-neighborhood, relations. Neighborhoods require free commerce and penetration by strangers and other groups if they are to thrive.

9. Police must understand that just as their task is to support the self-help capacities of neighborhoods when those capacities are used for appropriate ends, they must thwart self-help capacities of neighborhoods when they turn petty, mean, and tyrannical. Police are well-equipped for this. During the past two decades "constitutional policing," at first resisted by many police but later embraced and incorporated by the great chiefs and police leaders of the era, has empowered police to withstand parochial pressure. This does not mean that police will not have to be vigilant in resisting inappropriate pressures; it means that police executives have moved to instill the values and policies that will help them maintain constitutional practice. Justice is as important as security in policing.

These principles are a guide to considerations that should be addressed during the development of police and community collaboration to build safer communities.

Community Collaboration

Collaboration begins when the police department, community organizations, and neighborhood residents agree to work together to achieve the common goal of community safety. The central issue for the establishment of a collaborative community environment is to get residents and neighborhood institutions to share responsibility with their police for creating a safe community. The development of a collaborative effort should increase knowledge, understanding, trust and cooperation between the police and the citizens they serve. They are also created to orient police toward a more proactive and strategic approach to developing community safety. Collaboration is a way for departments to develop a sensitivity to citizen expectations, gain information about public safety issues, maintain an open dialogue during times of crisis, and achieve goals. Community collaboration requires police executives and managers to master interpersonal and group process skills and to develop a talent for recognizing and managing the potentials of intensifying community involvement, positive and negative, on organizational practice and culture (IACP, 1999).

Collaboration is built upon:

1. Knowledge and understanding of the parties involved.
2. Responsiveness to the needs of the community.
3. Trust, respect, and understanding between partners.
4. Communication consisting of an open and direct dialogue.

Community collaboration requires that police departments develop knowledge and understanding about the areas and people they serve and become skilled at diagnosing the issues affecting these neighborhoods. Communities are complex interactional settings whose public safety needs are subject to the forces of change within our society. Departments should develop timely and accurate information about the constituencies within their communities beyond developing data on crime and quality-of-life issues. From a strategic management perspective, the key value of this knowledge lies in terms of its "strategic" use (Dean & Gottschalk, 2007). To strategically manage their organizations, police executives must identify and monitor the factors creating change in their communities in order to develop the knowledge upon which to diagnose these issues, collaborate, set public safety objectives, and build partnerships. A department's leadership must also be administratively flexible to adjust their response to the changing nature of community needs.

One way to develop this knowledge is to create an accurate and timely **community profile** to define stakeholder constituencies and identify driving factors within their community. Developing and maintaining a community profile provides a structured way for identifying, gathering, and analyzing relevant information to support collaboration and problem solving. A department's community profile should not only define the various elements that make up and define the community but also identify the forces within the community that affect it and their underlying causes. This will serve as a basis for diagnosing these factors and lead to a fuller understanding of the community and its residents. A community profile should be descriptive and inclusive enough to enable the department to understand its relationship with its external environment. It should be considered a living document, not a static item that never changes after it is created but updated consistently.

Information needs for a community profile should include:

1. Description of the area population by race, ethnicity by number and percentage, and gender and age distribution.
2. Community institutions, religious and educational, and the contact persons for each of these.
3. Physical characteristics, such as boundaries, parks and recreation areas, name and number of buildings and streets.
4. Commercial properties, numbers of high-rise buildings, single-family units, transient lodgings, vacant and abandoned housing units, and population density.
5. Streets important to traffic and people movement. Alleyway, backyard, and rooftop conditions. Illegal and legal markets.
6. Location and identification of liaison for all correctional, confinement, treatment, and community-based assistance programs, that is, emergency family shelters, food banks, welfare services, and homeless shelters.
7. Listing by name of community service organizations and their contact persons.
   a. Professional associations
   b. Business associations
   c. Civic groups
   d. Fraternal associations
   e. Volunteer organizations for youths
   f. Day care centers
   g. Ethnic associations
   h. Athletic clubs
   i. Homeowner associations
   j. Parent-teacher associations
8. Governmental agencies: fire, sanitation, ambulance services, code enforcement, highway and street department, labor and welfare departments.
9. Offense-prone population: parole and probation clients, percentage of violent and property offenders, repeat quality-of-life offenders.
10. Gang/group activity: leaders, number and identity, ethnic composition, colors and symbols, affiliations and membership.

The information contained in the community profile should be an integral part of orientating new employees to the department and managers to their commands.

Police executives must also develop an understanding and responsiveness to the political, administrative, community, and justice constituencies' needs they serve. These include:

1. **Mayors and city managers** who set agendas and give policy and program direction to police chief executives. Understanding these individuals and responding to their major policy and program initiatives is essential for the successful management of the department's external environment and for executive survival.

2. **City and county council members** are elected officials that represent the entire community and who have special interests in issues affecting their electoral districts and individual citizens. They will expect the department to be sensitive to their constituents' concerns. The legal boundaries that conscribe these relationships must be understood by both the department and council members.

3. **Different neighborhoods and subcommunities** exist within most jurisdictions. The community profile must identify the different subneighborhoods and the majority ethnic and racial groupings that make up these areas. The issues relating to immigration, influx of new ethnic groups, and sizable increases in the population of present groups require the police to possess an operationally heightened degree of cultural awareness and tailor their response to a more varied set of subcultural needs. Subcommunities will have differing sets of leadership and concerns. Some are organized, have established formal leadership, and are vocal in expressing their concerns while others are disorganized and fail to express their needs. All neighborhoods, regardless of their ability to seek attention, must be understood and receive attention equally. Formal leaders may include such people as the pastor of a local church, an elementary school principal, or civic association leader. Informal leaders are residents respected in the neighborhood and who can influence opinion, but do not hold formal leadership positions in local organizations. Developing collaborative dialogues with residents and their spokespersons help departments realize potential issues and satisfy neighborhood differences and safety concerns.

4. **The business community** is the economic basis for a community. Leaders of major businesses frequently wield substantial political power and can be mobilized for political and financial support including resources. However, small independent businesses contribute to the social cohesiveness of neighborhoods, and their owners are often well respected by community residents. Destruction of these businesses during civil disturbances deprives residents of their services and economic contribution while resulting in creating hardships for residents.

5. **Civil service commissions** are responsible for the enforcement of civil service laws governing entry-level requirements, selection practices, promotional eligibility requirements, promotional practices, and discipline. Commissions also function as the appeal body for employees dissatisfied with discipline decisions. Police executives work with commissioners to revise archaic, cumbersome, and counterproductive laws and ordinances and educate them about the purposes and values of discipline practices.

6. **State and federal legislatures** recommend, draft, and debate to establish legislation needed to achieve public safety objectives and to ensure that crime and social legislation does not come forth that is damaging to public safety. The issues that pertain to law-making at the state level pertain with equal relevance to federal law-making.

7. **Federal and state law enforcement agencies** have locally based federal and state operations, including special task forces (FBI, DEA, ATF, INS, and DOJ). These agencies are important partners in addressing community public safety issues.

(IACP, 1999)

Collaboration efforts must also be built upon mutual trust, respect, and two-way communication. For example, a police chief executive of a 45-person department in northeast Florida explained to one of the authors that he meets either bi-weekly or weekly with 30 community leaders. Each of these individuals represents constituencies and residential groupings his department serves. During these meetings the chief shares information, gains awareness of issues, and discusses factors of mutual concern. The meetings are a proactive way for the chief to become aware of issues, address problems and community concerns with important stakeholders through direct dialogue, trust, and respect. Increasing stakeholder access to information coupled with invitations to proactively engage in solving issues of mutual concern enhance the development of a mutually beneficial collaborative alliance between the community and its police.

Community Partnerships

Community partnerships consists of a planned structured working arrangement designed to address a specific issue or problem that is affecting the community's public safety. It involves a formal process beyond that of collaboration. Forming community problem-solving partnerships between the police and neighborhood stakeholders represent what the late Stephen R. Covey (2008) identifies as a paradigm shift in policing. The new mind-set is about partnering for a sustainable civil society, representing a shift toward a community justice system for victims, for offenders, for the police, for judges, and for society at large. This shift requires everyone to be involved in creating safe and just communities. These relationships help to facilitate trust between community members and police organizations (Skogan, Steiner, DuBois, Gudell, & Fagan, 2002a, p. 10).

Covey (2008) suggests that community safety solutions should come from various pockets of the community, not just from those whose formal role is to provide protection. He suggests that communities must leave behind reactive systems and initiate proactive ones. Police and community stakeholders collaborating together in partnership can contribute to halting the spiral of crime and the development of safer neighborhoods. When citizens become co-producers of public safety it changes how they perceive themselves, their neighborhood, and the organizations that serve their community (Morabito, 2010). This paradigm shift is emphasizing the importance of the development of collective efficacy and the co-production of community safety.

It is important for police agencies to find ways to connect with members of the communities in which they serve through collaborative partnerships. Community partnerships can help develop ways to overcome citizens' negative perceptions of their police (Skogan et al., 2002a, p. 3). When police and locally credible community stakeholders work together in partnership in a focused and planned manner, more can be accomplished to create safer neighborhoods (Geller & Belsky, 2009). Many departments have implemented partnerships with minority residents in an effort to strengthen minority confidence in the police and increase their willingness to take part in crime-prevention activities (Wehrman & DeAngelis, 2011, p. 52). These collaborative efforts connect minority communities with law enforcement and create beneficial relationships between officers and citizens. For example, the Chicago Police Department formed an alliance with members of the Latino community that educates citizens about the law to help them avoid involvement in criminal activity (Skogan et al., 2002a, p. 12).

The process of building and sustaining partnerships with the community is an ongoing responsibility for the police chief executive. Trust must be established between participants because it is the sustaining quality to maintain this relationship. Citizen partners should be willing to:

1. Assume a sense of ownership for their community and its safety.
2. Provide the police with information about crime, criminals, and unsafe conditions.
3. Actively participate in community-based self-help activities that address sources of crime and disorder.
4. Be willing to join with the police and their neighbors to assist in development of the community's collective efficacy.
5. Be willing to participate with their neighbors in seeking help from other governmental resources besides the police.

The focus of this collaboration is the deterrence of specific kinds of crimes, mobilization of residents, and the development of environments inhospitable to crime. However, building community partnerships takes time, planning, communication, intention, willing participants, and mutual respect. Potential community partners include:

- Residents.
- Police officers.
- Police command staff.
- Community youth.
- Business leaders.
- Social clubs and organizations.
- Community organizations.
- Governmental agencies.
- Religious institutions.
- Schools.
- Elected or appointed officials.
- Criminal juvenile agencies.
- Media.
- Drug and alcohol treatment facilities.
- Informal community leaders.
- Representatives of racial, age, and economic diversity.

Community Leader/Stakeholder Identification

The process of identifying individuals as potential partners should be carefully thought out. One of the first tasks of developing community partnerships is to identify the public safety problems/issues to be addressed and ascertain as many individuals and organizations that have an interest in resolving these issues. Those claiming to be a spokesperson or leader at a community meeting may only represent themselves and their own ideas. However, successful partnerships need committed residents who can influence their neighbors and get things done. They need people who care about their community, who want to solve its problems, and who are willing to work on providing safety to their community. A good way to identify these individuals is to find out who has been involved in trying to address neighborhood problems and help their community improve. Individuals with a proven track record of leadership for effectively working with residents and residential groups to address problems should be given priority when building partnerships.

Community leaders are individuals who influence the attitudes and behavior of others within their community. They have a direct influence on those who are willing to listen to them. They often can affect segments of community life and assist police service delivery. These individuals usually fall into one of two leadership types, acknowledged or appointed. **Acknowledged leaders** are community-sanctioned grassroots persons living in the community whom residents respect and will most likely turn to in critical moments. Acknowledged leaders earn their position because residents often go to them when they need help with problems. They are part of the community's informal power structure (Miller, Hess, & Orthmann, 2014). Acknowledged leaders may include a pastor in a local church, a local team coach, or a small business owner. They may or may not have wide acceptance but may have the respect of a subgroup of residents and the potential to be a community leader.

Appointed leaders are individuals whose positions within the community are politically decided or designated, or set by official employment or by prominence.

APPOINTED LEADERS' CHARACTERISTICS

1. They are usually chosen and appointed by persons outside of the community.
2. They may or may not have personal knowledge of the community's problems since they may or may not be residents of the community.
3. They may have to prove themselves as effective leaders.
4. They may have to work extra hard to gain the community's trust.
5. They may not be able to mobilize community residents.

(NCPC, 1986)

The police should enlist the help of both types of leaders in creating secure communities. Including only appointed leaders when creating community partnerships can cause loss of community support. However, including only acknowledged leaders may deny needed access to local government service institutions and official resource networks available through appointed leaders' more formal contacts. The problem the department faces is to determine how both these leadership types can assist in solving community problems.

Successful partnerships enlist resident assistance in crime identification and prevention and other street-level problem-solving efforts. The basic aim is to get citizens and community institutions to share the responsibility for dealing with crime and crime-related problems.

Successful community partnership involve:

1. Stakeholders with a vested interest in the issue.
2. Chronic problem(s) that residents have a strong stake in addressing and that offers opportunity for organizing, planning and partnership building.
3. Informed and committed resident and police leadership.
4. Trust among and between partners.
5. Shared vision and common goals.

6. Expertise among partners to solve community problems.
7. Community organizations through which volunteers can work and be effective.
8. Organizations that can support local efforts and provide community residents with training, education, and technical assistance.
9. Teamwork strategies.
10. Open communication between participants and the police.
11. Motivated partners.
12. Sufficient means to implement and sustain the collaborative effort.
13. An action plan.

(Rinehart et al., 2001, p. 7)

When partnerships are organized with committed and active partners, the problem-solving process has more of a chance to succeed. The largest investment of time and resources should come from community volunteers, and secondarily, staff members of not-for-profit organizations. In this manner community stakeholders take responsibility for resolving their own problems with police assistance.

Problems that make developing partnerships difficult and can lead to failure include:

1. Non-existent communication between community participants and police.
2. Lack of informed and committed resident and police leadership.
3. Lack of community organizations through which neighborhood residents can take part.
4. The only community-based organizations that exist are concerned with serving clients, not in solving community problems.
5. Community residents are discouraged and feel that their neighborhood is lost and they are powerless.
6. Whether a group of dedicated individuals can actually make the neighborhood viable again.

Implementing a Partnership

The first step a department should take when implementing a community partnership is to identify what it intends to accomplish. In order for the partnership to work on community problems or issues, it must be clearly identified and defined. This task begins with the selection of a target neighborhood and the analysis of its public safety issues. Selection should be based upon an analysis of a variety of data sources and information obtained from both the department and the community. All aspects of the target problem or issue should be identified in priority order to be addressed by the partnership team. This process is identified as **scanning** in Problem-Oriented Policing. It involves:

•   Identifying recurring problems of concern to the residents of an area and the police.
•   Identifying the consequences of the problem for the residents and the police.
•   Prioritizing those problems based upon their impact on community safety.
•   Analyze the problems using a variety of data sources.
•   Identify community residents' perceptions of their safety and how they are affected by the problems in their area.

- Determine the frequency of problem occurrence and how long they have been taking place.
- Select the problem(s) for the partnership to address.
- Develop outcome goals relating to the resolution of the problem.

Once this has been accomplished, the next step is to identify key neighborhood stakeholders with skill sets and knowledge needed to affect the problem or issue selected for the group to work on. Once these individuals are identified they need to be approached and asked if they are willing to be members of the group who will focus on community safety issues. An important step in getting people interested and willing to join is to identify what is expected of them and its benefits. Next the department will need to convene the first meeting to clearly define group objectives and task responsibility. Each group member should be assigned an essential task(s) to perform and the time required to accomplish it. It is important that each member of the partnership be clear about their role, informed, feel included, and have a sense of ownership for the entire effort. Regular meetings, ongoing communication methods, and an evaluation process must be established to keep track of progress and achievements. Responsibilities must be shared among the members of the partnership to build commitment and a sense of accomplishment.

Next the group needs to develop an action plan for implementing the partnership project and the accomplishment of desired objectives. The **action plan** is a working document that serves as a tool to guide the collaboration of group members as they implement the problem response. An action plan identifies ***what*** will be done, by ***whom***, and ***when***. The action plan also should identify ***how*** the partnership will know if actions taken achieved desired outcomes. Rinehart et al. (2001, p. 4) recommend that the action plan should:

- Specify what activities and task should occur.
- Identify who has responsibility for each task.
- Establish the timeframe for the accomplishing the task and when to action will take place.
- Identify the resources that will be needed to accomplish the tasks and how these resources will be acquired.

This plan should be disseminated to all members of the partnership. It is a working document that should be changed as new information and the project evolves during implementation. The plan should be periodically reviewed, as to the relevance of the actions outlined and their consistency with desired outcomes. The last step is to design a means to evaluate what has been accomplished. Establishing appropriate quantitative and qualitative performance measures will help link partnership actions to specific outcomes. Monitoring, measurement, and evaluation are keys to partnership success. They let the partnership determine if they accomplished what they set out to do.

Valid and reliable **evaluation** requires:

1. **Identification of measurable outcomes (goals)**;
2. **Identification of measurable objectives (milestones, steps)** that will lead to the accomplishment of the desired outcomes; and
3. A **reporting system** for monitoring progress and maintaining **accountability**;
4. Assessment of **actual accomplishments** versus desired outcomes.

All partnership tasks should be conducted with evaluation in mind. Feedback systems and measurable objectives should always be part of action plans. Partnerships should avoid setting expectations that are unrealistic and unattainable by developing a strategy that incorporates realistic and attainable objectives as system elements. Goals and objectives (outcomes) should be established to provide a way to assess progress accurately, cite success, and identify tasks that work. Baseline measures that record the conditions for establishing the partnership before change is implemented should be identified so that a before-and-after comparison of relevant changes can be made.

Last, all performance measures should relate to the partnerships vision, mission, and goals. The design and implementation of evaluations depend upon the specific purpose they are intended to serve. Always measure what matters and what provides the information needed. All else is a waste of time, budget, and organizational resources.

Conclusion

The term "community" refers to a specific geographical area and the individuals, organizations, and agencies who live and function within that area. Creating and maintaining safe communities is a basic police function. Communities that are crime-ridden, disorderly, and disorganized are places where people lock themselves behind closed doors, stay off the streets, and are afraid to use public places. However, the police cannot create safe communities without the support, approval, and assistance of the community's residents. Peel recognized the importance of this relationship in his 1829 *Principles of Law Enforcement* and the concept of police–community collaboration has been reignited by Community Policing. Community Policing seeks to engage the community by involving residents as active participants in the identification and prevention of crime and disorder and other street-level revitalization efforts. This strategy requires police departments to actively seek to collaborate with the community in a planned manner, build partnerships, and develop mutual trust.

The capacity of neighborhood residents to protect themselves against crime and disorder requires the achievement of a "collective efficacy." Collective efficacy involves residents monitoring children and other persons in public areas, acting to prevent disorderly conduct, and confronting individuals who exploit or disturb public spaces (Sampson et al., 1997). These activities depend upon residents trusting each other and cooperating with themselves and trusting and cooperating with the police. Creating and supporting the development of collective efficacy is a worthwhile aim of police–community partnerships.

As first proposed by Wilson and Kelling (1982), Broken Windows theory hypothesizes that if the police maintained public order, they could simultaneously impact serious crime, citizen fear, and prevent communities from becoming unsafe. They stressed the importance of addressing and solving neighborhood problems to reduce the opportunity for crime and the fear of it among residents. Citizen fear, created by disorder, leads to weakened social controls, thus creating the conditions in which crime can flourish. The justification for this emphasis on public order crime is drawn from history that in the past the police had carried out such activities and that the community from which the police gained legitimacy saw these as important police functions (Weisburd & Braga, 2006).

Community partnership is an organizational strategy designed to create a working relationship between the police, residents, residents' groups, and social organizations in a defined neighborhood. The strategy calls for the development of a planned collaborative relationship between the police and residents that seeks to alter the nature of crime and anti-social behavior by building a neighborhood's collective efficacy. However, in order for the community residents to collaborate and form partnerships with the police, they must trust and believe in the legitimacy of their police department and approve of its efforts.

The police are viewed as legitimate when citizens believe that the police have moral authority to enforce the law and deserve respect, compliance, and support. Community residents will be more willing to work with the police when they view them as legitimate and consider their enforcement decisions as favorable and fair. The police need to think about how the community's perceptions of their legitimacy and use of procedural justice can affect the way they work with residents to address public safety issues. Procedural justice reflects the rational, neutral, and transparent decision making of police officers. It involves the belief that the police can be trusted to use their coercive authority in a trustworthy fashion. If the police intend to create collaborative partnerships with community residents, they must promote a culture of respect within their departments and clarify that mistreatment of citizens will not be tolerated. Police legitimacy is determined by public assessments of how the police exercise their authority. Legitimacy is crucial to respectful and effective relations between the police and the communities they serve.

KEY TERMS

Acknowledged leaders	Community leaders	Legitimacy
Action plan	Community partnership	Neighborhood
Appointed leaders	Community profile	Quality-of-life policing
Broken Windows	Community safety	Scanning
Collective efficacy	Evaluation	Vertical systems
Community	Horizontal systems	
Community collaboration	Hot Spot Policing Strategy	

References

Baker, A., & Rivera, M. (2010, October 27). Study finds street stops by N.Y. Police unjustified. *New York Times*, A22.

Braga, A.A., & Bond, B.J. (2008). Policing crime and disorder hot spots: A randomized controlled trial. *Criminology*, 46(3), 577–608.

Braga, A.A., & Brunson, R.K. (2015). The police and public discourse on "black-on-black" violence. *New Perspectives in Policing Bulletin*. Washington, DC: National Institute of Justice: John F. Kennedy School of Government, Harvard University.

Braga, A.A., Welsh, B.C., & Schell, C. (2015). Can policing disorder reduce crime? A systematic review and meta-analysis. *Journal of Research in Crime & Delinquency*, 52(4), 567–588.

Bratton, W.J., & Kelling, G.L. (2015, Winter). Why we need broken windows policing. *City Journal*, www.city-journal.org/html/why-we-need-broken-windows-policing-13696.html.

Bratton, W.J., & Tumin, Z. (2012). *Collaborate or perish: Reaching across boundaries in a net-worked world.* New York: Random House.

Carter, D.L. (2002). *The police and the community.* Upper Saddle River, NJ:Prentice Hall.

COPS Office. (2015). *President's task force on 21st century policing implementation guide: Moving from recommendations to action.* Washington, DC: Office of Community Oriented Policing Services.

Covey, S.R. (2008). A whole new mind-set on fighting crime. *The Police Chief, 75*(12), 16–18.

Dean, G., & Gottschalk, P. (2007). *Knowledge management in policing and law enforcement: Foundations, structures, applications.* London: Oxford University Press.

Fischer, C. (2014). *Legitimacy and procedural justice: A new element of police leadership.* Washington, DC: U.S. Department of Justice, Bureau of Justice Assistance.

Geller, B., & Belsky, L. (2009). *A policymakers guide to building our way out of crime.* Washington, DC: U.S. Dept. of Justice, Office of Community Oriented Policing Services.

Golub, A., Johnson, B.D., Taylor, A., & Eterno, J. (2003). Quality of life policing: Do offenders get the message? *Policing, 26*(4), 690–707.

Golub, A., Johnson, B.D., Taylor, A., & Eterno, J. (2004). Does quality of life policing widen the net? A partial analysis. *Justice Research & Policy, 6*(1), 19–42.

Hawdon, J.E., Ryan, J., & Griffin, S.P. (2003). Policing tactics and perceptions of police legitimacy. *Police Quarterly, 6*(4), 469–491.

Henry, V.E. (2002). *The Compstat paradigm: Management accountability in policing.* New York: Looseleaf Press.

International Association of Chiefs of Police. (1999). *Police leadership in the 21st century: Achieving & sustaining executive success: Recommendations from the President's first leadership conference.* Alexandria, VA, www.theiacp.org/Police-Leadership-in-the-21st-Century.

Katz, C.M., Webb, V.J., & Schaefer, D.R. (2001). An assessment of the impact of quality of life policing on crime and disorder. *Justice Quarterly, 18*(4), 825–876.

Kelling, G. (2015). An author's brief history of an idea. *Journal of Research in Crime & Delinquency, 52*(4), 626–629.

Kelling, G.L., & Stewart, J.K. (1989). Neighborhoods and police: The maintenance of civil authority. *Perspectives on Policing, No. 10.* Washington, DC: National Institute of Justice, John F. Kennedy School of Government, Harvard University.

Kennedy, D.M. (2011). *Don't shoot: One man, a street fellowship and the end of violence in inner-city America.* New York: Bloomsbury.

MacDonald, H. (2014, December 17). How broken windows policing puts fewer men in prison. *Time Magazine.* New York, NY.

Maguire, E.R., & Johnson, D. (2010). Measuring public perceptions of the police. *Policing, 33*(4), 703–730.

Maple, J., & Mitchell, C. (1999). *The crime fighter: Putting the bad guys out of business.* New York: Doubleday.

Mears, T. (2015). Broken windows, neighborhoods, and the legitimacy of law enforcement or why I fell in and out of love with Zimbardo. *Journal of Research in Crime & Delinquency, 52*(4), 609–625.

Miller, L.S., Hess, K.M., & Orthmann, C.H. (2014). *Community policing: Partnerships for problem solving.* Clifton Park, NY: Delmar.

Morabito, M.S. (2010). Understanding community policing as an innovation: Patterns of adoption. *Crime & Delinquency, 56*(4), 564–587.

National Crime Prevention Council. (1986). *Preventing crime in urban communities: Handbook and program profiles*. Washington, DC: NCPC.

Noland, J.J., Conti, N., & McDevitt, J. (2005). Situational policing. *FBI Law Enforcement Bulletin, 74*(11), 1–9.

Novak, K., Hartman, J., Holsinger, A., & Turner, M. (1999). The effects of aggressive policing of disorder on serious crime. *Policing, 22*, 171–190.

Neyroud, P. (2009). Legitimacy. In A. Wakefield, & J. Fleming (Eds.), *The Sage dictionary of policing* (pp. 190–192). London, UK: Sage.

Oates, D.J. (2016). Discussion of the Aurora Colorado Mass Shooting. *Presentation at the Southern Police Institute former Aurora the Police Chief*, October 3, 2016.

Peak, K.J., & R.W. Glensor (2012). *Community policing and problem solving: Strategies and practices*, 6th ed. Upper Saddle River, NJ: Prentice Hall.

President's Task Force on 21st Century Policing (2015). *Final report of President's task force on 21st century policing*. Washington, DC: Office of Community Oriented Policing Services.

Reith, Charles. (1956). *A new study of police history*. Edinburgh, Scotland: Oliver & Boyd.

Rinehart, T.A., Laszio, A.T., & Brisco, G.O. (2001). *Collaboration toolkit: How to build fix and sustain productive partnerships*. Washington, DC: US Department of Justice, Office of Community Policing.

Sampson, R.J. (2012). *Great American city: Chicago and the enduring neighborhood effect*. Chicago: University of Chicago Press.

Sampson, R.J., & Bartusch, D.J. (1998). Legal cynicism and (subcultural?) tolerance of deviance: The neighborhood context of racial differences. *Law & Society Review, 32*(4), 777–804.

Sampson, R.J., Raudenbush, S.W., & Earls, F. (1997). Neighborhoods and violent crime: A multilevel study of collective efficacy. *Science, 277*, 918–924.

Sherman, L. (1990). Police crackdowns: Initial and residual deterrence. In M. Tonry, & N. Morris (Eds.), *Crime and justice: A review of research—Vol. 12* (pp. 1–48). Chicago: University of Chicago Press.

Skogan, W., & Frydl, K. (Eds.) (2004). *Fairness and effectiveness in policing: The evidence*. Committee to Review Research on Police Policy and Practices. Committee on Law and Justice, Division of Behavioral and Social Sciences and Education. Washington, DC: The National Academies Press.

Skogan, W.G., Steiner, L., DuBois, J., Gudell, J.E., & Fagan, A. (2002a). *Community policing and "the new immigrants": Latinos in Chicago*. Washington, DC: U.S. Department of Justice, Office of Justice Programs, National Institute of Justice.

Sousa, W.H., & Kelling, G.L. (2006). Of broken windows, criminology and criminal justice. In D. Weisburd, & A.A. Braga (Eds.), *Police innovation: Contrasting perspectives* (pp. 17–97). Cambridge, UK: Cambridge University Press.

Sunshine, J., & Tyler, T.R. (2003). The role of procedural justice and legitimacy in shaping public support for policing. *Law & Society Review, 37*(3), 513–548.

Tyler, T.R. (2004). To better serve and protect: Improving police practices. *Annals of the American Academy of Political and Social Science, 593*, 84–99.

Tyler, T.R., & Fagan, J. (2008). Legitimacy and cooperation: Why do people help the police fight crime in their communities? *Ohio State Journal of Criminal Law, 6*, 231–275.

Tyler, T.R., & Huo, Y. (2002). *Trust in the law*. New York: Russell Sage Foundation.

Trojanowicz, R., & Bucqueroux, B. (1994). *Community policing: How to get started*. Cincinnati, OH: Anderson.

Vito, A.G., Higgins, G., Walsh, W.F., & Vito, G. (2012). The threat of methamphetamine use and production: evaluation results from a Kentucky law enforcement program. *International Journal of Police Science & Management, 14*(3), 1–12.

Walsh, W. (2001). Compstat: An analysis of an emerging police managerial paradigm. *Policing: An International Journal of Police Strategies & Management, 24*(3), 347–362.

Wehrman, M.M., & DeAngelis, J. (2011). Citizen willingness to participate in police-community partnerships: Exploring the influence of race and neighborhood context. *Police Quarterly, 14*(1), 48–69.

Weisburd, D., & Braga, A.A. (Eds.) (2006). *Police innovation: Contrasting perspectives.* Cambridge, UK: Cambridge University Press.

Weisburd, D., Davis, M., & Gill, C. (2015). Increasing collective efficacy and social capital at crime hot spots: New crime control tools for police. *Policing, 9*(3), 265–274.

Wilson, J.Q., & Kelling, G.L. (1982, March). The police and neighborhood safety: Broken windows. *Atlantic Monthly*, 29–38.

Wilson, J.Q., & Kelling, G.L. (1989, February). Making neighborhoods safe. *Atlantic Monthly*, 46–52.

Wolfe, S.E. (2011). The effect of low self-control on perceived police legitimacy. *Journal of Criminal Justice, 39*, 67–74.

Zhao, J.S., Tsai, C.-F., Ren, L., & Lai, Y.-L. (2012). Public satisfaction with police control of disorder crime: Does the public hold the police accountable? *Justice Quarterly, 31*(2), 394–420.

13 Future Challenges and Concerns

The police officer's mission is that of guardian: to protect. The rules of engagement evolve as the incident unfolds. Soldiers must follow orders. Police officers must make independent decisions. Soldiers come into communities as an outside, occupying force. Guardians are members of the community, protecting from within.
Susan Rahr, *President's Task Force on 21st Century Policing* (2015a, p. 10)

Learning Objectives

1. To understand the changing nature of policing.

2. To identify the issues driving change in policing.

3. To understand the factors involved in the use of deadly force.

4. To consider the relationship between organizational culture and good policing.

5. To identify the strategies for building community trust.

6. To identify the "Principles of Good Policing."

7. To examine the concept of legitimacy and how it affects both the police organization and the community.

8. To consider how to deal with budgetary issues.

9. To analyze the values of the "new generation" of police officers and how they affect supervisory styles.

10. To consider what is necessary for effective policing.

Introduction

The role of a strategic leader is to develop an organization that responds to the needs of the present as well as the future with the resources and capabilities of their organization. Understanding the present is difficult enough but preparing for and projecting what the future will bring is a challenging endeavor. If, however, as most strategic thinkers claim, that the past and present are a forecast of the future, policing can expect to face continued significant challenges. Chuck Wexler, Executive Director of the Police Executive Research Forum (2014), stated that policing in the 21st century changes more in a year than it changed in a decade a generation ago.

While still being accountable for traditional responsibilities such as calls for service and crime investigation, many departments have expanded their mission to include crime prevention, fear reduction, lowering crime rates, and creating effective communities. Rather than focusing on responding to crimes after they are committed, today's best police departments are looking for ways to be proactive. Progressive departments are emphasizing data analysis, technology, and analytical projection to assist in the development of crime control strategies and tactics. These changes are not just about finding new ways to reduce crime; they go deeper, to evaluating the basic mission of the police, and a reexamination of what people want from their police (PERF, 2014).

Successful police executives are driving organizational change using **strategic management**, an ongoing process that seeks opportunities to enhance operational efficiencies by identifying internal issues and external influences that hinder organizational sustainability. It focuses on management's responsibility for addressing these issues through the creation of a customer-focused, high-performance learning organization (Charrier, 2004). Communities are demanding more accountability, transparency, and oversight of their police in response to negative perceptions of police use of deadly force while reducing budgetary resources. Many crime control tactics used by the police that are based on Broken Windows theory are being challenged because of concerns of racial bias. Police use of force (especially deadly force) has become the catalyst of sustained protest, demonstrations, and municipal riots about the legitimacy of police treatment of minorities. These protests call for greater protection and rights for citizens, whether they are under suspicion or not. As a result, police departments are facing a more complex and changing environment than they were in the past.

Trust between law enforcement agencies and the people they protect and serve is essential in a democracy. It is key to the stability of our communities, the integrity of our criminal justice system, and the safe and effective delivery of policing services (PTF, 2015b). Recent events have exposed serious rifts in the relationships between local police and the communities they protect and serve. On December 18, 2014, President Barack Obama signed an executive order establishing the Task Force on 21st Century Policing. The President charged the task force with identifying best practices and offering recommendations on how policing practices can promote effective crime reduction while building public trust. This chapter will discuss identified trends and draw conclusions to guide police preparation for the future.

Issues in Police Management

American policing is at a critical juncture. Since the summer of 2014, the nation has seen a series of controversial cases, many of them captured on videos taken by the police, bystanders, or nearby security cameras of police officers using deadly force in questionable circumstances. These events have sparked protests across the country and soul-searching among police executives. While these incidents represent a small fraction of the millions of encounters that take place between the police and the public, their portrayal by the national media has galvanized negative opinions of police and launched a national movement around the slogan that "Black Lives Matter." As a result, the controversies surrounding the use of force and perceived mistreatment of minorities are the major issues threatening police–community relationships in many areas and have undermined citizens' trust and conceptions of police legitimacy. Police leaders must address and resolve this issue of "trust" for both the present and future because this upheaval in our society is continuing, and it is unlikely to abate soon. This is a critical responsibility because policing embodies and represents the ideal of the rule of law that governs civilized society (Covey, 2011).

Use of Deadly Force

Beginning with the death of Eric Gardner in New York City and Michael Brown in Ferguson, Missouri, at least a dozen other controversial uses of deadly force have received nation-wide and even international attention. In many of these cases, the officers' use of force had already been deemed legally "justified," and prosecutors have declined to press criminal charges. However, that did not mean that the uses of force observed in video recordings of these events look right to the ordinary citizen. PERF (2015) concluded that a fundamental change in how the American people view the issue of police use of force was occurring.

Fyfe (2015, pp. 522–523) in his research on the use of force notes several of the following determinants of police violence. Police/citizen interactions are uniquely urgent, involuntary, and public. Police cannot choose the times and places where they perform their services. They must deal with both the shock and substance of citizen problems as they occur. Many individuals who come to their attention do not seek or welcome it. Their actions take place in a public setting in circumstances beyond their control in front of audiences willing to show their disagreement and dissatisfaction with their efforts. Police must diagnose the situation and assess their potential response.

Unfortunately, he found that it is difficult to define the factors that led well-meaning police officers to make bad use of force decisions. Fyfe (2015, p. 526) suggests these decisions are often hastily considered and may be a product of what he identified as the "**split-second syndrome**." This syndrome serves both to inhibit the development of greater police diagnostic expertise and to provide after-the-fact justification for unnecessary police violence. He theorizes that this syndrome is a product of the following assumptions.

First, it assumes that no two police problems are precisely alike. As a result, there are no principles that may apply to the diagnosis of specific situations. Thus, no more can be asked of officers than that they respond as quickly as possible to problems, devising the best solutions they can on the spur of the moment. Second, because of these stresses and time constraints a high percentage of inappropriate decisions should be expected. Finally, because of these assumptions "the sole basis on which any use of force by the police needs to be justified is the officers' perception of the circumstances prevailing at the instant when they decide to apply force" (Fyfe, 2015, p. 527). He concludes that the acceptence of this syndrome lends approval to unnecessary police violence and the inability to consider whether the situation could have led to a successful, non-violent conclusion. It results in failure of the police to meet their highest obligation: the protection of human life. Nobel and Alpert (2015, p. 578) contend that there are very few instances where police have to make split-second use of force determinations. They maintain that officers should be trained and encouraged to reduce the need for making split-second decisions and to slow down the pace of the encounter to do so.

Adams (2015, pp. 534–546) reached several conclusions about what the research disclosed about police actual use of force:

Police use force infrequently. Between 2002 and 2011, only 1.6% of residents with police contact reported that police threatened or used force and only 1.2% of them stated that the police used excessive force during their exchange (Hyland, Langton, & Davis, 2015, p. 1)

Police use of force typically occurs at the lower end of the force spectrum, involving grabbing, pushing or shoving.

Use of force typically occurs when police are trying to make an arrest and the suspect is resisting.

Use of force appears to be unrelated to an officer's personal characteristics such as age, gender, and ethnicity.

Use of force is more likely to occur when police are dealing with persons under the influence of alcohol or drugs or with mentally ill individuals.

A small proportion of officers are disproportionately involved in use of force incidents.

The incidence of wrongful use of force by police is unknown.

The impact of differences in police organizations, including administrative policies, hiring, training, discipline, and use of technology on excessive use of force is unknown.

Influences of situational characteristics on police use of force and the transactional nature of these events are largely unknown.

Bolger (2015) conducted a meta-analysis of 44 studies published between 2001 and 2011 in which he confirms these conclusions. Bolger (2015, p. 483) reported that police use of force was more likely in encounters involving serious offenses, a resistant suspect, an arrest decision, when citizens are in conflict, when more officers are present, and during a police-initiatied encounter. These variables increase the probability that an officer will use force to subdue the suspect. In addition, minority, male, and/or lower-class suspects were more likely to be the targets of police use of force. While male officers were more likely to use force than females, the effect size for gender was substantially less than the encounter and suspect characteristics (Bolger, 2015, p. 484).

Deadly Force Policies

Fridell (2015, p. 548) points out that police executives cannot eliminate the necessity for the use of force but they can optimize it by: (1) the adoption of sound and effective policies, (2) implementation of mechanisms to promote policy adherence and accountability, and (3) training to ensure that officers have the knowledge, skills, and judgment to act under agency policy. The use of early intervention systems and appropriate reward structures for critical incidents should help avoid problems (Walker, Alpert, & Kenney, 2000).

Chief executives who wish to improve on their use of force policies should begin by reviewing their department's current policies. These policies should meet all current legal standards and advise officers what they may do in situations involving force. Policies are goal-oriented general statements of intent, designed to assist department personnel through problems and give direction that will assist in mission accomplishment. Departments should:

- Establish policies that guide the most critical decisions made by personnel.
- Make certain that personnel are trained in what the policies mean and how to apply them.
- Hold personnel accountable for abiding by policy.
- Continually review policies to ensure that they respond to community needs and that they hold personnel properly accountable as new issues are identified.

(Fyfe, Greene, Walsh, Wilson, & McLaren, 1997)

Procedural justice requires that these policies should be explained to the public so they understand the obligations and boundaries for officers' application of force. The department must also ensure through established policy and administration that credible investigatory procedures are followed in deadly force incidents. Criminal investigations are often subject to open-record laws following the determination that no prosecution will result. When this happens or by subpoena in a civil manner, it will be disclosed if the department did a thorough and unbiased effort in policing itself. Administrators should also cultivate strong professional relationships with all involved in this process. This includes the prosecutor, medical examiner, corner, and the media. Departments should also seek to educate the public regarding the use of force policy. In communities that have experienced confrontations with the police, the public should be educated in the appropriate manner to behave during traffic stops and contacts with the police. Educating at-risk groups may prevent the possibility of violent confrontations occurring. The culture of the department needs to be assessed and changed to support the policy.

For example, a study of seven police departments determined that police occupational attitudes influenced citizen complaints. Officers with negative attitudes toward management generated more complaints regarding discourtesy, use of force, and total complaints. Officers who believed that their departments' use of force policy increased the likelihood of receiving complaints got them. These variables combined with belief in the traditional crime fighting or "thin blue line" role of the police were the most powerful predictors of citizen complaints about procedural unjust encounters with officers (Terrill & Paoline, 2015, p. 204). These findings imply that police managers should pay attention to the attitudes and grumblings of their officers (especially the line staff) rather than simply write them off because they play a major role in how citizens perceive the legitimacy of police departments. In addition, an examination of self-reported use of force incidents from the Austin (TX) police department determined high neighborhood crime levels impacted use of force. In addition, citizen resistance was the single most important factor in elevated levels of police force (Lee, Vaughn, & Lim, 2014, p. 497).

The International Association of Chiefs of Police has played a central role in the research, development, and creation of model policies and leading practices regarding the use of force by law enforcement officers. To support agencies, the IACP has created a single webpage with model polices and other publications that address issues related to law enforcement use of force. Besides IACP's resources, many other organizations, such as CALEA and state accreditation boards, have developed policies governing the use of force that could prove valuable to law enforcement agencies.

The Police Executive Research Forum (2016) has offered 30 principles on the use of force (see Table 13.1). For example, Principle No. 2 calls for the use of force policies to exceed

TABLE 13.1 PERF 30 Principles for Use of Force

1. The sanctity of human life should be at the heart of everything an agency does.

2. Agencies should continue to develop best policies, practices, and training on use-of-force issues that go beyond the minimum requirements of *Graham v. Connor.*

3. Police use of force must meet the test of proportionality.

4. Adopt de-escalation as formal agency policy.

5. The Critical Decision-Making Model provides a new way to approach critical incidents.

6. Duty to intervene: Officers need to prevent other officers from using excessive force.

7. Respect the sanctity of life by promptly rendering first aid.

8. Shooting at vehicles must be prohibited.

9. Prohibit use of deadly force against individuals who pose a danger only to themselves.

10. Document use-of-force incidents, and review data and enforcement practices to ensure that they are fair and non-discriminatory.

11. To build understanding and trust, agencies should issue regular reports to the public on use of force.

12. All critical police incidents resulting in death or serious bodily injury should be reviewed by specially trained personnel.

13. Agencies need to be transparent in providing information following use-of-force incidents.

14. Training academy content and culture must reflect agency values.

15. Officers should be trained to use a Critical Decision-Making Model.

16. Use Distance, Cover, and Time to replace outdated concepts such as the "21-foot rule" and "drawing a line in the sand."

17. De-escalation should be a core theme of an agency's training program.

18. De-escalation starts with effective communications.

19. Mental Illness: Implement a comprehensive agency training program on dealing with people with mental health issues.

20. Tactical training and mental health training need to be interwoven to improve response to critical incidents.

21. Community-based outreach teams can be a valuable component to agencies' mental health response.

22. Provide a prompt supervisory response to critical incidents to reduce the likelihood of unnecessary force.

23. Training as teams can improve performance in the field.

24. Scenario-based training should be prevalent, challenging, and realistic.

25. Officers need access to and training in less-lethal options.

26. Agencies should consider new options for chemical spray.

27. An ECW deployment that is not effective does not mean that officers should automatically move to their firearms.

28. Personal protection shields enhance officer safety and may support de-escalation efforts during critical incidents, including situations involving persons with knives, baseball bats, or other improvised weapons that are not firearms.

29. Well-trained call-takers and dispatchers are essential to the police response to critical incidents.

30. Educate the families of persons with mental illness on communicating with call-takers.

the "objective reasonableness" standard established in the U.S. Supreme Court decision *Graham v. Connor*. As a result of this decision, departments issued policies directing officers to create a buffer zone of 21 feet when faced with potential danger any time a person within this area is armed with a knife. Unfortunately, the "21-foot rule" has been taught informally in police training academies and sometimes, it has morphed into an incorrect way of thinking. Instead of seeing the 21-foot rule as a general warning to think defensively and protect themselves when confronted by a person with a knife, some officers came to see the rule as a legal justification to shoot a person with a knife less than 21 feet away. So instead of protecting officers' safety, the rule has been cited to justify the use of deadly force in incidents when other tactics might have resolved the situation without deadly force (PERF, 2015).

The PERF guidelines call for extending this zone to give officers time to assess their options to resolve incidents without use of force. They also advocate methods to "slow things down" and de-escalate situations—asking questions in a normal tone of voice while summoning additional resources, if necessary and possible. The ultimate aim of these principles is to ensure that police use of force is proportional to the threat faced and to respect the sanctity of human life.

Less Than Lethal Force Use

Police have always been encouraged to use less than lethal force to subdue suspects besides avoiding injury to themselves and others. Data from a medium-sized police department revealed Tasers were more likely to be used in response to verbal resistance or suspect flight and not when faced with physical resistance or threatened with a weapon. Police were more likely to use a Taser on non-White and male suspects—controlling for the level of resistance, call type, and other factors (Crow & Adrion, 2011, pp. 380–381). In their comprehensive review of a national study, Alpert and Dunham (2012, pp. 251–253) made the following recommendations regarding the use of a conductive energy device (CEDs—Tasers) by the police:

- If injury reduction is the primary goal, agencies should forbid the use of less than lethal weapons (OC spray & CEDs) on passive resisters. They should only be used as possible response alternatives to active threats of resistance.
- Multiple applications of CEDs should be prohibited when they prove ineffective or create an unacceptable health risk.
- CED policies should require officers to assess continued resistance after each standard cycle and limit their use to no more than 3 standard cycles of total activation time against the same subject.
- Following use of a CED, officers should examine the suspect for signs of distress and have them medically examined at the earliest possible time.
- Training on these principles could lead to fewer problems with CED deployment.

Recent studies have examined the effect of official policies on the use of less than lethal force by police. An analysis of data from a national use of force study sponsored by the National Institute of Justice (NIJ) and administered by the Police Executive Research Forum (PERF) concluded that when the policies toward the use of CEDs were less restrictive, they resulted in fewer police shootings (Ferdick, Kaminski, Cooney, & Sevigny, 2014, p. 351).

Terrill and Paoline (2016) analyzed 3,340 use of force incidents from three agencies and determined that the agency with the most restrictive less than lethal force policy used it less often than two other agencies with less restrictive policies The resistance faced by the officer should be considered in Taser policy making and training.

Dealing with police use of force (both lethal and less than lethal) is a continuing issue for police leadership and a challenge to police legitimacy. This problem has motivated not only an analysis of the actual use of force incidents but also of recruitment, policy development, organizational culture, and management of force applications. Unless the manner in which police officers use and are held accountable for the use of force are improved, police leadership will continue to be challenged by this issue. The last two years have taught us that community oversight in the age of the Internet is a powerful force. The public's demands for increased accountability and transparency will continue to work their will on our 18,000 police departments (PERF, 2015, p. 10).

Principles of Good Policing

Throughout the last two decades there has been a constant attempt to suggest ways of enhancing police legitimancy, reducing civil disobediance and incidents of violence between police and citizens, and improving the relationship between the police and the communites they serve. A powerful force affecting the solution of these problems is how police offices continue to view themselves as the front-line operatives who are soldiers in a "war against crime." This is a common perception held by both citizens and officers and supported in the popular media. This perception took root and developed during the 20th century's reform era that emphasized crime fighting as the primary task of police. However, research has consistently found the majority of day-to-day police work comprises such activities as community service, crime prevention and maintaining order, not law enforcement per se (Crank & Langworthy, 1992, p. 344).

An underlying theme of the President's Task Force on 21st Century Policing addresses this issue by suggesting that the culture of policing must change. They advise that police can build trust and legitimacy in the eyes of the citizens they serve by embracing a culture of guardianship, not that of the warrior. In Plato's "Republic" the greatest amount of power is given to those called **Guardians** who serve and protect democracy. Only those with the most impeccable character are chosen to bear the responsibility of protecting democracy (PTF, p. 11). The Task Force calls for policing to adopt a culture of guardinaship that protects the dignity and human rights of all, to be protectors and champions of the Constitution. However, this cultural change and role rethinking will require redirection of recruitment, training, leadership; significant budgetary resources; and commitment throughout policing to ensure that internal and external policies, practices, and procedures support this effort.

In 2015, the International Association of Chiefs of Police held a national policy summit on police–community relations because of events in Missouri, New York, and Ohio that strained community–police relationships. The report issued by the summit outlines a series of tangible strategies and steps for law enforcement executives to build trust in their communities. Those strategies include (IACP, 2015, p. x)

> ***Recommended Strategy 1***: Begin to redefine policing in a 21st century democratic society utilizing shared definitions of roles, responsibilities, and priorities. Understanding

law enforcement's role of enforcing the rule of law, state laws/statutes, and municipal ordinances changes in the world we live in requires adjustments to our approach to policing. Law enforcement leaders must take the lead in working with the community to define innovative ways to police in the 21st century.

Recommended Strategy 2: Strengthen and/or rebuild the capacity of police agencies to develop legitimate, sustainable relationships with their communities, and with unique segments within the community.

Recommended Strategy 3: Implement meaningful ways to define and measure success in community-police relationships as a community.

The US Department of Justice (2003, pp. 19–20) developed a set of principles of good policing, which it suggested can be the springboard for a department's culture change. They propose a road to implementing the guardianship ideal:

- Police departments must preserve and advance the principles of democracy. All societies must have a system for maintaining order. Police officers in this country, however, must not only know how to maintain order, but must do so in a manner consistent with our democratic form of government. Therefore, it is incumbent upon the police to enforce the law and deliver a variety of other services in a manner that not only preserves, but also extends precious American values. It is in this context that the police become the living expression of the meaning and potential of a democratic form of government.

- The police must not only respect, but also protect the rights guaranteed to each citizen by the Constitution. To the extent each officer considers his or her responsibility to include protection of the constitutionally guaranteed rights of all individuals, the police become the most important employees in the vast structure of government.

- The police should place its highest value on the preservation of human life. Above all, the police department must believe that human life is our most precious resource. Therefore, the department, in all aspects of its operations, will place its highest priority on the protection of life. This belief must be manifested in at least two ways. First, the allocation of resources and the response to demands for service must give top priority to those situations that threaten life. Second, even though society authorizes the police to use deadly force, the use of such force must not only be justified under the law, but must also be consistent with the philosophy of rational and humane social control.

- The police department believes that the prevention of crime is its number one operational priority. The department's primary mission must be the prevention of crime. Logic makes it clear that it is better to prevent a crime than to put the resources of the department into motion after a crime has been committed. Such an operational response should result in an improved quality of life for citizens, and a reduction in the fear that is generated by both the reality and perception of crime.

- The police should involve the community in the delivery of its services. It is clear that the police cannot be successful in achieving their mission without the support and involvement of the people they serve. Crime is not solely a police problem, and it should not be considered as such. Rather, crime must be responded to as a community problem. Thus, it is important for the police department to involve the community in its operations.

This sharing of responsibility involves providing a mechanism for the community to collaborate with the police both in the identification of community problems and determining the most appropriate strategies for resolving them. It is counterproductive for the police to isolate themselves from the community and not allow citizens the opportunity to work with them.

- The police are accountable to the community they serve. Police departments also are not entities unto themselves. Rather, they are a part of government and exists only for the purpose of serving the public to which it must be accountable. An important element of accountability is openness. Secrecy in police work is not only undesirable but unwarranted. Accountability means being responsive to the problems and needs of citizens. It also means managing police resources in the most cost-effective manner. It must be remembered that the power to police comes from the consent of those being policed.

- Police departments should be committed to professionalism in all aspects of their operations. The role of the professional organization is to serve its clients. The police department must view its role as serving the citizens of the community. A professional organization also adheres to a code of ethics. The police department must be guided by the Law Enforcement Code of Ethics. A profession polices itself. The police department must ensure that it maintains a system designed to promote the highest level of discipline among its members.

- The police department will maintain the highest standards of integrity. The society invests in its police the highest level of trust. The police, in turn, enter into a contractual arrangement with society to uphold that trust. The police must always be mindful of this contractual arrangement and never violate that trust. Each member of the police department must recognize that he or she is held to a higher standard than the private citizen. They must recognize that, besides representing the department, they also represent the law enforcement profession and government. They are the personifications of the law. Their conduct, both on and off duty, must be beyond reproach. There must not be even a perception in the public's mind that the department's ethics are open to question.

- Recognizing that society is undergoing massive changes, police agencies are confronted with a great challenge. The essence of that challenge is to respond to problems created by social change, while providing the stability that holds a society together during a period of uncertainty.

- By setting forth a clear set of values, articulating what it believes in, the police department has a foundation to guide itself. Such a foundation also allows for organizational flexibility. In addition, a set of values provides the community with a means of assessing its police department without having to become involved in technical operations. Value statements serve as the linkage between the ongoing operations of a police department and the community's ability not only to participate, but also to understand the reason for police department strategies.

These principles challenge police leadership to come to terms with the changing environment in which their organizations live and their legitimacy is being challenged. Meeting this challenge is necessary if a department wishes to develop a strategic approach to the factors in our society that are affecting policing today and tomorrow.

Legitimacy

As defined earlier in this text, police legitimacy is at the heart of the problem of reducing violence between police and citizens. This has and will continue to be an issue all police leaders will face because it shapes the behavior of citizens toward their organizations. **Legitimacy** is present when citizens believe that the police have moral authority to enforce the law and deserve respect and compliance with their initiatives (Gau, 2013, p. 760). People will voluntarily obey the law when they support it and believe in the legitimacy of the authority enforcing it. Thus, they will accept police decisions when they believe that they are legitimate and to the degree they consider the decisions as favorable and fair. If they view the police procedures and practice as discriminatory and unfair, the results will be alienation, dissatisfaction, defiance, and a lack of public cooperation. The legitimacy of the police is linked to public judgments about the fairness of processes through which the police decide and exercise authority. If citizens believe that police actions are morally justified and appropriate to the circumstances, they are legitimate.

Satisfaction with police control of disorder has been found to be significantly related to citizens' overall satisfaction with crime prevention (Zhao, Tsai, Ren, & Lai, 2012, p. 414). Visability is another factor in this process. When citizens see the police doing their job and quality service is provided, legitimacy is enhanced (see Hawdon, Ryan, & Griffin, 2003, p. 485; Maguire & Johnson, 2010). Citizens cooperate with the police when they believe that police performance in fighting crime is effective and that there is a credible threat of punishment for crime (Tyler & Fagan, 2008, p. 263). In a free society citizen cooperation and trust are necessary factors in the acceptance of the police.

Kane (2005) studied variations in violent crime arrest rates in New York City (1975–1996) to determine if they could be explained by indicators of compromised police legitimacy (official misconduct and over-policing). Increases in police misconduct predicted increases in violent crime within precincts marked by high levels of disadvantage. It was recommended that police administrators pay specific attention to the use of aggressive methods in such neighborhoods because they may aggravate the level of violent crime in communities stressed by extreme disadvantage (Kane, 2005, p. 492).

These conclusions are supported by a study of calls for service following a use of force incident in Milwaukee, WI. Following the widely publicized police beating of an unarmed Black man, Frank Jobe, 911 calls to the police dramatically declined by an estimated 22,000 calls over a one-year period. It is possible that publicized cases of police violence not only threaten police legitimacy but also the very safety of a community (Desmond, Papachristos, & Kirk, 2016).

Promoting legitimacy may also facilitate order maintenance. A survey conducted by Wolfe (2011) found that persons exhibiting low self-control were more likely to hold negative perceptions of police procedural justice. Such persons may also be more likely to be treated unfairly by the police because they challenge police actions and decisions. However, the results also showed that, if the police follow the tenets of procedural justice, they would gain voluntary compliance and lower levels of offending from people who have low self-control (Wolfe, 2011, p. 72).

Procedural Justice

Legitimacy is bound to procedural justice. Procedural justice is concerned with the officer's use of rational, neutral, and transparent decision making. It provides tangible evidence that the police can be trusted to use their coercive authority in a trustworthy fashion (Gau, 2013, p. 760). As a social psychological construct, procedural justice is grounded in citizen perceptions and the actual behavior exercised by the police (Gau, Corsaro, Stewart, & Brunson, 2012, p. 333).

To demonstrate procedural justice, the police should explain their views and behavior when working with the community before deciding on a course of action to resolve problems, providing evidence of their neutral and objective decision making and intention to treat people in a like manner with dignity and respect. For example, in the City of Boston, the police received praise and support for releasing a video of their killing of a knife-wielding man under terrorist surveillance. The police released the video to representatives of the African American community and the public while explaining their reasons for taking the action they did in this case (Marcelo, 2015).

There are several factors related to citizen perceptions of procedural justice in policing. First is the quality of police decision making. Do the police accurately apply the law and are their decisions based upon the facts? Do they try to understand these facts in a situation before acting? Do they give honest explanations to citizens for their actions? In similar situations, do the police consistently apply rules to different people and treat them the same? The second factor is the quality of treatment by the police. Do they take people's needs and concerns into account? Do they respect and show concern for the rights of citizens? Do they treat people with dignity and respect (Dai, Frank, & Sun, 2011, p. 160)?

Procedural justice is also tied to moral principles (Bayles, 1990). The first principle is impartiality or neutrality (Dolan, Edlin, Tsuchiya, & Wailoo, 2007, p. 160). Officer decisions should be made without bias or self-interest. The second is giving citizens the opportunity to be heard, to present information and support their position. "Citizen voice" means that the persons affected by an official decision should contribute to the process (Dolan et al., 2007, p. 160). Third, actions should be transparent (Dolan et al., 2007, p. 161). Officers should give the reasons for their actions to citizens. The fourth involves adherence to formal justice—consistency, adherence to precedent and conformity to rules (Dolan et al., 2007, p. 162). Fifth, decisions should be made on the basis of accurate information (Dolan et al., 2007, p. 160). Sixth is the reversibility of the decision. Citizens should have a right to be heard and appeal the outcome of the decision (Dolan et al., 2007, p. 160).

Police administrators should understand that they have more control over how their officers treat citizens than they have over crime. When citizens feel that the police represent their values, they identify and cooperate with them (Sunshine & Tyler, 2003, p. 543). For example, Wells (2007, p. 615) surveyed three groups of citizens who had contact with the police: victims of crime, drivers involved in traffic accidents, and drivers who received citations. The results showed that measures of procedural justice (professionalism, competence, contact-specific behaviors) were strongly related to positive citizen ratings of officer performance across all three groups. Operating with an eye toward procedural justice enhances police authority and legitimacy.

Research findings support the conclusion that how the police operate affects public perceptions of legitimacy. Gau (2013) analyzed data from the national Police-Public Contact Survey to examine whether consent searches affected citizens' attitudes of legitimacy toward the police. Consent searches give the police an expedited way to check vehicles for contraband. Yet, consent searches can cause citizens to question officer motives for the traffic stop and damage their perceptions of procedural justice and police legitimacy. On this basis, Gau

(2013, p. 760) recommended that police executives should examine the frequency of consent searches in their departments and have written policies to evaluate this approach. She also endorses conducting focus groups with officers and community stakeholders to examine their feelings about requests for consent searches during traffic stops to determine how the process can be conducted in a manner that does not damage citizen perceptions of legitimacy. Police as guardians must be sensitive to citizens' judgments regarding the fairness of a procedure and maintain control over their behavior. Widespread use of stop and frisk leads to questioning of procedural justice and thus undermines police legitimacy. When such methods are used, the police must adhere to strict standards of professionalism and make sure that equity and fairness are paramount.

What the majority of this research and the recommendations of the federal resports suggest is that police leaders must "promote a culture of respect within the department and clarify that mistreatment of citizens will not be tolerated within the organization" (Gau & Brunson, 2010, p. 274). **Communication** is a major implementation factor in the accomplishment of this suggestion. A department's leadership team must work at informing and guiding their personnel in understanding these concepts, objectives, and performance indicators. A meta-analysis of studies on police legitimacy confirms this conclusion. It found that regardless of the crime strategy promoted by the police, it was positively affected by the "adoption of a dialogue that actively operationalizes the key principles of procedural justice to advance citizen perceptions of legitimacy" (Mazerolle, Bennett, Davis, Sargeant, & Manning, 2013, p. 266). Citizens' perceptions of procedural fairness by the police may overcome the influence that negative neighborhood and social environments have upon this assessment—particularly among citizens who have been victimized (Nix, Wolfe, Rojek, & Kaminsky, 2015, p. 632; Nix, Wolfe, Rojek, & Kaminsky, 2015). The essence of procedural justice is that when citizens see the police administering the law in a neutral and professional manner, they can gain the trust of the community even when they are not giving people exactly what they want (Fischer, 2014, p. 41). Citizen perceptions of fairness determines their satisfaction with police encounters, whether they will obey the law, and trust and work with the police in the future (Rosenbaum, et al., 2011).

The final report of the **President's Task Force on 21st Century Policing** (2015a) warned police leaders that unless they understand how the operational nature of their departments interrealte with the communites they serve and gain collaboration and support for their methods, their departments will never be able to provide true public safety. Specifically, as noted above, this requires a change in police culture from the crime-fighter **warrior** self-image to that of democratic guardians who value the dignity and human rights of citizens. This rethinking of the role of police in a democracy requires leadership and commitment across law enforcement organizations to ensure internal and external policies, practices, and procedures that guide individual officers and make organizations more accountable to the communities they serve (President's Task Force on 21st Century Policing, 2015a, p. 2.).

As Sir Robert Peel understood so well, community expectations and needs play a major role in the development of what police departments should do now and in the future. For example, despite the absence of documented success, random preventive patrol and the use of 911 systems are a continued core of police operations in the majority of the nation's police departments. Citizens have come to expect a rapid response to their calls for service and police departments are now chained to satisfying this expectation. Police departments primarily engaging in the strategies and tactics (i.e., Community Policing, Compstat, etc.) we have presented in this text because they are expected to do so by the "sovereigns" in their institutional environment and their actions contribute to "myth building" processes (Crank, 2003, p. 189). **Sovereigns** are actors whose views can significantly impact the police organization. They include individuals from federal, state, and local law enforcement agencies, national and local media, law enforcement employee and community organizations, medical providers, and elected representatives (Matusiak, 2014, p. 9). For example, it is accepted by all of the sovereigns listed above as a fact that "Community policing is the 'right way' to do police business because its underlying values of building positive linkages to the community are taken for granted" and they link the organization to its broader societal context (Crank, 2003, p. 193). This position also reflects the fact that as the most visible agents of local and state government police in a democracy are expected to ensure domestic security and safety. However, improperly used or uncontrolled, they become subversive of the system they are sworn to protect.

The implementation guide for the President's Task Force on 21st Century Policing (2015b, pp. 2–3) contains several underlying themes on which specific recommendations for the future of policing are based.

1. **Change the culture of policing.** In a republic that honors the core of democracy—the greatest amount of power is given to those called Guardians. This calls for law enforcement to protect the dignity and human rights of all, to be the protectors and champions of the Constitution. This rethinking of the role of police in a democracy requires leadership and commitment across law enforcement organizations to ensure internal and external policies, practices, and procedures that guide individual officers and make organizations more accountable to the communities they serve.
2. **Embrace community policing as a philosphy and a way of doing business**. The commitment to work with communities to tackle the immediate and longer-term causes of crime and joint problems solving reduces crime and improves quality of life. It also makes officers safer and increases the likelihood of individuals to abide by the law.
3. **Ensure fair and impartial policing.** Procedural justice is based on four principles: 1) treating people with dignity and respect, 2) giving individuals "voice" during encounters, 3) being neutral and transparent in decisionmaking, and 4) conveying trustworthy motives. Besides practicing procedural justice, understanding the negative impact of explicit and implicit bias on police-community relations and then taking constructive actions to train officers and the community in how to recognize and mitigate are key factors.
4. **Build community capital**. Trust and legitimacy grow from positive interactions based on more than just enforcement interactions. Law enforcement agencies can achieve trust and legitimacy by establishing a positive presence at community activities and events, taking part in proactive problem solving, and ensuring that communites have a voice and seat at the table with working with officers.
5. **Pay attention to officer wellness and safety**. Police officers face all kinds of threats and stresses that have a direct impact on their safety and well being. Ensure that officers have access to the tools that will keep them safe, such as bulletproof vests and tactical first aid kits and training. Promote officer wellness through physical, social, and mental health support.

6.   **Technolgy both new and emerging are changing the way we police**. It improves efficiency and transparency but also raises privacy concerns and has a significant price tag. Body-worn cameras, less than lethal use of force technologies, communication, and social media all require a legal and pragmatic review of policies, practices, and procedures. These policies, practices, and procedures should be developed with input from the community and constitutional scholars.

Budgetary Issues

A constant administrative problem that will have a direct impact on departmental strategic redirection and the above suggestions now and in the future is budgetary issues. The ability of the police department's leadership to redirect and use its resources and assests is determined by the budget of the political subdivision in which it serves. The budget has a direct impact upon the police executives' ability to provide public safety and accomplish their goals. Because of several years of economic downturns on municipal tax bases, police executives past, present, and future have had to continually deal with less and less budgetary resources and be more creative with what they have been given. In a analysis of economic impact on police agencies the Police Executive Research Forum (2010, pp. 11–13) reported:

- Nearly a quarter of American cities surveyed have made cuts to their public safety budgets.
- Over one-third of the agencies that applied for COPS officer hiring funding reported an operating budget drop of greater than 5 percent between 2009 and 2011.
- Nearly 12,000 police officers and sheriff's deputies will be laid off.
- An estimated 28,000 officers and deputies in 2010 have faced week-long furloughs.
- Some departments have stopped responding to all motor vehicle thefts, burglar alarms and non-injury motor vehicle accidents.
- Departments also report decreases in investigations of property crimes, fugitive tracking, a variety of white collar crimes, and even low-level narcotics cases.

In 2010, a PERF study found that nearly half (47%) of the responding agencies it surveyed showed that budget cuts had already caused or will cause changes in the services they provide to their communities. In response to their fininancial environment, many agencies have greatly reduced their staffing and training expenditures and services to the community. The effects of such reductions will influence the capacity of law enforcement departments to provide services, in the same ways, as they have in the past. All of which will have a negative impact on a department's ability to serve the community now and in the future.

The National Institute of Justice (2011) has provided several suggestions for police leaders facing budget cutbacks, noting that circumstances call for the use of strategic management. They suggest that police leadership (National Institute of Justice, 2011, pp. ii, 6–8):

- **Think long term**: Develop a strategic plan with a long-term time frame.
- **Do not just cut costs, look for revenue opportunities**: Departments may charge user fees for some specialized services provided.

- **Invite innovation**: Turn this threat into an opportunity to find cost-effective methods.
- **Focus on what is kept, rather than on what has been cut**: Plan what you are doing with the funds you have retained. Budget for outcomes.
- **Allocate budget dollars for your top goals**.

Many of the cost-saving budgetary adjustments discussed in various studies suggest organizational transformation through the use of strategic operational strategies, the systematic use of partnerships and problem-solving techniques, to proactively address the immediate conditions that give rise to public safety issues such as crime, social disorder, and fear of crime. The three tenets of Community Policing—community partnerships, organizational transformation, and problem solving—are of increased importance when facing budget cuts that reduce the number of officers on the streets. The National Institute of Justice (2011) also recommends the NYPD's Compstat and Maryland's StateStat as methods to establish accountability in budgeting and performance. Tying goal accomplishment to available funding and command responsibility is a strategic managment issue that must be dealt with now in policing and in the future.

The recognition and acceptance of the impact of this present economic reality is a more important reason for the development of strategic management practices to ensure the effective and efficient delivery of police services. Police nation-wide will need to evaluate, adapt, and redevelop how they do their job to ensure appropriate levels of public safety

Recruitment/Retention

In addition to dealing with the impact of the financial crises, departments are also faced with the challenge to recruit qualified individuals to fill their ranks. Although recruitment was addressed in Chapter 9, it is identified here because it is continuous problem for both the present and future of policing. Organizations need to identify and hire the right people to maintain current and future levels of performance. Shifting societal demands have created a demand for individuals who are critical thinkers and problem solvers. These new officers represent the department's future. Unfortunately, current issues with police legitimacy and media coverage of demonstrations against the police use of force have resulted in qualified individuals no longer considering a police career.

However, it has also been found that the present generation of police recruits has attributes that are distinctly different from those of their precedessors. Labled "**Millennials**," these individuals are considered "conscientious and independent in their thinking while also more tolerant of differences than those of other generations" (Batts, Smoot, & Scrivner, 2012, p. 3). They are not necessarily working for money but are noted for their altruism that creates a desire to make the world a better place and give back to society via a team-oriented approach to work (Malcolm, 2016). These individuals can multitask, articuluate their career values, use technology, and value diversity. They place a greater value on balancing work and family, experiencing comfort with questioning authority, and challenging the traditional chain of command, demanding ongoing performance feedback, expecting transparency and timely outcome measures that show what is working, and relying on instant feedback from electronic communication and social networking. This generation also requires a management style that is distinctly different from the traditional methods used in the past. Police leadership needs to understand them, utilize them properly, or lose them to the organization (Batts et al., 2012, p. 4).

Traditional police managers and supervisors may view this new generation as "whiners" and their managerial methods may cause problems. Several questions arise from this potential conflict (Batts et al., 2012, pp. 10–11):

- Are they a generation that expects to be empowered and make too many demands for information and feedback?
- Is it equally likely that they are seeking clarification of roles and responsibilites but in ways perceived as challenges that make supervisors uncomfortable?
- Do they want a lucrative, easy ride or are they seeking meaningful work and the opportunity to advance?
- Are they "risk adverse" and hesitant to go "hands-on" or are they using sensible risk management?
- Do they expect on-going accolades for work or are they seeking honesty and authenticity from their superiors?
- Does their questioning of rules mean actual resistance or do they wish to understand the rules and learn the history of why they exist?

These factors suggest the need for changes in management style that encourage managers to engage in dialogues with their subordinates that will explain, instruct, and mentor rather than autocratically issue orders and expect unquestioning (or uncaring) compliance. This challenge requires a reevaluation of current supervisory training and development practices and management techniques discussed earlier in this text.

Internal Organizational Legitimacy

Just as in community relationships, legitimacy within the organization is also tied to fairness but within the workplace. Employees are more willing to follow organizational rules when they believe they are legitimate. Perceptions of organizational fairness creates a "reservoir of support" that is vital to organizational survival during a time of crisis. It is linked to the use of open and participatory forms of leadership and the fairness of resource allocation procedures within the organization. Legitimacy provides a framework to evaluate procedures as just or unjust. Studies show that the exercising of legitimate authority with subordinates promotes a host of positive outcomes and feelings in employees (Keyes, Hysom, & Lupo, 2000). Employees should be involved in the development of the department's vision and mission to gain their support and accountability. The organization's internal procedural justice begins with the transparent creation of its core values and the development of its policies, protocols, and decision-making processes (*President's Task Force on 21st Century Policing*, 2015b, p. 13).

The department's leaders should model the way for their employees by engaging in actions and behaviors that promote organizational legitimacy. To stay relevant, modern law enforcement leaders will have to become more adaptive. They need to be self-aware of who they are, what they believe and value, and act upon them while interacting with others. They should use their personal identification with their employees as a way to create meaningfulness at work. This style of leadership can become the basis of the culture of the organization.

Authentic leaders are guided by a set of values based upon "what is right and fair" for both themselves and organizational personnel. In this manner, the organizational values of their employees model those demonstrated by their leader. The leader's ethical behavior sends a strong message to followers that affects what they attend to, what they think, how they construct their own roles, and how they behave. The authentic leader is to raise optimism and build upon individual strengths rather than draw attention to weaknesses. By sponsoring positive emotions, the authentic leader promotes positive behaviors such as creativity, coping with adversity, commitment, satisfaction, handling stress, and providing motivation, and promoting quality performance.

Blader and Tyler (2003) note several aspects of procedural justice that affect employees regarding how they are treated by their organization. For example, employees wish to see that decisions made at work are made in an unbiased, impartial manner. They wish to be treated fairly in evaluations and promotions regarding their dignity and rights. Fairness promotes feelings of inclusion and group importance. These perceptions have a formal and informal basis. Formal sources of procedural justice spring from the official rules, policy, and procedures of the department; are structural; and are often constant across time, situations, and individuals. Informal bases of procedural justice in organizations are more dynamic, based upon the perceptions of the employees, their supervisor, and the personal relationship that develops between them (Blader & Tyler, 2003, pp. 114–115). This research shows that the manner in which people are treated within their organization affects their treatment of organizational clients.

The Ferguson Effect

The "Ferguson Effect" refers to a perceived negative response in the performance of law enforcement officers due to increased scrutiny and bad publicity in the media. This effect is alleged to extend to two areas of policing: (1) The police are disengaging from vigorous activities (or even arrests) and thus crime rates are increasing, and (2) The lack of desire by police officers to collaborate with community members to prevent crime (see MacDonald, 2016, pp. 57–59). In addition, it has been suggested that such "depolicing" is attributable to changes in the law, departmental policies, implementation of new policing strategies, civil suits, establishment of consent decrees on departments, and line of duty deaths (see Oliver, 2015).

A study by Nix and Wolfe (2015) was recently conducted to determine the effect of bad publicity on officer motivation. Their survey of 567 officers found that officers who were less motivated because of negative publicity also expressed less self-legitimacy (the confidence they have in themselves as a law enforcement officer). This is unfortunate because officers who view their own authority as legitimate are more likely to engage in positive behaviors for their department and the community they serve—such as observing fairness in procedures. The best way for departments to counter bad publicity is to provide organizational justice for officers (Nix & Wolfe, 2015, p. 20). Subsequent analysis of these data also demonstrated that deputies who felt that their supervisors practiced organizational fairness were less likely to lack motivation, perceive more on-the-job danger, believe their colleagues feel negative effects of Ferguson, and that citizens were less likely to support them (Nix & Wolfe, 2016). Again, how officers are treated by their departments affects the nature of their job performance.

Rosenfeld (2015) examined whether events in Ferguson affected crime rates in St. Louis, MO. He found no credible effect on homicides, a mixed result for violent crimes, but a temporal (but not causative) effect upon property crimes. He cautions police departments to monitor fluctuations in the crime rate and to apply evidence-based practices to any problems that occur. Similarly, a time series analysis of police officers killed in the line of duty found no evidence of a Ferguson Effect for the period August 2014 (following the shooting of Michael Brown in Ferguson, MO) to March 2016 (Maguire, Nix, & Campbell, 2016).

Legitimacy envelops the police organization and the communities they serve—both externally and internally. The findings on legitimacy confirm that how people are treated directly relates to their expectations and performance both within the department and the community. It is apparent that sponsoring the feeling of legitimacy among all concerned will affect not only how police agencies are perceived but also how they perform. Organizational justice and self-legitimacy are important predictors of willingness to engage with the community. Treatment and support within law enforcement agencies can trump negative publicity in the media.

Effective Policing

Besides what has been identified above, the continuing challenge facing police leadership is the need to provide an effective level of public safety to the community in which they serve for today and tomorrow. The general theme of this book is that a fundamental rethinking is taking place in the manner by which this challenge is accomplished. We have entitled this organizational redirection Strategic Policing. **Strategic policing** is a continuing process of enhancing the effectiveness of a police department through its use of the latest information and analysis techniques to develop targeted, innovative strategies to address public safety issues (Moore & Stephens, 1991).

Many of today's police leaders base their organizational stewardship on leadership perceptions that emerged from demands of the Reform Era of policing when operational environments were simpler and based upon the principles of Scientific Management. That leadership paradigm holds that organizational effectiveness can be achieved solely through the control or motivation of organizational personnel instead of changing processes and structure. It created top-down bureaucratically controlled organizations locked into providing public safety through three operational strategies: random patrol, rapid response to calls for service, and reactive post-event investigation. The present environmental reality of policing is complex and demands a new proactive paradigm. Today's public safety issues and limited police resources have created the need for a strategic redirection in both leadership and administration that will affect both present and future operations of police organizations.

A consistent finding that has emerged out of the police operational experimentation and research of the past 20 years is that effective policing requires police leaders to think strategically and use a variety of tactics, treat and supervise their organization in a more purposeful and humane manner, collaborate with the citizens they serve, and achieve legitimacy by upholding democratic principles. Citizens expect their police departments to be professional, accountable, transparent, and self-monitoring (Walker & Archbold, 2014). However, this raises the question: Can police leadership develop and sustain an effective response to the driving forces their organizations are facing with their current level of capabilities, personnel, and resources?

Research noted throughout this book establishes that effective police organizations can and must adapt to their environment. Strategic police leadership requires that executives proactively develop and implement an organizational direction that allows their departments to meet the demands of their operational environments. Experience informs us that this can be accomplished by departments acquiring, creating, and transforming information into intelligence that they disseminate to all operational decision makers within their organization. This intelligence-generating process provides operational decision makers with timely and accurate intelligence upon which to evaluate and prioritize community needs. This becomes the basis for planning and developing operational tactics and management practices to meet changing demands. Departments engaging in this process continually assess and evaluate their strategies, tactics, objectives, and accomplishments in crime strategy meetings. Properly conducted, these meetings should override the tactical compartmentalization of traditional policing and have the entire department take ownership for problem identification, developing problem solutions, and tactical response. In this manner, strategically managed police departments become, in practice and accomplishments, learning organizations that engage in:

- Systematic problem solving.
- Experimentation with new approaches.
- Learning from their own experiences and past practices.
- Learning from the experiences and best practices of others.
- Transferring of intelligence quickly and efficiently throughout the organization.
- Engaging in continual dialogue, double-loop learning, operational flexibility.

In these organizations the chief and leadership team continually seek to understand the pattern of relationships that exist internally and externally with the department. They actively promote creativity and proactive policing, while empowering their operational commanders to solve problems at all levels of the organization, and develop problem-oriented tactics to help prevent and solve crime. Strategic management prevents these departments from becoming status-quo, crises-driven organizations through in-depth information gathering, analysis, strategy and tactical formulation, and assessment based upon real-time data.

Strategically managed departments also engage the community and rely on both police and non-police resources in their problem-solving efforts. They reinforce or change the department's operations to respond to driving forces through planning, communication, networking, and strategy development. **Strategic leaders** establish an organizational-wide shared vision, mission, objectives, outcomes, and culture that has meaning for all members of the department and mobilizes their commitment. This organizational redirection is shifting the dominant principle of organizational control from supervision and management to strategic leadership and organizational learning.

Conclusion

Effective police organizations are led by individuals who set direction for today and tomorrow. Their community service delivery is value-driven based upon objectives and outcomes that reflect the department's vison of effectiveness. Command accountability is clearly established and practiced within the parameters of ethics and professional standards. In these organizations, **continuous improvement** is achieved through ongoing measurement, evaluation, analysis, and dialogue. The effective police organization is an adaptable department that has developed the capacity to anticipate change and restructures its operational strategies to respond to these anticipated needs. It engages in a continuous process of determining what is required of the department and what must be done to accomplish it effectively. Administrators are continually engaged in the process of making sure their organization's capabilities fit the demands of its current and future environments.

The issues raised in this chapter address these concerns and provide information on how they can be effectively managed. The foundation upon which traditional police organizations can be transformed to strategically focused ones is based upon the following tasks:

1. Creation of a strategic vision.
2. Mobilization of commitment.
3. Institutionalization of change.
4. Measurement of progress.

It should be remembered that a department's vision, objectives, strategy, and execution are never final. Elements of the strategic management process involve evaluating performance, monitoring changes in the environment, and making adjustments. Follow-up, assessment, and ongoing searches for ways to improve are normal everyday managerial activities. What happens to crime and the quality of safety in a community is always a product of the department's organizational learning and strategic thinking (More et al., 2012). These changes will not be easily accomplished because they call for a somewhat radical change in how police agencies have traditionally operated. This is the challenge for the future—using strategic management concepts to guide police leadership, management, and community engagement. A summary of strategic policing strategies is presented in Table 8.1, p. 343.

KEY TERMS

Authentic leaders
Budgetary issues
Communication
Continuous improvement
Deadly force
Effective police organizations
Ferguson Effect
Guardians
Institutional sovereigns

Internal organizational legitimacy
Legitimacy
Less than lethal force
Millennials
President's Task Force on 21st Century Policing
Principles of Good Policing
Procedural justice

Sovereigns
Split-second syndrome
Strategic leaders
Strategic management
Strategic Policing
Trust
Use of force
Warrior

References

Adams, K. (2015). What we know about police use of force. In R.G. Dunham, & G.P. Alpert (Eds.), *Critical issues in policing: Contemporary readings,* 7th ed. (pp. 532–546). Long Grove, IL: Waveland Press.

Alpert, G.P., & Dunham, R.G. (2012). Policy and training recommendations related to police use of CEDs: Overview of findings from a comprehensive national study. *Police Quarterly, 13*(3), 235–259.

Batts, A.W., Smoot, S.M., & Scrivner, E. (2012). *Police leadership challenges in a changing world.* Washington, DC: Harvard Kennedy School; National Institute of Justice.

Bayles, M. (1990). *Procedural justice: Allocating to individuals.* Dordrecht, Netherlands: Kluwer Academic Publishers.

Blader, S.L., & Tyler, T.R. (2003). What constitutes fairness in work settings? A four-component model of procedural justice. *Human Resource Management Review, 13,* 107–126.

Bolger, P.C. (2015). Just following orders: A meta-analysis of the correlates of American police officer use of force decisions. *American Journal of Criminal Justice, 40,* 466–492.

Charrier, K. (2004). Strategic management in policing: The role of the strategic manager. *Police Chief, 71,* 60–70.Community Oriented Policing Services. (2011). *The Impact of the economic downturn on American police agencies.* Washington, DC: U. S. Department of Justice.

Covey, S.M.R. (2011). Policing at the speed of trust. *The Police Chief, 78*(10), 58–70.

Crank, J.P. (2003). An institutional theory of police: A review of the state of the art. *Policing, 26*(2), 187–207.

Crank, J.P., & Langworthy, R. (1992). An institutional perspective of policing. *Journal of Criminal Law & Criminology,* 338–363.

Crow, M.S., & Adrion, B. (2011). Focal concerns and police use of force: Examining the factors associated with Taser use. *Police Quarterly, 14*(4), 366–387.

Dai, M., Frank, J., & Sun, I. (2011). Procedural justice during police-citizen encounters: The effects of process-based policing on citizen compliance and demeanor. *Journal of Criminal Justice, 39,* 159–168.

Desmond, M., Papachristos, A., & Kirk, D. (2016). Police violence and citizen crime reporting in the black community. *American Sociological Review, 81*(5), 857–876.

Dolan, P., Edlin, R., Tsuchiya, A., & Wailoo, A. (2007). It ain't what you do, It's the way that you do it: Characteristics of procedural justice and their Importance in social decision-making. *Journal of Economic Behavior & Organization, 64,* 157–170.

Ferdick, F.V., Kaminski, R.J., Cooney, M.D., & Sevigny, E.L. (2014). The influence of agency policies on conducted energy device use and police use of deadly force. *Police Quarterly, 17*(4), 328–358.

Fischer, C. (2014). *Legitimacy and procedural justice: The New Orleans case study.* Washington, DC: Police Executive Research Forum.

Fridell, L.A. (2015). Use-of-force policy, policy enforcement, and training. In R.D. Dunham, & G.P. Alpert (Eds.), *Critical issues in policing: Contemporary readings,* 7th ed. (pp. 548–566). Long Grove, IL: Waveland Press.

Fyfe, J.J. (2015). The split-second syndrome and other determinants of police violence. In R.G. Dunham, & G.P. Alpert (Eds.), *Critical issues in policing: Contemporary Readings*, 7th ed. (pp. 517–531). Long Grove, IL: Waveland Press.

Fyfe, J.J., Greene, J.R., Walsh, W., Wilson, O., & McLaren, R. (1997). *Police administration*. New York: McGraw-Hill.

Gau, J.M. (2013). Consent searches as a threat to procedural justice and police legitimacy: An analysis of consent requests during traffic stops. *Criminal Justice Policy Review, 24*(6), 759–777.

Gau, J.M., & Brunson, R.K. (2010). Procedural justice and order maintenance policing: A study of inner-city young men's perceptions of police legitimacy. *Justice Quarterly, 27*(2), 255–279.

Gau, J., Corsaro, N., Stewart, E.A., & Brunson, R.K. (2012). Examining macro-level impacts on procedural justice and police legitimacy. *Journal of Criminal Justice, 40*, 333–343.

Hawdon, J.E., Ryan, J., & Griffin, S.P. (2003). Policing tactics and perceptions of police legitimacy. *Police Quarterly, 6*(4), 469–491.

Hyland, S. Langton, L., & Davis, E. (2015). *Police use of nonfatal force, 2002–11*, Washington, DC: Bureau of Justice Statistics.

International Association Chiefs of Police. (2015). *National policy summit on community-police relations* Alexandria, VA: IACP.

Kane, R.J. (2005). Compromised police legitimacy as a predictor of violent crime in structurally disadvantaged communities. *Criminology, 43*(2), 469–498.

Keyes, C., Hysom, S., & Lupo, K. (2000). The positive organization: Leadership legitimacy, employee well-being, and the bottom line. *The Psychologist-Manager Journal, 4*(2), 143–153.

Lee, H., Vaughn, M.S., & Lim, H. (2014). The imact of neighborhood crime levels on police use of force: Examination of micro and meso levels. *Journal of Criminal Justice, 42*(6). 491–499.

MacDonald, H. (2016). *The war on cops: How the new attack on law and order makes everyone less safe*. New York: Encounter Books.

Maguire, E.R., & Johnson, D. (2010). Measuring public perceptions of the police. *Policing, 33*(4), 703–730.

Maguire, E.R., Nix, J., & Campbell, B.A. (2016). A war on cops? The effects of Ferguson on the number of U.S. police officers murdered in the line of duty. *Justice Quarterly, 35*(5), 739–758.

Malcolm, H. (2016). Millennials value happy workplace over better pay. *USA Today* p. 4B.

Marcelo, P (2015, June 18). Boston praised for releasing video in police killings. *AOL.Com*, www.aol.com/article/2015/06/18/boston-praised-for-releasing-video-in-police-killings/21198105/.

Matusiak, M.C. (2014). Dimensionality of local police chiefs' institutional sovereigns. *Policing and Society: An International Journal of Research and Policy*, 1–18.

Mazerolle, L., Bennett, S., Davis, J., Sargeant, E., & Manning, M. (2013). Procedural justice and police legitimacy: A systematic review of the research evidence. *Journal of Experimental Criminology, 9*, 245–274.

Moore, M., & Stephens, D. (1991). *Beyond command and control: The strategic management of police departments*. Washington, DC: Police Executive Research Forum.

More, H.W., Vito, G.F., & Walsh, W.F. (2012). *Organizational behavior and management in law enforcement*. Upper Saddle River, NJ: Prentice Hall.

National Institute of Justice. (2011). *Strategic cutback management: Law enforcement leadership for lean times*. Washington, DC: U.S. Department of Justice.

Nix, J., & Wolfe, S.E. (2015). The impact of negative publicity on police self-legitimacy. *Justice Quarterly*, 34(1), 84-108.

Nix, J., & Wolfe, S.E. (2016). Sensitivity to the Ferguson effect: The role of managerial organizational justice. *Journal of Criminal Justice*, 47, 12–20.Nix, J., Wolfe, S.E., Rojek, J., & Kaminsky, R.J. (2015). Trust in the police: The influence of procedural justice and perceived collective efficacy. *Crime & Delinquency*, 61(4), 610–640.

Nobel, J., & Alpert, G. (2015). State-created danger: Should police officers be accountable for reckless tactical decision making? In R.G. Dunham, & G.P. Alpert (Eds.), *Critical issues in policing: Contemporary rings*, 7th ed. (pp. 567–582). Prospect Heights, IL: Waveland Press.

Oliver, W.M. (2015). Depolicing: Rhetoric or reality? *Criminal Justice Policy Review*, 28(5), 437–461.

Police Executive Research Forum. (2010). *Is the Economic downturn fundamentally changing how we police?* Washington, DC: Police Executive Research Forum.

Police Executive Research Forum. (2014). *Future trends in policing*. Washington, DC: Office of Community Oriented Policing Services.

Police Executive Research Forum. (2015). *Re-Engineering training on police use of force*. Washington, DC: Police Executive Research Forum.

Police Executive Research Forum. (2016). *Use of force: Taking police to a higher standard—30 guiding principles*. Washington, DC: Police Executive Research Forum.

President's Task Force on 21st Century Policing. (2015a). *Final report of the President's task force on 21st century policing*. Washington, DC: Office of Community Oriented Police Services.

President's Task Force on 21st Century Policing. (2015b). *President's task force on 21st century policing, implementing guide*. Washington, DC: Office of Community Oriented Police Services.

Rosenbaum, D.P., Shuck, A., Lawrence, D., Harnett, S., McDevitt, J., & Posick, C. (2011). *Community-based indicators of police performance: Introducing the platform's public satisfaction survey*. Washington, DC: National Police Research Platform, National Institute of Justice.

Rosenfeld, R. (2015). *Was there a "Ferguson Effect" on crime in St. Louis?* Washington, DC: The Sentencing Project.

Sunshine, J., & Tyler, T.R. (2003). The role of procedural justice and legitimacy in shaping public support for policing. *Law & Society Review*, 37(3), 513–548.

Terrill, W., & Paoline, E.A. (2015). Citizens' complaints as threats to police legitimacy: The role of officers' occupational attitudes. *Journal of Contemporary Criminal Justice*, 31(2), 192–211.

Terrill, W., & Paoline, E.A. (2016). Police use of less than lethal force: Does administrative policy matter? *Justice Quarterly*. doi:10.1080/07418825.2016.1147593.

Tyler, T.R., & Fagan, J. (2008). Legitimacy and cooperation: Why do people help the police fight crime in their communities? *Ohio State Journal of Criminal Law*, 6, 231–275.

US Department of Justice, Community Relations Service. (2003). *Principles of good policing: Avoiding violence between police and citizens*. Washington, DC: Department of Justice.

Walker, S., Alpert, G.P., & Kenney, D.J. (2000). Early warning systems for police: Concept, history, and issues. *Police Quarterly*, 3(2), 132–152.

Walker, S., & Archbold, C. (2014). *The new world of police accountability*, 2nd ed. Newbury Park, CA: Sage.

Wells, W. (2007). Type of contact and evaluation of police officers: The effects of procedural justice across three types of police-citizen contacts. *Journal of Criminal Justice, 35,* 612–621.

Wolfe, S.E. (2011). The effect of low self-control on perceived police legitimacy. *Journal of Criminal Justice, 39,* 67–74.

Zhao, J.S., Tsai, C.-F., Ren, L., & Lai, Y.-L. (2012). Public satisfaction with police control of disorder crime: Does the public hold the police accountable? *Justice Quarterly, 31*(2), 394–420.

Index

Page numbers in italic indicate a figure and page numbers in bold indicate a table on the corresponding page.

Made in the USA
Coppell, TX
27 August 2024